KT-549-597

who has devoted decades to the service of not just the Labour Party,
but women everywhere … a fierce, unrelenting campaigner for
women's rights who has dedicated every ounce of her being to achieve
change' Sarah Champion, *Labour List*

'A Wom... Work... f... ... hi... ... hi... ...'d
recom...
promoting... ...has
fought h... ...et
Harr...

ABOUT THE AUTHOR

Harriet Harman was elected as Labour MP for Peckham in 1982. Joining a House of Commons which was 97 per cent male, she had three children while in Parliament. She has been politics' most prominent champion for women's rights, introducing the National Childcare Strategy, the Equality Act and changing the law on domestic violence. She was the first woman to represent the Labour Party at Prime Minister's Questions. As the longest-serving woman MP in parliament she is now the Mother of the House.

A Woman's Work

HARRIET HARMAN

PENGUIN BOOKS

PENGUIN BOOKS

UK | USA | Canada | Ireland | Australia
India | New Zealand | South Africa

Penguin Books is part of the Penguin Random House group of companies
whose addresses can be found at global.penguinrandomhouse.com.

First published by Allen Lane 2017
Published in Penguin Books 2018
001

Copyright © Harriet Harman, 2017, 2018

The moral right of the author has been asserted

Set in 10.68/16.10 pt Dante MT Std
Typeset by Jouve (UK), Milton Keynes
Printed in Great Britain by Clays Ltd, St Ives plc

A CIP catalogue record for this book is available from the British Library

ISBN: 978-0-141-98386-8

www.greenpenguin.co.uk

MIX
Paper from
responsible sources
FSC® C018179

Penguin Random House is committed to a
sustainable future for our business, our readers
and our planet. This book is made from Forest
Stewardship Council® certified paper.

Contents

Prologue
Aiming to be Equal

There were four daughters in our family in St John's Wood, north-west London. Born in 1950, I was the third. We were all roughly two years apart and, though it was a house full of girls, there the similarity with *Little Women* ended. Family life for us children was dominated not just by our closeness but by our intense competitiveness. It felt like both a blessing and a torment to be part of a group of sisters who were all so near in age. I couldn't imagine what it must be like to be an only child, like the girl up the road we were friends with. I pitied her and thought she was being described as a 'lonely child'. It seemed so normal to fight constantly that I was baffled when my mother lost her temper with one of my elder sisters, Sarah, for throwing a knife at me as we carved balsa wood.

Our father was a doctor and our mother had qualified as a lawyer. Unusually for parents bringing up daughters in the fifties, ours were determined that we should stand on our own two feet and never be dependent. It wasn't just our mother who thought this but our father, too. The fact that his own mother had been a doctor – which was very unusual at that time – must have played a part in his view.

We had to get an education so we could earn a living. A good income and standard of living were worthless if they came from dependence on a man's earnings rather than on our own. Men were not to be depended on. A husband might have a heart attack or run off with a younger woman. And we should never depend on state benefits, which were paid for by the work of others. We had to learn to drive so we wouldn't end up getting in a car with a drunk boyfriend. Dependency was undesirable and even

I

dangerous. Self-reliance was essential. We were not supposed to envy the children of enormously rich parents. We should instead feel sorry for them because, dependent on money which they hadn't worked for but which had been earned by their parents, their lives would be blighted by their having no incentive to work. And we should feel sorry, too, for young women who were exceptionally beautiful – they'd just rely on their looks, never get a proper job and then, all too soon, their beauty would fade and they'd be left with nothing.

And we had to have our own opinions, and not just follow the views of others. I remember my mother telling me that most people thought that if a man said something it was more likely to be right than if a woman said something, but that she didn't agree with that. It struck me as bizarre that anyone would think it. But she was warning us about such views – and not to accept them.

My mother's upbringing had been very different to ours. For someone of her generation – she was born in 1918 – education was thought to be 'wasted on a girl'. It was important for a boy to be educated but, for middle-class girls, education was not just unnecessary, it was downright undesirable. No husband would want a wife who was 'too clever by half'. But my mother, Anna, was determined to, and did, go to university. Very few people went in those days, and only a tiny minority were women. My mother went to Oxford, one of only three women in her year to study law. The criminal-law tutor refused to teach them, pronouncing it to be a waste of his time, so the university had to arrange for a lecturer from London to come down to Oxford to teach my mother and her two fellow women students.

After Oxford, she studied as a postgraduate at the London School of Economics (LSE) under the radical socialist academic Harold Laski. During the war, she went to work for the Workers' Educational Association (WEA), a job which took her to live as a lodger with a family of factory workers in Northampton. Her work there and in the surrounding towns and villages brought educational opportunities to men and women working in the textile and footwear industries in the East Midlands, men and women with whom I would work more than fifty years later.

My mother qualified as a barrister but gave it up when she married my father and had children. She became a full-time wife and mother – as most women did, if their husband earned enough to support the family – and her barrister's wig and black robe were unceremoniously consigned to our dressing-up box. Years later, when we'd left school, she, with my father's encouragement, retrained as a solicitor. It was easier for a woman to be a solicitor rather than a barrister. Barristers get work through a solicitor, and in those days the predominantly male solicitors were reluctant to send work to a woman barrister, fearing that their clients would think they were getting only second best. I vividly remember one morning seeing my mother studying a law book she had propped up against the back of the electric stove. While my father, who had by this time retired, was reading the morning paper, my mother was cooking his breakfast (kippers) and preparing his supper (curry). The smell was terrible. I thought, You won't catch me doing that!

She says that hearing about her distant relative, Louisa Martindale, who was a suffragette, had been a big influence on her. It had given my mother the surprising, and subversive, idea that women could 'do things' – though Louisa had had to remain unmarried in order to do what she did.

I never thought of myself as being particularly influenced by my mother. On the contrary, I was one of many in my generation who were in rebellion against the lives our mothers ended up leading. My life was certainly not going to be one dominated by the wifely duties of cooking and looking after a husband. We didn't really discuss politics at home, probably to avoid arguments with my father, who was a traditional One-nation Tory. But looking back, it can't be a coincidence that so much of my politics echoes my mother's.

My mother was a strong Liberal and a great admirer of the then leader of the Liberal party, Jo Grimond. In the sixties, when she was in her forties, she stood for election as a Liberal candidate for the London County Council and then as a parliamentary candidate in Welwyn and Hatfield. She thinks she was selected as the latter only because none of the men wanted to run, as there was no chance of a Liberal winning in that constituency. We daughters would sit around the table, stuffing copies of her election address into envelopes. Though I don't remember even reading it at the time, it was full of radical demands, such as calling for an end to the sharp difference in pay and status between manual and skilled workers. This was a change that, forty years later, my husband, Jack Dromey, as a Transport and General Workers Union (TGWU) official, negotiated for public sector workers, demanding equal treatment for men and women, manual workers and white-collar workers. Her election address also laid a heavy emphasis on educational opportunities for all.

She didn't win: the Liberal vote was squeezed between the moderate Labour candidate and the successful One-nation Tory. And being a candidate, with the evening meetings that entailed, was incompatible with the duties of a middle-class wife. She was supposed to be at home cooking our father's supper and keeping everything running smoothly in the family. Though she remained active in her support of the Liberals, she never stood for any elected position again.

While our parents were undoubtedly keen that we should be educated and independent, we were also expected to find a good husband – 'good' being defined by his professional status and earning power. But men at that time didn't want a 'career woman' for a wife. So we sisters grew up with mixed messages. Though our lives were to be different from those of our mother's generation, for whom the family role had been the only priority, we were not to sacrifice our role in the family altogether. Career women – lacking a husband and children – were pitied rather than admired. And along with the conflicting expectations of us came contradictory pointers about how we were supposed to behave. We weren't supposed to be submissive, but neither should we be too assertive. No one liked a woman who was a 'show-off'. To encourage us to work hard at school we were treated to approving reports of our parents' friends' daughters who'd done well in their exams, but alongside these came reports of those for whom 'doing well' seemed to be having married a rich man. We heard cautionary tales of friends' daughters who were doomed by virtue of making the mistake of doing a secretarial course. They would be condemned for ever after to taking dictation from their boss and never have the opportunity to work their way up the ladder. But the most cautionary of all was the tale of the unmarried mother, condemned to have neither a husband nor a career. The one consistent message that came across loud and clear at every turn was: Don't get pregnant!

To reinforce our sense of independence, each of us was given our own post office account which we could access once we were sixteen. Our father put in £50, a considerable sum at the time. The idea behind it was that we might, one day, need money for something we wouldn't want to tell our parents about, or ask for money to buy. Sometimes it was ironically referred to as our 'abortion money'. (Abortion was, at that time, illegal in the UK, and it was not legalized and made available on the NHS until 1967.)

Wanting us to get the best possible education, my parents sent me to St Paul's, a girls' public day school in west London. It was an exceptional school academically but I had a turbulent time there. I hated its smug sense of superiority, which was at odds with the changing mood of the sixties. It was totally out of touch with what was going on in the rest of the country. Even when Labour won the 1964 General Election, the mock-election at St Paul's saw the Tory candidate win twice as many votes as the Labour one.

The school pushed the girls to succeed academically, and many did. But even though, despite myself, the education rubbed off on me, I felt suffocated. You were expected to work hard, but being argumentative or opinionated was anathema to the teachers. You had to learn, but never challenge. In every subject, knowledge was promulgated and we were to learn it. I was in 'resistance mode' much of the time, which took the form of not doing my homework and talking throughout lessons with my friends, particularly Kate Wilson, who has continued to be one of my closest friends for over fifty years now. Kate comes from a progressive Quaker family. No wonder, then, that she didn't fit into St Paul's either.

My sister Sarah hated it so much she left early, but I managed to last until A-levels. I set off for York University to study politics, trying to be intelligent but not too clever, trying to be independent but hoping that at some point I'd find a husband – and, above all, determined not to get pregnant.

Having felt out of sympathy with the prevailing culture at school, I fitted in no better at university. Established in 1963, York was then one of the dynamic new universities, had a great reputation, and most of the students seemed excited to be there. But though I'd been keen to leave home, I was miserable as soon as I arrived, missing the closeness of my family and my tightly knit group of schoolfriends. I probably appeared confident, but I wasn't ready to leave home and sat in my room under my Che Guevara poster, listening to gloomy songs by Leonard Cohen. I didn't like the course and couldn't see the point of learning about the structures of different legislative assemblies.

Although I instinctively identified with the left, I wasn't particularly interested in party politics at this point, and certainly not in studying it – or, indeed, studying anything at all. I just was expected, and expecting, to go to university and get a degree and I didn't want to continue with any of the three subjects (French, Spanish and geography) which I had taken reluctantly at A level. I arrived at the choice of a politics course by a process of elimination.

Despite marching through York in protest at the Bloody Sunday killings in Belfast in 1972, I didn't get involved in student politics. The Labour Club seemed plodding and old-fashioned. The rest of the left was splintered into various Trotskyite groups who seemed interested only in fighting each other and, of course, I wouldn't have been seen dead anywhere near the Conservative Club. Just as I'd failed to take up the opportunities that were undeniably there at my secondary school, I trod water at York.

At the end of my final exams, I was delighted ceremonially to throw into the rubbish bin all my notes and my thesis (a comparison between the Peloponnesian War, as told by Thucydides, and the Vietnam War). My low profile as a student was underlined to me when, some years later, I met up with the academic and broadcaster Laurie Taylor, who was the boyfriend of my friend Anna Coote. I reminded him that I'd been in his seminar group for a sociology module. He had absolutely no memory of my being there.

Towards the end of my time at York, one of my tutors, T. V. Sathyamurthy, called me in to talk about my final degree. He told me that I was borderline between a 2:1 and a 2:2 but that if I had sex with him it would definitely be a 2:1. I found him repulsive and had no doubt that, if that was what it took to get a 2:1, I'd settle for a 2:2. I had no commitment to the course and my family's hopes were not pinned on my achieving any academic distinction, so I had no hesitation in repelling his advances. Despite rejecting him, I ended up with a 2:1 anyway. A friend who'd done the same course had the same experience. But she had worked hard, was from a working-class family living in a small town and all her family's hopes were riding on her. She didn't dare risk returning home with a 2:2 and so had succumbed to his pressure to have sex with him. It was only years later that we discovered he'd tried the same thing with both of us. At the time, neither of us had even considered telling anyone else. There wasn't anyone to complain to, he'd only deny it, and though it was vile, it seemed to be just the way things were. I would have hoped that, by now, things would have changed, but reports in the *Guardian* in August and October 2016 cite surveys of university students which show a painfully similar pattern of impunity and abuse, so, evidently, more still needs to be done.

I headed back to London with a degree, but I was still none the wiser about what I would do with my life. In the end, all of us four daughters ended up qualifying as solicitors, despite having done very different courses at university. Doing legal training while we tried to work out what we really wanted to do was the default option in our family. It was a qualification which would give us the opportunity to do something with our lives.

I enrolled in the College of Law at Lancaster Gate. In the seventies, it was Part 1 for six months, two years of in-work training, articles of clerkship, and then back to the College of Law for six months of Part 2. Part 1 was statute and case law; no analysis or theory, just learning by heart. To this day, I can remember great chunks of the criminal statutes and case law. Many of my fellow students found it terribly restrictive after the academic freedom of university, but I immediately loved it. I liked how logical it was: the problem-solving, working out who should take responsibility, the weird new concepts 'Fee Simple' and 'Consideration'. I loved the strange human stories that formed the basis of our ancient laws: the snail at the bottom of the ginger-beer bottle, the sheep escaping and destroying the neighbour's crops, the murders, theft and fraud. What was guilt and what was innocence? Who would take responsibility when things went wrong? Although I had hated Latin at school, some of it had stuck with me and I loved learning the concepts locked in Latin phrases such as *mens rea, res ipsa loquitur, sui generis*, phrases which became useful for me again when I became Solicitor General three decades later. Unlike the stiflingly elite St Paul's and the narrow social base of even a new university like York, the College of Law attracted a surprisingly broad range of people, all hoping to be solicitors. I sat next to a taxi driver who, after his daytime legal studies, drove his cab at night to support his wife and child. At the college, I made friends and discovered for the first time, and to my surprise, that I had a capacity for hard work.

The good times at the College of Law gave way to bad times in my articles of clerkship at Knapp-Fishers, in Great Peter Street, Westminster. I'd looked through the *Law Society Gazette*, where articles of clerkship were advertised. Many of the firms ruled out women applicants in their ads, setting out the qualities needed in the 'right man for the job'. This was just before the Sex Discrimination Act outlawed such practices in 1975. My sister Sarah, who was applying for articles of clerkship at around the same time, telephoned a solicitors' firm, hopeful because she knew they had a woman articled clerk. They told her she couldn't apply because she was a woman. She said she understood that they already had a woman solicitor, and they replied that this was precisely the reason. 'We've already got one woman,' they said, 'so we can't have another. You'd only fight!' There was no concept of female solidarity in those days. Women were seen as rivals to each other, mostly in pursuit of the best husband, a form of divide and rule which didn't suit women and which sustained a status quo favourable to men. The women's movement challenged those attitudes and the Sex Discrimination Act changed the law.

My parents suggested I look for articles of clerkship in a firm with a wide variety of legal work and an established reputation so that, when I qualified, I would have the greatest choice of jobs. Knapp-Fishers was a solid, conventional Westminster firm. Their biggest client was Courage Brewery, for whom they did legal work on contracts, conveyancing and planning applications, as well as dealing with the directors' wills and divorces. This included acting on behalf of Courage against pub tenants whom they wanted to evict. The evidence we would present to the County Court on Courage's behalf in support of an application for an eviction order consisted of reams of unfathomable computer print-outs which purported to show that there was a gap between the volume of beer that had been delivered to a pub landlord and what the landlord had accounted for to Courage. Unable to afford their own lawyer, or accountant, there was no way the landlord could challenge it. For the landlords, eviction spelt not just the loss of their job – and often also their wife's job at the bar – but also their family home; they would also be tainted with the suspicion that they'd been dishonest. I hated the work, but I was stuck there for two years because, if I left, I would have no chance of qualifying. No one would take on an articled clerk who'd walked out on or been rejected by their firm. This meant that articled clerks were particularly powerless, and the very few of us who were young women were particularly vulnerable.

Articled clerks would spend time in the different departments of the firm, sitting in the room of each partner. One day I was standing by the window, looking out into Great Peter Street and, as I took a call from a client, the partner, Roger Maddison, crept up behind me and groped me, causing me to let out a scream in shock. When I came off the phone he rebuked me for shrieking while a client was on the phone. Of course, I didn't complain to anyone. Just as when I was at university, it never crossed my mind that complaining would do anything other than make things worse for me. I don't think I even told my soulmate, one of the other articled clerks, Julie Holman. I was just counting the days until the two years of my articles of clerkship were over. I spent a lot of time smoking in the post room with Julie, which kept me going. Without her, I'd never have stuck it out. There were a few women assistant solicitors at the firm, but it was clear that they would never become partners in what was still very much a man's world.

You would hope that legal professionals preying on junior women members of the profession would now be a thing of the past, or that, if it did happen, the victim would be supported in her complaint. But that is not the case. As recently as 2015, barrister Charlotte Proudman tweeted her objection to a senior solicitor's leering response to her photograph on LinkedIn. The pattern Charlotte Proudman described echoes my experiences with a predatory lecturer and a lecherous boss. Charlotte Proudman didn't beat about the bush in the complaint she made. She pointed out to the senior solicitor that she was 'on LinkedIn for business purposes and not to be approached about my physical appearance or objectified by sexist men', adding: 'The eroticization of women's physical appearance is a way of exercising power over women. It silences women's professional attributes, as their physical appearance becomes the subject.'

However, in the media storm that then erupted she encountered more criticism than he did. Reporting the story, the *Daily Mail* coined a new term, dubbing her a 'feminazi', and the *Sunday Times* described her as 'the most divisive woman in Britain'. She stood by her complaint, but it's disappointing that even many of those who agreed that the man was in the wrong couldn't resist adding, disapprovingly, that she shouldn't have complained publicly. The fact that she exposed what was happening and argued that it mattered only unleashed more criticism of her. She explained that with training opportunities for barristers (pupillages) in short supply, some young female law graduates feel pressured to have sex with senior male barristers as a condition of getting a place in their chambers and that some are vulnerable to pressure to have 'transactional sex'.

It is the age-old story of coercive pressure being put upon young women by older men in positions of power. Where young women are trying to break into a field dominated by older men, there are inevitably men who'll seek to abuse their power for sexual purposes. Criticism heaped on a woman who dares to complain deters other women from following suit and thereby reinforces the impunity of the men. Unless we support complainants and deal with the substance of their complaint rather than vilifying them, they will not dare to speak out and will endure assaults in silence, and young women will still be taken advantage of by unscrupulous men in thirty years' time.

Later, I found this to be true in politics, too. When I became a Labour MP, young women friends who worked in politics complained to me about uninvited sexual propositions and lunges from some of my male colleagues – though I, personally, and mercifully, did not have this experience with men MPs.

There was, however, one occasion when I was an MP where I was groped. In 1991, when Peter Hain had just been elected MP for Neath, he invited me to be the guest speaker at his constituency annual dinner at the Neath Working Men's Club. After I spoke, I accepted an invitation to dance from one of the senior members of his party, feeling I couldn't refuse, as it would appear rude. Taking advantage of the darkness of the hall, he rubbed himself all over me and groped me horribly. The dance seemed to go on for ever. But, once again, I felt I couldn't complain. This time, my reluctance was not because I was junior and vulnerable but because I was senior – an MP and the guest of honour at the dinner. To have said anything would have caused a huge row and overshadowed Peter's dinner. The Neath women, who themselves were at the time protesting that the club did not allow women to be members and still had a men-only bar, would have been mortified on my behalf. I did tell Peter, who was outraged, but I made him promise not to say anything to anyone, as I felt embarrassed and dreaded it becoming public.

My friends would talk about their bitter disappointment that Labour MPs would use their position of authority to be sexual predators. And yet, still it didn't occur to them, or to me, that such things could be reported. To whom? It was an abuse of power in a working environment and deeply resented, but there was no sense, at that time, that we could do anything about it.

Essentially, this has always been the problem with the inequality of power, with a male hierarchy and young women in junior roles. The women didn't dare challenge the men whose support would be crucial in enabling them to go forward in their career. Any complaint would see the men closing ranks. And the women had no expectation of any solidarity from other women, who would be apprehensive about supporting a junior woman against a male hierarchy and themselves be caught in the backlash.

Sexual harassment of young women by older men was endemic in society. I got the sense that, on the one hand, the men knew that what they were doing was wrong but did it anyway, knowing they could get away with it. On the other, they rationalized it to themselves as just a 'bit of fun' and pretended to themselves that they didn't know how revolted and intimidated women were, and still are, by such predatory behaviour. For the most part, the law is now there to protect women from it, but what is needed is a culture change so that women know that they can report it, that they will not be ostracized for doing so, that their complaint will be properly investigated and, if justified, will result in action being taken against the predator.

Another thing that helped me endure the time I was an articled clerk at Knapp-Fisher was the work I did as a volunteer at a legal advice centre. I was living in Fulham at that time and every Tuesday evening Fulham Legal Advice Centre's door on the Fulham Road was open to local people who had legal problems but couldn't afford a lawyer. I thought it was wonderful that the lawyers there were helping people with debt, housing and employment problems, and was proud to be a volunteer. It was at this time, in the mid-seventies, that the Law Centres Movement was gathering force, with a network of Law Centres being set up all around the country, lobbying the Law Society and government for more legal services for people on low incomes. At one of the Annual General Meetings (AGM) of the Fulham Legal Advice Centre there was a presentation by fellow members of the Law Centres Movement from Brent Law Centre. This is where I first met Jack Dromey. Jack told the AGM how he'd brought together the local tenants' associations, trade unions and radical lawyers to set up a Law Centre dedicated to helping not just individuals but the whole community, by working with local groups. They weren't giving help only to individuals to protect them in an unfair society, they were, by empowering groups of people, trying to make society itself fairer. It was not just about using the law to protect people from the system but using it to expose injustice and to try to change the system. I was transfixed. This was the way I could use my legal qualification in the cause of social justice and tackling inequality. I started volunteering after my work at Knapp-Fishers at evening sessions at Brent Law Centre. Where Knapp-Fishers had been about using the law to protect the status quo, Brent was about using the law to challenge it. While Fulham Legal Advice Centre was philanthropic and did good work, Brent was radical. I'd found my spiritual home.

The working set-up at Brent couldn't have been more different from Knapp-Fishers. Knapp-Fishers was a stifling, reactionary hierarchy with men at the top and women at the bottom, whereas Brent was a group of men and women working together on equal terms. Conventional wisdom had it that the better you were at your job, the more you were paid. But here, in a semi-derelict building in Harlesden, was a group of top-flight lawyers working for a fraction of what they could have got in a City firm of solicitors, yet they had turned their backs on it. The lawyers Jamie Ritchie and Mike Kellas worked as a team with what would now be described as community organizers, like Patrick Lefevre, trade union activists (Jack Dromey) and tenants' activists (Irene Bannon and Pam Scotcher). Irene and Pam were both 'unmarried mothers' but bore no resemblance to the downtrodden stereotypes I'd heard about as a child. They were vibrant and dynamic women doing great work in the Law Centre and in their local communities in addition to bringing up their children.

PART ONE

*Upheaval: The Rise of the
Women's Movement (Birth–1996)*

Enlisting in the Women's Movement

Although it was less than ten miles from Knapp-Fisher, it felt to me as if Brent Law Centre was on a different planet. The legal standards were unflinchingly high but, unlike Knapp-Fisher, they were using this legal expertise to protect, rather than oppress, the underdog; they were a team of women and men working together in the cause of progress.

The Law Centre was advertising for another lawyer and, as I had just qualified as a solicitor, Jack encouraged me to apply. I got the job and started working with him in a back room so small our two desks had to be pushed together. I was doing the legal work and, from his side of the desks, Jack boomed down the phone to the tenants' associations' leaders and trade unionists in the area. His desk was always covered with piles of papers – leaflets advertising meetings, minutes of previous meetings – which he stuffed into envelopes by hand and sent out in huge mailshots. He took me with him to meet all the tenants and trade unionists and soon we were spending all our time together. It was an exciting world, very different from the one I was used to, and without a doubt it was where I wanted to be and what I wanted to be doing.

The Law Centre's progressive principles infused the way in which they worked as well as the work they did. Most law firms, like the one I'd trained in, were steeply hierarchical, with well-paid male lawyers dictating letters and documents typed out by low-paid women secretaries. The secretaries were trapped at the bottom of the firm and, just as my parents had warned, had no chance to 'work their way up the ladder'. But at Brent Law Centre, the idea of women secretaries 'servicing' male bosses was rejected as male subjugation of women. The solution was that everyone would be self-servicing and do their own typing, with no one working *for* anyone else. So off we all went to Oxford Street, to a Sight and Sound typing course. Jack, Jamie and Patrick were the only men in the class, and I could hardly type for laughing at the sight of Jack, in his trademark leather jacket, his huge hands daintily tapping the keyboard. My touch-typing is excellent to this day.

In 1976, shortly after I'd started work at Brent Law Centre, a strike broke out at Trico-Folberth, a factory which made windscreen wipers, in the neighbouring borough of Brentford. The Equal Pay Act and the Sex Discrimination Act had come into force the previous year, giving women rights to equal pay and outlawing sex discrimination. These laws were put through by Labour Cabinet minister Barbara Castle and heralded a new era of social change.

Women of my generation had smarted to see men-only job ads – as I had when I was applying to firms of solicitors. Now such ads were banned and all jobs had to be open to women as well as men. Firms could no longer advertise one rate of pay for men and a lower rate for women. The Labour government was officially saying, for the first time, that women had the right to be treated as equal to men, and had passed a law to back us up. The importance of these new laws went far beyond giving women new legal rights – it was government leading cultural change.

At the time of the strike, the women who worked at Trico earned between £30 and £40 a week, about £6 less than the men. When the Equal Pay Act came into force, they felt they no longer had to put up with it. With this new promise of fairness and equality and in the strong belief that their work was no less valuable than that of the men, the women, and their union, the Amalgamated Union of Engineering Workers (AUEW), made a claim for the same rate as the men and started negotiating. The management resisted and, when talks broke down, four hundred women walked out on strike. All but a handful of the men continued to work.

The strikers were led by the dignified, matronly figures of Betty

Aiston and Eileen Ward, and by Sally Groves, one of the younger women. John Inwood of AUEW, Roger Butler, its full-time official and Jack, as secretary of the local Trades Council, were the only men on the strike committee. I was strongly supportive of the Trico women and keen to use my legal skills to help them and, at Jack's suggestion, they invited me to become their legal adviser.

The local young women with no prospect of further or higher education went straight from school to work in the factory. The youngest of the strikers was eighteen, the oldest eighty-two. Most women there couldn't afford to retire, as they had worked part-time when their children were young. This meant they were excluded from the workplace pension scheme, which was open only to full-timers, and that they hadn't paid the full National Insurance contribution 'stamp' and therefore had no entitlement to the basic state pension. The legacy of lower pay and part-time work for women means that, still today, there are women without adequate pensions having to continue to work into their late sixties and seventies.

With most of the men still working, production at the factory continued, so the women set up a picket line to appeal to the men not to go into work and to try to persuade the lorry drivers bringing in supplies to turn back. Some of the drivers did, but most didn't.

As the first strike for equal pay after the Equal Pay Act and Sex Discrimination Acts came into force, Trico hit the newspaper headlines. And it drew support from the women's movement.

The women's movement, never a single organization, was formed out of the growing belief among women from all walks of life that the inequality which women had always endured was wrong and must be challenged. The Trico women saw themselves, and were seen by other women, as a symbol of the new resistance to the status quo. But with the men continuing to work, the strike dragged on for weeks. To keep production going and to avoid the picket line, the company started bringing the delivery lorries in at night – so the women kept the picket line going through the night.

The Trico picket line looked very different from the usual sight of a row of men standing in front of a factory gate. It was made up of middle-aged women and younger ones, some of whom wore hot pants. The Trico women often faced real physical risks as they stood in the path of the delivery lorries. Even though some of the women were forbidden by their husbands to picket at night, they were adamant and they knew it was up to them to run the picketing. It was their fight, and though they welcomed support from the wider women's movement, they did not want their dispute to be taken over. However, they were happy for the women from the McVities factory further down the road to bring them biscuits while they were on the picket line.

One night, when the strike had dragged on for eighteen weeks, journalists from the BBC were there as a convoy of delivery lorries arrived, and the police, who had been called in by the management, were filmed dragging the women roughly away from the factory entrance. Seeing this on the TV news later that night, the men working at the factory became so angry that they, too, walked out. Production came to a halt and the management started to look for a settlement. The strikers won, and a big social event, which had been planned to raise support for the strike in its twenty-first week, became a victory party. Feminist supporters from the women's movement joined the strikers in their celebration, and in so doing revealed a wide cultural divide. The Trico women were dressed in their finest glittering dresses; the radical feminists came in dungarees. I certainly wasn't in dungarees. I, too, was committing the ideological error – as some saw it in those early days of the women's movement – of dressing up for the occasion, in my case, in a Laura Ashley frock.

Jack had challenged the police about their manhandling of the women pickets that night and was arrested. I went to the police station to arrange his bail. He was prosecuted on two charges in the local magistrates' court. As I had seen it happen, I gave evidence for him and automatically assumed that, on that basis, he'd be acquitted on both charges. I was a solicitor, and therefore an Officer of the Court whose word would be trusted. But, as it turned out, the fact that I was on the side of the striking workers was more important to the court than the fact that I was a solicitor. Faced with the choice of believing the evidence of the police witness or my evidence as a radical solicitor acting for the strikers, the magistrates went with the police version. It was a moment that signalled to me that I was no longer seen by the establishment as 'one of them'. Jack was acquitted of assaulting the police – a serious charge for which he could have faced prison – but found guilty of the lesser charge of using threatening words and behaviour. Many of those involved in strikes in the seventies and eighties ended up with a criminal record. And that was no trivial matter: it would count against you in future job applications and, as Jack found later, when applying for a visa to visit the US.

The summer the Trico dispute was settled saw the start of a strike at Grunwick, a film-processing factory just around the corner from Brent Law Centre. Most of the employees were Asian women who wanted to join a union to protect them from management bullying. Jayaben Desai, a tiny, soft-spoken, middle-aged woman, led the walk-out, which was the start of a strike for union recognition that was to last nearly two years. The strike was notable not just because the majority of the workers were women but because they were Asian. Now, with the growth of trade unionism in the public sector, most trade union members are women and many are black and Asian. But, back then, most trade union activism was carried out by white men. Most of the Grunwick workers were of Indian origin and had come to Britain after having been expelled from Uganda. They were from the mercantile and administrative classes and, though they embraced hard work, they refused to accept being pushed around by management. Mahmood Ahmed was secretary to the strike committee, Jack, as Secretary of the Brent Trades Council, was a member of it and, once again, I was legal adviser. Grunwick became a national cause célèbre and, over the months, I got to know the trade union leaders and activists who came to

Brent from all around the country to join the picket line to demon-strate their support for the strikers. I made regular visits to Willesden Green police station to arrange bail for arrested picket-ers, among them Arthur Scargill, who'd led a group of more than a thousand miners to join the picket.

Although the Labour government supported the strikers' object-ive of union recognition, the strike was highly controversial. It was a stand-off between an employer and his workers, and the dispute spilled out into the surrounding streets. There were mass pickets following the arrest of eighty-four of the picketers, and then the Cricklewood post office workers came out in solidarity, refusing to deliver post to Grunwick. The obligations of the post office are laid down in law, and the hundred Cricklewood post office workers, members of the Union of Communication Workers (UCW), were suspended from work and threatened with the sack. These were white workers putting their jobs at risk to help newly arrived immi-grant workers. It was unprecedented, and a huge national news story.

Despite attempts by the independent Advisory, Conciliation and Arbitration Service (ACAS) to broker a settlement, and a court of inquiry ruling that the Grunwick workers should get trade union representation and that the striking workers should be reinstated in their jobs, the management at Grunwick resisted. The strike was called off, the strikers defeated. Yet although the strike failed in its objectives, the Grunwick dispute was to have a profound political impact. It became a potent and enduring symbol of the workers' struggle. Thousands of people from all around the country had come to Brent to support the strike and would never forget the part they played in it. The backing of the Trades Union Congress (TUC) demonstrated the emerging commitment of the trade union move-ment to equality at work for people from ethnic minority communities, and the defeat of the strikers paved the way for the right to trade union recognition which would be introduced into law by the Labour government over twenty years later.

I was now practising as a lawyer, but in a very different way to that my parents had envisaged when I went off to law school. Instead of being part of the establishment, I was becoming more and more deeply involved in challenging it.

Jack and I had both been caught up in a battle that we cared passionately about, and we were together all the time, in meetings and on picket lines. We never once went on a 'date' but, by now, we were a couple. One night when I was back home having supper with my parents, a news report from Grunwick came on the television. The commentary was about the disorder in the local streets, and Jack was reported as being at the centre of it all and it was mentioned that he had been convicted of a criminal offence. The newspapers had for months been carrying lurid stories depicting Jack as subversive and dangerous and had dubbed him 'Jack of All Disputes'. My father grumbled his disapproval – especially for 'that Jack Dromey'. But Jack and I were already living together – though my parents didn't know it – so I said nothing.

My father took the stereotypical view of working-class Irish Catholics that they drank and had too many children and, worse, that they might support the IRA. The fact that Jack came from an immigrant Irish working-class family was then another reason for arousing my father's disapproval of him. But in the seventies things were changing. London was becoming freer from the rigid class divisions that had characterized my parents' generation. Young people were getting together on the basis of their work and their beliefs, rather than just sticking with people from a similar background to them. Jack's life was going to be very different from that of his traditional working-class parents, just as mine was going to be very different from that of my traditional middle-class parents. A short while later I told my parents that Jack and I were living together. They invited us over to supper and then came over to supper at our home in Brent.

My job and my partner were very different from what my parents had hoped for me. I was working in a Law Centre rather than in a respectable solicitors' practice. And Jack could not have been further from the professional middle-class husband they had envisaged. And the last straw was that Jack and I were living together without being married at a time when cohabitation was thoroughly disapproved of. Unsurprisingly, then, the atmosphere at these suppers started off tense, but after a while it thawed, as my parents realized that, whatever they thought, Jack and I were a couple and that, far from inciting me to denounce them, Jack wanted us all to be on good terms.

Of all the things that were changing for me in the seventies, it was the women's movement which was to have the biggest and most far-reaching impact.

This was a time when women were thoroughly constrained, told what we could and, more often, couldn't do. You can't expect the same pay as a man, you can't expect to be treated equally at work, you can't expect men to play their part at home, you can't object if your husband beats you, you can't expect to be valued if you're not young and pretty, you can't expect to be taken seriously intellectually if you are. And I, along with many young women back then, had an equally strong corresponding conviction that we were not going to put up with it.

The women's movement was developing rapidly, finding support among both middle-class and working-class women. At its heart was the idea that women were not inferior to men and should not be subordinate to them. We wanted to be equal. The movement had many different strands, but perhaps three were dominant: the radical feminists involved in 'consciousness raising'; those women who were keen to tackle issues of domestic violence; and those campaigning for women's rights.

The radical feminist consciousness-raising sessions were, typically, weekly women-only discussion groups focusing on key gender issues such as equality at work, equal opportunities in education and access to abortion. They also included the politics of sexuality, emphasizing the importance of women defining their own sexuality rather than having it defined for them by men. And for some, the focus was on supporting lesbianism. There were

Annual Women's Liberation conferences and Women's Liberation marches, but I was uncomfortable about sitting in a group discussing sex so I didn't get involved in these.

As for the second strand, the women organizing around challenging rape and domestic violence, this was a time when a woman who was raped was likely to be blamed as 'having brought it on herself' and when a man beating his wife was treated as a private matter: 'Who knows what goes on behind closed doors?' The national standard bearer challenging domestic violence then was Erin Pizzey, who set up Chiswick Women's Aid in west London in 1971. All around the country, women were getting together to set up women's refuges, including my sister Sarah, by this time a lawyer, who was involved in establishing a refuge in Canterbury. Women were beginning to be critical of the police and the courts for not taking domestic violence or sexual offences seriously and were demanding changes in the law.

The third strand was the fight for women's rights. Firmly rooted in feminist ideology, it concentrated its efforts on winning very practical rights for women and on challenging the laws and structures within which men's 'superior' status was entrenched.

Although there was a sense that we were all part of the same movement, and a great deal of shared thinking, there were also different views within and between these different strands of the women's movement. Some, for example, argued that women who stayed at home to look after their children should be paid 'wages for housework'. Others, as I did, saw this as entrenching the role of women in the home and argued that what was important was not that women be paid for working in the home but that they be paid properly for going out to work and that men should play a bigger role in the home and in caring for their children.

Some women campaigned for round-the-clock crèche facilities so that women could work the same hours as men did, while others, including me, argued that, while childcare provision should be made more widely available, the way forward was not to consign children to twenty-four-hour crèches but to campaign for longer maternity leave, for part-time workers to have equal rights to full-time workers, and for men to take on more responsibility in the home.

There were conflicting views on fatherhood. In the women's rights strand of the movement, we wanted men to do more within the family home and in the care of their children. We saw this as important not just for the sake of the father, and for the sake of the child, who would benefit from having a strong relationship with both parents, but also for the mother. It was essential as a precondition of women's equality at work that men should share in the work at home. So long as women retained the lion's share of responsibility for children, they would never, we believed, be equal in the world outside. The 'division of labour' in the home entrenched inequality at work. An active and engaged father was necessary for the mother's liberation. So we argued for the father to be present at the birth of his children, and for the right to paternity leave and paternity pay. Others, however, particularly many of the women working on tackling domestic violence, saw fathers, all too often, as a threat from which the family needed protection rather than as a parent whose involvement needed to be encouraged. They felt it was better to marginalize men from this role and to focus on the ability of women to bring up their children successfully on their own.

There were also divisions between women lawyers. We all vigorously opposed the notion that a man could avoid a rape conviction by saying, 'When a woman says no, she means yes,' or by arguing that, if the victim had had a number of previous sexual partners, she must have consented to sex, or that she had 'brought it on herself' by, for example, wearing a short skirt. But while some women barristers refused to represent defendants who sought to run these defences, others did represent them, on the basis that every suspect has the right to defend themselves in the way they want.

Some who were working hard to establish women's refuges argued that women victims of domestic violence should be warned that the police could not be trusted, would not help them and that reporting their abuse would only put them in greater danger. Others, including me, argued that we should campaign to make the law enforcement agencies tackle the issue and that deterring women from reporting domestic violence would only serve to prolong the impunity of abusive men.

There were also sharp disagreements on the issue of pornography. Some women argued that it was male exploitation of women and should be banned, others that it was about women expressing their own sexuality and that we should protect freedom of expression and oppose censorship. On prostitution, some argued for a woman's right to choose to be a 'sex worker' and called for it to be licensed. Others, including me, saw prostitution as the exploitation by men of vulnerable women and wanted the men paying for sex to be prosecuted.

And there were different views on the laws that were then in place to protect women, like those which, arising from the Factory Acts of 1831 and 1833, prevented women from being employed in certain factory jobs, or the laws that kept women from serving on the front line of the armed services. Some argued that we should be campaigning to keep and strengthen these protections for women; others that, rather than protection, such restrictions were a limitation on women and so should be abolished, and that women should have the same right as men to be in the armed forces, take part in boxing matches, and perform any job in a factory.

And we had different views about the role of men in our personal lives. Many of us searched for a 'new man' or tried to turn our partner into someone with whom we could be a genuinely equal partner in all things, both inside and outside the home. Others thought this was unrealistic, that men were a write-off and it was better for women to give up any idea of men changing and instead get on with living a life without them.

However, although we didn't hold the same views on these issues, we all passionately believed in the centrality of the issues themselves, and debated them vigorously. While we didn't always agree among ourselves on certain points, as women, we all agreed that it was for us to discuss and decide on these questions and held the radical and subversive view that what mattered was what *we* thought and that we would not be told by men either what we should do or what we should think. The women's movement spawned a multiplicity of organizations both at national and local levels, and networks of women grew within existing organizations. Unlike in the US, which had the National Organisation of Women, there was no single organization in the UK. But despite that, we felt the exhilaration of being part of the great force which was the emerging women's movement. There were no limits to our ambition. The bigger the obstacle, the more determined we were. The more we were told we couldn't do something, the stronger we fought to do it. We were convinced we could challenge the old order and bring about seismic change in our own lives, in society and in the economy.

Paradoxically, with the women's movement growing, by the end of the decade we found ourselves in unequivocal opposition to our first woman prime minister. Far from seeing Margaret Thatcher's move to Number Ten in 1979 as a step forward, we loathed her. Britain's first woman prime minister was not from the Labour party, the party of equality, but from the Tory party. For us, left-wing feminists in a left-wing movement, the election of a right-wing Tory as the first woman prime minister was an excruciating blow. It was undeniable that, symbolically, the appointment of a woman to lead the country was of huge importance. It sent out the message that there was no job that a woman could not do. But Margaret Thatcher was not a feminist determined to use her high office on behalf of other women. Her approach was to beat the men in her party on their own terms and show that she could do this *despite* being a woman. And we believed that the Conservative policies she pursued undermined opportunities for women. She cut back the public services women often rely on, for example, home helps for the elderly. She opposed rules requiring employers to treat women equally. But she, the champion of women as housewives, was elected to govern, while we, who championed women at work, languished in opposition. We certainly didn't celebrate her move to Number Ten as a breakthrough for women; instead, we campaigned to highlight the ways in which her government's policies would hit women hardest, and marched under banners proclaiming, 'The First Lady Puts Women Last.'

It was the fight for women's rights that drew me into the women's movement. Discrimination against women was not just endemic, it was perfectly legal. In the first few years of the seventies, employers would advertise for male workers, and women doing the same jobs as men would be paid the lower 'women's' rate. A married woman would be expected to give up her own name and take her husband's. She could not sign a mortgage on her own, nor even a television-rental agreement. A married woman could not have a private bank account because her income had to be added on to her husband's tax return. Because marriage conferred on a man the 'right' to have sex with his wife, a married man could not be charged with raping his wife, even if they were separated. Men-only boardrooms and men-only working men's clubs were the norm. A lone woman would be refused service at a hotel bar on the assumption that, if she was on her own, she could be there only in order to pick up a man – so she must be a prostitute.

We were angry that, in every sense, women were second-class citizens. The women's movement was the tide that challenged this. At the epicentre was the Women's Rights Committee of the National Council for Civil Liberties. The NCCL was a members' organization founded on an alliance between libertarians and trade unionists. The Women's Rights Committee blazed a trail, highlighting discrimination and inequality, mapping out the policy changes needed and campaigning for them. As well as being pivotal in drawing up the new Sex Discrimination Act, passed in 1975, which formed the basis of my work with the Trico women, they campaigned for and won many other rights, including that women's income be treated separately for tax purposes.

They changed the civil service recruitment rules through the test case of Belinda Price in 1977. Belinda had taken a degree in her late twenties after having children and had applied for a job in the civil service. But she was excluded because there was a maximum age of twenty-five. She applied to the Equal Opportunities Commission for legal help, but they turned her down on the basis that the rule applied to men as well as women. But the new Sex Discrimination Act outlawed actions which, though they applied to both men and women, in their impact disproportionately hit women. The NCCL took up her case, arguing that it was indirect discrimination that penalized women because it was they who were more likely to be the applicants excluded by the age limit as they were more likely to embark on a career later because of taking time off to look after children. Belinda Price won her case, and the maximum age limit for joining the civil service was abolished in 1978.

Over the road from the Law Courts in the Strand was El Vino, a bar where the elite of the legal profession and Fleet Street journalists met to drink after work. Women were allowed to go in but not to order a drink. El Vino was a symbol not just of women being excluded from buying a drink but from the higher ranks of the legal profession and the press. With the Sex Discrimination Act newly in force, the Women's Rights Committee decided to challenge this as discrimination in the 'provision of services'. Two members of the committee – Anna Coote, a journalist, and Tess Gill, a radical lawyer – went up to the bar and ordered a drink. When they were refused service, they took the case to court. Their demand to be served, and their court case, was criticized by the right – they were simply making a fuss about a trivial issue – and by some on the left, who said that buying a drink in a central London wine bar was irrelevant to the mass of working women. The pair were lambasted in the press. But the point was that El Vino's ban embodied the view not only that the centre of the legal and journalistic professions was men-only but that women were only allowed anywhere at the behest of men, and women on their own in a bar, or similar, were thought to have no role other than that of prostitute. The NCCL was keen to confront discrimination wherever it found it. Anna and Tess won the case. And this was seen by women around the country, who were starting to refuse to accept the way things had always been and to challenge the exclusively male networks which ran everything from the law, to politics, to business, to the media and trade unions. Instead of women simply suffering on their own, there was now a vocal protest movement demanding change. Hundreds of thousands of women played their part in many different ways over the decades to follow. And many more who could not themselves take part saw other women fighting for them and felt empowered.

Jack was heavily involved in the NCCL, both on its executive and, in particular, in its work against internment in Northern Ireland. As I was a committed feminist and the work I was doing at Brent Law Centre was also about helping women enforce their rights, Jack introduced me to the members of the Women's Rights Committee in 1974. Both Anna Coote and Tess Gill were founder members, as were Christine Jackson, who ran the Cobden Trust (the research arm of the NCCL), Catherine (Cash) Scorer, the NCCL Northern Ireland Officer, and Bill Birtles, a barrister and the only man on the committee. Patricia Hewitt had become the first NCCL Women's Officer in 1972. They were well-known nationally and I had heard all about their work and was in awe of it.

The aim was threefold: to inform women of their rights, to help enforce these rights and to press for full legal, political, economic and social equality for women. Bill, Patricia and Tess prepared draft clauses for the Sex Discrimination Bill. Anna and Tess wrote the *NCCL Guide to Women's Rights*, which went into every bookshop. We all went to Manchester for the first meeting of the newly established Equal Opportunities Commission, set up under the Sex Discrimination Act, held specifically for women's organizations in 1975. After that, they invited me to join the Women's Rights Committee. The committee would meet after work in rotation in members' homes, where, despite our ideological rejection of women's domestic role, there was stiff competition over the cooking. We enjoyed the contradiction that, as feminists who wanted women's role to be more than domestic, we put such a huge effort into it. Even so, as we were seen in the press as very much part of the movement that was challenging the notion of male superiority, we were stigmatized as 'bra-burning man-haters'. Though some of the women's movement certainly were, we weren't. While many radical feminists rejected make-up and wore dungarees, I, for one, was wearing black eyeliner and a miniskirt.

It was intoxicating for me to be on the NCCL Women's Rights Committee. I found the women's movement electrifying. Angry at inequality, we had the sense that by working together we could make great changes. I was thrilled to be working with Tess, Anna and Patricia, who seemed to me to combine a great mission with a sense of fun, and to be both fearless and glamorous. It was a wonderful, close-knit and creative group. We were firm friends as well as close work colleagues, and our work, social and personal lives became interwoven. Patricia married Bill Birtles. Anna married Laurie Taylor, an academic and broadcaster who was also involved in the NCCL. Christine Jackson was married to a Labour MP, Peter Jackson. Tess was married to leading trade union General Secretary Ken Gill. I was with Jack. At supper in each other's homes we talked about how we would challenge injustice and spearhead change.

When I'd been on the NCCL Women's Rights Committee for a few months, the legal officer resigned, creating a vacancy, and Jack suggested I apply. The role was one that was nationally recognized at that time and had a high public profile. Even though I was a member of the Women's Rights Committee and had been doing similar work at a local level at Brent Law Centre, I had never dreamt that I could step up and do that job. But with the moral support of my sister Sarah and of Jack, I applied and got the job.

With Patricia having been promoted to General Secretary, and Jack, Tess and Anna on the NCCL executive, I had plenty of help in finding my feet, which was essential, as, though I was only in my twenties, I was handling High Court cases, challenging the police and the government and speaking publicly for the NCCL. Within a month of being appointed NCCL legal officer, I was told by Patricia that I was to go on the *Jimmy Young Show* on BBC Radio 2, which had at the time millions of listeners, to talk about the need for a new right to privacy. It was a long way from my work in Brent Law Centre, let alone Knapp-Fisher, and most experts you heard talking on the radio back then were men. I was certainly no expert on the campaign for privacy rights and, having never been on the radio before, felt daunted by the prospect. Patricia gave me a copy of the pamphlet she'd just written to learn overnight and told me to sit calmly in the studio with my hands folded in my lap. It was the first of thousands of TV and radio interviews over the decades that followed. Patricia was keen that the NCCL should have a high profile and, as legal officer, I was catapulted into the front line. There was no point in shouting or emoting. We had no power at the NCCL other than the strength of our arguments. There was no such thing as media training in those days, and certainly not for people like us, so we developed our own approach, which was to ensure that we knew the facts and to put our case clearly and persuasively at every opportunity.

I appeared as a guest on *Any Questions*, the Friday-night political panel show on Radio 4, and from 1979 on BBC TV's *Question Time*, which was hosted at that time by Robin Day, in his trademark spotted bow-tie. In 1980, I was invited on what was at that time a new programme, *Newsnight*, and over the following years I went on just about every national and local radio and TV station. I got to know the newspaper and television legal correspondents, foremost among whom were the *Times*'s Marcel Berlins and, later, Frances Gibb, and Joshua Rozenberg at the BBC.

As NCCL legal officer, I took some of the first Equal Pay and Sex Discrimination Act cases, which would set out how the new laws would work in practice. This further strengthened the links between me, as a woman lawyer, and women working in factories. One such case was that of Brenda Clarke, a Birmingham woman who worked in the Kynoch munitions factory. There were redundancies at the factory in 1981, and her union, the TGWU, had negotiated an agreement that redundancy was to be on a 'last in first out' basis, but with the usual provision that all the part-timers were to be made redundant in the first instance. All the part-timers were women and most of the full-timers were men. So what the redundancy agreement meant, in effect, was that the women would be made redundant before the men.

The women part-timers were all TGWU members but they had not been part of the negotiations and so had had no say in the decision. Brenda Clarke wrote to the NCCL, and her heartfelt hand-written letter pointing out that the women's work was important to them and to their household budgets arrived on my desk. It was not just 'pin money' and, indeed, for those who were lone parents, it was their only source of income. I phoned the TGWU National Women's Officer, Marie Patterson, whom I knew, asking her to step in on behalf of the women, but she refused, saying that the redundancy agreement had been locally negotiated. She would not acknowledge that it was sex discrimination, and warned me that it would be 'anti-union' if I took up the women's case. Though we dreaded being seen as 'anti-union', the Women's Rights Committee did not hesitate and decided that the NCCL would support the women. I instructed the radical barrister Stephen Sedley to represent them at the industrial tribunal, citing both the employer and the union as the respondents.

Brenda was as far from the stereotype of a London radical feminist as you could get, a soft-spoken, hard-working married woman in her thirties, but like so many women, hearing that they were now entitled to be treated equally to men, she was no longer prepared to see women's jobs tossed aside as if they were of no importance and was determined to stand up for herself and the other women in her workplace, taking on not just the management but the men in the factory and her own union. That was an incredibly courageous thing to do and, when we won the case, it laid down for the first time that treating part-timers less favourably than full-timers was unlawful; it was indirect discrimination in breach of the Sex Discrimination Act.

The leadership role Brenda had taken on in fighting for women against their employer, their male colleagues and their union gave her the confidence and determination to go on to become a Labour councillor on Birmingham City Council, part of the growing minority of women who were becoming local councillors. At that time, in the late seventies, 80 per cent of the councillors in Birmingham were men. In the decades ahead, I would always be delighted to bump into Brenda, and I often did, whenever I was campaigning in the West Midlands.

The number of women becoming activists in their place of work was growing inexorably, and this, as it had with Brenda Clarke, crossed over into political activism. All around the country, women campaigners were getting to know each other and working together in the cause of equality. But while it was often reported in the newspapers, it remained firmly on the margins of what was regarded as real politics or real trade unionism, which continued to be seen as something that was done only by men.

My role as NCCL legal officer involved working not just on issues of women's rights but on a whole range of civil liberties. We felt that we were fighting for and enhancing the fundamental rights which underpin democracy in the UK and using the law to protect vulnerable individuals against the government's abuse of its powers. But the government, and the establishment in general, took the view that we were subversive and dangerous. Indeed, it later became clear that, because of our work at the NCCL, Jack, Patricia Hewitt and I had been under surveillance by the security services.

One of the legal cases which brought me into the most direct conflict with the 'powers that be' was our challenge to a new experiment which the Home Office was trying out to deal with disruptive prisoners. Unruly prisoners were now to be put in Control Units for six months' solitary confinement instead of the one month laid down in the law governing prison regimes.

Fighting this case on behalf of two prisoners who were in the first such unit was to have ramifications for me which would last years. I came to public attention as a radical lawyer fighting human rights cases against the government, but I was nearly 'struck off' as a solicitor, I attracted the open hostility of both the government and the judiciary, and I was pursued by a violent stalker. We lost the case against the government on the Control Units but, with the stoical support of my boss, Patricia Hewitt, we defeated the establishment's attacks on me in the European Court of Human Rights.

The problems arose when the NCCL launched a legal action against the Home Office on behalf of two of the men in the Control Units. In cases which go to the civil courts there's a process called Discovery of Documents, which requires each side to show the other all documents relevant to the case in advance of the hearing. The rationale behind this is that before the trial starts, as many as possible of the facts and issues in the case will be clear to both sides and to the court. As the lawyer for the prisoners, I applied to the Home Office to see all their documents. The Home Office was one of the most secretive of government departments, so I was not surprised when at first the government lawyers sent me just a handful. However, like all government departments, the Home Office puts everything in writing, so I knew they were not complying with the rules which oblige lawyers to ensure their clients offer full disclosure. Clearly, I was going to have to drag these documents out of them in order to be able to see what they said about the proposed regime and its compliance, or otherwise, with the Prison Rules. Eventually, I received more and, after a while, the floor of my office was covered with the documents as I read and sorted through them. As I did, I saw references to yet more documents which hadn't been sent to me, so I made further requests. And so it went on until we had the full picture.

The Labour Home Secretary at the time when the Control Units regime was developed was Roy Jenkins, who was a progressive on prison issues, yet, behind his back, his department had devised a repressive and, in our view, illegal regime of solitary confinement.

I could see in the documents that he had asked for assurances that the regime was not going to be inhumane but he had been fobbed off by the civil servants. Seeing the obvious progressive instincts of the Home Secretary being undermined by his department's attempts to keep him in the dark reinforced my commitment to the NCCL's policy calling for a Freedom of Information Act, something Labour would introduce in 2000. It was clearly necessary not just to prevent ministers from keeping secrets from the public but to prevent civil servants keeping secrets from their minister.

The new documents showed that the prison medical officer was worried about the effect such a long period of solitary confinement was having on prisoners and revealed that the prison chaplain had protested vehemently and threatened to resign over the inhumanity of the Control Units. It was all material which we needed to set out to the court. Seeing the documents they had tried to keep back leave the Home Office and go into the hands of the NCCL had obviously been the cause of major consternation in the government; it was evident that the Home Office was unhappy at the prospect of this material coming under scrutiny. But the rules of Discovery, which I was fully aware of, are very clear. When you receive documents under this process, they are confidential; you can use them for the case but for no other purpose.

The prisoners' case against the Home Office was heard in the High Court in the Strand, and we were once again represented by Stephen Sedley QC, who was married to Ann Sedley, who was later to become the NCCL Women's Rights Officer. To explain to the judge what was going on in the Control Units, Stephen read out the relevant sections of the documents. Despite the fact that the documents clearly showed that the regime prescribed six months' solitary confinement when the Prison Rules limited it to one month, we lost the case. However, during the course of the hearing a number of journalists were sitting in the reporters' box, scribbling notes as Stephen Sedley read out to the court the documents revealing that there were major concerns, not least within the prison service itself, about what a draconian regime the Control

Units were. One of those journalists was the *Guardian*'s David Leigh. Because so much documentation had been read out, and so quickly, David asked if he could come to my office the next day to check his notes for his report. I agreed but was emphatic that he should see only the parts of the documents which had been read out in court. My view was that those were in the public domain and so it wouldn't be a breach of the Discovery rules to show them to him. The next day, the *Guardian* printed a devastating two-page article showing what had been going on in the Control Units. The Home Office was furious and the Attorney General, Michael Havers QC, authorized them to launch a case against me for contempt of court. The Law Society, of which I was a member and which should have defended me, cravenly took the government's side and embarked on disciplinary proceedings against me to take away my practising certificate.

It is hard to overstate how horrifying all this was. I was a recently qualified lawyer. I'd toiled through my law exams and my grim articles of clerkship. I was in a job I loved, my legal career was just taking off, and now it looked as though it was going to end in the public disgrace of being found guilty of contempt. Not only that, it would seriously damage the NCCL, which had a strict rule that, although we could protest, all our activity must be within the law. I believed that because the documents were in the public domain, a contempt case which said it was wrong to have shown them to a journalist would fail. But my solicitor, Michael Seifert, spelt it out to me. He was a member of the Communist party and gave a steely Marxist analysis. 'The courts will have a choice between the NCCL legal officer and the Home Office,' he said. 'Who do you think they'll choose? Not you!'

The NCCL was a thorn in the side of the government. We took cases challenging them on the right to demonstrate. We raised questions about internment in Northern Ireland and set up an independent commission of inquiry into Bloody Sunday, exposing the official inquiry, by Lord Widgery, as a whitewash. We persistently shone a light on what we saw as government abuse of their powers.

The Home Office seemed delighted that it had, as it saw it, caught me, and the NCCL, out. The establishment is always looking for an opportunity to move against radical lawyers who challenge the status quo, as they are doing today with the firm Leigh Day, which is taking on the government and multinationals on human rights and environmental law.

I got on with my work and tried to explain the story to a baffled media, which, on this occasion, were firmly on my side. Most of the newspapers disapproved of the NCCL, but they disapproved even more of any restrictions on the press. The practice of journalists sitting in court and reporting the proceedings was well established. Justice was not only to be done, it had to be seen to be done. They couldn't get their heads around the idea that I was being prosecuted for showing a journalist documents which had already been read out in open court. They kept asking if the court had been sitting in camera (a private sitting where the judge has ruled that the press and public be excluded). It hadn't. They asked if the documents I'd shown the journalist were ones which hadn't been read out. They weren't.

This time, instead of acting for the defendant, as I usually did, I was the defendant and I was to be the one in the dock. It felt as if a steamroller was heading towards me, and I was terrified. The night before the case was due to start I got a call from Mike Seifert, who told me that the government's lawyers had called him, saying that, if I apologized and made a public admission that what I'd done was wrong, they'd drop the case. I was desperate to avoid the dock but convinced I'd done nothing wrong. I called Patricia about it. She asked, 'Well, do you think you have done anything illegal or wrong?' I said no, of course not. 'Right,' she said. 'We fight on and we fight to win.' So despite his warning that I was heading for a conviction, I told Mike we were not accepting the offer and that the case would go to court.

The next day the case was heard in the High Court on the Strand. Patricia decided we should not sneak into court through the back door and we walked defiantly up the steps to the front doors, determined to show that we had nothing to be ashamed of, that this was a fight of principle.

As Mike had predicted, the high court found me guilty of contempt. We appealed and, three months later, the case came before the legendary Lord Justice Denning. (It was he who had, in 1977, issued a notable rebuke to government, using the phrase 'Be ye never so high, the law is above you' in one of his judgements.) But although Denning had a reputation for holding the government to account, Mike gloomily predicted that he would choose the Home Office. Again, he was right.

Lord Denning's judgement was a thoroughgoing defence of 'the Establishment'. He said that confidential documents had been exposed to the 'ravages of outsiders' and that he regarded the use of the documents to be 'highly detrimental to the good ordering of our society . . . they were used so as to launch a wholly unjustified attack on ministers and high civil servants who were doing their best to deal with a wicked criminal who had harassed society'. He added: 'The danger of disclosure is that critics – of one political colour or another – will seize on this confidential information in order to seek changes in government policy, or to condemn it. So the machinery of government will be hampered or even thwarted.' Lord Denning said I had acted 'unprofessionally and irresponsibly'.

We appealed again, this time to the House of Lords Judicial Committee (the precursor of the Supreme Court), and lost again when they ruled in favour of the Home Office by three to two. Having gone through all the avenues of appeal in the UK and failing, we then appealed to the European Court of Human Rights, claiming that the conviction breached my right to freedom of expression. We had to wait four years before the case came to court in Strasbourg. It was carried out on the basis of legal arguments, so I didn't have to give evidence, but I did go to the hearing in June 1986.

The European Court of Human Rights in Strasbourg found in my favour, and against the government. In a judgement which relied on the common sense which had escaped the UK courts, they ruled that I couldn't have breached confidentiality because, having been read out in court, the documents were already in the public domain.

The European Court ordered the government to pay all our legal costs and, finally, the threat of disciplinary action by the Law Society was lifted. By the time the European Court found in my favour, even the establishment had stopped trying to justify taking out a case of contempt of court against me. After the European Court ruling, I found myself standing next to Sir Michael Havers while we were waiting for a vote. He asked whether I was enjoying being in the House of Commons and said how awful it must have been for me to face such an unjustified prosecution. I reminded him that it had been his decision to take the case against me. He implied that it had not really been his decision but that of the Home Office. But a contempt case can be launched only with the explicit consent of the Attorney General and, as such, it was very much his responsibility. He launched an oppressive prosecution against me for exposing a harsh, hidden prison regime and then expected to be able to brush it aside. I thought it was pitiful.

After we lost the case against the Control Units, one of the inmates had become obsessed with me; he was what the police would now-adays describe as a 'fixated individual'. And his obsession was stoked constantly by my high profile in the media and the regular reports of my contempt of court case. He wrote hundreds of threatening letters, sending most to my office at the House of Commons but putting some through our letterbox at home. Sometimes I'd see him watching our house from the other side of the road. He phoned my office and our home and came to my advice surgeries. He was menacing and angry. Having been his solicitor, I was fully aware of every detail of his record of violent crime. I knew that he didn't just threaten violence, he carried it out.

It was frightening, coming home on my own to a deserted street in the small hours of the morning after late votes in the House of Commons, fearing that he might be lurking somewhere. But he had been my client, and I'd been defending him against the authorities, so I was reluctant to call the police. Neither did I want to be accused of absorbing hard-pressed local police resources when so many of my constituents couldn't get the protection they needed from the police. I didn't want it to be thought that I was getting preferential treatment. And I worried it might make the stalking worse and that my taking action against him was exactly what he wanted, as it would keep open a connection between me and him. I had too much on my plate and couldn't see how I could deal with it so, although I told Jack about my fears, I did nothing. But I always knew when he was back in prison because those were the times I got respite from the stalking, his letters and his phone calls.

This went on for years until one day in 1989 my office told me that the Maudsley – the local psychiatric hospital – had called and wanted to speak to me urgently. I phoned them back, to be told that my stalker was a patient there. He was Scottish but told them he'd come to live in the local area 'to be near me' and that he was going to kill me. They told me that they were breaching patient confidentiality to tell me this because they judged that his mental condition meant that he was a serious threat. They said they hadn't called the police because of patient confidentiality but that I should do so, as I was in danger. I was exasperated. They'd told me, but they wouldn't tell the police, who were the only people in a position to do anything about it. After hearing the Maudsley's warning I was now really scared, but they wouldn't take the next step to help me get it sorted out. I did what they suggested and called the police, who sent an officer around straight away. As I tipped out the carrier bags full of just some of the letters, which I'd kept, they were aghast that I'd done nothing about it before. And I felt they were worried and didn't want something to happen to me 'on their patch'. They immediately arrested him and he was remanded in custody. It was such a relief. It was not until then that I allowed myself to recognize how frightened I'd become.

However, although after his arrest he didn't come to my home again or write me any more letters, he launched a legal action against the police for wrongful arrest, claiming that I had pressurized them into arresting him. I was sure this was his way of getting me into the witness box so he could cross-examine me and re-establish the connection he felt there was between us. The police had charged him with threatening to kill me but they had no option but to drop the case when the Maudsley refused to give evidence, on the grounds that he was their patient and they felt it would interfere with his treatment. The newspapers, which couldn't be told about the threats he had made at the Maudsley, and which were largely hostile to the NCCL, portrayed the situation as me abusing my power against an innocent victim. My stalker was the victim and I was a Labour MP, throwing my weight around. It led to more hostile publicity for me, but at least he never contacted me again and at last I could stop looking over my shoulder.

The law now protects victims of stalking, and I was an avid backer of Labour MP Janet Anderson's Protection from Harassment Act in 1997. I would hope that, nowadays, the newspapers would recognize that, far from it being a case of me abusing my power, it was a case of me suffering the terrifying ordeal of being stalked.

The NCCL was not affiliated to any political party. Neither was the women's movement. But from the time I'd started work at Fulham Legal Advice Centre, I'd been a member of the Labour party. It was to the Labour party that I looked to pursue the feminist agenda about which I felt so passionate. Labour was the party which was radical and progressive. The Conservative party represented the defence of the status quo and the Labour party stood for change. Labour was against inequality and social injustice, and that's what the women's movement was fighting against, too. And Labour was the alternative party of government to the Conservatives. And I believed then, as I still do now, that Labour had to be in government to make the changes that were needed. We could only go so far by pursuing progress in the courts or through marches and demonstrations. We had to get into government to make the wholesale change the women's movement demanded for women at work, for childcare, in tackling domestic violence and for equality more generally.

The women's movement wanted to do more than propose political change, we wanted to play our part in carrying it out, too. We backed the Labour party but we were quite clear that we also wanted to change it, to challenge the male hierarchy and make Labour a political party fit to represent the aspirations of women and one which would thereby become a government fit for a country in which women regarded themselves as equal. Like every aspect of society, the Labour party was male-dominated from top to bottom. Though we women worked hard as grass-roots members of the party, the decision-making was done by men, whether in parliament, in the National Executive Committee, in local councils or in the constituency committees. But, in the spirit of the women's movement, it was anathema to us that we, as women, would remain 'outsiders' and should forever be petitioning men rather than making the decisions ourselves. We wanted to be on the inside, in Parliament, in the NEC and in councils, participating in the decision-making.

It was our enormous ambition that we would change politics and through this the world of work, the law and family life. We were inspired by the sense that our cause was just, so the scale of the odds we were facing served only to make us more determined.

In the early eighties, women were setting up Women's Sections in local Labour parties all around the country. This was not always easy, as permission to establish one had to be given by the invariably male-dominated General Committee of the local party. More women party members were becoming active, standing for election for positions such as Chair and Secretary of Constituency Labour parties and trying to get more women selected as councillors and as candidates for Parliament. I joined the Brent Women's Section, as Jack and I were living in Brent at the time.

A leading light in the Fulham Labour party at that time was a young local woman called Francine Bates, who later worked for Ed Balls when he was a Cabinet minister. She'd set up the Fulham

Women's Section in 1980 and, to help get it going, wanted to have a woman in the selection contest for the Labour candidate to stand for Fulham in the 1983 General Election. Knowing I'd lived in Fulham and been a member of the party there, and of my work on the NCCL Women's Rights Committee, she invited me to be the Women's Section candidate for the selection. There was no expectation we would win the selection, but it would help galvanize a fledgling Women's Section. I didn't hesitate.

The clear favourite was the leader of the local council, Tony Powell. With no pressure of expectation, and with no rivalry from Tony's campaign – the people running it felt that we had no chance – we ran an exuberant and friendly campaign. I made speeches at each of the wards. Francine, her mother and a network of local women rang up the women members of the local party, canvassing support for me and urging them to come to the selection meetings and vote to nominate me. For a woman member, to get a phone call asking her to come along and 'do her bit' for women by supporting a woman candidate gave that woman a special role and a sense of purpose. They managed to gather a few nominations for me, in addition to the nomination from the Women's Section, and organized within the constituency party's Executive Committee to get me on to the shortlist. With my group of women supporters, I went along to make a speech at the final selection conference in front of the members of the General Committee. To no one's surprise, Tony Powell was selected. But to our amazement, I came second, losing by just one vote.

With the warmth of the women in that constituency party and the unexpected success of our campaign, for the first time the thought came into my head that perhaps I should really try to become an MP. As Labour women, we were always complaining about the lack of women MPs and urging women to put themselves forward. Out of 269 Labour MPs there were only 11 women – 4 per cent. We had to change this. Patricia had been selected to stand for Labour in a safe seat. Perhaps I, too, should go for selection.

*

I had taken up the role of secretary of our local Queen's Park branch of the Labour party ward where Jack and I lived in the London Borough of Brent. One typical Saturday morning in 1981, in a scene which bore more than a passing resemblance to that of my mother cooking my father's kippers, I was ironing in the kitchen and Jack was reading *Labour Weekly* – the party's newspaper, which was sent to all members – when he spotted an advert saying that Peckham constituency Labour party was looking for a new candidate for the next General Election. Their current MP, Harry Lamborn, was in his late sixties and unwell, and had told them he was retiring. Jack said I should go for it.

It was a safe Labour seat less than a mile from Westminster, so the competition was going to be intense. But, as in Fulham, there were women throughout the London Labour party wanting to end the male domination of Labour in Parliament, so at least some of the members would be interested in the idea of having a woman MP. Audrey Wise, a former Labour MP who was nationally known, and a left-wing firebrand who had lost her seat of Coventry South West in the 1979 General Election, announced that she was putting in for it. She was such a popular figure in the Labour party that, on hearing that she had thrown her hat into the ring, and thinking she would inevitably win, many other leading figures decided not to apply. But I pressed on with my application, as did 119 others, including Jeremy Corbyn, who did not get any nominations in Peckham but went on to be selected as Labour's candidate in Islington North.

At about the same time, Woolwich constituency Labour party were looking for a new candidate, too, to replace their current MP, who'd defected to the SDP. Audrey had applied for this constituency as well. As luck would have it, the process of the Woolwich selection was running a couple of weeks ahead of Peckham's. Audrey made the shortlist for both. The Woolwich selection meeting took place first and Audrey won. Peckham was a seat with a bigger Labour majority but, having won the Woolwich selection, she went with the 'bird in the hand' option. All the national figures who'd decided not to apply because Audrey was standing gnashed their teeth, because now Peckham was left with a shortlist of relative minnows. But it was too late for them to apply, as the Peckham deadline had closed, and the selection proceeded with the original shortlist. The local party members started to think about who they'd select now that Audrey was out of the running. I and the other hopefuls went around each of the eight ward meetings, seeking nominations.

The first I went to was in Newington ward, off the Walworth Road. This was dominated by two formidable Labour families, the Wentworths and the Kennedys. George and Ellen Wentworth had eleven children, six girls and five boys. George worked long hours in a range of jobs and was a trade union activist. Ellen was a school 'dinner lady' (as they were known at the time) and active in the General, Municipal, Boilermakers and Allied Trade Union (GMB). Their son John (who went on to become a head teacher at one of the most successful primary schools in south London) thought I'd be a good MP and urged his family to take a close look at me in the selection meeting. To everyone's surprise, Newington ward nominated me. With a nomination from one of the eight wards, I was now firmly in the race.

Over the years, I came to know and admire the Wentworth family. I ended up with three children but was less able to cope than they were with eleven. And I was on an MP's salary, which allowed me to buy in help. Ellen told me that, at one point, five of her children had chickenpox at the same time. In those days, the father wasn't expected to share responsibility for things such as looking after sick children. I'd found it impossible when my three children had chickenpox one holiday! Shopping and cooking for Ellen's large family was a massive exercise and when the children were older she would use their old pram to bring back sacks of potatoes from the market. She told me that once she'd stopped to chat on her way home from East Street Market and, feeling the weight of the potatoes in the pram, found she was automatically rocking it. She had a no-nonsense approach to keeping order which I envied but couldn't emulate. Finding it hard to get my children to sleep when they were young, I asked her advice. She said that any of her children who didn't want to go to bed were told they'd be put in the garden in their pyjamas until they agreed to come in and get into their cosy beds.

Near to the Wentworths in Newington ward lived the Kennedys. John Kennedy worked in the post office and his wife, Frances, in catering in the House of Commons. Their son Roy (who was later to become a local councillor, senior party organizer and then Labour peer) worked in Whitehall Clothiers on the Walworth Road. They were such a welcoming family. Like Jack's parents, they were from Ireland and were determined to see their children get on in life. I remember, one evening when I was out canvassing, the Kennedys offered to look after my young son until I'd finished for the night and I left him in their warm embrace. With his red hair, he looked as if he could be the latest member of their family.

Down the road in Camberwell ward lived Margaret Prosser, who at that time was bringing up her three children on her own in a small flat on the third floor of a council block. I knew her because she was strongly Labour, a feminist and involved with the Southwark Law Centre. (She went on to be TGWU Women's Officer and then Deputy General Secretary and a Labour peer.) She, too, backed me, and that meant I was well and truly off.

The trade unions played a key role in the Labour party at that time so I rang up the secretaries of the local trade union branches who were affiliated to the Peckham party and asked to meet them in order to seek their backing. I met up with printers, dockers, postal workers, council workers, health workers, bus workers and engineers to listen to their concerns and ask for their support. As at Fulham, there was little pressure on me because I was not expected to win. Most of the people I met already knew of me from having seen me on television. I was so different to Harry Lamborn that they were intrigued and, as there was a developing sense that the party needed to change, they were open to giving me a fair hearing. Along with the other candidates, I went for a drink in the bar of the old Labour Club, in a run-down house in Camberwell Grove.

I would have felt daunted doing that on my own, but Jack came with me, and the fact that so many of them knew of him from Grunwick meant that they were prepared to take me seriously. Nowadays, a woman garnering votes for a selection in a Labour Club via her well-known trade unionist boyfriend would be frowned upon but, back then, we thought nothing of it.

However, it wasn't all straightforward. The nomination meeting for the Friary ward was held in the community centre in the middle of the Friary Estate. I had prepared carefully, talking to everyone I knew in the ward in advance, making sure I was fully in the picture about all the local issues and ready to tell them what I would do as their MP.

To look my best for all the meetings I'd have to go to for the selection contest, I'd taken every item of clothing I had to the dry cleaner's and, that evening, the clothes were hanging in my car. I parked my Mini outside the community centre and went in. I didn't win their nomination, and when I came out my car had been broken into and every piece of clothing stolen. I ran back in and was told that leaving anything visible in a car in a dark place was asking for it. They pointed out that there was a lot I didn't know about life in Peckham and I'd need to learn fast if I was to become the MP representing the constituency and inspiring the trust of local people. There was much good-natured chortling as they suggested I keep an eye out for anyone who was wearing my clothes.

I pressed on, undeterred. I'd never been the favourite to win the selection but even when I didn't win branch nominations there was no question of me pulling out of the race. If we were going to make women's voices heard in the Labour party, we'd have to start somewhere. We were in no doubt that it would be a long haul. And, anyway, I now had to do my best to justify the leap of faith Newington ward had taken in nominating me.

In the end, forty-two members of the Peckham Labour General Committee, all local members elected by the 366 members across the eight wards in the constituency, met for the selection meeting in the tenants' hall on the Camden Estate in the heart of Peckham. It was an icy night and the ground was so slippery I had to cling on to the handrail as I climbed up the dark stairs to the tenants' hall. The freezing weather had given me the idea for the speech I would make there. We were warm and cosy in the hall but, just a few yards away, in the flats on the walkways of that very estate and the other estates all around us, were elderly people and families with young children who were shivering with the cold, going to bed in the early evening because they couldn't afford the heating. Pensioner and child poverty were massive problems in the area. I promised that I would fight to get the Labour party into power so we could have a government which would end such poverty and that I would work with the Peckham Labour party to make that happen.

Each candidate had to go in separately to make their speech and answer questions. It was reported back to me that the speeches of the other candidates were a combination of setting out their own qualities and high-level political analysis. My speech reiterated the basic reasons why we were all in the Labour party and what we wanted to achieve: a fairer, more equal society. I was full of adrenalin, excited as well as nervous, and then I heard one of my supporters lean forward to a man sitting in front of him to whisper loudly, 'See, I told you she was the one!' The General Committee members filled in the ballot papers, the party officers counted them and came back in to announce that I'd won, beating Chris Mullin (who later became MP for Sunderland South) by twenty-three to nineteen in the final round.

I was delighted but full of a sense that my work had only just begun, so I set about building support in the local party, justifying the confidence of those who'd backed me and winning over those who'd backed other candidates. Inevitably, when there's fierce competition for selection, party members divide into different camps. It's hard to reach out to people who you know have fought against you. As the winning candidate, I was determined to try to get my opponents and my supporters back on good terms, mostly by working with them on local issues.

I went to meetings of the local tenants' associations on the housing estates and of the trade unions at local workplaces. I visited schools, Social Security offices, council offices and pensioner groups. I campaigned against poor housing conditions – getting into a row with the Southwark councillors for my 'Stamp Out Damp' campaign, which criticized the council for leaving families with young children in substandard flats. I worked with the newly formed Southwark Childcare Campaign, run by my friend Linda Smith. Together with members of the Peckham Labour party I went on endless demonstrations: 'Save London Transport', and in support of the striking health service workers, which started with a picket of the Maudsley Hospital and continued with a march down the Walworth Road to Elephant and Castle. We helped organize the South-east Region TUC march against women's unemployment, arguing with the police in the process, as we wanted to march down Whitehall at the same time as the rehearsals for the Trooping of the Colour ceremony. With Southwark Labour members, I joined the Woman's Right to Work march (I was legal adviser to the Action Committee for a Woman's Right to Work) and the May Day Labour movement march.

As Peckham's candidate, I also attended numerous conferences, including, in 1982 alone, the Peckham Young Socialists conference on the Alternative Economic Strategy, the two-hundred-strong biannual meeting of Southwark Pensioners Action Group (addressed by Jack Jones), the National Childcare Campaign conference (which was attended by only three Labour MPs and no Tories) and the Women's Fightback conference on part-time workers.

I was an activist, engaged with other activists in a whirl of Labour movement activity. The women's movement was dynamic and growing. But though the national demonstrations against the government were well attended, whatever the issue, I always saw the same people there. It was clear that we were not winning the support of the wider public, and without their backing we would not replace the government against whom we were fighting. Building support for demonstrations was all well and good, but we needed to be in power if we were to change the things we wanted to change. And with the Tories in the ascendancy and Labour in the doldrums, that seemed a faraway prospect.

From the late seventies right through until the early nineties, the Labour party was beset by over a decade of struggle against 'entryism'. Militant, a sectarian hard-left 'party within a party' was growing in strength. Militant had a macho, bullying culture and espoused policies that alienated the mainstream of Labour's voters, such as nationalizing the top two hundred private companies in the country. They organized within local constituency Labour parties and trade unions with the objective of taking over the Labour party, rather than reaching out to win more votes and take over government. I started to write a monthly newsletter to report on my work to the Peckham Labour party. Neither Labour candidates nor MPs usually did this, but I was following the practice of Patricia Hewitt, who as NCCL General Secretary had always done a monthly written report to the Executive Committee to record her work and shape discussion. I was trying to keep the backing of those members who'd voted for me and win the support of those who hadn't. Even so, the atmosphere in the local party became increasingly unpleasant as MPs and the National Executive Committee fought to contain and then expel the Militant Tendency. Reports in the papers about Labour's turmoil eclipsed all the other things they were trying to do. The only thing the public got to see about us was our internal warfare.

Though I was a seasoned campaigner, I was relatively inexperienced politically, so it was a struggle to take up a leadership position against this background of deepening conflict within the party. And there was mounting misery for people living in the constituency. Government cuts to Southwark council's funding meant that the council had to pare back vital services. The estates in Peckham had been well built but now it took longer for the council to undertake routine repairs. A broken front door would mean that a family remained insecure in their home for weeks. A cracked window would leave a flat chilly for months. Broken lifts went unrepaired, so tenants had to walk up the stairs, some of them carrying children, buggies and shopping, and elderly tenants became trapped and increasingly isolated on upper floors. Broken lights on housing estates and landings left people afraid to go out at night. Blocked-up refuse systems meant that rubbish blew around, dismaying houseproud tenants. Just as we are starting to see again now, with the current government's cuts to council housing budgets, the repair and maintenance backlog just grew and grew until, by the time Labour got back into government in 1997, there were billions of pounds' worth of maintenance to be done, even before we started to upgrade the homes with central heating, better bathrooms and kitchens, new entryphones and rubbish disposal schemes.

The cuts to the council, alongside rising demand for services such as home helps for the elderly and housing repairs, created conflict between the council and local people, between the council and its employees, and exacerbated the rows within the Labour party. The reality was that the council cuts in jobs and vital services were not the fault of the Labour council but that of the Tory government, which was squeezing the budget of a council in a deprived area. I, and the centre left of the party locally, wanted to do what we could to protect the most vulnerable from the effects of the cuts and to make sure everyone knew that it was the fault of the government. But the sectarian left and many of the council union activists blamed the Labour council and fought against them. So, in addition to the cuts compounding the deprivation in the local community, they were also undermining local political cohesion.

The local area went downhill: more and more were unemployed, police numbers were cut, estate entry systems were poorly maintained. At one point, there were so many attacks on milkmen delivering on the Gloucester Grove Estate that they refused to do their rounds there. The postmen would no longer deliver to the North Peckham Estate. I convened meetings between the postmen, the milkmen, the police, the tenants and the council to have such deliveries re-started, ensuring that the milkmen and postmen got the reassurance they needed.

While relations between the police and the tenants' leaders were often good, most local people viewed the police with hostility. There were also problems with squatters, many of whom came from a middle-class background and showed little regard for the working-class community they were living in. The prevalence of squatters, led locally by Piers Corbyn, who'd become active in the Squatters' Rights movement in the seventies, undermined the sense of community, as they came and went and local tenants no longer knew who their neighbours were. In later years, the council became more effective at boarding up empty properties, repairing and re-letting them more quickly and putting in entryphones so that tenants and tradesmen felt more secure.

Earlier generations had worked in the food factories in the north of the borough, in the print industry and in the docks, but by the time I was elected in 1982 jobs were being lost both in the public sector and in the private sector. There was a big brewery, the Camberwell Pride, in the heart of Peckham, and it employed hundreds of local men. It was closed down and lay derelict, a blight on the area, for nearly two decades, until the building was converted into stylish flats. This pattern was repeated all over Southwark. Father had followed son into these workplaces, and local women worked in a whole range of trades, from the clothing industry, to catering, to administrative and clerical jobs. And when a member of the family became unemployed, it caused not just financial hardship but anger and despair. Unemployment hit young people, who felt they'd been thrown on to the scrapheap before they'd even begun. It caused tensions in families when the husband had no work to go to, and the woman was often then put in the position of having to give up her work because, if she carried on, the family would not be classed as unemployed, would not be able to claim unemployment benefit, and would be worse off. Unemployment for a man undermined his status as breadwinner. The woman resented having to give up her job. The whole family suffered when they saw a son or daughter continually applying for jobs, unsuccessfully, along with hundreds of others. Nationally, by 1983, the number of jobless had risen to 3 million, of whom 1 million were young people.

It was these concerns which brought people in to Harry Lamborn MP's fortnightly advice surgeries. His wife, Lilian, who worked as his secretary, was at the surgeries to help him, bringing an expanding file stuffed with all his most recent cases. I'd sit at the table with him and listen. Nearly all of the constituents who came were council tenants with housing problems. Harry would say, 'Leave it with me,' and Lil would follow it up with a letter to the council. Nowadays, constituents expect to be told exactly what I am proposing to do. So after I, or one of my advice surgery team, have listened to their problem, we tell them that I will write on their behalf to the council, or the UK Border Agency, or whoever they are complaining about, and that they will be sent confirmation in writing as soon as I've done so. But there was no service delivery culture then, and certainly not from the council officers. Many tenants would come with a fistful of recorded-delivery slips from letters they'd sent to which there'd been no reply, or even acknowledgement. They queued up to see their MP just to get a reply to their letters from the council. And while the council struggled with internal Labour warfare, the problem of no response carried on well into the early nineties.

Constituents would always dress smartly when they came to the advice surgery to meet Harry, as they did when I became MP. As they are expecting to meet someone who is going to be able to help solve their problem, I followed suit, and always took care with what I was wearing when I went to my constituency engagements. It was a leap of faith for careworn constituents to put their trust in a young woman – and one who didn't at all look like the traditional idea of an MP. So I felt my clothes had to send out the message: 'I am a competent professional, you can rely on me.'

However, as the newly selected candidate, and even when I became the new MP, there was no way I was able to stem the tide of rising economic deprivation and political bitterness. Over the ensuing years, many Labour party members stopped coming to local meetings. People don't join a party which stands for peace and justice in order to attend meetings where everyone is shouting abuse at each other. The monthly meetings became an ordeal. And the contest in 1981 for the deputy leadership between Tony Benn and Denis Healey had stoked up the already bitter in-fighting. Harry Lamborn, who, for a period, had been Denis Healey's ministerial aide when Healey was Chancellor of the Exchequer (1974–9), became a particular target for local ultra-leftists, for whom Denis Healey was public enemy number one. At a meeting in 1982, after I was selected to stand, Harry was there as the soon-to-be-retiring MP. He had become painfully thin and was obviously seriously ill. As soon as he started to speak, some members in the meeting started to chant, 'Resign! Resign!' Here was a thoroughly decent local man who'd only ever worked for the cause of local people and who everyone could see was now gravely ill being attacked in a Labour meeting. But humanity was not a consideration in the pursuit of left sectarianism. I was disgusted by this cruelty to a dying man on the part of those who called themselves progressive.

Some retiring MPs made life hard for their successors, especially if they were coming in with different politics, as I was. Harry was a traditionalist, a working-class man who'd become a councillor and then the MP for the area he was born and brought up in. In the neighbouring constituency of Bermondsey, the retiring MP Bob Mellish denounced Labour's by-election candidate, Peter Tatchell, and that contributed to Tatchell losing the by-election brought about by Mellish's resignation in 1983. In contrast, Harry was unfailingly helpful, introducing me to the constituents attending his advice surgery, explaining that I would be the Labour candidate to be their MP at the next election and recommending me to them.

The ugly and divisive politics that were being played out in the meetings of Peckham Labour party of the eighties afflicted Labour up and down the country, too. It appalled decent local Labour activists. Members were intimidated and felt threatened, and many stopped coming to meetings. Who in their right mind would want to spend an evening after a hard day at work hearing Labour MPs denounced as traitors and being shouted at if they didn't vote in the way the ultra-left had, in advance of the meeting, decided was the correct way? And, of course, Labour party infighting turned the public off voting for us. Who would want to vote for a party that denounced its own MPs and was more interested in publicly tearing itself apart than in speaking up about the real-life problems the people in the country were facing?

And it wasn't just confined to meetings. The house of local members Jimmy and Vicky Naish nearly went up in flames when Jimmy's scooter, parked outside, was set on fire. At that time, Vicky was the chair of the Local Government Committee and was told in an anonymous phone call that the bike had been torched because she 'didn't do what she was told'. And it wasn't just the hard left that local members had to contend with. There were also threats of violence from the far right. Bill Skelly, a local trade union activist and party member who later became a councillor, was chased down the road by National Front skinheads throwing bricks at him after a union branch meeting at our local Labour Club. Rod Robertson, a National Association of Local Government Officers (NALGO) official and secretary of the local Trades Council, was told as he went into a meeting that he would get his head kicked in when he came back outside.

At one point, the dispute between the Labour council and the local unions about the pay and conditions of council manual workers spilled over into the Peckham General Management Committee. Some of the trade union delegates to the committee turned on me. I wasn't involved in the council/trade union negotiations, but I got caught in the crossfire. This was later in the eighties, when I was an MP and had three small children. I was exhausted by the combination of having a young family, late nights in the House of Commons and demanding constituency work. So though it was a problem within my own constituency, I felt I couldn't sort it out. From his involvement in Grunwick and his work in the TGWU, Jack knew all the London trade unionists, including the local ones.

He offered to call them together and get them to back off in their attacks on me. Though I knew I should really have been fighting my own battles and not relying on a man, let alone my husband, I was worn down so gratefully took up his offer. He convened a meeting at the Labour Club of the key trade unionists. I waited at home apprehensively to hear what had happened. Jack returned and reported that there had had a 'full and frank discussion'. While the battles in the local party between the hard left and everyone else continued unabated, the trade union attacks on me stopped abruptly.

I was sustained throughout this time by the strong backing of a group of long-standing local party members. Vicky Naish cared for her elderly mother, father and aunt and kept them active and engaged, folding my campaign leaflets and putting them in envelopes. If I was out campaigning in her neighbourhood at the weekend, she was always happy for me to drop off any of the children with her. Vicky later became a councillor and Mayor of Southwark, and she still helps at my advice surgeries. Mary Ellery, who also later became a councillor, folded leaflets with her four children at her kitchen table on the Camden Estate. Local tenants' activists, like Sandy Cameron and Maria Williams from the North Peckham Estate and Ali Balli from the Gloucester Grove Estate, would help with leaflet deliveries and come with me on visits around their estates. The women members of the Peckham party, who ranged from those in their eighties to those in their teens, were all touched by the sense of being part of the women's movement and wanting change in the Labour party.

I'd been to the National Labour Women's Conference in 1981 in Buxton. We'd all shuffled in our seats, grumbling, when the only man to speak, Labour leader Michael Foot, spoke for nearly an hour to the six hundred women assembled there without once mentioning women. The next National Labour Women's Conference, in June 1982, had doubled in size and I went with local party members Mabel Goldwin and Di Robinson. They were older women from the local area, and party stalwarts. Although they wouldn't describe themselves as feminists, they were strongly for women's rights. With twelve hundred women attending, the conference was abuzz. It passed, with a narrow majority, a resolution demanding positive action to give women equality in the Labour party. These demands included a woman on every shortlist for parliamentary candidates, the women's conference being given the right to table five resolutions for debate at the annual conference, and the NEC Women's Section being elected by women at the women's conference instead of by party members as a whole. The women's conference had only 'advisory' status, but the resolution showed the growing demand for more women MPs and for women to have a greater say. It was about asserting women's political independence, rejecting the notion that they were simply wives or mothers.

Peckham Labour party had not one but two Women's Sections: Peckham North and Peckham South. They organized meetings on 'a woman's right to work', on unequal pay, on childcare and domestic violence, and held self-defence classes for women. While this may not have always succeeded in making women skilled enough to fight off an attacker, it was evidence that women were no longer prepared to put up with being victims of male assault and would look to defend themselves and fight for their right to walk safely in the streets. Women were battling for the right to be involved in politics and the right to work. One of the problems at the time, however, was that many unemployed women didn't feature in the jobless figures. Unemployment was a major problem: 3 million people were registered as unemployed nationally, fifteen thousand in Southwark, but neither figure took into account the thousands of women who were looking for work. They were invisible in the jobless statistics because, if they were married or lone parents, they simply didn't count as unemployed. If her husband was in work, a woman's joblessness was not counted.

This problem was compounded when the Conservative government tightened the rules in 1989 as to who could register as unemployed in such a way that women with children would be unable to do so unless they were able to show that they had a nursery place or someone to care for their children while they were at work. This was the 'availability to work' test. But there were no nurseries, and making arrangements for a friend or relative to give up their work to care for your child was, of course, not practical if you didn't have a job already. It was just another way to conceal the true level of unemployment and cut the cost of unemployment benefit. The Tories, believing that women's main role was in the home, had never supported women's right to work. One of the things Labour changed when we were in government was to make women fully visible in the employment and unemployment statistics. We had to be able to see women's unemployment if we were to tackle it.

But back in the eighties the priority for the trade unions and the mainstream of Labour was men at work. In the spirit of the women's movement, Labour women began openly to challenge this, and women's resentment that our role at work was still not sufficiently recognized and valued by the trade union movement grew; it was felt that, although the Labour movement had always fought for men's jobs, it didn't care about women's right to work. An article in *Peckham Labour News* in May 1982 angrily complained: 'For generations, women have supported men in the home and at work. We have backed them in the Labour movement and in the unions. Behind the scenes, we have done the hard graft which kept things running. That is the kind of support that, from now on, men must earn and not expect.'

Though trade union members were very much at the heart of the Labour party, and unions were affiliated to the NEC, women in the Labour party were beginning to complain openly about the unions' leadership. Trade unions negotiated with employers for 'the family wage' for men, and meant by it sufficient pay for a man, his wife and their children. We challenged this because, by definition, it meant that if the man was earning 'the family wage', women's pay was not important; she was working only for 'pin money'. Our attack on the concept of the family wage was criticized as threatening to undermine men's pay, but we were insistent that the trade unions, which represented women as well as men at work, should fight as hard for their women members as they did for the men.

In 1982, while I was starting to get to grips with my work as the newly selected parliamentary candidate and still working at the NCCL, Jack and I decided to have a baby. We thought we could have the baby in good time before the General Election, which was not expected for another two years. Life was non-stop political meetings and campaigning, but I had no idea of the reality of life as an MP. Nor did Jack or I have any idea of the reality of life with a baby. There was no route map for a woman parliamentary candidate who wanted to start a family, so we just went ahead and did it.

Once I was pregnant, we decided to get married. My being young and a woman was going to cause enough of a flurry in the political world, and I didn't want the added fuss of my being an unmarried mother. I didn't want to offend anyone in the local party or any of my future constituents who would prefer their MP to be a 'respectable' married woman. There was still, at that time, deep disapproval of couples who lived together without being married, let alone of those who had a baby out of wedlock. And I knew my parents would be upset if I didn't marry now that I was pregnant. They had put pressure on my sister Sarah when she had a baby without being married to the father. I don't think this was out of moral disapproval, they were worried that the child might suffer by having been born 'out of wedlock', so Sarah relented and got married. However, alongside this persistently strong societal disapproval of having a baby out of wedlock, there was strong disproval of marriage in the women's movement.

In the women's movement, we saw marriage as the embodiment of patriarchy, 'ownership' of the woman passing from her father to her husband. All the traditional symbols of marriage reinforced this. The woman was 'given away' by her father to her husband. At the wedding, her father would make a speech, and then the best man. The bride and her female relatives and friends would applaud and say nothing. The marriage vows included one that the woman would 'obey' her husband. She would relinquish her father's surname and take her husband's. On occasion, she might even be addressed by his first name as well as his surname. (My mother used to receive letters addressed to Mrs John Harman.) Wearing a ring on the fourth finger of your left hand marked you out as a married woman. Only very few men, in those days, wore a ring, as on marriage a man's status wouldn't change. The woman's father was the head of the household in which she had grown up, and her husband was the head of her household for her married life. I used to cringe when I heard a woman say that she was engaged. I thought a woman whose description of herself was as a 'fiancée' was a pitiful thing. But despite this, for the sake of my parents and my constituency, we got married.

We made sure it was as low key as humanly possible. Jack and I never described ourselves as engaged and wouldn't have dreamt of having an engagement party or an engagement ring. Our wedding, in August 1982, was not in a church but at Willesden Registry Office. There was no wedding ring, no white dress, no flowers, no vowing to obey, no father giving me away. Neither my, nor Jack's, parents were invited. This was not out of any hostility to them, far from it. We just didn't want any fuss made. So there were no guests, not even my sisters – only Anna Coote and the Chair of Brent Trades Council, Irish militant trade unionist and communist Tom Durkin to act as our witnesses. It didn't occur to me to wonder whether my, or Jack's, parents might have liked us to have a 'proper' wedding which they, other friends and relatives could attend. We thought it was enough that we were getting married.

I did, however, buy a dress. Chatting to the shop assistant, I told her it was for my wedding. Seeing my obvious pregnancy, she was full of embarrassment and sympathy for me, clearly thinking this was a 'shotgun wedding', and brought me a selection of white dresses to try on which would conceal my bump in the wedding photos. She needn't have worried. I was thrilled with my bump and, anyway, there was to be no wedding photographer. Her consternation was complete when the dress I chose was hot pink. In order to make sure that my future constituents were aware that I was now married and respectable, Jack and I did pop into a local photographer's shop and sent the resulting picture off to the *Willesden and Brent Chronicle* and the *South London Press*. It looked like the sort of picture you might have taken in a photo booth.

After our wedding, Jack and I sped off for a holiday in France. We certainly never called it a 'honeymoon', but I told the Peckham Labour party I'd be away and we drove around La Rochelle, Arcachon and Les Landes. It is a lovely area but, for me, still racked as I was with pregnancy nausea, the seafood, undercooked pigeon breasts and ripe, smelly cheese for which it's famous were a torture. All I wanted was dry bread and water. Jack stopped the car regularly so I could lean out and be sick. One day, we had a coffee (water for me) by a beautiful lake. Having been out of touch with the UK for so long and starved of news, we were excited to see in a newsagent's a three-day-old copy of *The Times*. Jack read it first and as he did I saw, in the front-page 'News in Brief' section, a headline for a story inside: 'Labour MP Dies'. 'Quick,' I said, my heart sinking. 'Who is it?'

Sadly, it was Harry Lamborn. Instead of him retiring at the General Election some years in the future, there would have to be a by-election to fill the vacancy and elect the new MP within a couple of months. I was Labour's selected candidate, but I was pregnant. There'd never been a pregnant candidate in a General Election before, let alone in the heightened atmosphere of a by-election. I was delighted to have been selected as a candidate in a safe Labour seat and the last thing I wanted was to give it up, but the thought of having a baby was daunting enough; to be pregnant in a by-election felt impossible. I wavered. But of course the whole idea behind the women's movement was to break new ground and challenge the notion of all the things women supposedly couldn't do. And Jack was adamant that I shouldn't step down.

I called the local party secretary, we commiserated over Harry's death and discussed the likely date of the by-election and the campaign, but although my pregnancy was well known to everyone, neither of us mentioned it. We just didn't know how to talk about it. It was the elephant in the room on that call – and by the time we returned from France I felt as heavy as an elephant and I was only going to get bigger. We didn't cut short our holiday and return for the funeral, and I regret that. Even though, in those days, it was much harder to change ferry bookings and cancel hotels, it would have been proper to show my respect and attend the funeral of the MP who I was going to take over from, alongside his grieving family and all the party members who were going to work so hard to get me elected. At that time, I overdid the rejection of tradition and ceremony.

At my next antenatal appointment at Guy's Hospital I asked the obstetrician whether she thought it was all right for me to stand in the forthcoming by-election, by which time I'd be five months pregnant. She asked what it entailed and I told her: working all hours, going up and down stairs all day and very little sleep. She said that was excellent exercise and that I'd get no sleep when the baby came anyway, so it would be good practice.

We were in the middle of moving into our new home in Southwark when the campaign got underway. Roy Hattersley, then deputy leader of the Labour party, came to Peckham to launch the campaign in October 1982, and Clive Soley, then MP for Hammersmith, whom I'd known since I set up the Labour Campaign for Criminal Justice, a group which linked my NCCL work with the Labour party, was my 'minder'. Frank Dobson, then an MP in Camden, came down regularly to campaign with me, and my friend Glenys Thornton, a Labour activist, was indefatigable as my 'candidate's aide'. Glenys (who was later made a Labour peer) was the best candidate's aide I could have had. She was determined to keep me going and looking smart, so there was always a packet of sandwiches and a spare pair of tights in her handbag. The by-election was exciting, and campaigning alongside Glenys was fun. But I was sick, not just in the morning but throughout the day, my back ached and I felt the sort of exhaustion that sleep can't even touch.

The Social Democrat (SDP) candidate, the charismatic former Labour minister and MP for Lincoln Dick Taverne, was my main challenger in the by-election. With the SDP newly formed and Labour deep in internecine warfare, it was not beyond the realms of possibility that Labour would lose Peckham and, indeed, four months later, the SDP's Liberal partners did succeed in beating Labour in the by-election in the neighbouring Bermondsey constituency, previously a rock-solid Labour seat. With hardly any Conservative voters in Peckham, the Tory candidate, John Redwood, stood no chance.

As our campaign got under way, reports started to come back to our HQ that Taverne's team were telling residents not to vote for me as I was pregnant and so wouldn't be able to do the job. It proved counterproductive. The working-class women constituents were affronted. Jack reported back that the women stall-holders in East Street Market, who had always had to work hard as well as bringing up their children, had taken offence at a woman being criticized in that way.

I continually came across evidence that, far from counting against me, the fact that I was a woman and was being criticized by men for being pregnant gave voters a connection with me that they didn't feel they had with 'normal politicians'. It was engendering female solidarity for me from my women constituents. And this connection with women voters was reinforced on election day, when, about ten minutes before the polls closed, I knocked on the door of a third-floor flat on the Glebe Estate. Our campaign records showed that the couple living there hadn't yet voted. The door was answered by a woman with a chubby baby in her arms. She said her husband would be voting on his way home from work and that she'd been planning to vote when he got back, but he was late and she couldn't leave the flat because, as well as the baby, she had a two-year-old asleep in the bedroom. The baby beamed at me, and she handed him to me to admire. I said I'd look after the baby and stay in the flat so she could pop down to the community centre to vote. She threw on her coat and rushed out. I felt honoured. I knew that she would never have left a male candidate alone in her home with her precious children. And, understandably, no male candidate would have offered. It wasn't that I needed her one extra vote. It was that I wanted her to know that her vote – as a woman – was as important to me as the vote of her husband.

That was just one of so many encounters which reinforced in me the belief that I had a particular mandate from women, and that it mattered to them and was important that I was different from the men politicians. It spurred me on every day. When I got to Parliament, young and pregnant, I was an 'out-group' of one. But outside Parliament, more and more women were working as well as having children and, instead of struggling on their own, they could increasingly hear, see and experience the fact that the women's movement was backing them.

Labour won the Peckham by-election with a convincing majority, but the atmosphere at the local school where the votes were counted was ugly, with the National Front making threats and physically shoving people. They'd run a vicious, racist campaign, and the menace of violence encountered by our canvassers was there in all its repulsiveness as the results were declared. Their chants nearly drowned out my acceptance speech and, dressed in my pink wedding dress, which was now doubling up as my election victory outfit, I had to shout to make myself heard. Usually – and quite rightly – in their acceptance speech the winner finds positive things to say about the defeated candidates. But I lashed out at the SDP for the way they had campaigned against me as a pregnant woman. My father later complained to me about this; he felt I'd been ungracious. But after such a bitter campaign, being magnanimous was the last thing on my mind. I was fighting the world and hitting out in all directions. There was no precedent for what I was doing. Again, I found myself in a position where I couldn't work out which conventions I should obey and which I should flout and, on occasion, my breaching of long-standing conventions caused much disapproval. Looking back at the by-election, I felt too angry and defensive at the time to be generous to my opponents. And saying what I did on live TV at the count showed that, though I was embattled, I was going to denounce my detractors and soldier on.

There was a sackful of letters waiting for me when I got to the House of Commons. They were evenly divided between enthusiastic congratulations on my election victory and angry denunciations of my acceptance speech. Some said that I had no right to be in the House of Commons, that my children would truant from school and I should stay at home. I hoped they were wrong, but the accusation that my career would make me an unfit mother was to haunt me.

2.

A Pioneer in Parliament

I was elected on Thursday 28 October 1982. While I knew little about the political processes within the Parliamentary Labour Party (PLP), I knew exactly what I was coming into Parliament to do. I was there for women, for social justice and to fight the Tory government. The women's movement's political agenda had long been honed in meetings of women up and down the country. It was well-developed and coherent. We wanted equality, in work and in politics. We wanted childcare, maternity rights, for domestic violence to be taken seriously and for women to play an equal part in political decision-making. But my certainty of what I was in Parliament to do was not matched by an understanding of how to do it. And I had no idea how hard I'd find it to go from a small, supportive organization led by women into a big, largely hostile one dominated by men. And this at the same time as becoming a mother for the first time.

Most MPs arrive in the House of Commons as one of a group of new MPs after a General Election. The different intakes from each General Election tend to work and socialize together, networking and learning the ropes as they go along. But as a by-election winner, you arrive 'mid-term'. Nowadays, the House of Commons offers new MPs training sessions to help them find their way through the parliamentary processes, for example how to use the House of Commons library, but there was nothing like that then. For the first few months I paid my secretary out of my salary, not knowing there was a secretarial allowance you could claim.

I arrived to 'take my seat' in the House of Commons on the same day as one other new MP, Labour's John Spellar, who had won the

Birmingham Northfields by-election. John was a trade unionist from the West Midlands, and from the right wing of the AEUW, and it seemed to me that, while he fitted seamlessly into the West Midlands group of MPs and the trade union group of MPs, I fitted in nowhere.

However, I was of great interest to the Tory MPs because many of them wanted me to be their 'pair'. At that time, there was a 'pairing system' whereby the MPs from the government party didn't have to be in the House of Commons for the votes, which usually started at about 7 p.m. and often finished after midnight, if they could tell their Whips they had a 'pair' – a Labour MP who would stay off the same votes. With one Tory and one Labour MP off the vote, the Labour absence would counterbalance the absent Tory MP and so the outcome would not be affected. With the government party having, by definition, more MPs than the Opposition, there were many Tory MPs who couldn't get a pair and would roam the corridors of the House of Commons late at night wishing they had a Labour mate.

I had all the attributes to be a perfect 'pair'. I represented a Labour seat with a big majority and was therefore unlikely to be pitched out at the next General Election and leave my pair in the lurch. I was young, so likely to be in the House for many years and, best of all, I was six months pregnant and therefore could, they expected, be counted upon to want to be at home as much as possible. Such was the enthusiasm to be my pair that two Tory MPs, Norman Lamont and Sheila Faith, wanting to get ahead of the competition, wrote to me during the by-election campaign. It would have taken a political earthquake for the Tory candidate to win in Peckham but, even so, it would be a slap in the face for their candidate to see Tory MPs anticipating his defeat. So I immediately released the letters to the press. I was roundly criticized for this and accused of breaching confidentiality. But I was at war with the Tories and keen to do anything I could to embarrass them. I wasn't going to keep their secrets.

When I arrived at the House of Commons, the interest in me as a potential pair remained intense. It was usual for MPs to inherit the pair of their predecessor. Alan Clark, the flamboyant Tory minister (and later diarist) had been Harry Lamborn's pair and was deeply disgruntled at being trapped in the House of Commons after Harry died. When I turned up there was a letter waiting for me from him, telling me he was my pair. But there was also a letter from Judy Hurd, who was married to Douglas Hurd MP. She explained that she was his second wife and that he had had three sons with his first but that they had just had their first child together and were planning to have more. She wrote to me, as she said, 'woman to woman', and pleaded with me to abandon Alan Clark and choose her husband instead. I loathed Tory MPs, as they were against everything we stood for. We were for gay rights; they brought in Section 28, which banned teachers talking about homosexuality at school. They supported the apartheid regime in South Africa; we wanted it overthrown. They were cutting the NHS as people were dying on hospital waiting lists. We were fighting for fuller employment and decent housing for all, and they remained deaf to arguments about the pain and suffering caused by rising unemployment and homelessness. I hadn't come into Parliament to make life easier for any of them. Quite the opposite. I was there to fight against everything they stood for. This was at the height of Thatcherism, and the battle lines then could not have been clearer. But Judy Hurd's letter was heartfelt, describing the strain put on marriages by the late hours of the Commons and how much she wanted this, his second marriage, to work. In the end, I replied that I would be Douglas Hurd's pair and wrote to Alan Clark to turn him down. The next night, he caught up with me in the members' cloakroom as we came in to vote. He was distraught, complaining that, with no pair, endless nights in the Commons stretched ahead of him. I explained that it was because Judy Hurd had written to me and he quickly suggested that he would get his wife to write to me and that they would have another baby, too, if it meant I'd be his pair. He was only half joking.

Newly elected MPs have to swear allegiance to the Queen and

sign in a book made of parchment which is laid out on the table in front of the Speaker. This is the moment of an MP's formal accept-ance into the House of Commons. After a General Election, it takes over a week for all 650 MPs to be sworn in. The process takes place at the start of the Commons day, or in a break when the House is not sitting. First in the queue are the members of the Cabinet, then junior ministers, then the Leader of the Opposition and Shadow Cabinet, after that government backbenchers and, finally, Oppos-ition backbenchers. I've been sworn in nine times now but, for me, it never ceases to be a solemn moment. I think of the great respon-sibility I have to my constituents, what a privilege it is to represent them and what an extraordinary institution the House of Com-mons is. And having been in both the Cabinet and the Shadow Cabinet, and been an Opposition backbencher and a government backbencher, I've been in every place in the queue. The feeling doesn't vary. But the first time I was there was when I had won the by-election, and introduction to the House of a by-election winner is a high-profile political occasion.

It was a few days after the by-election and the House of Com-mons was packed. I was acutely aware that nearly everyone there was male. It really was a men's club. Of the MPs at the time, 97 per cent were men; there were only seventeen women, eleven of whom were Labour. Of the eight Tory MPs, one was the Prime Minister, Margaret Thatcher, and none of them was, like me, a young femi-nist. We had planned, and indeed were fighting for, more women in Parliament, but it felt strange to find myself actually being there. There were more MPs called John than there were women. I stood at the 'bar of the House', the line on the carpet at the end of the Commons Chamber, the MPs were crowded on to the benches on both sides of the House, and the journalists were leaning forward in the press gallery, directly in front of the bar of the House, high up above the Speaker's Chair. And above us, on both sides, the pub-lic gallery was rammed. I could feel all eyes on me. The Speaker called for order – the sign for MPs to fall silent – and then called out my name. Flanked by two MPs, Jo Richardson and Clive Soley, I processed down the centre of the House of Commons. Four steps, then a little bow to the Speaker. Another four steps, then another bow, with the Labour side cheering our party's victory. But I was very much the odd one out. I was a Labour MP in a Tory-dominated Parliament. I was a London Labour MP in Tory London. I was a woman in a male-dominated Parliament. And I was pregnant. Wearing a dark red velvet maternity dress, I took my seat on the Labour benches among the grey suits of the House of Commons.

One organizing principle of the women's movement was that we should meet together as women, without men, to formulate our demands and press for change. The view was that we had to work together as women, not as individuals, and that we should meet without men. Any man in a meeting would only dominate it. Women had to be 'the engine of our own liberation'. In councils all over the country, Labour women were setting up women's committees. Coming into Parliament, I thought we needed a Parliamentary Labour Party Women's Committee to be the parliamentary wing of the women's movement. We were so outnumbered in the Commons at that time, it was obvious that we had to work collectively as women MPs to raise women's issues in the House, to form a link with women outside Parliament, and to work towards bringing more women into Parliament. I didn't tell the Chief Whip, or the Chair of the PLP, or the Secretary of the PLP, let alone ask their permission. I didn't know them and, anyway, they were all men and I wasn't going to ask men if it was all right for us to meet together as women. The women's movement was not about seeking permission from the men in authority; we were bent on challenging that authority. I booked one of the small rooms off Westminster Hall and invited all ten other Labour women MPs to come to a meeting to establish a PLP Women's Committee. To me it was an obvious move, but it was greeted with annoyance by nearly all of the men. And Joan Lester, Labour's spokesperson on women, was worried that it might be seen as undermining her position. The women's movement beyond Parliament was delighted and the men in the PLP were annoyed with me, and that set the pattern for many years to come.

After that first meeting I asked the secretary of the PLP, Bryan Davies, to list the Women's Committee in 'the whip', the PLP bulletin notification of future meetings and, despite grumblings, after the 1983 General Election, meetings of the Women's Committee began to appear. There were protests that the PLP should not be advertising a meeting which excluded most of its members, but I pointed out that there were many meetings on the whip which I couldn't attend, such as the miners' group of MPs, or the Scottish group of MPs. No one objected to these meetings excluding certain members. So despite the ill-feeling, the PLP Women's Committee was now official. I was in Parliament to pursue the policy agenda of the women's movement and we were building the structures to deliver it.

It would have been pointless biding my time, going through the processes, building up support first. I would never have got through the hurdles. I was always being told that it would be best for me to keep my head down and learn the ropes for the first few years, before even contemplating making any suggestions. Over the following years, the Women's PLP grew in strength as more women were elected to Parliament. It became a vital political axis when Labour was in opposition. Alongside Joyce Gould, the most senior woman in the party's HQ and a strong feminist, and the women in the trade unions and at the grass roots, the Women's PLP fought for organizational change to open up the party to women, and for change in our policies so that they reflected women's demands. And it played a crucial role when we were in government, too, encouraging the new Labour women MPs, supporting women ministers and forming the bedrock of our drive to make the government deliver for women. Over time, with women such as Jean Corston, Lorna Fitzsimons and Fiona MacTaggart taking up the chair of the Women's PLP, it came to be seen as a very significant role in Parliament and in the party. It's sometimes hard to remember now, but in the eighties, while politics included discussion of the mines, motorways and money supply, issues such as maternity leave, childcare and domestic violence were just not on the political agenda.

I saw it as my duty, as a feminist in Parliament, to speak up in defence of women any time there was an example of discrimination. These protests set me at odds with the establishment, for example when I complained, as I often did, about such things as employers discriminating at work, or police inaction, or court leniency on issues of domestic violence. But sometimes it also set me against my own side, for instance when it meant challenging the trade unions and fellow Labour representatives. One example was what happened to one of the first women firefighters in London.

Lynne Gunning was one of only five women in the London Fire Brigade in 1985. When she was posted as a lone woman among men at the Soho fire station, she was forced to watch masturbation and had urine thrown over her. Fireman Langford was dismissed by the Fire Service management, but the Fire Brigades Union (FBU) – and it was her union, too – appealed on his behalf to the Fire Authority, which was run by the Labour-controlled Greater London Council (GLC), and they reinstated him. I protested and led a delegation to the General Secretary of the FBU, Ken Cameron. It was considered disloyal for a Labour MP to side with management against any union, let alone one which was affiliated to the Labour party, and especially when it was in support of a sacking. And it was frowned upon to challenge a Labour council, particularly at a time when the GLC was under attack from the Thatcher government. But I felt I had to take action to support a woman who was breaking into what had always been an exclusively male occupation and take issue with the sort of harassment which drives women out, and his dismissal was reaffirmed. Sexual harassment remains a problem, and though there is much greater understanding of it now, when it happens it makes a woman's life at work a misery and is far from being harmless banter. And I could tell it mattered to women to see a Labour politician protesting about the things that they deeply resented, because the more I spoke up, the more women would write to me, or come up to me in the street, and say, 'That happened to me, too. Keep at it.'

Taking action in cases like this prompted derision from newspapers, which regarded me as a 'humourless feminist'. That characterization, which is still common today, has the effect of minimizing the behaviour objected to and stigmatizing those of us who complain. The message is clear: Speak up, and you'll pay a price. But the women's movement was gaining strength and there was growing and voluble support among women for what I was doing, so I kept it up, despite the criticism.

As part of my determination to push for women's rights, I remained fiercely focused on campaigning to get Labour into government. We had to be in government to change what we were protesting about. But the party was convulsed by ever more bitter internal divisions. It became increasingly obvious that we had to both end the in-fighting and develop policies which would be popular as well as radical. In addition to the efforts made by the NEC, by Michael Foot as leader and then by his successor, Neil Kinnock, there were members all around the country working at local level to sort out the party. So to bring all of them together and to create a policy discussion, the Labour Co-ordinating Committee had been set up in 1978. I became active in it and was elected to its National Committee. It was not Westminster-based, being a network of Labour local councillors, trade unionists and constituency activists. We came from the left, centre left and centre right of the party and had joined together in an effort to defeat the ultra-left, who advocated policies such as nationalization of the top public companies, which the public just would not accept. The key movers and shakers were Peter Hain (not yet an MP), Cherie Booth, whom I got to know well as the only other woman elected on the National Committee, and Hilary Benn, who became an MP but was then council leader in Ealing. The joke was that he'd been a beneficiary of the 'women's' vote.

Throughout the eighties, Labour had strong support in what were seen as our 'heartlands' of Scotland, the north, the north-west, the Midlands and Wales. But it was a different matter with people across the south-west, East Anglia, the south-east and the rural shires. With them, the Labour party seemed to have no connection. And we couldn't get elected without the support of those areas. The NHS was being starved of funds, waiting lists grew ever longer and some of my constituents died waiting for operations for perfectly treatable conditions. Unemployment soared and the jobless were castigated by the Tory government for being idle and feckless. But the Labour party was immobilized by internal arguments. And I was exasperated that, while local people suffered, the ultra-left was less interested in fighting the Tories and more concerned with seizing control of the party. Going around the country, I listened to what people were saying about why Labour didn't appeal to them and became increasingly convinced that we needed to change.

All this time, our Peckham General Management Committee still met in the Labour Club in the large, dilapidated Georgian house on Camberwell Grove owned by the Peckham party. The overwhelming majority of local Labour party members were decent, caring people, but it only took a few people, intent on pushing the divide that ran through the party, to turn the atmosphere ugly. Our meetings were dominated by angry arguments. In a room in the basement where we held our meetings there was a bar which helped finance the party by selling cut-price beer, and members would gather before meetings to have a drink. By the time the meeting got under way some of the more aggressive members would have got thoroughly drunk, and the debate would quickly descend into shouting and threats. The bar stayed open at the end of the room we were meeting in and drinks continued to be ordered. It was not just unpleasant, it was a thoroughly intimidating atmosphere, especially for the women.

The conflict spilled over into acrimony on the council. Rows blazed between the Labour councillors, who, on a falling budget, were trying to protect the most vulnerable and manage their services and their employees, and the council workers' trade unions, who were striving for improved pay and conditions and who were affiliated to the local Labour party. Before council meetings a throng of trade unionists and sectarian leftists would gather on the steps of the town hall in Peckham Road and the councillors would have to push their way through, past threats and spitting. Concerned about security, the council staff suggested opening up the back door to the town hall, in Havil Street, to let the councillors in. They were particularly worried about Councillor Mary Ellery, who is barely five feet tall. Mary is married to Norman Ellery, who was a caretaker on their estate, a council employee and a trade unionist. They were a distinctive couple, with Norman being over six feet tall. But Mary refused to be relegated to the back door, and Norman agreed, insisting that, as an elected councillor, she would go up the steps and through the front door, and he would go with her.

You had to be tough to be a Labour councillor in London at that time, and most of them were. Many had been born into large families where there was very little money and things were not easy. Mary was one of nine children. Bill Skelly, another Labour councillor, was the youngest of eleven children. The councillors were deeply and passionately committed to the Labour party, not least because of their belief in the NHS. In their large families, where many children of previous generations had died of tuberculosis, theirs was the first generation which could go to the doctor and be given free treatment. They were also in full support of council housing, in which most of them lived. But being a Labour councillor was an ordeal. The ugly threats were not confined to the Labour Club and outside the town hall, they erupted inside the council chamber, too. Protesters bayed at the councillors from the public gallery. At one meeting, at which agreement had been reached to evict squatters from her estate, protesters chanted at Mary Ellery, who was Chair of Housing, from the gallery, calling her a fascist. But she knew the eviction orders were what the local tenants wanted. They'd waited to be allocated a flat and scrimped and saved to pay the rent. They didn't want squatters to jump the queue and live rent-free. In addition, most of the squatters didn't work and kept the tenants awake at night with noisy parties.

Later, after a relentless stream of worsening problems being reported to the London region of the Labour party, which culminated in an imitation gun being pulled in the Labour Club (which, by this time, had moved to Camberwell Church Street), the General Committee of the Peckham party was suspended in 1987. The branches within the Peckham Labour party were still allowed to meet. So, for the following two years, until the suspension was lifted, I'd go to the branch meetings to report on my work, as would the councillors, but there were no General Committee meetings. Ultimately, by the mid-nineties, its finances had descended into such chaos that the club was closed and the building sold. It should have been a disappointment for our local party no longer to have its own social club and meeting rooms but, in fact, it was a blessed relief. The General Committee was reinstated, but it has never been able to afford its own building again, and the party has to rent local meeting rooms.

Locally, there were two completely different sides to Labour. The violence and sectarian politics were grim but, through it all, there were local members of long standing who were deeply loyal to the party, grounded within the neighbourhood, who went about doing good in their area and improving the lives of their local community. They wanted, above all, for Labour to get back into government. Under the Tories, it was always the communities these Labour councillors represented, made up of the poorest people, who were the first to suffer. Whatever I and other local party members did to support the council against the twin problems of Tory cuts and ultra-left attacks, without a Labour government the problems in Peckham were only going to get worse.

Throughout the eighties, as the country, under Margaret Thatcher, became more divided and hostility to the government deepened in strong Labour areas, we'd seen our vote in Labour strongholds increase and Tory support in Labour areas collapse. We were ahead of the Tories in the national polls. But this masked the fact that, despite the strengthening of our support in Labour areas, our support in the crucial areas which had previously been marginal between Labour and the Tories was slipping away. And when it came to women voters, we trailed behind the Tories. In 1983, Labour lagged by 12 per cent with men voters, but by 20 per cent on votes from women. We would never get into government to change things for women unless we could get women to vote for us. And we wouldn't do that without radical change.

Both locally and nationally, there was lots of marching, and there were many demonstrations and instances of left activism inspired by hatred of the Tory government. In 1983, a quarter of a million people gathered in Trafalgar Square for the People's March for Jobs. Thousands of people came out on to the streets to support the miners' strike in 1984 and 1985, and to oppose the poll tax in 1989. However, as Neil Kinnock used to say, 'Never mistake the enthusiasm of the minority for the support of the majority.' We lacked broad-based support. The demos and marches grabbed the headlines, but Labour seemed to have become increasingly out of touch with most people's lives. We were an angry minority. At the weekends, we'd be marching and demonstrating, while most people were doing things like going shopping, taking their kids to football and just trying to getting on in their lives. The more they saw on TV of our marches and rallies, the more different they felt from us. And that was a problem, because we weren't going to be able to change anything, whether it was meeting the demands of the women's movement or anything else, if we remained in Opposition.

I'd always seen my politics as being firmly on the left. That's why I was in the Labour party and why I fought for women's rights. But I always believed that the only way you can put your principles into action and bring about the change you want is to get into power. But the party was out of touch with the voters. The *Peckham Labour News* was, in the early eighties, so full of polemics about internal party organization, about Polaris, about the demand for nationalization and of loathing for the United States, it made scarcely a reference to the issues which dominated my advice surgeries. There was a climate of bullying and intimidation, but I felt that, as a Labour MP, I shouldn't duck my responsibility to challenge the sectarianism and speak out about the way I saw things. Incredible though it seems, some in the party thought, that despite the fact that we had lost, the General Election in 1983 had been a success for Labour by virtue of us having such left-wing policies in our manifesto. But I pulled no punches in my monthly written report to my General Committee. Under the heading 'Facing the Facts' I described the defeat as devastating, wrote that our base of support was declining and that we were further back than at any time since 1931. If we were ever to get back into government, I insisted, we had to change.

The press lobby is a crucial part of the House of Commons. A distinguished, select corps of political journalists – 'lobby correspondents' – sit high up above the Chamber in the House of Commons press gallery to report on parliament. Their coveted press lobby passes also give them access to the Members' Lobby, where they wait around to talk to MPs and get off-the-record comments. (There's a convention that MPs can speak to lobby correspondents on 'lobby terms', which means that, when they quote it, the journalist will not mention the MP by name except with the MP's explicit permission.) It's how a great deal of political reporting is done and shapes the political agenda.

From my perch on the male-dominated benches of the House of Commons, I'd look up at the press gallery and see a solid mass of male political journalists and political editors. The Parliament I entered in 1982, 97 per cent of whose members were men, was reported on by a press lobby of whom 95 per cent were men. They were not the least interested in the women's agenda which Jo Richardson MP had been so valiantly espousing in parliament, and neither were they disposed to listen to what I had to say. The *Mirror*'s Julia Langdon and Channel 4's Elinor Goodman were rare exceptions as senior women in the lobby. So while it was hard enough to do my work in such a male-dominated Parliament, it was made still harder by the fact that it would not be taken seriously by the overwhelmingly male press lobby. It was, to me, no surprise that polls consistently showed that women in the country felt so little connection with what was going on in Parliament. It was a boys' club being reported on by a boys' club.

Although the press lobby in Parliament remains highly influential, it was of even greater importance back in the eighties and nineties, as it had a monopoly on reporting what went on. Hansard, the official written record of Parliament, was published a day or so after a debate, but it was what lobby journalists wrote in the following day's papers that set the agenda. From 1978, there was sound recording and then, in 1989, televising of Parliament. But the broadcasting of proceedings in Parliament was very limited and was controlled by the media correspondents in the lobby. The public heard about what was being said and done in Parliament only through the press lobby. They defined the Commons; they were the single lens through which the public saw the work of their MPs. I developed a theory that the journalists would pick out men of the same age and height as themselves and say how clever they were, thereby reflecting credit on themselves. I was only half joking. And while, as a novelty, I attracted the attention of the male press lobby, most of them had no interest in, or understanding of, the women's movement agenda I was in Parliament to pursue – the issues of childcare, domestic violence, maternity leave, equal pay and women's representation – and when I did appear in their columns it was usually to be trivialized.

Unable to get the press lobby to report sensibly on my work in Parliament, I turned to the local press and to the 'women's pages' of national papers. To encourage the local and regional press I'd include a regional breakdown of statistics or local examples – a nursery opening or an old people's home closing. I'd always be prepared to follow up with a 'down the line' interview on local radio or TV. I embargoed my press statements to coincide with their copy deadlines and gave interviews to features editors of local newspapers. I found them a much fairer conduit for the arguments I was making. Widespread coverage in the local papers was important because, while politicians tend to be more concerned about reporting in the national papers, polls show that people are more likely to pay more attention to what's in their local newspapers. And, unlike the lobby, they were listening to what I was trying to say.

Because there were so few women in the exclusive club of the political press lobby, I was delighted whenever a new woman arrived. Knowing it would be hard for them as they, too, were pioneers in a man's world, I wanted to help them find their feet and make progress. I saw this as my responsibility as a feminist. But I was also hopeful they would understand, and report on, the agenda I was in politics to pursue. So, seeing them newly arrived, self-consciously standing in the Members' Lobby, I would rush up, introduce myself, make friends with them and give them news to report.

They were in a small minority, just as I was. And the male hegemony in the lobby was reinforced by customs such as the political editors' Friday-afternoon golfing session, which did not, of course, include any of the women. The successor to that tradition is the regular lobby versus MPs football match. So even though our jobs were very different – and their job was to critique mine – we supported each other as women. If they worked on a Sunday newspaper, I'd call them on a Friday to give them an exclusive story so they could have a good hit in their paper without having to write a story on a Saturday when their children were off school. Getting into the lobby was hard, but then it was difficult, too, for these women to get their stories into their newspapers, so I never gave a story to a male journalist if there was a woman on the paper I could give it to.

It was a delight to me to see one new reporter arrive in the lobby and confidently start reporting on TV: 'Jackie Ashley, ITN News'. She was a breath of fresh air, so different from the men, a feminist of my generation who bent over backwards to get women MPs and our agenda on to the news. She married Andrew Marr – another political journalist (who later went on to be BBC Political Editor) – and I soon spotted a bump under her dress. As she stood around in the Members' Lobby looking for stories, one Tory MP complained that the sight of her 'pregnant belly' was distasteful and asked that pregnant women should not be allowed in. She recounts that one senior member of the ITN management, when told she was pregnant, said it would ruin her promising career and offered her the phone number of a good abortion clinic. She was horrified, as it was very much a planned pregnancy.

When she went off on maternity leave, I looked forward to her return and to seeing once again her gleaming blonde hair, so distinctive up in the gallery, and hearing her incisive political reports. But just when I was wondering when she'd be back she called me, saying she wouldn't be returning because, although she'd persuaded ITN to let her come back part-time, the lobby wouldn't allow her a part-time lobby pass. She was at the start of a promising career and was really upset. It was so typical of the many obstacles put in the path of the women that I immediately flew into 'outrage' mode. Jackie was a jewel in the crown of the press lobby, women in the gallery were as rare as hen's teeth, and they were making it impossible for her to return from her maternity leave. Denying her a pass because she worked part-time was indirect sex discrimination. I rang to protest to the Sergeant at Arms, the Commons official responsible for security and issuing passes. He said a part-time pass was impossible. Some weeks later she called to say that they'd relented and she was back up in the gallery. It's hard enough for anyone to come back to work after maternity leave, but what guts it must have taken for her to persist and challenge the House and the lobby powers-that-be, all with a new baby.

The hours of the House of Commons at that time, hard enough for me as a woman MP with young children, were even worse for a woman journalist with young children. The journalists stayed until the last vote and then often got stories by meeting MPs in the bar afterwards. Monday to Thursday, the last vote was never before 10 p.m., and often it could be 11.30 p.m. or 1 a.m. The journalists needed to stay on every night – it wouldn't do to miss a breaking story. Sadly for me and for the world of political reporting, after she had her second child, Jackie left the lobby. She later went to work at the *Guardian*. It was the same with nearly all the young women who came into the lobby. It's a great professional achievement for any journalist to get into the lobby, and they'd arrive full of enthusiasm. I'd see a new one appear in the Members' Lobby, then share their delight when I noticed their dresses getting baggier, with a baby on the way. They'd come back to the lobby after they'd had the baby, but the hours would grind them down and by the time they had their second child it would be too tempting for them to take the next job they saw advertised on the news desk or in features, which would allow them to pursue their profession without having to work until late at night.

There were so many brilliant young women journalists who'd blaze a trail in the lobby but, instead of going up the ladder to become political editor, they'd leave and go on to other things. It's a great breakthrough that the most prestigious post in political journalism – BBC Political Editor – is now held by a woman, Laura Kuenssberg, and the position of *Guardian* political editor is now a job-share between two women, Anushka Asthana and Heather Stewart. The hegemony of the press lobby has been dented by live broadcasting of the Chamber and the ability of MPs to communicate directly from the House of Commons on Twitter and Facebook, but the press gallery remains influential and needs to change. And men still outnumber women in the lobby by three to one. It's wrong that the largely male world of Parliament is still reported to the men and women of this country through predominantly male eyes. And I think there is a lost generation of female political editors – Lucy Ward, Gaby Hinsliff, Rosemary Bennet, Kathy Newman, Allegra Stratton, Ann Perkins, Rosa Prince, to name just a few.

To try to expose what I saw as the problem of male domination of the lobby, to make the point that it created unbalanced political reporting and that there was not equality for women journalists, I published a gender breakdown of the number of political editors and lobby correspondents. The women in the lobby were delighted, but it infuriated most of the men, who took it as a personal criticism. Later, in 1998, the still small number of women in the press lobby started going out to dinner together once a month to foster mutual support and solidarity. Sometimes they'd invite a female minister or MP. This also met with open hostility from the men in the lobby. They'd shown precious little interest in us but they were suspicious when the women got together.

I tried my best with the men in the lobby and had perfectly amicable relationships with some of them. But unlike the male MPs, I never had a drink with them between, or after, late-night votes, instead dashing back to the children. When journalists invited me to lunch, that didn't work out either. Long lunches seemed to take too much time, when I was trying to get as much done as I could during the day in order to be able to rush home in the evening. And I certainly couldn't drink at lunchtime, so I was a disappointment to them and got a reputation as being stand-offish. The *Independent* echoed what most of the lobby wrote continually about me when they described me in their Diary as an 'arrogant, icy airhead'. This was in 2002, and showed that, even twenty years after I'd entered Parliament, my relations with them still had a long way to go.

One of the issues which, though not exactly top of my agenda, worried me when I became an MP was what to wear. The men had the dark, or grey, suit as a default 'uniform'. I wanted to look smart but would have looked ridiculous in the matronly attire worn by some of the older Labour women MPs. Being an MP was a deeply serious job: I wasn't going for a night out, so I mustn't look too glamorous. To inspire confidence in my constituents, I had to look professional. In a way, it was more straightforward when I was pregnant; I just resorted to the enormous, tent-like maternity dresses of the time, swathes of fabric protecting people from the sight of the bump.

There was, in those days, no standard dress for a woman

professional or a woman in public life which I could adopt – there were so few of us, let alone of my age, and because there was a pretty constant stream of comments about what I was wearing, I wanted to get it right. In March 1984 Terry Dicks, Conservative MP for Hayes and Harlington, called on the Speaker to 'make it known' that he would not call me to speak in the House of Commons as I was too 'scruffy'. He said, 'There ought to be a rule as in some clubs and restaurants, where you must wear a collar and tie and a suit or you are not admitted,' and complained that 'any resemblance between [me] and a lady was entirely coincidental'.

As more women started to come into the world of work in professional positions, there began a discussion about what we should or could wear, and talk of 'power dressing'. The idea was that you would feel more powerful if you wore a jacket with large shoulder pads.

I was trying to work out how women would want to see a woman MP in the public eye dressed. Along with other younger Labour women, I looked for advice from Barbara Follett, a Labour feminist who later became MP for Stevenage. Of course, when they discovered this, the newspapers mocked it as 'Folletting'. But on her advice I abandoned my Laura Ashley floral frocks, took to wearing structured jackets, shiny, high-heeled shoes and carrying a smart briefcase instead of my overstuffed handbag. And it did make me feel more professional and less out of place.

There were so few of us in any meeting or on any political occasion, we had to avoid disappearing into the sea of grey suits. Folletting put us in brightly coloured jackets. If you've fought your way in against the odds, there's no point being invisible once you're there. And in the struggle and grind of politics, it was a welcome bit of light relief for us to have a laugh together and talk about clothes and make-up.

Later, in 1991, during one of my regular visits to marginal constituencies, I went to campaign with the newly selected Labour candidate for Cambridge, Anne Campbell. I was delighted to be going out to campaign with another woman, who I'd heard was my age and a working mother like me. She'd set up an organization called Childcare Links to bring together childcare providers, employers and the local council so that mothers searching for childcare would have a 'one-stop shop'. She went on to win the seat for Labour and be a major voice in the House of Commons. But I still remember the first time I saw her, standing at Cambridge station. All the other party members were dressed in an assembly of anoraks and overcoats, but she stood out, glowing, in her smart burgundy jacket. A deeply serious academic, she, too, had obviously been 'Folletted'.

The pictures of the new Labour women voted into the Commons in 1997 show nearly all of us proudly wearing our bright jackets. Now that women MPs are such an integral part of the House of Commons, what we wear is less of an issue, more a matter of choice, but everything we did or said then was like walking a tightrope, and we were trying to avoid getting it wrong.

I worked right up until our first son was due, in February 1983. I reckoned that I might as well do as much as I could before the birth to give me more time with the baby afterwards. I now think it would have been better to have taken at least a couple of weeks off before the birth, to get my head out of work mode and do some 'nesting'. But it may be that nothing can prepare you for the birth of your first child. Three months after I was elected, our first son was born and I was instantly smitten. I looked at him sleeping peacefully in his Perspex cot among the rows of babies in the hospital nursery and hoped there were no other mothers about – I felt such a great wave of pity for them because, compared to mine, their babies looked awful. Hopefully, they wouldn't see Harry and realize how ugly their own baby was! But of course a part of me knew that the other mothers would be having the same hormone-fuelled feelings I was. I left hospital sniffing the air, wondering if it was pure enough for my baby to breathe and started worrying even more about everything. I had to look after this baby and change the world to make it good enough for him. And this even extended to shielding him from Margaret Thatcher.

One night, we were voting late and, unusually, I had Harry with me. I was walking down the long corridor beside the House of Commons Library when I spotted the Prime Minister with a group of aides at the other end. She had clearly seen me carrying the baby and was bearing down on me. I was gripped by the sense that I couldn't bear her eyes to fall on my perfect baby. I pulled his blanket over his face to shield him from her gaze and then, as I passed a room off the corridor, dived into it.

When I went back to the House of Commons to vote, about six weeks after our son was born, I felt even more, if that were possible, like a fish out of water than I had when I was first elected. These were lonely times for me in the House, and I was torn between Westminster, my constituency and my home. Although most of the Labour MPs were fathers themselves, and no doubt loving and committed, there could be no sharing of problems and parental chat between me and them. I couldn't talk to them about how hard I found breastfeeding to start with, and then, the anguish about when and how to wean the baby. I felt I couldn't share with them the joy of the miracle of the first steps and words, as most of them were hundreds of miles away from their home and children and their wives were holding the fort. And though many tried to be supportive as I struggled with my new roles, many were not. One night, soon after coming back, I was suffering from mastitis and I told the Whips, explaining that I couldn't vote. This promptly appeared in the papers the next day. Having mastitis is really upsetting and I was embarrassed to see it reported in the papers. From then on, I resolved to tell the Whips nothing personal. That made it harder to get the flexibility that the other MPs took for granted, but I couldn't trust them.

A while later, a rumour started to circulate that I had fed the baby in the Chamber. I never did; it took all my courage to go into the Chamber to speak. Yet the rumour also found its way into the newspapers and became an urban myth. Ironically, there are still women to this day who come up and tell me how pleased they were that I did it, that it gave them the strength to insist on feeding their babies more openly. No woman MP has yet brought a baby into the Chamber, let alone fed it there. Many women councillors had already, at that time, taken their babies into the council chamber if they were breastfeeding them, without any ill-effects on local democracy or the baby. And one day a woman will sit and feed her baby on the green benches, and I'll be delighted when that happens.

Another night not long after our son was born, I went into the House of Commons to vote. The next day I got a call from the Sergeant at Arms. He'd received a complaint from a member that I'd taken the baby through the Division Lobby, which MPs walk through to have their vote counted. It was alleged that I had hidden the baby under my coat, and I was to be reprimanded. Only members are allowed in the Division Lobby, and babies are not members, so it was against the rules. I felt bitter that a Labour MP (since it was about our Division Lobby, it had to be one of my own side), had, just after I'd come back from having a baby, gone behind my back to make a complaint about me. Why hadn't they said something to me? Why did it even matter to them if I *had* taken my baby through under my coat? Why hadn't they asked to see my new baby to admire him rather than making a complaint? It felt like yet another example of hostility to me as a new mother in Parliament and, worse, hostility to the baby with whom I was besotted. And in any case, I hadn't taken the baby through the lobby. It wasn't a baby under my coat but the 'baby fat' I still had after my pregnancy. I miserably protested my innocence to the Sergeant at Arms, mortified at having to explain the real reason to him. And it reminded me that it was far too soon for me to be back voting.

Though incidents like this might seem small, they made me feel alienated from the House and from most of my fellow MPs. Excluding babies from the Division Lobby was an absurd and oppressive rule, especially then, when there were so many late-night, and all-night, sittings. But I consoled myself that, though it was miserable for me, I could make it better for other women in the future and it reinforced my determination that, in the coming years, when other women MPs arrived and had babies, I would go out of my way to be demonstrably welcoming and encouraging to them. For any of them who'd suffered any slight or meanness, I wanted to help be the antidote. Even now, when it's not unusual to see a pregnant MP and, thanks to Labour MP Lucy Powell and Lib Dem Jo Swinson, the ban on babies in the lobby has been lifted, it's still hard to manage the competing demands of being a mother with being an MP, especially if your constituency home is miles from Westminster, so I want to help them make the next steps of progress on their journey as MPs.

I was a constant presence on the radio and on television, including programmes such as *Question Time* and *Any Questions*, and from breakfast TV through to *Newsnight*, whether it was on the issue of the safety of people in old people's homes, people on hospital waiting lists dying unnecessarily, the lack of nursery places, the scourge of domestic violence, or the problems of unemployment and low pay. And I was permanently ready to speak up to denounce the latest of the many examples of discrimination or injustice.

There was, at that time, a casual acceptance not only of sexism and sexual harassment but also of homophobia and racism. Any time this was challenged, it was described as banter and the critic was accused of lacking a sense of humour. But tackling discrimination was at the heart of my politics so I publicly protested at every example I came across. One such was in Guy's Hospital rag magazine, published as part of their annual rag week to raise money for local charities. This was what appeared in the joke section: 'How do you get a hundred Jews in a mini? One in the driver's seat and ninety-nine in the ashtray,' and 'How do you stop a Pakistani spitting? Turn the grill down.' I complained to the hospital and referred the matter to the Director of Public Prosecutions. The *South London Press* ran an editorial condemning me for overreacting and being humourless. But the Jewish community and local black and Asian organizations were deeply appreciative when the hospital apologized.

Every time I stuck my head above the parapet, I'd be lambasted by the press. The Tories decried my protests as 'political correctness gone mad'. And in this they were supported by some in Labour's ranks, who continued to regard me as a humourless feminist, unable to see 'the joke'. But I'd always get strong support from those on whose behalf I was protesting. I knew my protests heartened those who were suffering as a result of such attitudes and were welcomed by party members who were pleased to see Labour MPs challenging them. The only way I could avoid the criticism was to keep quiet, and I wasn't going to let the press shut me up.

I became accustomed to being criticized in the press, as did all Labour MPs at the time, but I was taken apart for being a feminist as well. I never complained, thinking that it would only make things worse, yet one article so aggrieved me that I just could not let it stand. A story in the *Yorkshire Post* described me as 'lazy'. And I knew from personal experience, as well as from talking to many others, that working mothers are the least lazy people of all. I wrote, threatening to sue. They protested that they had simply been quoting one of my Labour MP colleagues, who, of course, was not named. I didn't doubt that this was the case but insisted that they had to take responsibility for printing something which was not true. They backed down, apologized and paid me compensation, but I smarted at the knowledge that a Labour MP colleague could – and would – go behind my back and criticize me to the press.

In the eighties and nineties I was battling on so many fronts for women outside Parliament, for maternity rights, support for breastfeeding, childcare and equal pay, and I lived with the constant fear that my arguments would be undermined if my colleagues were able to say I wasn't doing my job properly or to depict my arguments about Parliament as self-serving and as drawing attention to myself. My priority in terms of the workings of Parliament at that time was to end the late-night and all-night sittings and I was already getting a lot of flak for and making too little progress on that.

It had long been the women's movement's view that the hours of the House of Commons were anachronistic and should change. We believed they were designed for men for whom being an MP was their second job, that those long night sittings were hard for women with young children and that Parliament was setting a bad example to employers about 'family-friendly working'. We were arguing that the law should require employers to make work more family friendly, but how could Parliament tell employers to do what it was so strikingly failing to do itself?

As well as the late hours, there was a difference in the work patterns of the Tory and the Labour MPs at that time. Tory constituencies were concentrated in the south, nearer to the House of Commons. Labour MPs had so much further to travel from their homes in their constituencies in the north, in Scotland and in Wales. More Tory MPs had second jobs. Many were barristers or company directors, and would come into the House only during the course of the afternoon. By early Monday evening the Palace of Westminster would fill up. There were far fewer offices for MPs than there are now. Most had to share and some had no office at all and had to work in the House of Commons Library. And at night, the Members' Dining Room, the Tea Room, the Smoke Room, the bars and the canteen would be packed, while, even though business was still going on, the Chamber would be virtually empty. On the occasions when there was some highly controversial business late at night, the Chamber would become full and the MP speaking would have to compete with the sort of hubbub you'd find in a pub just before closing time. I wasn't at ease speaking in the Chamber, but I especially dreaded winding up a debate from the front bench which would involve speaking late at night, when inebriated jeers would be aimed at the earnest points I was trying to make. Drunken late nights in parliament happened all the time. But it was never mentioned in the Chamber. It was 'unparliamentary' even to imply it.

The culture of drunkenness in the House of Commons wasn't challenged until 1983, when Clare Short, then a new MP, criticized the minister Alan Clark for making a statement in the House when he was drunk. She said, 'It is disrespectful to the House and to the Office that he holds that he should come here in this condition.' He was scarcely coherent and slurring his words, and Clare didn't even directly refer to drink, but it was she who was reprimanded, for breaking the rule that it's unparliamentary for an MP to allege that another is drunk. Later, in his diaries, Alan Clark admitted that he had been drunk at the time.

Whether it was a minister speaking at the dispatch box, a backbencher making a speech or just MPs sitting in on a debate, when people had been drinking the quality of the debate and the atmosphere was, inevitably, affected. Most drank in the evening and, even if they were not 'drunk', they were no longer sober. It became a vicious circle. The later the House was sitting, the more they would drink. And the more they had drunk, the longer their speeches became. There was not, as yet, comprehensive television or radio broadcasting of Parliament, so MPs were not concerned that their constituents would see them. And the press gallery newspaper reporters were not going to say anything against this culture, because most of them were, themselves, part of it. People often remark that the behaviour they now see in the House of Commons is boorish, but it's nothing now compared to what it was then.

By the time it got beyond 10 p.m., most MPs were well past their best. It made no sense, in terms of the quality of the work, for the House to sit so late. And the hours certainly made it more difficult to be an MP if you were a woman with young children, there being in those days no expectation that fathers would share equally in caring for young children. We felt we needed women with children as MPs to give women in the country a voice, and to do that we needed not only to change the selection process to get women in but also to make it less of an ordeal once you got there, so we needed to change the hours. Starting on Monday at 2.30 p.m. makes sense, as it allows MPs to spend Sunday night with their family in their constituency and travel to London in time for Monday's votes. But once in London for the working week, there is, aside from the requirements of doing another job, no reason for the House not to start at 9 a.m. and finish at a reasonable hour, like most other work-places. If the House wasn't sitting on Friday, it made sense to start early on Thursday and finish in time to enable MPs to get back home, ready to start their constituency work on Friday morning.

As soon as I arrived in the House of Commons I started pressing for the hours to be changed. I made the argument as carefully as I could, especially taking into account the differing situations of MPs outside London. I argued to maintain Monday's two-thirty start and to end Thursdays sittings early to help out-of-London MPs. I argued that this was important for women MPs but also for men, who were effectively exiled from their families by the hours. I pressed for House recesses to coincide with half-term. I proposed that the long summer recess that ran from the end of July to the beginning of October should start and finish earlier to fit in with Scottish MPs, whose children went back to school after the sum-mer holidays in mid-August, when the House had only just risen for the summer recess.

I pointed out that staffing costs made it more expensive for the public purse for the House to be sitting late at night, that the pres-ent hours dated back only to 1945, that there was no evidence that late hours helped hold the government to account, that if they wanted to do second jobs, MPs could do them in the evenings and at weekends.

I had hoped that MPs would support my call for change, espe-cially fellow Labour MPs, many of whom didn't have second jobs and lived outside London. But there was overwhelming resistance to any change. Out-of-London MPs argued that, because they couldn't get back to their homes in the evening, they needed to be in the House of Commons, otherwise they'd have nothing to do except sit in their flat. They felt this would mean being pitched out of the cosy sociability of nights at the House of Commons. It became personal, with some MPs accusing me of proposing change which would threaten their marriage, as their wives wouldn't trust them being out and about in London in the evening. I argued that, even if the House was not sitting at night, the bars and dining rooms could stay open. By putting the case for change in terms of it being more family friendly, they felt I was implying they weren't good parents. The MPs with outside jobs, mostly Tories, were implacably opposed to changing the hours, as it would affect their income.

A change in the hours wasn't just my argument, it was a long-standing demand of the women's movement but, as I pressed the argument in the House, it became deeply unpopular, and me with it. No one likes a newcomer who arrives and immediately starts demanding change. I was seen as criticizing an institution I had only just joined and, by implication, finding fault with my PLP colleagues and exposing them to public disapproval. I was accused of being self-serving and self-centred, of being London-centric and not understanding the life of out-of-London MPs. One MP echoed the sentiments of many when he said that I knew what the hours were before I came to the House and if I 'couldn't stand the heat, I should stay out of the kitchen'. No doubt he thought I should never have left my own kitchen in the first place.

Though I never argued for fewer hours, only for earlier sitting times, the press lobby sided with the MPs and cast my argument as one from a lazy MP who wanted to work less. I was accused of ignoring the plight of ordinary working-class women who worked unsocial hours and focusing selfishly on my own situation. One Scottish Labour MP said he wouldn't support change because, although he acknowledged it would help 'London women', earlier sittings wouldn't help him see more of his children. I reminded him that I was arguing for the House recesses to coincide with Scottish school holidays, which would help him, and protested that, as socialists, we are not supposed to be concerned only about issues in so far as they coincided with our own interests.

In 1990 I published 'Time, Gentlemen, Please. The case for changing the sitting times of the House of Commons'. Using the research resources of the House of Commons library, I reported that, in 1989, the House sat after 10.30 p.m. on 123 days and after midnight on 76 days. Nearly three quarters of sitting days finished after 10 p.m., a quarter after midnight, and a tenth after 2 a.m. By this time, I had three children, aged six, four and two. Bearing in mind how exhausted I was and how thoroughly counterproductive late sitting hours were, it is remarkable how reasonable my tone was in 'Time, Gentlemen, Please'. But the title, implying as it did that the Commons was a gentlemen's club or a bar, increased the antipathy towards me on the part of those MPs who were comfortable with the status quo.

As I struggled to cope with the late sittings, it was not just that my fellow MPs were feeling angry with me – I was angry, too, bitter against those among my colleagues who opposed change. But bolstered by the arrival of more Labour women MPs, particularly Joan Ruddock and Hilary Armstrong, and with the support of Neil Kinnock and then John Smith, the pressure to change the hours began to grow. It was never just about Parliament being more family friendly, it was also about modernizing it, turning it into a twentieth-century legislative body rather than it remaining a nineteenth-century gentlemen's club.

By 1991 pressure for change had grown to such an extent that the government set up the Joplin Committee to carry out a review. I was jubilant that, at last, here was the prospect of change. But my delight was quickly dampened when I discovered that the Whips hadn't nominated me to be on the committee; Labour was to be represented by Hilary Armstrong. I'd taken the argument on and, now there was the possibility of doing something, I was to be excluded. I was resentful, but now I think that to go forward we needed to move into consensual mode, and I'd been too much of a protagonist. Hilary backed changing the hours but had had fewer rows about it. She, of course, did a great job and proposals came forward to change the hours in just the way I'd set out in 'Time, Gentleman, Please'. Although it took until 2002, they were finally voted through.*

---

* However, the backlash rumbled on and the opponents of the change managed to pull back on some of the progress by pushing through a vote in 2004 that we

On other issues, less has changed. The Whips still arrange House of Commons votes so they don't come in the middle of a big football match. I discovered this when, one night in 1986 when I was waiting for a vote, I found the normally busy House of Commons corridors deserted. I couldn't work out where everyone was, until I heard a huge cheer erupting out of a committee room I was passing. It was the World Cup. Special screens had been set up in a number of committee rooms. I could hear the roars and groans and the cheerful camaraderie. Whatever grapevine got them all to the committee room, I was not on it.

I made frequent speeches in the Chamber of the House of Commons. The older members, the Commons grandees, used to listen to each other with mutual respect, but the atmosphere was hostile when I spoke. I always prepared my speeches carefully and I was never inflammatory for the sake of it, but my comments would be received with sexist jeers and barracking. Tony Marlow, a Tory MP, was rebuked by the Speaker, Betty Boothroyd, for calling me a 'stupid cow', but for the most part such jibes went unchecked. In 1985, after I'd made a serious speech about cuts in local public services, the Tory MP Jerry Hayes dripped condescension, starting his speech with: 'What a remarkable little speech that was from the Member for Peckham. I am sure that it will go down well with the Labour Party Women's Committee, but it will not cut much ice in the House.' I hadn't, in that speech, even mentioned women, but the Tories were determined to put me in my place and, often, my own side joined in. When the TV cameras were first allowed into the Chamber I was able to see for the first time the reaction of my fellow Labour MPs when I was speaking from the front bench. It was mortifying to see that, instead of backing me up, they'd be shuffling in their seats, looking embarrassed. Sometimes, I saw on the broadcast footage that they were joining the Tories in laughing

---

sit until ten on Tuesdays as well as on Mondays. (This was reverted to 7 p.m. in a vote in 2012.)

at me. That was before MPs became accustomed to the fact that they were in camera shot even when they weren't speaking.

Though there was precious little change inside the House of Commons, outside, it was a different story. The women's movement and feminism were growing in strength and confidence and so was the Labour party women's organization. It was undoubtedly exciting to be part of it. But, lonely in the House of Commons, exhausted by the late nights of voting, distressed by the bloodletting in the Labour Party, worried about not spending enough time at home or at work, I was often tempted to give up. However, Jack and my friends in the women's movement refused to countenance it.

I was holding the flag for women in Parliament. If I gave up, it would, they said, send a terrible message to other women struggling for progress. There were important things for me to do in Parliament, they said. I'd feel better once we got to the next House of Commons recess, and so on, and so on. And so many of my women constituents started conversations with 'As a woman, I know you'll understand . . .' I felt I couldn't walk out on them.

I longed for the arrival of more women for personal reasons. I missed working in a female environment. It would have been so much more bearable to sit out the long night hours if there had been other women there, and of a similar age. But, above all, I wanted there to be more Labour women MPs for political reasons. It's hard to bring about change when you are in a tiny minority. I'd hoped that, after my by-election in 1982, the General Election would bring many other Labour women into Westminster. Among others, Patricia Hewitt was the candidate in a safe Labour seat in Leicester, and Kate Hoey was standing in the Dulwich seat next door to mine. But Labour's election result was so disastrous – we lost 60 seats, falling from having 269 MPs in 1979 to having only 209. Many MPs lost their seats, and Patricia and Kate, along with many other Labour candidates, didn't get elected. Even Audrey Wise lost in what had been a safe Labour seat in Woolwich.

With Labour's result being so bad, we lost some of our long-standing Labour women MPs. My report to the Peckham

Women's Sections after the 1983 General Election was bleak. Joan Lestor, our spokesperson on women, had lost her seat in Slough. We'd lost Helen McElhone from Glasgow, leaving the forty-one-strong contingent of Scottish Labour MPs with only one woman – Judith Hart – who was due to retire in 1987. Ann Taylor lost in Bolton to the Tories. I was still one of only twelve Labour women MPs so, as well as working with Labour women to change the rules to get more women selected, I also encouraged women I knew to try for Labour constituencies.

After the 1983 election, Neil Kinnock became leader of the Labour party in a hard-fought contest against Roy Hattersley, Eric Heffer and Peter Shore. Roy Hattersley became deputy, defeating Michael Meacher. The prospects for the party were not good, with commentators predicting that Labour would fall into third place behind the SDP–Liberal Alliance and would never again be in government. Neil Kinnock had a mountain to climb, but I had confidence in him, feeling that, because of his political instincts and his personal qualities there was no one better suited to take on the task. Neil came from the Bevanite tradition of the Labour party, a leftist movement led by Aneurin Bevan in the fifties, which was never marred by the kind of sectarianism that characterized the ultra-left. He wanted vigorous debate and for the members' voices to be heard but he was also determined that party unity should be restored. He was strongly critical of the lack of solidarity shown by the ultra-left to anyone not of their doctrinal purity and firmly believed that the politics of focusing only on passing resolutions in Labour General Committee meetings had to give way to setting the party on a path to get back into government. He was an outstanding orator, electrifying the party on the eve of the 1983 General Election with his iconic speech, in which he said that, if the Tories got into government again, 'I warn you not to be young. I warn you not to fall ill. And I warn you not to grow old.'

Neil Kinnock took on the leadership at a time when the party was sliding backwards. We'd hoped that, after our defeat in 1979, if we redoubled our efforts, we'd get back into government next time. But with the party moving even further away from the public and immersing itself in in-fighting, the marginals we lost in 1979 had, by 1983, turned into safe Tory seats. With the backing of the trade unions, whose members were suffering so much under the Tory government, Neil embarked on a process of modernizing the party's policy and organization and reconnecting Labour with the public. And that was no easy task. It took courage for anyone to stand out against the threats and bitterness that had started in the late seventies and which, by the early eighties, was ripping through the Labour party. To get us out of that quagmire, what it required from the leader was nothing less than huge personal and political commitment, intelligence and courage. But that is what we got with Neil Kinnock. He was attacked mercilessly both by the ultra-left of the party and by the Tory-supporting press. But he earned my enduring respect and admiration and that of many others. And only someone with his leftist antecedents and personal and political courage could have succeeded in that task. Although he resigned after the 1992 General Election defeat, he had laid the basis for our subsequent victories. When, in 1997, I watched on TV as Tony Blair walked into Downing Street, I remembered how much we owed Neil for what he did to make that possible. And I imagined what a bittersweet moment it must have been for him. He had done more than anyone to rescue the party and set it on the path to government, but it was not to be he who made that walk into Number Ten.

In March 1984 a vacancy arose on the front bench when Frank Field voted against the whip and subsequently resigned. I got a message to call Patricia Hewitt, who was then Neil Kinnock's press secretary. I was to come down to Neil's office to see him right away. She didn't say what it was about. I'd never been in to see him before and, thinking I must have done something wrong, wearily made my way to his office. I was feeling ill and this seemed like the straw that was going to break the camel's back. I was ushered into Neil's room and he said he wanted to appoint me to the front bench, which was the last thing I had expected. He suggested that I come back to him with my answer. Patricia was waiting for me, beaming, as I left. It had obviously been her suggestion. I said I didn't think I could do it. I couldn't even think straight because I had such a headache, and I might have some awful illness, and after less than a year and a half I hadn't yet worked out how to be a backbencher, let alone a frontbencher. And I was struggling to do it all with a young baby. She said this was a big opportunity for me and that if I didn't grab it another chance might not come, that the ministers on our front bench were mostly old and nearly exclusively male, and that the party needed me to do my bit at this difficult time. Three of the ten other Labour women MPs were already on the front bench but most of the others were heading into retirement and I was needed.

She said I was probably just getting flu, I'd soon be better and that I would kick myself if I didn't take the job. Suggesting I go home, she said she'd tell Neil I'd do it and, feeling too weak to argue, I did so and went to bed. It was announced in the newspapers the next day that I was to be Shadow Minister for Social Services under Shadow Secretary of State Michael Meacher.

It was typical of Patricia's political commitment and personal loyalty that when the Shadow ministerial vacancy occurred, she used her position in the Labour leader's office to look for an opportunity to push forward for women, and for me. She could have been forgiven if she'd felt resentful that her former employee was now an MP when the political failings of the Labour party had denied her the chance to get elected. But instead she engineered my promotion, and her commitment to the cause and her support for me gave me my first, early step on the front-bench ladder.

I continued to feel unwell and, some weeks later, I discovered why. I was pregnant again. I wasn't going to feel better until November, by which time I'd be a new MP with a front-bench job and two babies under the age of two. (My pregnancies were particularly badly timed for my political work. The first time I was pregnant, I fought a by-election. My first baby was only four months old when I fought my first General Election. My second pregnancy coincided with me moving on to the front bench for the first time. And the next General Election was called in 1987, when my third child was only four months old.) However, we wanted another child, and I felt it was a privilege to be able to work in such great causes as the Labour party and the women's movement.

Living the struggle of balancing work and family undoubtedly added an extra dimension to my commitment to campaign for rights for part-time workers, maternity pay and leave and flexible working rights. But I was anxious to guard against the perception that my family responsibilities undermined my ability to be an MP and meant that I was too busy with my own family to help others. I felt that my constituents wanted a woman who could, from her own life experience, understand their concerns but also one they could rely on and would be superhuman in fighting for them. So even when I was scarcely coping, I never admitted it but emphasized instead that I was strong, capable and determined in their cause. Presenting that face to the outside world helped me live up to my responsibilities, but it gave many women the false impression that I was, somehow, superhuman, when I was anything but.

Often, juggling young children with working in the House of Commons and in my constituency felt as if it was just too much. Now, it is expected that MPs and ministers will take a period of leave when they have a baby. It is so normal, there would be surprise if they didn't. And that has made the business of being an MP and a minister having babies, though still not easy, much less fraught. But in the eighties, with me the only MP having babies, there was no maternity leave from the front bench, let alone from the pressing needs of my constituents. When it came to things like setting up the Women's PLP, making demands on behalf of women in the party or in public, I was bold. But I didn't feel able to demand change when it was for myself. I was too much on the defensive to insist on formal maternity leave, feeling I had to give the impression that I was coping with everything, fearing that any sign that I wasn't would unleash a torrent of accusations that I wasn't doing my job properly. So my written reports to my constituency party were full of 'business as usual'. My January 1985 report reassures my local party that 'the baby and I are in good health and so I have been able to do a considerable amount of work from home during my "maternity leave".' Though I fantasized about giving up, I couldn't. I'd be breaking the promise I had made to my constituents when I stood for election, I'd be letting down the Labour party and the women's movement. Once you've picked up the flag as a pioneer, you can't easily throw it down. And the whole point is that you are carrying it for others, not for yourself.

I already had a public presence and was regularly on TV when I was at the NCCL before I was elected. But in the years after I became an MP, my public profile grew. When I was out and about, in the street or on a train, women were starting to smile at me and come up and talk to me about their lives. They were teachers, carers, shop or factory workers, all trying to balance work and home, and they said how pleased they were to see someone talking publicly about the issues they themselves were wrestling with every day, coping with the demands of home, husband and work. They urged me to keep on speaking up about those issues in Parliament. That was a constant reinforcement of my mandate. I could see that I was giving them a voice representing their lives in politics. But my heart would sink if a woman came up to me, as they sometimes did, and said, 'I don't know how you do it' or 'I don't envy you, doing all that.' I know they only meant to be friendly, but I heard it as 'I wouldn't do that.'

3.

Throwing Open the Doors of Politics

I now had national responsibility on the front bench, and it was an opportunity to work with Labour councillors all around the country. Labour wasn't in government but we held power in many local councils where women councillors, though still a small minority, were, despite the Tory cuts, innovating and putting their Labour and feminist values into practice. In Scotland, Strathclyde Regional Council developed a ground-breaking childcare strategy of provision for all children, not just those in 'problem families'. Manchester Council turned a women's cloakroom in the town hall into a crèche for the children of council workers and councillors. Rita Stringfellow, one of the rare women council leaders, made childcare a priority for her North Tyneside council. Margaret Hodge, leader of Islington council, developed its childcare. Tessa Jowell pushed forward on services in her Camden council and put childcare to the top of the agenda. It was exciting to see the policies we cared about turned into action. I visited nurseries, crèches and playgroups. I went out on visits with home helps and to old people's homes. Seeing what Labour councils were doing helped us develop the policies we would put in our manifesto and implement when Labour finally got into government in 1997.

The Labour councils were working against the odds, as central government cuts bit deeper into their budgets. I wanted us to get our message across about the dreadful impact the Tories were having on council services and, as Shadow Minister for Social Services, it was my job to hold the Tories to account. I innovated by, for the first time, collecting data on public services and putting them into league tables, which enabled people to see what was being done, area by area. I did all this by asking questions in Parliament, which ministers have to answer in writing, factually and within a specific time. When I got their responses I commissioned the House of Commons library to draw up the figures into league tables by local authority. The first was on home helps. From my own constituency, I knew of their invaluable work going to the homes of the elderly. They helped with cleaning, which was so important to houseproud people no longer able to do their own housework. They helped with bathing and making meals, did shopping and collected pensions in cash from local post offices. They were trusted and caring and provided elderly people with much-needed company. But the cuts being imposed by the Tory government were forcing the councils to reduce services at the very time when, with people living longer, demand was growing. The first league table I published was the Home Help League Table, which showed, by local authority, the number of home helps per thousand people over the age of sixty-five.

The guidelines that the government had issued to local councils specified that there should be at least twelve home helps per thousand residents over sixty-five years old. But my findings showed that, out of 108 councils in England, only eighteen complied with these guidelines.

The results of the Home Helps League Table were reported in every regional newspaper and I followed up with interviews on all the regional TV and radio stations. I'd hit on a way of highlighting Labour's concerns and getting them into the news. And the league table showed that Labour councils were investing far more in home helps than Tory councils, though the results also annoyed some Labour councils, which were competitive between themselves and didn't like to be compared unfavourably with one another.

I pressed on, and my next league table was on childcare – the number of nursery places per hundred children under the age of five – to highlight the need for more nursery provision. Once again it showed Labour councils ahead of Tory ones, but it also exposed the woeful lack of provision generally. Southwark council came eleventh out of 108 local authorities, but with only four nursery places for every hundred children under five. They were not even scratching the surface. The unmet demand was huge.

What I was doing got some Labour councillors up in arms; they complained that I didn't realize how hard it was to maintain existing provision for childcare at a time of cuts, let alone increase it. But the league tables were strongly supported by party members, and the one on childcare by women in particular, so I continued to do them year after year, knowing that they would lay the basis for an improvement in services. And, by this time, I'd found another important ally for this work: Tessa Jowell, in her position as the new chair of the Association of Metropolitan Authorities (AMA) Social Services Committee. On one occasion, in 1986, when I was pregnant with my third child, I'd gone to speak at an AMA conference she was chairing in Nottingham. I arrived feeling exhausted and sick, and the very last thing I felt capable of doing was making an authoritative speech to hundreds of expert chairs and directors of Social Services. Tessa instantly spotted the 'end of tether' signs, having no doubt experienced them herself, as she had children of about the same age as mine. She ushered me into her hotel room and on to her bed, where I lay, flat out, while we worked out what I would say. And instead of pressing me to mingle with all the delegates in advance, she fuelled me up with herb tea and only at the last minute took me to the stage, then bundled me on to a train home as soon as I'd finished.

Our third child, Amy, was born in January 1987 and the General Election was called for June that year, so it was to be the first election where I was on the front bench and expected to be part of the national campaign team. Patricia Hewitt held Amy at the side of the platform when I joined the photo call for our manifesto launch. It was a joy to leave the hostile atmosphere of the House of Commons and go on the road with my five-month-old baby, where she was enthusiastically welcomed in the mother and toddler groups and playgroups I visited all around the country. Because of all the publicity around the league table, the mothers I met there already knew of me and that I was a champion for the services which were so important to them. And they were of course delighted that I'd brought my baby with me. My sisters Sarah and Virginia took it in turns to come on the road with me, as did my sister's elder son. For the first time, as part of our General Election campaign, Labour launched a Manifesto for Women, full of promises of maternity leave and nursery care. When it came to that launch, Neil Kinnock spotted Amy in the wings and swung her up on to his shoulders for the photo call. Despite what, for me, was an enjoyable campaign, it was dispiriting that no one thought Labour had any chance of winning and, indeed, we lost – our third defeat in a row. Although I was re-elected in Peckham with a healthy majority, it was depressing to face up to another five years of Tory government and miserable to sit with my constituents in my advice surgery on the Friday morning after the election defeat knowing that their problems, with housing, hospital waiting lists and low pay, would only continue to grow.

After the defeat, the NCCL Women's Committee, of which I was still a member, went off for a weekend at Anna Coote's mother's home in the countryside. We made plans for our future work – more cases on equal pay, more research on domestic violence – and enjoyed all being together. I was confident that I'd be reappointed as a Shadow minister. I knew I'd done well and expected that Shadow Cabinet members would bid for me to join their team. Jack Straw rang to say he was going to be Shadow Secretary of State for Education and asked me to be his deputy. It was a step up from the more junior role I'd had in the Department of Social Services (DSS) team as Shadow Social Services Minister, but I had no hesitation in declining. I wanted the children's primary-school teachers to see me as one of the mums, not as a politician pronouncing on education. Luckily, another call came in, this time from Robin Cook. I didn't know him well, but he was hugely impressive and a much admired parliamentary performer. He told me he was going to be the Shadow Secretary of State for Health and wanted me to be his deputy. I agreed, and we went on to work together for the next five years. There was never a dull moment working with Robin. He was clever, strategic, incredibly hard-working and had a brilliant dry wit. Though we didn't socialize together, we formed a close political relationship which lasted until his untimely death of a heart attack in 2005. Our dynamic and collegiate team was completed by Karen Buck, the Labour HQ health researcher (who later became MP for Westminster North), and Anna Healy from the Labour HQ press office, who was to become my head of office when I was elected Deputy Leader twenty years later.

Once again, I set about compiling league tables. Every constituency advice surgery had been bringing in complaints about people waiting for treatment at King's College Hospital. One young couple said that the woman's mother had been waiting over a year for a cataract operation. Unable to see properly, she'd become housebound and they feared that, even when she had the operation, she'd have lost her confidence and never go out on her own again. An elderly woman passed me a letter about her hip-replacement operation. King's had at last given her a date, but it was in two years' time. She wept as she whispered to me that because of the pain in her hip she could no longer get upstairs to her toilet and bedroom. She felt humiliated by having to use a bucket and wait for her daughter to empty it, and sleeping on the sofa made her hip worse.

Often, constituents would get so desperate, waiting in pain, that relatives would club together and borrow money to pay for the operation to be done privately. But it left debt for the family and guilt for the patient. And many, even with the help of friends and relatives, couldn't afford to go private, so they suffered for months on end from perfectly treatable conditions. On one of my regular visit to Guy's Hospital a cardiac surgeon pointed to his operating list, which was pinned up on the wall in his office. The names and addresses on it included many in my constituency. He pointed to a name a third of the way up and said, 'All those below this will die before I can operate on them. Completely avoidable deaths.' I was horrified to see the names and addresses of people on the estates I knew so well.

I tabled parliamentary questions asking the Health Minister to list the waiting times within each speciality for each health authority. All were bad, although some were worse than others. The longest waits were in orthopaedics, in cataract operations and cardiac surgery. With the help of Karen Buck and the House of Commons Library, I drew up and published the league table of the length of time people had to spend on hospital waiting lists in each health authority area. Measuring the waiting times, not just the number of people on the waiting list, and ranking the health authorities brought into political focus a picture of what was going on all around the country. Our 1997 election manifesto promised to cut the 1.3 million people on the waiting lists by a hundred thousand. And we then moved on to double the budget of the NHS and to set a target to cut average waiting times from eighteen months to under eighteen weeks. The 'target culture' proved controversial with the medical profession, who felt it overrode their clinical judgement as to which patients to treat first. But I passionately defended the targets, remembering the tears of my constituents and the names on the list of those who needed cardiac surgery who would be dead before they got their operation.

My constituents complained that, even when they'd waited so long for an operation, often it would be cancelled on the day. King's College Hospital told me they had too many people coming into Accident & Emergency who urgently needed to be admitted and this didn't leave enough beds for those due to be operated upon, so they had no option but to cancel operations. So I did a league table of cancelled operations by health authority.

The Department of Health had a huge press office, as well as thousands of civil servants working to support it. I had just Karen, Anna and one parliamentary assistant. It was a David and Goliath situation, but we were full of enthusiasm and commitment. The government press offices worked office hours. At weekends and on bank holidays, they only had a skeleton duty rota. Government ministers heaved a sigh of relief when it came to bank holidays and Commons recesses, and went off to their constituency or to their homes outside London. So that's when we'd launch our attacks. The government press offices dominated the news agenda during the week, but we could ambush them at weekends and in recesses. The ministers were remote, but my home phone number was given at the end of every press statement we issued, there for any journalist to ring if they had follow-up queries. Anna embargoed our press releases for Saturday's papers and made sure we gave each of the regions a tailor-made press release showing how they compared with other regions. By the time the government press machine cranked back into action on the Monday, we'd have already done all the follow-up radio and television interviews and the story, and our accompanying line of argument, would be well established. This was a highly productive period for me. It was still a struggle to combine my work with looking after the children and I felt no more at home in Parliament, but wherever I went around the country, people knew of my work and were warm and supportive. But still, what I wanted, above all, was for Labour to get into government. Having lost three elections, it was unthinkable we would lose yet another.

I was still only one of twenty-one Labour women in Parliament. One who was to make a huge impact was Clare Short. I hardly knew her before she was elected in 1983, as I had not come across her in the women's movement and she had not come to the House of Commons as an avowed feminist. I felt that, for her, the only true struggle was against injustice based on class, rather than on gender. (Although, later, when she was chair of the NEC Women's Committee and, for a brief period, our Shadow Minister for Women, she played a key role in backing measures to increase the number of Labour women MPs.) With her outspoken and progressive views, she was a beacon to many women in the country during her time as an MP. She was our first (and Labour's best) International Development Secretary when we got into government and broke new ground with her campaign against topless women being pictured on page three of the *Sun* newspaper. That campaign saw her vilified in the press, and in parliament, but she received strong support from women. From all around the country, women of all ages and backgrounds wrote, pouring out their hearts to her; she later published their letters in a book, *Dear Clare*. When I was pregnant for the second time in 1984, I kept it secret for as long as I could. My first child was less than two years old, and I was already being criticized in the press lobby for neither doing my job properly nor being a proper mother. I dreaded the disapproval that would rain down on me about this second pregnancy.

One night when we were voting late, I was in the Lady Members' Room, which was an anteroom to the ladies' toilet, hovering in my regular place, close to the toilet, as I kept being sick. Clare rushed in to use the toilet, spotted how awful I looked and asked what was wrong. I didn't want to complain about my pregnancy, as it had been planned and I knew she'd wanted to have children with her husband, Alex Lyon, but I blurted out that I was miserable because I was feeling dreadful as I was pregnant again. She said that it was a wonderful thing and was warm and reinforcing. Nowadays, that would be what was expected from another MP, but back then, it wasn't, and I greatly appreciated it.

On another night, again in the Lady Members' Room, I heard her talking on the phone about something that was going on in her Birmingham constituency. It concerned a girl of ten years old who'd grown up living with her grandmother. She'd gone on a visit to her father, who'd moved to Germany, and he had then kept her there and not allowed her to return home to her granny, who she lived with. The child had written anguished letters to her granny, who had then come repeatedly to see Clare to ask for her help. The child scarcely saw her father but was being used as a babysitter for his new child. A court had ordered that she should live with her granny, but international enforcement was slow and ineffective at that time and the authorities Clare wrote to could do nothing. Clare thought about what she'd do if it was a member of her own family and concluded, if it was, she herself would go and get her. So she went over to Germany and to the girl's school at picking-up time. She asked the child if she wanted to go back to her granny and she leapt into Clare's arms. Although Clare didn't have the child's passport, she brought her back, showing her birth certificate at the airport.

It was vintage Clare. Even decades later, when I have a constituent who has suffered an injustice, for example when a young journalist was arrested and thrown into jail in Indonesia, and where the usual processes can't sort it out, I 'channel' Clare's attitude of simply doing whatever it takes.

Though we were still a tiny minority in Parliament, the new Labour women who were coming in were making a big difference, to politics and to me. They were a generation of politicians that was completely different from the men they replaced, and not just in age and in gender. The first day back after the 1987 General Election was as miserable as it always is after a defeat. That day was just for 'swearing in' and there was to be no 'business' in the House, so I had, unusually, brought Amy in with me. A young, willowy, blonde woman came up to me in the Members' Lobby and introduced herself as Mo Mowlam. I had heard of her, as the NEC had chosen her to be Labour's candidate in the constituency of Redcar, but I hadn't yet met her, as she'd been selected just before the General Election, when James Tinn, an MP since 1964, stood down at the last minute. James Tinn had worked at the coke ovens of the steel industry before becoming an MP and had been a prominent member of his trade union, the National Union of Blastfurnacemen (NUB). Mo was so completely different. Even all these years later, I can remember the scene. In among all the Tories and the dark suits, here was Mo in a floaty, blue floral dress, bursting with energy and enthusiasm. She swept Amy out of my arms and disappeared off with her. They returned a few minutes later, Amy chortling as Mo sucked her far from clean fingers. Whether you were four months or ninety-four years old, Mo would engage with you with a unique directness.

A handful of women were now joining Labour MPs who'd come

from heavy industry or from working in the mines. The unions were effective in getting their leading men into Parliament, but not their female members, so most of the new women came in not through the trade unions but as Labour activists, mainly with backgrounds of working in education or public services. With their arrival, Labour, in Parliament, was starting to become more representative of the country as a whole, with women as well as men, and with professionals such as Mo, who'd worked in higher education, alongside men from manufacturing. This was important because one of the reasons we continued to lose elections was not just because we could not appeal to people outside our heartlands of Scotland, Wales and the north, but because we couldn't get women to vote for us. In 1983 we were trailing the Tories in votes from men (they had a lead among men of 12 per cent), but our position with women was woeful. Crucially, we needed more of the women's vote, and the way to do this was by pursuing women-friendly policies and to have more women visible in our party. This would not only play a key role in extinguishing the Tories' poll lead among women, it would embody the connection between the women's movement and politics which I felt would move Labour forward and broaden our appeal.

My own work as Labour's Shadow Health Minister and in the constituency was going well, and I continued to work with others in the women's movement, in the trade union movement, and with the growing band of Labour women on local councils who were blazing a trail on issues such as childcare and domestic violence.

Margaret Thatcher's growing unpopularity reached crisis point with the imposition of the poll tax (in Scotland in 1989; and in England and Wales in 1990) and she was ousted and replaced by John Major in 1990. Labour was desperate to win the next General Election and, as 1992 approached and we were ahead in the national polls, we were hopeful. I campaigned all around the country, especially with our women candidates.

In the run-up to the 1992 election, one of the campaign visits I went on was to Salford. I'd heard of Hazel Blears, our candidate standing there; she was a dynamic, local working-class woman who'd qualified as a solicitor and was a local councillor. The constituency was held by the Tories, but it was on our list of key marginal seats to win back. Together with Glenys Kinnock, I joined Hazel in a local community centre. Afterwards, Glenys and I returned to London optimistic that we'd win the seat and that Hazel Blears would be elected and make a huge splash in Parliament. But she didn't win. And we didn't even get the hung Parliament that we'd hoped for. The Tories got yet another majority, their fourth in a row. We hadn't done enough to allay people's concerns that, while Labour stood up for the poor, we didn't represent the people in the middle. In addition, voters felt that we couldn't be trusted with the economy.

Neil Kinnock was replaced in July 1992 as Labour leader by John Smith, who carried on Kinnock's work to modernize the party and broaden our appeal among the voters. With the support of the new Labour MPs whom I'd helped in the General Election campaign, I was finally elected on to the Shadow Cabinet, after eight years on the front bench. It was exciting to be in the Treasury team, to be appointed to be Shadow Chief Secretary, with Gordon Brown as Shadow Chancellor. But it was miserable to face yet another term of Tory government. Yet again, our work would be protesting against the government; we would not be able to implement any of our policies. I would remain unable to protect my constituents or put our agenda for women into action. With a mountain to climb at work, I continued to struggle to reconcile my two identities as a politician and as a mother.

Things in the party were improving steadily, but I worried that my children were missing out because of the time and energy my work absorbed. I loved my work but longed to spend more time with my children. And although now many women MPs have babies, at that time, I was the only woman in Parliament who'd had her babies while being an MP – until the new women arrived in 1997, by which time my eldest child was fourteen. After dropping the children off at school, I would tear off into the House of Commons, looking wistfully at the mothers in the playground as they exchanged priceless maternal wisdom, networking and supporting each other. I was sure that they knew the secret of how to get children to bed, how to protect but not over-protect them, how to encourage them to share their toys, to eat things other than Nutella sandwiches, how to make them work hard at school but not pressurize them, how to help them become happy adults. I was certain, as a result of not sharing in this network of knowledge, that I was getting it all wrong. Luckily, two of my sisters had children the same age as mine, and I spent time with them at weekends and in the holidays, which was very important to me. But neither lived in London, so the precious wisdom I got from them was diluted by distance. On my daily drive to the House of Commons up the Walworth Road, I would pass the building society where Diane Wilkinson, a member of the local Labour party, worked part-time. She and her husband Kevin, who was a TGWU activist as well as local party member, had two lovely daughters. I used to look at the building society wondering why it was that I was in a job where I had to work such challenging hours and why I, too, wasn't working part-time. If, as I sat at the traffic lights, a mother crossed in front of me with a baby strapped to her chest, it would send a dagger through me, as I asked myself why I, unlike her, was at the wheel of my car, driving away from my baby.

My maternal guilt was exacerbated by the contrast between my life and that of what I imagined to be the wonderful 'earth mother', who was able to flex her work around her deeply contented children, or who didn't work at all.

One of my particular bugbears at the time were proponents of 'attachment mothering', mothers who wrote books about how children are ruined unless the mother is continuously there with them. (There appeared to be no equivalent theory about 'attachment fathering'.) I could avoid buying their books, but then they'd appear on breakfast TV or radio talking about it. How, I wondered, did they manage to do 'attachment mothering' while also writing books, posing for photoshoots with their adorable 'attached' children and broadcasting through my car radio? Why couldn't they just do it quietly at home instead of persecuting us guilty working mothers?

Another thing that haunted me was reading press reports about women who, having reached the top of their profession, 'saw the light' and gave it all up for the sake of their children. One example which gave me sleepless nights was Brenda Barnes in 1997. Newspapers reported that Brenda was giving up her job as chief executive officer of PepsiCo for the sake of her children. She had three. And so did I. But she was putting her children first while I was going into the Cabinet. Reading her interviews, I was tortured by guilt.

I know most mothers have mixed feelings going back to work after having a baby and working when their children are young, but I certainly made heavy weather of it. I'm sure I'd have been less tormented if I'd been in a woman-dominated environment, such as there had been in the NCCL, sharing the ups and downs of working motherhood with the likes of Tess, Patricia and Anna. It's hard and confusing to be a mother and, whatever job you're in, whether in a factory or an office, it's harder if you don't have any opportunity to talk your problems through with other women in the same situation.

In retrospect, I think my ideal pattern would have been to have a year's maternity leave for each child, on full pay. Then I would have liked to have been able to work part-time and flexibly from home until the youngest started school, and then to work term times until they were teenagers – all with no detriment to future progress in my career, of course. Unfortunately for me, and for just about all other working mothers, we are not in a position to decide our own work patterns so as to be able to work in a way which we think is in the best interests of our children. Work patterns are usually on a take-it-or-leave-it basis. And if you choose to advance your career, you're likely to be in competition with men who don't have the same family demands. We are still far away from the time when fathers expect, and are expected, to take an equal share of responsibility for the day-to-day care of their children. With children, the mother's work pattern still changes irrevocably. His generally remains the same, or he works even more. Most women struggle on, doing the best they can in the circumstances and with the choices they make between the demands of their work and their finances and time at home. This will only change fundamentally when employers allow more flexibility for families and when, and if, men take an equal part in the responsibility for caring for their children and their older relatives. In my thirty years in Parliament, I worked to enact laws such as doubling maternity leave, the right to request flexible working hours, equality for part-timers and paternity leave for fathers, and these are all important things. But maternity leave is still too short, maternity pay too low, and work too inflexible. Patterns at work and at home need to be altered in order for everyone to experience greater change.

Balancing work and family life is not just a question of how much time you spend at work and how much at home. It's about what's going on in your head. It's dealing with the challenge of leaving thoughts of home behind when you're at work and leaving thoughts of work behind when you're at home. It's hard. It takes a conscious effort not to take parental worries into work, and it's pointless being at home if your mind is still on work. Children can tell if a parent is at home physically but still at work mentally.

When my children were young we didn't have email or the internet intruding from work into our home life. We did, of course, have a phone, and I was obsessive about not answering it until the children had gone to bed. I missed out on the 24/7 conversations that bound my male parliamentary colleagues together even when they were not working. But I felt that I gave enough of myself to the job already.

One of the ways I tried to cope with my maternal anxieties was to have fixed rituals, certain times I protected for the family, come what may. For example, I'd always pick up the children from school on a Friday. I moved the local advice surgeries from Friday evening, when Harry Lamborn had held them, to Tuesday evenings and Friday mornings. I felt it was essential, at least one day a week, to be part of the special ambiance of the primary-school playground at picking-up time. For work, I wore a 'uniform' to convey that I was smart, professional and competent. For school, I had a 'uniform' to convey to the children, the world (and myself) that I was exclusively focused on them. No high heels, no suit, no briefcase; instead, a tracksuit, trainers and a plastic bag for bringing home school artwork or collecting leaves for sticking into pictures. I was the opposite of a 'yummy mummy'.

For a long while, I had a tradition of the 'Friday cake'. Over coffee, one enviable earth-mother type told me she baked a cake for her family every week. I decided to do this every Friday. I'm not a great baker, and it was certainly never 'Bake-off' standard, but it meant so much to me to join the children in front of the TV with the smells of baking wafting through the house. It didn't make me a great mother, but it was weekly, it was tangible and I was trying. As the children grew older, the Friday cake ritual evolved into the Friday-night takeaway. South London is blessed with takeaway restaurants from every continent and country, including Chinese, Indian, Thai and Italian. Full of food colouring and additives, the meals were far from healthy eating, but this was a family ritual that was precious to me.

Another important fixture on the weekly calendar was the Sunday supper-time visit from my parents. My parents began bringing 'meals on wheels' to us to help when the children were small. They would come over, bringing one of my mother's amazing casseroles in the boot of their car – and an extra one for us for during the week. The children could relax with their grandparents and the family pets were fussed over. At one stage, we had pet rats and one of our sons appeared on a Sunday night with one of them in his dressing-gown pocket. This was thoroughly approved of by my father, who said that, in his view, every child in a dressing-gown should have a pet rodent in their pocket. Sunday nights felt a million miles from Westminster, and that's what made them so valuable. The Sunday-night ritual continues to this day and is highly valued by three generations, and sometimes four.

The House usually worked during school half-term, and I'd see, on my way to work, troops of sightseeing parents with young children swarming around Westminster. As the police held the public back to let me drive into the House of Commons, I wished it was me and my children out there. But I did what I could, and carved out time for the children in half-terms, and they knew that, once I'd promised them we'd do something, I'd stick to it.

During one half-term in 1989, the ambulance workers were out on strike. Robin Cook, and I as his deputy, were strongly backing them and condemning the government for undermining their pay and pensions. I'd been planning to be in the House of Commons on Monday at 5 p.m., instead of the usual 9.30 a.m., so I could take my son and his friend Mark to the Bromley Odeon for the afternoon screening of the recently released film *The Bear*. At ten o'clock I received a message on my pager from the Whips telling me that the Health Secretary was going to make an urgent Oral Statement on the ambulance strike to the House at half past three. Robin was marooned in his constituency in Edinburgh. All the flights were cancelled because of the weather, so I had to come in right away, prepare for the statement and lead for the Opposition as Robin's deputy. My office called with the same message: I had to come in immediately. While I was on the phone, Robin called me and left the same message.

It would have been quite simple to change our plans and go to the cinema the following day, but I felt I just could not cancel today's trip. My maternal self-esteem, precarious at the best of times, would have collapsed altogether if I turned into one of those parents who let their children down because of sudden work demands. But there was no way I could explain this to Robin or to the Whips.

The very last thing I could tell them would be that I couldn't respond to a government statement on the ambulance strike because I was going to the cinema. I'd be bound to see myself vilified in the following day's newspapers. My assistant called me again to say that the Whips were becoming increasingly aggressive and demanding to know where I was. I told him to stall them and say that he couldn't reach me. I couldn't face speaking to Robin or the Whips myself, so I didn't pick up their calls. We went off to the cinema, my nerves in shreds but pretending to the children that everything was as normal. I felt terrible that I wasn't there, standing up for the ambulance drivers. I was letting down all my Labour colleagues, who would be counting on me to land blows on the government. And I felt sure that, when they found out, I'd be sacked. You can't just 'go missing' from the front bench. (Indeed, some years later, in 1995, Ann Clwyd was sacked from her position in Labour's Shadow Foreign Affairs team for missing some key votes while on an unauthorized but important visit to Iraq to investigate and expose Saddam Hussein's persecution of the Iraqi people.)

My pager rumbled menacingly in my bag throughout the film. Despite the fact that it was the main release for half term and consisted of live footage of bears, it did not go down well with the boys. Shortly after it started, the 'Daddy' bear started having sex with the 'Mummy' bear. Mark thought he was attacking her and started to cry. Then there was a landslide and a boulder fell down the mountain and killed the 'Mummy' bear. We watched as her head was stoved in, and the film ended, but by then both children were crying loudly as we made our way back to the car. After I got back home, I listened to my messages. The situation was dire. My assistant had left numerous messages, of ever-increasing desperation, culminating in him saying that the Whips had shouted at him, telling him that he was useless, as he didn't even know where his MP was, and saying that he should be sacked. Robin's messages descended into icy fury, culminating with an instruction that as soon as his flight arrived and he got to the House of Commons I was to meet him there. I was certain I would be sacked from the front bench and denounced across the board. Robin was the most congenial of bosses, but he believed in being there for the cause and doing the job properly.

When I went into his room to find him, his face was red with anger. 'Where were you?' he asked. I just couldn't find the words to explain about the cinema trip. My mind went blank. Any attempt at explanation would just have made things even worse – if that was possible – and I wasn't going to lie. All I could think of to say was 'I was not available.' After a moment's pause, Robin's furious expression turned into one of conspiratorial glee. 'In that case, we'll say no more about it,' he said, his eyes twinkling. He positively beamed at me as I hurried out of the room. It dawned on me that he must have assumed that I was having an affair. He never did say another word about it, becoming even more friendly with me than usual because of our shared 'secret' and, no doubt, his belief that I, too, was one of the 'gang'. I began to notice some of the Whips looking at me with new and comradely approval and I assumed he'd told them about this supposed affair.

As it turned out, Frank Dobson, a long-standing London MP who had a great expertise on health issues, had stood in for me to give the Opposition's response on the ambulance strike statement and had done an excellent job. For me, the episode underlined two things. Firstly, while children will never forget a broken promise, there's always someone who can stand in for you at work. And secondly, that while it would, in the eyes of my colleagues, have been beyond the pale for me to be absent because of my children, falling down in my duties because of an affair was not only understood by my male colleagues but thoroughly approved of.

Later, during the course of the ambulance dispute, I came across one of the very few women MPs who had young children at the time in tears behind the Speaker's Chair. She said that she'd felt terrible leaving home early on the Monday morning, telling her children she couldn't go to their sports day, as she'd promised, because she'd told her local ambulance workers that she'd speak up for them in the statement being made in the House of Commons that day. She was distraught because, now, although she'd been in the Chamber and had tried to speak, the Speaker hadn't called her. She'd let her children down for nothing. She'd have felt guilty if she hadn't tried to speak and had let the ambulance workers down. She now felt guilty for disappointing her children. There was just no way to 'get it right'. And her situation was even worse than mine, because her constituency was hundreds of miles from Westminster and she had to be away from home from Monday until Friday. At least I could go home to my children every night and be there for them in the morning.

Another thing I would always do was sit up in the gallery at the local swimming pool on Sunday mornings with the other parents as we watched our children learning to swim. My eyes were focused like a laser on my own child as they started just walking through the water, and then, as the weeks went on, I'd see, with each one, the miracle of their little feet lifting off the floor of the pool as they learned to float. All the mothers were the same. But I'd notice, disapprovingly, that if a father was there he would often be deeply engrossed in the Sunday newspapers. How could they encourage their child if they weren't watching? The modern equivalent is the father with his children at the playground, his eyes glued to his iPhone.

Despite all this, I still found the gear change between the different pace of work and being at home a challenge. When I was working I had to be focused, adrenalized, setting goals and going full out to achieve them. I'd walk briskly from meeting to meeting, talking to my colleagues or to my advisers, or on the phone. You can't be like that with a toddler. Walking even a few yards down the street can take time. First climbing on to the wall and walking along it, then climbing off it, then stopping for fifteen minutes to watch a digger. Being at work is all about getting things done. Family time needs to include time doing nothing, except perhaps relaxing together in front of the TV. It was my mindset I had to change on my daily transitions between work and home, doing my best to set up a barrier between the two. But, inevitably, real drama at work, or at home, would sometimes crash through.

Although I was caught up in my own struggles, I knew that just about every mother, whatever her work pattern, or, indeed, even if she is not working, worries that she's not getting it right. Even those mothers who seem to radiate how well they are managing to bring up their children, whether balancing this with work or not, can feel after a time that they haven't managed so well, after all. One friend of mine, who was a top mathematician at university and then highly successful at work, gave up her job when she had her children – a boy and a girl. They were a lovely family, and I was envious at the time that they all seemed so relentlessly contented, she being always there for them and the children thriving at school and then at university. Her daughter achieved the first-class honours degree that had been predicted. Having finished university, she returned to the family home – but then did nothing. My friend bemoaned to me the fact that her daughter showed no sign of looking for a job or wanting to earn a living, and when she urged her to do so, her daughter retaliated by saying, 'But you've never worked, Mum.' It just goes to show that there's no right way to be a mother but so many ways to get it wrong.

On the other side of the scale, at every constituency visit and every advice surgery, I'd hear from women who wanted to go out to work and couldn't, or were working part-time and were frustrated at being held back as a result. Women with young babies in their arms came to talk about issues such as housing or benefits. But it was the women with a toddler wriggling in their buggy who really wanted to work. Young single mothers would tell me that they were going mad cooped up in a one-bed flat on the tenth floor of a council block. They wanted to work so they could set a good example to their child, show them that life was not about being dependent on benefits. They wanted to improve their children's standard of living. For them, the issue was the lack of childcare. It's hard to imagine it now but, in the eighties and nineties, the only way to get a child into a council nursery was if the parent was judged incapable of caring for it. If you had mental health problems or posed a threat to your child, a nursery place was yours, but not if you simply wanted to work and earn a living. There was a small network of childminders, but with no financial help for mothers to pay their fees, most mothers who would be working in low-paid jobs just couldn't afford them. The few private nurseries there were at the time were unaffordable so, for most mothers, it was a council nursery or nothing.

One mother, at the end of her tether, came to one of my advice surgeries, feeling unable to cope with being with her boisterous two-year-old son all day in her one-bedroom flat. In good weather, at least she could take him to the park – which didn't cost anything. The final straw came for her when it had been raining for a week and they'd been stuck indoors; she couldn't afford to take him anywhere other than the park. I contacted Southwark's Social Services department, urging them to find a nursery place for her son. They assessed her as being at breaking point, and he went to the local nursery. She was delighted, he settled in well, and she got a job. Her life was transformed. A few months later she was back in my advice surgery. She looked like a different woman. Her hair was washed and styled and she was wearing smart clothes. I greeted her, telling her she looked terrific. That, she said, was the problem. She'd taken her son to the nursery that morning and the staff had said how great she looked. She'd said she felt great, and they said how pleased they were for her that she was now coping – but because of this her son was no longer eligible for a nursery place. She then had to give up her job and found herself back at square one. And I couldn't help locally, because although Labour's policy now was to support childcare, we couldn't get into government so we had no chance of achieving it.

I battled for childcare at every opportunity. I spoke about it in my first speech in the House of Commons in 1982, then I used my first question to then prime minister Margaret Thatcher to call for care for school-age children in the school holidays and at half-term. She smirked and answered in a condescending voice that school-holiday provision was not a role for the government, which was the cue for Tory MPs to laugh and jeer. Even some Labour MPs sniggered. And Keith Waterhouse wrote in his column in the *Daily Mirror* the next day about the absurdity of my asking a question which had nothing to do with government. But despite my humiliation in parliament, I knew that it mattered very much not just to women in my constituency but to women all around the country and that at least they would see that someone was speaking up for them. Yet while I pushed for the services which other mothers wanted to enable them to go out to work, I, who could afford childcare, wished I was working less. Perhaps I could have 'coasted' when the children were young. Some MPs did. One told me that, because we were doomed to be out of government for so long and he had a large, young family, he would use those years to earn money as a barrister and take time with the children, and then come on to the front bench when it looked like we were going to get into government. I strongly disapproved of this line of reasoning. If we all did this, Labour would never get into government. But part of me envied his strategic approach and it certainly worked for him, as he did, ultimately, get into the Cabinet. I, however, had committed myself to being in Parliament, to speak out on women's causes and to try to get Labour back into government. No one was making me work this hard. No one was making me work at all. Jack didn't earn a huge amount as a trade union officer, but plenty of other trade union officers raised their families on their salary alone. But with my commitment to my work, I was doomed to fail to resolve the tension I felt between my punishing hours at work and my desire to be at home.

Being a mother myself gave me a particular platform for arguing for maternity rights and childcare. But there were pitfalls, too. I had to avoid giving the impression that I was doing it for myself, for my own benefit. From 1983, I campaigned for there to be a nursery in the House of Commons but at the same time I had to guard against news coverage of this eclipsing the demand for more childcare for all mothers. Political journalists sometimes found it easier to report on (and pillory) the Commons nursery campaign than write about the childcare needs of the majority of women all around the country. Hostile journalists portrayed it as self-serving, and for middle-class women. But it wasn't a contradiction to want childcare for ourselves as well as for the women in our constituencies. In the end, it was only in 2010, and because Speaker John Bercow insisted on it, that a nursery was opened in the House of Commons. It's a pleasure now to see MPs and Commons staff taking their toddlers through the throng of the coffee area in Portcullis House where MPs have their offices. From my office on the corner of Parliament Square, I can look into the nursery on the first floor of the neighbouring building and, as I do, I often think how great it would have been if it had been there for my children. I started campaigning for the House of Commons nursery when they were babies, but it didn't open until my youngest was twenty-three years old.

When I arrived in the House of Commons some of my fellow Labour MPs advised me not to speak up on women's issues, warning I would be 'pigeonholed' and be seen as having narrow interests. To be taken seriously, they counselled, I should abandon my fixation with women's issues and get into the mainstream. I protested that half the population were women, so campaigning on their behalf couldn't be narrow. One of the main reasons I'd come into politics was to help broaden it to represent women. If women MPs like Jo Richardson and I didn't speak up for women, who would? Certainly not the men. It would have been perverse if, having got into politics through the women's movement, I abandoned it as soon as I got elected. While I did not hesitate to reject their advice, their message was clear: I was not a serious politician; as far as they were concerned, I was indeed narrow in my interests; and they disapproved of me 'banging on about women'. But that was never the view of Neil Kinnock, and it changed with the growing number of women who came into Parliament over the following decades.

Women in the Labour party were continuing to build the case for making progress on issues like childcare, and the arguments of the women's movement continued to gain momentum in the country, but Parliament lagged behind. I'd never wanted to be one of a tiny minority of women – indeed, the idea was to get many more women into the House of Commons for us all to argue for women's causes. Yet the House of Commons remained much as it had always been and Labour continued to fall behind the Tories with women voters.

While the number of women MPs was scarcely increasing, our argument that there should be more continued to grow in strength. It brought together many strands of thinking: we thought it was unfair for women to be barred because they were women – that was discrimination; women should have the right to put themselves forward and be considered alongside men on equal terms; a male-dominated Parliament was old-fashioned, out of date, reflecting a time when the public sphere was exclusively male. In general, we thought that having more women in Parliament was a necessary part of the modernization of the UK's democratic institutions and that increasing our number was vital if Parliament was to fulfil its claim to be representative. It would be intolerable if one part of the country was simply not represented; in the same way, it is intolerable for a whole gender, the majority of the population, to be unrepresented. We argued that it would boost the quality of MPs to have them selected from the whole of the population, that widening the pool from which MPs are drawn is meritocratic. Politics would never reflect women's concerns unless women MPs were there in sufficient number. The public policy agenda was blind to women's very different lives, and men, however sympathetic they were, could not articulate this. From women's pensions, to women's health issues, to opportunities for girls to play sports, it was not just that these issues could not get on to the public policy agenda of a male-dominated Parliament, it was also that men wouldn't make the right arguments in support of them. We had to make our own case. In addition, we felt that the male domination of Parliament was a drag anchor on women's progress outside Westminster. Parliament should be a beacon leading the cause of women's progress; it should not simply reinforce the status quo, keeping in place the notion in women and men alike that women are second-class citizens. And if women were to be in government, they had to get into Parliament. A male-dominated Parliament guaranteed a male-dominated government.

The usual pattern in the Labour party was that a woman would apply for a safe seat, a man would be selected and the woman would then go off and stand as candidate for Labour in a seat we couldn't win. We had plenty of women candidates but, like my mother in the Liberal party in the sixties, they fought the seats where their party had no chance. So when my parliamentary neighbour John Silkin, MP for the rock-solid Labour constituency of Deptford, announced in 1986 that he was retiring, I wanted to do what I could to help a woman take over his seat and wrote to Joan Ruddock saying that Deptford was wide open and urging her to go for it. Then I rang her.

I'd never met her before, so I was writing to her out of the blue, but I'd admired Joan, who, as the leader of the Campaign for Nuclear Disarmament (CND), had long been in the national media. She combined passion for her cause with a calm ability to set out her arguments. I knew she was Labour, as she'd been the Labour candidate in the Tory stronghold of Newbury in 1979. She'd tried to get selected as our candidate in the Labour stronghold of Torfaen, in her native Wales, but they had selected a man. I told Joan I thought that she would be a brilliant MP and that Labour in London was, unlike Wales at that time, open to sending women to Parliament. I wanted to redress the effect of the old boys' network in order to tackle the discrimination against women that it perpetuated. But though I was keen for her to be selected, I didn't 'put in a good word for her', or 'twist someone's arm'. I simply gave her the encouragement to put herself forward in a constituency I thought she would suit. I didn't have any particular influence in that local party and, anyway, I believed it was their right to choose, not mine, as a neighbouring MP. I deplored the old boys' network, believing it to be one of the most significant ways in which the male status quo was maintained. In the women's movement, we didn't want to ape the way the men sustained their unfair advantages, we wanted to change the system so that it was open and fair to everyone. Also, the reality is that an MP who gets in with the help of people higher up in the party is not as good an MP as someone who's fought their own way in. You'll never be up to the task of standing up for your constituents if you can't stand on your own two feet to get selected.

In the end, Joan did apply, was selected and, in 1987, she joined the ranks of Labour MPs as one of twenty-one women. She was a massive asset to Parliament. She was in the vanguard of the environmental movement and an assiduous local MP but of great importance to me was that she was an uncompromising feminist and a true 'sister' in politics. We worked together in the PLP for the next twenty-eight years. And then another safe Labour seat next door to my constituency fell vacant and I suggested to Kate Hoey that she go for it. I'd worked closely with Kate, as she'd stood for Dulwich in my borough of Southwark in 1983 and 1987, but lost both times. I'd urged her to move on from Dulwich and seek selection in a safer seat so she could join us in Parliament, but she refused, vowing to stand by the constituency party members who'd worked so hard for her. Then, in 1989, my neighbouring MP in Lambeth, Stuart Holland, announced that he was standing down to take up a teaching post at the European Institute at the University of Florence. It was shocking to me that an MP would give up his seat this way and thereby run the risk of Labour losing the by-election, but at the time we were so deep in the political wilderness that many Labour MPs thought they could be doing something more worthwhile elsewhere. At the funeral of long-standing local councillor and former mayor of Southwark Mabel Goldwin, I stood next to Kate. Prayers were being said over the coffin as it was lowered into the grave but I found myself whispering in Kate's ear that she really must put in for Vauxhall. Kate whispered back that she'd think about it. It felt unseemly to be plotting at a graveside, but I reassured myself that Mabel, who was a pioneer as a female councillor in Southwark, would have been keen to see Kate go for it. Kate did so, and was selected. Again, it wasn't that I 'fixed' it for her; my part was simply to encourage women to stand for selection to Parliament.

I learned something about campaigning in that by-election.

Leading figures from the PLP came out to campaign with Kate, including Denis Healey. We set off to visit Vauxhall City Farm, with Denis in ebullient form. There were hordes of photographers following him as we mingled with the goats and the sheep, but not many voters. One of the pens housed a friendly old pig. I spotted its big red cheeks and bushy eyebrows. I looked at Denis, with his big red cheeks and bushy eyebrows and, trying to be helpful, whispered a warning to him not to go anywhere near the pig. He whispered back that I should watch him and see how to get a by-election on to the front pages. To my horror, but to the delight of the assembled photographers, he leapt over the sty wall, crouched down and posed with his face pressed next to the pig's. Both he and the pig were beaming and the picture went straight to the front page of the *Evening Standard* – alongside Labour's pledge of support for the city farm. Denis had no vanity. He was there to get publicity and, if it meant leaping into a sty and cosying up to a pig, so be it.

That was an important lesson. A visit by a frontbencher should not just be a private boost for the morale of the Labour candidate, it must get into the local papers and show the party is out and about. Personal dignity is not the issue. If I go campaigning to meet women at an indoor bowls session, I'll immediately kick off my shoes and hurl a ball across the mat. And if it's a pink one, so much the better. If I'm campaigning in a leisure centre, I will always get on an exercise bike; if it's in a children's playground, I'll go down the slide. I still do this. In 2015, it was basketball in Great Yarmouth with our local candidate Lara Norris. And I clung on to another local candidate, Lee Sheriff, as we took to the skating rink on a campaign visit to Carlisle.

By 1992, by which time I'd been in Parliament for a decade, there were still only thirty-seven women in the PLP and sixty overall in Parliament, making it 91 per cent male. It didn't feel as if we were moving fast enough. We did, though, finally, in 1992, with London continuing to move to Labour, unseat the Tory MP in Dulwich, when Tessa Jowell, having replaced Kate Hoey as our candidate, was elected. Again, she'd previously stood in a Tory stronghold with no chance of succeeding. But with Tessa in Dulwich, Kate in Vauxhall, Joan in Deptford and me in Peckham, by 1994, south London was racing ahead in being represented by women, with all three of my neighbours women Labour MPs.

Throughout the eighties, however, though I had solid and invaluable support from women outside Parliament, from my friends, my family, women in the party and the wider women's movement, it nonetheless remained a lonely task for the handful of us who were fighting, in Parliament, for women's rights. Witnessing my political and maternal struggles, and with the clear objective of helping to ensure that I survived and pressed on, a group of women came to have supper with me in the Commons once a month. It consisted of Patricia Hewitt, Margaret Hodge (then leader of Islington council), Tessa Jowell and Anna Coote. We ate in the Churchill Room, one of the Commons dining rooms, planning the next steps to be taken by the women's movement. Under portraits of Churchill and countless other men, we talked through our ideas about the women's movement, how to move our party forward and make it more electable. This monthly get-together gave me ideas for campaigns but, more importantly, it gave me maternal and political solidarity, filling what would otherwise have been lonely hours. Our male colleagues, however, regarded us with suspicion and made pointed comments as they passed us to get to their own tables.

Women didn't want an endless parade of men telling them things. I remember hearing Margaret Beckett, when she was Shadow Chief Secretary to the Treasury, talking on Radio 4's *Woman's Hour* about the economy and thinking that it was such a breath of fresh air, a breakthrough moment, to hear a Labour woman talking with absolute authority and clarity about the economy on a programme for women. It was what we needed to do to get our message over to those women who weren't listening to us, let alone prepared to vote for us.

The twenty-four Shadow Cabinet members were elected by Labour MPs. In 1989 we still had only one woman in the Shadow Cabinet, Jo Richardson, who was Minister for Women. We thought that would never change, that we'd never get more women in, unless we changed the rules about Shadow Cabinet voting. So, at a Shadow Cabinet awayday in Eastbourne, Deborah Mattinson, a polling and political analyst, and Patricia Hewitt – still Neil Kinnock's press secretary – did a presentation setting out all the data on women's reluctance to vote for a male-dominated Labour party. Deborah Mattinson, who with Philip Gould had set up Gould Mattinson (later to become Opinion Leader Research), was very much part of the Labour 'sisterhood'. Deborah was pivotal, not only in the analysis of women's voting patterns and devising strategies to increase their support for us, but also, with Gould Mattinson, in forming the basis, in 1987, of the Shadow Communications Agency, a group of people working in advertising and marketing who volunteered to help the party bring our communications strategy up to the standards of those used throughout the professions, business and industry.

Deborah broke new ground by setting up focus groups in which women, in the absence of men, discussed what they thought about politics. In a women-only group with a woman moderator, there was no danger of men dominating the agenda by doing all the talking and, sure enough, women's discussions about politics are very different from those of men. Her analysis of women's attitudes and voting patterns became key to our discussions about how we could advance the cause of women in the Labour party and persuade women to vote for us. The results of Deborah's work in focus groups showed that women felt little connection with Labour. They didn't feel the party understood their lives, their hopes or their concerns. They felt we were a party for men in cloth caps, for trade unionists and for people in the north, not for them. As women pressing for change, we had long known this. But Deborah quantified it forensically. Hitherto, our argument about making Labour a party for women had been based on principle rather than electoral expedience. We had argued that we should have policies which delivered equality for women, and more women's representation in the Labour party, because it was right in principle. Deborah's research gave us the opportunity to begin to argue forcibly that, even if men didn't like the idea of women marching forward in the party, they needed us to help Labour win women's votes. Without these, the party would remain in opposition.

We started from a really low base. In the 1983 General Election, 46 per cent of women voted Tory and only 26 per cent Labour, giving the Tories an election-clinching 20 per cent lead. So long as this continued to be the case, the men could remain at the top of our party, but they would forever be Shadow ministers, never ministers. The idea of changing the party to make space for women was still hugely controversial but, suddenly, we began to make progress. By 1997 we had turned the Tories' 20 per cent poll lead among women into a 12 per cent poll lead among women for us, delivering a General Election landslide, this time, for Labour.

The profound organizational and policy change we embarked upon started under the leadership of Neil Kinnock, who considered getting more women into senior positions a critical part of modernizing the party. He strongly supported our proposal to have three women in the Shadow Cabinet and, with his cajoling, it went through on a vote of the PLP in 1990. There was deep resentment from frontbenchers and backbenchers alike. Backbenchers complained that it would interfere with their choice of who should be in the Shadow Cabinet and would undermine its quality. Junior male frontbenchers who wanted to get into the Shadow Cabinet felt it would reduce their chances. The fact that we proposed that the women's places should be in addition to existing positions in the Shadow Cabinet did nothing to dampen the fury. One would-be member of the Shadow Cabinet complained to me that, now, he wouldn't have a chance, as he didn't wear a skirt – but an additional three women in the Shadow Cabinet would still leave room for twenty-four men, not wearing skirts.

However, despite the resentment, with Neil's backing, the rule change went ahead; now, any ballot paper that did not contain votes for three women would be discounted, meaning that every Labour MP had to choose three women to vote for. It became known in the PLP as the 'Assisted Places Scheme', a derogatory reference to the highly unpopular (with Labour MPs) government scheme to pay for low-income children to go to private school. In the House of Commons bars it was denounced as the 'Tarts' Charter'.

Opponents of the new scheme hatched a plan to 'dump' their votes on the most 'useless' women, in the hope that, if the votes could be spread out thinly, no woman would win enough to be elected. Some MPs actually wanted a 'useless' woman to be elected, thinking that, then, the whole scheme could be discredited and abandoned. There were, within the PLP at that time, 'slates' for election to the Shadow Cabinet, with different groupings of Labour MPs organizing in support of a list of their preferred candidates. 'Dumping' votes for women was the opposite of the 'slate'; it was about who they *didn't* want elected. Many of them identified East London MP Mildred Gordon as the best candidate for 'useless' woman. She had come late into Parliament and, though she was a hard-working local MP, had not particularly made her mark. So many MPs voted for her she was nearly elected. This sudden apparent show of support for Mildred exposed her to ridicule. It was a horrible thing to have done: so mean, indeed, that nobody dared admit to her face that they'd 'dumped' their votes on her, which meant that she was amazed and happy to have nearly got into the Shadow Cabinet, believing that at last her abilities had been recognized, while hostile MPs sniggered behind her back.

I stood for the Shadow Cabinet in 1990. But even though I'd been in the Commons for eight years and had worked successfully as a member of the junior front-bench team for six, and though they had agreed that they needed more women, I didn't get elected. They had to put up with the new scheme, but at least they could ensure that I was not a beneficiary of it. Those of us who'd argued for the new system felt the full force of the backlash. It was reported in the newspapers that some of my male colleagues had started calling me 'Harridan Harman'. And Joan Ruddock was spitefully referred to as 'the Widow Ruddock', her estranged husband having died in a road accident. Pushing for positive action for women in the PLP was, for a woman, not the path to popularity. John Prescott, in what was an uncharacteristic understatement, said, 'There clearly was a resentment among some MPs who didn't want to be told who they should vote for in a sexual way.'

As I rushed home to check on the children after or between late-night votes, I burnt with indignation at the thought of what my colleagues were saying about me in the House of Commons bars. And it was horrible to see the reports of anonymous hostile briefings against me in the papers, leaving me in no doubt that, any time I tripped up, they'd be on me like a pack of wolves. I wouldn't be getting their votes for anything. But at least we now had four women in the Shadow Cabinet.

The opposition within the party slowed our efforts. Often, it felt as if we were taking two steps forward, then one step back. We were making progress, but it was laborious. Despite the backlash, we never for one moment doubted that we had to press on. It was hard, but it had to be done. From right back to the seventies, this had been our aim, and we weren't just going to give up. And the women in the party were willing us on. Although our rule changes, such as the one that laid down that there had to be a woman on every parliamentary shortlist, were having precious little effect, the general argument that we needed more women MPs was gaining momentum in the party, in all regions. And throughout the country, women were putting themselves forward in greater numbers and with greater determination. In 1992, we did see some more women elected to the Labour benches. Although only thirteen were newly elected (taking our numbers up from eleven, ten years earlier, to thirty-seven), they were an intake of women who would make a significant impact in the PLP, in Parliament and in government. In the north-west, Jane Kennedy, Angela Eagle, Janet Anderson and Ann Coffey were elected. Jane had fought off Militant in Merseyside; Angela had beaten the Tories and went on to become a leading figure on our National Executive; Janet became our Minister for Women and brought an anti-stalking bill into law;

and Ann was at the heart of government for years, first in 1997 as Tony Blair's Parliamentary Private Secretary (PPS) and then from 2007 as PPS to Alistair Darling during the years of the global financial crisis, and was crucial in the campaign to get the hours at which the House of Commons sat changed. In the south-west, Jean Corston was elected. She went on to become the first woman to chair the PLP, and the first chair of the new Joint Committee on Human Rights, and produced a pioneering work in 2007 on the issue of women in prison, which I pressed the Home Office to commission. A number of the key recommendations in the Corston Report were implemented. Helen Jackson came in as the only woman MP from the male stronghold of Sheffield and played an important role in the Women's PLP. Barbara Roche, Tessa Jowell and Bridget Prentice joined us from London constituencies. Barbara, an eminent barrister, held a number of ministerial offices, most notably on immigration; Tessa went on to be in the Cabinet and a major figure in bringing the Olympics to London in 2012; Bridgit was a minister in the Department of Constitutional Affairs. Ann Campbell joined us from Cambridge, playing a key role in developing our policy on childcare, and Estelle Morris, who later served in the Cabinet as Education Secretary, was elected in Yardley in Birmingham. These women formed a strong cohort within Parliament supportive of all and any arguments on women. They were the advance guard of the one hundred and one women Labour MPs who would be elected in 1997. They not only made a major contribution as individuals but also in what would, after 1997, become a significant number of women in Parliament – enough to ensure that our agenda was taken seriously.

The demand for more Labour women MPs swelled. There was growing activism in the Women's Sections in constituencies, among women in trade unions, among women councillors and on the Labour Women's Action Committee. But each time we put forward a proposal to increase the number of women MPs, it was the same story. Men expressed fury, and were backed by some women, who denounced it as patronizing. There'd then be a huge row, new rules would be instituted, but nothing would change in practice. Men would still win the selections for safe Labour seats.

Since the eighties, the alliance of women in the party had been arguing for a rule change that would end men-only shortlists and require every shortlist for selection to include at least one woman. The idea caused outrage. The politics behind the proposal made men feel that they were being disparaged simply for being men.

As the woman MP most associated with this proposal, I was, once more, the obvious target for their hostility. Any progress I had been making in building bridges with more of the men was washed away. They said I was accusing them of failing to represent the women in their constituency. More than that, it was not unusual for MPs to build support in their region by giving backing to men in neighbouring seats. And many wanted to choose their successors and had been nurturing a 'favourite son'. Some of these men felt that the 'interference' of putting a woman on each shortlist threatened to bring all this to an end. Regional hostility was exposed. I was told that, as a Londoner, I didn't understand the north, that northern women didn't want to be MPs. One MP even said there weren't any women in the Labour party in the north. Of course, this was nonsense. While the men worked shifts in physically demanding jobs, the women ran the local Labour parties, as well as looking after the children and older relatives. This was the network that was nurtured by women like Hilary Armstrong, who, when she became MP for North-west Durham in 1987, pushed for more women MPs in the north. But when I made public the number of Labour women MPs by region and ranked the regions in a 'woman-friendly' league table, I became *persona non grata* with many of the Labour men in the north, in Wales and in Scotland. Criticism came not only from our own side, but from the Tories, too, who denounced our attempt to recruit more women MPs as 'political correctness gone mad'. Every time I went on the radio to defend our quest, one of the very few Tory women MPs – in 1992, they still had only twenty in total – was put up to argue against me, saying that it was patronizing to women and discriminatory against men and that, anyway, we didn't need any more. And the press took up the hue and cry against us, deriding me as 'Harriet Harperson'. I began to dread going in to vote, when groups of my male colleagues would turn on me in the Division Lobby.

In 1988, the Labour conference had agreed to change the rules to ensure that there was a woman on every shortlist for selection. However, the angry men in the Labour party needn't have worried at that point. They were able to frustrate the objective of the rule change by making sure that the woman who was chosen for the shortlist would be the one who was least likely to pose a challenge to the 'favourite son'. So it would either be a woman from the local party who was least likely to attract support, or a woman from miles away who had no local connections. Men duly continued to be selected.

As it became clear, in the late eighties, that having a woman on every shortlist would not increase the number of women selected in winnable seats, momentum grew among women in the constituency parties, in the trade unions, and between MPs and councillors, that we should have all-women shortlists (AWS). Women in the trade union movement had grown impatient at exclusively male national executives presiding over unions in which there was a growing number of women members and had instigated reserved seats for women. A group of these women in the unions got together, meeting at least every month, to plan how they could get their unions to throw their weight in the party behind all-women shortlists for Parliament. They were Angela Eagle in the Confederation of Health Service Employees (COHSE), Margaret Prosser in the TGWU, Bernie Hillon in the Union of Shop, Distributive and Allied Workers (USDAW) and Maureen Rooney in the Amalgamated Engineering and Electrical Union (AEEU). Their unions, with members across the public and the private sector, between them wielded the majority of the block vote at the Labour conference. If they opposed AWS, there was no chance, but with their backing it could go through.

The original proposal was that wherever a man was retiring, and in all the new seats which we hoped to win at the next election, there should be a woman-only shortlist. Putting a woman into every Labour seat where there was a vacancy would have been the quickest way to bring about an increase in the number of Labour women MPs, but the proposal met with so much opposition we watered it down, now asking that in 50 per cent, in total, of retirement seats and of the seats we hoped to win, only women would be able to apply.

This was a political innovation which no other party in a Westminster-style democracy anywhere in the world had tried before. It was bitterly opposed. Many local constituency Labour parties denounced it; they said it interfered with their free choice of candidate. Inevitably, many women joined the opposition to it, declaring that they didn't want special treatment for women. They were rewarded, being fêted by the men, and they were used as a stick to beat us with. Another complaint was that we would end up with a poorer quality of MP because excellent men would be ruled out in favour of inferior women. We carried on, arguing that, as things stood, the judgements prevailing in selection couldn't be solely in terms of merit. How could they be, when 86 per cent of Labour MPs were men and only 14 per cent women? How could that be a reflection purely of the comparative merits of men and women in the Labour party of 1992? There was nothing comfortable in our decision to exclude men from shortlists and thus restrict the choice for local party members. We argued for it as the last resort because we had, over many years, tried everything else to get women Labour candidates into safe or winnable seats and nothing had worked.

We were well organized and there was a network of constituency and trade union women all around the country in support of AWS. But many party members, although convinced that we needed more women MPs, didn't want to exclude men from any of the selections. We'd won the argument that the objective of more women MPs was a good one, but not for the all-women shortlists that were necessary to achieve it. To make it happen, we needed a rule change to be voted through at Labour's annual conference in 1993. In the end, we did it by combining the AWS rule change with another constitutional measure which was a key part of modernizing the Labour party – that the election of the leader of the party be done on a 'one member, one vote' (OMOV) basis, thereby ending the block votes of the trade union leaders.

It was the Tories' constant refrain that the Labour party was run by the unions. At a time when many believed that trade union power held back our economy and undermined our democracy, the notion of trade union domination of the party damaged us in the eyes of the voters. Under OMOV, the trade unions would still have a third of the votes to elect the Labour leader, but those votes would be cast by individual members, not by the General Secretary or the Union Executive. John Smith had made tackling the block vote a key objective of his leadership, so it stood a good chance of being passed. If we combined the strong support of AWS with the strong support for OMOV, that would, we hoped, outweigh the opponents of AWS. Many women played key roles in bringing us to this point, including Clare Short, who'd been the women's spokesperson and chair of the NEC Women's Committee, Ann Pettifor, who'd been a leading light in the Labour Women's Action Committee, Barbara Follett, who'd set up Emily's List, and Hilary Armstrong, who as well as being MP for North-west Durham was an active member of the MSF. We also had active support from within Labour HQ from the then Director of Organization, Joyce Gould.

The Conference Arrangements Committee put OMOV and AWS together in a 'composite motion' of constitutional changes and we went in for the conference debate with our hearts in our mouths.

John Prescott, at that time Labour Deputy Leader, gave a rousing speech in support of the composite resolution to conclude the debate, saying that John Smith's head was on the block and he'd be humiliated if the conference rejected OMOV. And it was ironic that, just as union leaders were voting to reduce their influence in the party, it was that block vote which, thanks to Angela, Margaret and the trade union women's network, delivered the vote for AWS and got the resolution through. The next day's headlines were all about OMOV. But we women were jubilant about the AWS. It had slipped through largely unnoticed in the controversy over OMOV.

However, the way we had got AWS only increased the unpopularity of the policy. The new rules came into place and Party HQ asked the Labour party in the regions, Scotland and Wales to identify constituencies that were willing to have an AWS. Even many of those Labour members who supported the principle didn't want AWS in their own constituency. In the many constituency Labour parties who fought against having an all-women shortlist, the arguments were myriad, ranging from 'We've had a woman MP in the past, which proves we don't discriminate, so we shouldn't be forced to have one now' through 'We've had a woman MP before, so we've done our bit and it's someone else's turn now' to 'We've never had a woman MP so that means we don't want one.' Arguments broke out in every region and in every constituency. Those opposed to AWS said they were protecting constituencies from a diktat from HQ and the rights of the regions, Scotland and Wales against London. It was very much a case of 'I'm in favour of women MPs but . . .' Women who argued for their constituency to have an AWS were accused of being self-serving, so women who did want to become MPs often fought shy of calling for an AWS on their own patch in case the unpopularity of the measure caused them to lose out in the selection.

The hostility to me, as a key proponent of AWS, intensified, both in the PLP and in the press. One would-be MP protested furiously to me that I'd ruined his life. He told me that some years earlier he'd moved his wife and children to what he described as a 'god-forsaken part of the country', which they hated, in order to be in position to take over from the ailing and elderly current Labour MP there, and now, just when the aged MP was finally looking as though he was about to give up his seat, he wouldn't even be able to apply. I felt sorry for his wife and children. It was wounding to be criticized in the press and made me feel that I was constantly on the defensive, which in turn led the press to portray me as stuck-up and unfriendly. It was hard to know that I engendered hostility in so many of my work colleagues and it made me even more miserable working in Parliament. But I saw it as an inevitable consequence of pressing for the change that we needed and so I carried on.

It was definitely one of those times when the end justifies the means. It reminded me of how Barbara Castle had got the Equal Pay Act on to the statute book in 1970 in the face of opposition from her Cabinet colleagues. She told me that the Labour government had been bringing forward the Prices and Incomes policy, which was highly controversial. They were in government with a majority of only one. After months of pressing for it, Barbara still hadn't got agreement for the Equal Pay Bill so, sitting on the front bench as it came to the vote on the Prices and Incomes policy, she calmly told the Chief Whip that she would not vote for it – and so they would not get it through – unless they promised to agree to her Equal Pay Bill. They caved in, and the Equal Pay Bill was brought forward and became law. Unable to persuade her colleagues, she'd threatened them instead. I was shocked when she told me this one day when we were having tea in the House of Lords, shortly after we'd got into government. I couldn't imagine that I would ever threaten our precious Labour government. But later, after years in government facing battles with Cabinet colleagues, I understood exactly why she had done it. She had been determined to get the change implemented, whatever it took. And in our quest to have more women Labour MPs selected, so were we.

After the 1993 conference resolution, the party got on with the process of selecting our candidates for the next General Election, implementing the policy of all-women shortlists. Each Labour party regional board drew up a list of those constituencies that they proposed should be AWS and submitted them to the National Executive Committee. If a town had two constituencies, then one would be nominated for an AWS and one would be 'open'. If there was already a woman MP in a local area, they'd suggest an AWS in another. The idea was to ensure that there were some women MPs in every area in every region. Some local parties who found themselves ordered to have an AWS settled down afterwards and accepted it. Others continued to fight back. In 1995, two men took the party to an industrial tribunal, arguing that, by being excluded, by an AWS, from going for a selection, they'd suffered from an unlawful breach of the Sex Discrimination Act. They won their case, and the AWS policy was struck down. By that time, most of our women candidates had already been selected. But it meant more controversy swirling around AWS and, ultimately, in government, we had to change the law to allow us to continue with it. John Spellar, a long-term opponent of quotas for women, formed the Labour Campaign for Real Equality, to challenge and reverse our progress.

As if the row in the party wasn't enough, the press kept up a vigorous denunciation of AWS, the *Daily Mail* running a 'Quota Watch' column dedicated to ridiculing the women who'd been selected from AWS. One such was Candy Atherton, in Falmouth and Camborne, a three-way marginal in Cornwall. We had come third in 1992, when the Tories won the seat with former Olympic athlete Sebastian Coe. But we hoped to win it in 1997 and, unusually, the officers of the local party offered to select a woman candidate so they could have the first woman Labour MP in Cornwall. They selected the ebullient, blonde Candy Atherton from an all-women shortlist. But within the local party, antagonism against having an AWS erupted, and some members and local councillors threatened that, unless the party reran the selection, they would resign. There was terrible coverage in the local media, with local party members denouncing Candy for having been selected from an all-women shortlist. However, Candy was undaunted and the party, nationally, held firm. A few party members resigned in protest but, deeming it hopeless to try to win them over, and with the General Election fast approaching, Candy set about mobilizing local women to join the party and become active. Many who had been put off by the domination of the local party by older, old-fashioned men rallied around her. The public row that had raged in the local papers actually helped her gain support and achieve success in this and, by the time of the General Election, she had hundreds of new members and activists campaigning for her.

Nationally, Labour women gave Candy vociferous backing and, as the election drew near, we decided to support her with a women's campaign visit. Instead of trying to brush over the AWS row, we were going to highlight the fact that she was a woman – and that we wanted women to vote for her. Because so many women MPs, peers and activists wanted to come, it turned out to be cheaper for the party to charter a plane than to send us all by train. So, at the crack of dawn, we took off from Northolt airfield. There was a jubilant atmosphere on board, and the jollity of the occasion was ensured by the presence of Labour activist and my former by-election minder Glenys Thornton. But we flew into serious turbulence, and grew quiet. As the tiny plane was tossed around, the silence was broken by Margaret Hodge, who grimly pointed out that the number of MPs on board meant that, if the plane went down, the nominations having closed, it could cost us the General Election. There was much nervous laughter.

Luckily for all involved – though perhaps not the Tories – we arrived safely at Newquay and, as convention dictates when campaigning in Cornwall, ate vast quantities of Cornish pasties. To our delight, Candy did get elected and she took her seat on the Labour benches as the only Cornish Labour MP, the first since John Dunwoody in the sixties, and the only Cornish woman MP from any party.

The Falmouth and Cambourne election campaign worked out better than we could have hoped, but hostility to all-women shortlists was to cost us our safest Labour seat, in South Wales. Despite the efforts of many Welsh Labour women activists, the contingent of Labour MPs sent to Westminster remained resolutely male. Even after the 2001 General Election, out of thirty-four Welsh

Labour MPs, only three were women. Llew Smith, the Labour MP for Blaenau Gwent, announced that he was not going to fight another election. Blaenau Gwent was not only a Labour stronghold but a male bastion. It had come second from the bottom in the league table of women councillors that I'd drawn up in 1999; of their Labour council, 93 per cent were men and only 7 per cent were women. If we wanted a woman MP, we were unlikely to get one in Blaenau Gwent without an AWS.

The NEC ordered one and stood firm, despite the torrent of protests from the local party. Maggie Jones, who'd been born and brought up in South Wales but was now a London-based employee of Unison, the public service union, was selected from an AWS and immediately labelled a Blairite London imposition on the local party and the local people. Local opponents of the AWS didn't want to be seen to be arguing against her as a woman, but the label of her as a Blairite and as a Londoner stuck. Llew Smith came out against the AWS, and eight of the twelve members of the local constituency party executive resigned in protest.

The Welsh Assembly member (AM) for Blaenau Gwent, Peter Law, had been hoping to become the MP. Barred from the selection as he was a man, he resigned from the Labour party and stood as an independent in the 2005 General Election. Labour voters abandoned Maggie and she lost to Peter Law by over nine thousand votes in what had been a Labour stronghold. Peter Law had been a popular Labour AM, and the party in Wales, including our MPs, failed to come out in support of the AWS.

With the Blaenau Gwent defeat, the opponents of AWS had a field day. And when, at subsequent elections, we wanted more constituencies for AWS in the South Wales valleys, the party's nerve cracked and they backed down. So, while Scotland steadily increased the number of women MPs (until all but one of the Labour MPs was wiped out in the SNP landslide of 2015), Wales was left behind. By 2015, though, thanks to AWS, eight out of twenty-five of Wales's Labour MPs were women. But there's still never been an AWS or a woman MP for Blaenau Gwent.

Though there was, and still is, deep hostility to AWS, the results it produced proved a turning point in the history of women's advance both in politics and in the country. The percentage of women in the PLP was to jump from 7 per cent in 1992 to 24 per cent in 1997, with the number of Labour women MPs having climbed from eleven when I was elected in 1982, to twenty in 1992, and then having jumped to a hundred and one in 1997. Though the Tories have had a woman prime minister, their resistance to adopting AWS means that they have yet to make substantial progress on getting a fairer gender balance among their MPs. Despite the fall in the number of our MPs in 2015, Labour still has more women MPs than all the other parties put together.

John Smith was elected leader of the Labour party in 1992, and the process of modernizing our policy and the party's organization which had been started by Neil Kinnock continued. Tony Blair, appointed by John Smith as Shadow Employment Minister, set about changing our policy on trade union legislation. He pledged not to repeal the new Tory laws which had required, since 1984, that there be a ballot before a union could go on strike and for general secretaries to be elected by a secret ballot rather than appointed by a union's National Executive. We'd campaigned ardently against these laws in the eighties when the Tories brought them in and had voted against them. The trade union leaders opposed them, seeing them as unwarranted and as hostile government intervention in the internal affairs of trade unions. We backed the trade union leaders, but the laws were popular with the public and were supported by most trade union members and Labour voters. Tony's change of policy caused uproar in the party at the outset but, before long, a majority of the party recognized that insisting on scrapping a popular measure was not the way to get elected and, albeit reluctantly, accepted it.

John Smith gave me, as my first job in the Shadow Cabinet, the role of Shadow Chief Secretary to the Treasury and deputy to the new Shadow Chancellor, Gordon Brown. I'd been working with

Gordon since 1983, and we had both, in different ways, striven to make Labour electable. After my appointment as his deputy, we would work together closely for the next eighteen years, initially as he reframed and modernized Labour's economic policy.

We needed economic growth in order to generate the tax revenues needed to renew public services in the UK and to create the jobs that would tackle the poverty of children in workless households. Gordon developed the mantra that, to have growth, we needed to build the supply side of the economy. He was determined that our economic policy, which had been our electoral Achilles' heel over so many years, would shift from taxing and spending the proceeds of growth to focus instead on increasing the rate of economic growth. He wanted to move beyond the idea that our economic policy was only about taxing the rich more and spending more on benefits. Government policy should not just be about dividing up the cake but about increasing the size of the cake as well. This was the background to his 'endogenous growth' speech in 1994, in which he said that economic growth could come not just through increasing demand but through increasing the capacity of the economy by investment in people, through education and training; in industry, through research and development; and in infrastructure, like roads and public transport. He was lampooned over the jargon he used but persisted with his line of argument.

This was a huge change. For so long, the only thing people knew about Labour's approach to the economy was that we would raise taxes and use the money to improve benefits and public services. The public perception was that they would have to pay more in taxes and that, subsequently, their money would be thrown down the drain. We were told this on doorsteps whenever we were out campaigning, and it was made clear to us in all the opinion polls. Now, our weekly Treasury team meetings would always begin with Gordon intoning that Labour was not just about taxing and spending but about investment. To get our message across, we had to invoke the supply-side investment strategy as the frame for every point we made. The political appeal of this approach was evident.

We changed the dividing line between us and the Tories so that, instead of the public perception being 'Labour will tax you more and make you worse off,' it would be 'Labour will make the economy grow more and make you better off.'

I had no hesitation in backing this approach. I'd heard too many voters saying that they wouldn't vote for us because of our policies on tax. But neither were they happy with the way the economy was struggling under the Tories, and this new approach won their support. It was resisted by many Labour traditionalists, who felt comfortable arguing solely for higher taxes on the rich. Within the party, Gordon was to pay a high price for this essential modernization of our economic policy. As its architect, he became the prime target for the backlash, and this dented his popularity in the party and undermined the chance for him to become its next leader.

My contribution to our new economic policy was to insist that when we invested in people, industry and infrastructure, we should recognize the role of women as well as men. This was an argument that had a long history in the women's movement and which Patricia Hewitt and I had set out in an article we'd written for *Tribune* in 1981. Now, eleven years later, I was in Labour's Treasury team, so I could do something about it. I argued that our policy should ensure that there were apprenticeships and training programmes for women, too, investment in sectors where women worked as well as those which were traditionally male dominated. I argued that the economic infrastructure we were going to invest in needed to include childcare as well as 'hard infrastructure' such as roads and railways. The women's movement had long argued that childcare was not just something that women wanted but something that was necessary for the economy as a whole. Within the Treasury team, I pressed for it to be seen not just as a social provision but as economic policy, for it to be recognized as something that was as vital for women in terms of getting to work as the roads and the buses they travelled on.

The childcare lobby, made up of organizations such as the Daycare Trust, the Kids Club network and the Fawcett Society, strongly supported this line of argument, and Gordon did, too, despite the fact that the mainstream majority of economic and political reporters at that time showed little interest. If mothers with young children could get the childcare and training they needed, they would be able to get back to work. Instead of claiming benefits, they would be paying taxes and in a position to set up businesses which would help the economy to grow. With mothers working, there'd be fewer children in poverty.

There was the democratic argument: women constituted half the electorate, and they wanted childcare. There was the social policy argument: hundreds of thousands of children would be kept from poverty. And now we had added the economic argument: the provision of childcare would help the economy grow and reduce the burden of benefits on the public purse.

I produced numerous policy papers laced with statistics and graphs to show the massive demand for childcare and with calculations of the number of women who, with childcare, could move from 'economic inactivity' into work. I made speeches saying that childcare would help employers because it would give them a wider pool of employees to choose from and help their existing employees to stay in work after they'd had children. I met with the Confederation of British Industry (CBI) and the Federation of Small Businesses (FSB) and went to the annual conferences of the trade unions to highlight this argument.

The Tory government had taken Britain into the European Exchange Rate Mechanism (ERM) in 1990, and by 1992 our economy was struggling. It was evident to everyone that the pound was overvalued. Every commentator had a view on it but, as Labour's Treasury team, we were not commentators, we were, potentially, part of the next government and what we said could be the straw that was going to break the pound's back. We were certainly not going to say publicly that the pound was overvalued and then take the blame for the devaluation that would inevitably follow our falling out of the ERM.

When Gordon, in TV interviews, dodged the question, he looked like he knew the answer but was simply choosing not to say. Everyone knew he was deeply immersed in economics. He looked as if he wasn't answering because he was too clever. When I did the same, it was assumed that I didn't know the answer. I looked as if I wasn't answering because I was too stupid. A series of interviews culminated in my being grilled by Jeremy Paxman on *Newsnight*. I looked vacuous and evasive, even to my own eyes. My already non-existent economic credibility was in tatters. I could sense that the enemies I had built up over my years of campaigning on women's issues were rubbing their hands in glee as they saw me stumbling.

Yet I fell to a new low in an interview on Channel 4's *A Week in Politics*, a highly influential Saturday-evening programme anchored by well-respected presenters Andrew Rawnsley and Vincent Hanna. Unusually, despite the fact that the interview would take place on a Saturday, in the early evening, I had agreed to do it. I drove myself to the studio, my then five-year-old daughter strapped in the back of the car. The entire way, we had a vibrant discussion about the different and very lovely colours of the manes of her My Little Ponies. As we drew nearer, my delight at the ponies became overlaid with a sense of foreboding. This was going to be an important, high-profile interview, and I had no idea what its focus was going to be. I'd had no briefing, I had no researcher, either with me or on the end of a phone line. The whole thing was a textbook example of what not to do.

The interview lasted ten minutes – which was long for a political interview – but it felt like an hour. It was a disaster. It wasn't just that I couldn't answer the questions, I didn't even understand them. As I came off the set, I caught sight of the programme researcher. He should have been delighted. The questions he'd prepared for the interview had floored me. But instead, he looked distraught. It was a twenty-three-year-old Ed Miliband, dismayed to have played a part in exposing a Labour Shadow minister.

Smarting from the criticism that followed this TV interview, I sought the advice of Patricia Hewitt. She said she knew of a young

TV researcher who would be an ideal special adviser for me and would help me get back on track – Ed Miliband! She knew him because she'd worked with his brother, David, in the Institute for Public Policy Research. I called Ed and, after a long discussion with him, he agreed to leave his job at Channel 4 and come and work for me. Unfortunately, there was bad news looming: I was voted off the Shadow Cabinet. You can make yourself unpopular with your colleagues and survive if you're doing a brilliant job. You can survive even if you're doing a bad job if you're popular with your colleagues. But if you're doing a bad job and are unpopular with your colleagues, you can't survive. So, having been elected to the Shadow Cabinet only in 1992, I was voted out the following year.

The newspapers gloated over my downfall. I sat glumly with Ed and Gordon and floated the idea that I should 'retreat' to the job of Shadow Women's Minister, outside the Shadow Cabinet. Gordon was adamant I should do no such thing. 'If they scent blood, it'll be the end of you!' he said. 'You've got to fight back.' But I felt humiliated and now, in addition, mortified that I'd messed up Ed's career. He'd left his secure, well-paid job in TV and, only one month later, because I was out of a job, so was he.

I was astonished when John Smith rang me the day after the Shadow Cabinet results and told me that, whatever the PLP thought, he was going to override the vote and keep me in my job and in the Shadow Cabinet. This was unprecedented. Though, now, all the members of the Shadow Cabinet are chosen by the leader of the party, back then, the right of the PLP to choose them was sacrosanct. By ignoring them, John Smith was using up much of his political credit and risking a PLP revolt. I was so grateful to him, and overwhelmed by his generosity in sticking his neck out for me. Looking back, I think his decision must have been a combination of the fact that Gordon had pressed him to keep me and him recognizing that I was a well-known public face, particularly among women. And John was father to three daughters. The pride with which he spoke about them told me that, if any young woman were to face a setback, he'd be there to give them another chance.

I thanked him profusely and pledged that I would work to justify his faith in me. I'd have a mountain to climb to rescue my reputation and I'd used up one of my political nine lives, but Gordon's backing and John Smith's leadership qualities had given me a reprieve.

I remained Shadow Chief Secretary to the Treasury during the aftermath of Black Wednesday, 16 September 1992, when the UK was ejected from the ERM. Public finances groaned under the weight of rising unemployment and the £3.3 billion cost to the reserves of the sterling devaluation. The public fumed as the bosses of the privatized utilities industries – gas, water and telecoms – put up their charges and awarded themselves massive bonuses.

My brief centred on public spending. Ed drafted parliamentary questions and crunched the numbers that came back to expose the fact that, despite the Tories' rhetoric about having cut public spending, it had in fact risen. We calculated that they'd implemented no fewer than twenty-two separate tax increases and embarked on a 'Twenty-two Tory Tax Rises' campaign to show that the Tories were not, in practice, the low-tax party. This was an epic break with past Labour orthodoxy. Hitherto, we'd always campaigned for more taxes, in order to provide better public services. Now we were parking our guns on the Tory lawn, criticizing them for raising taxes. The Labour party could see this was hurting the Tories, but many remained unsure whether this was the right ground for us to fight the Tories on.

With unemployment stubbornly high, public spending on benefits was high, too, so we developed the argument that Tory economic mismanagement had pushed up taxes. The Tories' failure on the economy had led to a hike in public spending and the subsequent imposition of higher taxes to deal with this. For once, we took a break from our argument that the problem was that the rich weren't taxed enough, which used to make everyone, even those who couldn't possibly be described as rich, think we'd put their taxes up. Our case was simply that the Tories had raised taxes for middle- and lower-income families.

We'd established a strong new line of attack, encroaching into the Tories' heartland issue of tax. It worked really well with the public and that gave our members at local level a new confidence on the doorstep and a fresh connection with their voters. I went campaigning in a by-election for a council seat in the Black Country in the West Midlands and picked up a leaflet the local party were delivering. It was one they'd written and printed themselves, not one they'd been sent by HQ, and it railed against Tory tax increases! I knew then that the party was ready to buy into the idea that we, Labour, could attack the Tories on tax. This reversed my political fortunes, too. Having been booted off the Shadow Cabinet a year earlier, I was voted back on in 1994, and not just scraping on but bouncing up to be fifth out of twenty-five. It was Tony's first Shadow Cabinet reshuffle and he made me Shadow Secretary of State for Employment.

Ed Miliband continued to do exceptionally well as my special adviser. I had a strong sense, shaped through my work with Gordon, of where we needed to take the Labour party economically, but it is hard to overstate the difference an extremely intelligent, committed, hard-working and – in Ed's case – thoroughly nice, political adviser can make. Ed had a crystal-clear idea of what I needed to do, an eerie ability to understand what I would want to do and the commitment to make it happen. He drafted parliamentary questions, policy papers and speeches for me. One night I went home exhausted, even though I had an important speech to make in the House of Commons the next day, leaving Ed, as usual, toiling in the office until late. Returning to the office the following morning, I found the speech which he'd left on my desk at 3 a.m. It not only made all the arguments but read as though I had written it. While I'd been peacefully sleeping in my bed, he'd been my alter ego – only one with considerably more economic expertise. We made some final tweaks to the speech, worked out how I'd respond to interventions and he walked with me to the door of the Chamber. The speech, like all those Ed wrote for me, was a great success.

It couldn't last. I began to notice that Gordon, usually solemn and businesslike at team meetings, was now smiling winningly at Ed and respectfully seeking his views. I knew that my days as Ed's boss were numbered. And sure enough, Gordon poached him from me in 1994. It was a blow but I was pleased to see Ed moving up and to know that Gordon would have someone working for him of intelligence and integrity who would never engage in the divisive machinations some of the other political advisers did.

Tony and Gordon hammered out the policy that, for the first two years of a Labour government, we would spend no more than the Tories had planned to spend, and would not put up the basic or the higher rate of tax. It felt like we were really beginning to show the public how Labour would do things differently, how we'd deliver on our progressive priorities without hitting people with extra taxes. I felt a sense of renewed hope among the people at my advice surgeries.

Although these arguments were winning us support on the ground, they were fiercely contested by many in the party. For decades, the entire basis of Labour's opposition to the Tory government was that the Tories didn't spend enough or tax enough. High spending on vital public services – and levying the taxes to pay for it – was our raison d'être. Though it was popular with the public, our new approach was disliked by politicians and commentators on both the left and the right. The ultra-left saw the new pledge to stick to the Tories' spending and taxing levels as a betrayal of Labour's socialist principles, and the Tories, in this echoed by *The Times* and the *Telegraph*, said we'd never stick to it.

The party remained nervous. If Labour didn't stand for higher taxes, what did we stand for? Jack Straw complained to me that every left-of-centre party in Europe backed high taxes and spending and the party would never wear it, but, whatever the situation in other left parties in Europe, I was convinced that, unless we came to terms with the electorate's fears about Labour's tax plans, we would continue to lose elections and my constituents would remain under the yoke of a Tory government. In any case, higher taxes were a means to an end (the end being equality and good public services), not an end in themselves. I backed Gordon unequivocally as he came under sustained attack. Up until now, he'd been a universally popular figure in the party, but his stance on tax and spending dented his popularity. He was embattled, but he held the line and laid out the argument with absolute determination. And he was solidly backed by Tony.

These were all changes that were being made in response to the growing sense within the party after 1992 that Labour had to change if we were ever to move into power. The arguments, like those that I'd been making, not least in my reports to my constituency party as far back as 1983, were gaining ground. And the momentum of the women's movement continued to gather pace. The struggle to make Labour electable was to forge one of the most important and enduring partnerships in the history of the Labour party – that between Tony Blair and Gordon Brown.

I knew Tony before he was elected in 1983, because I knew his wife, Cherie. Gordon Brown had been elected for the first time in the same election and, although I knew many activists in Scotland, I hadn't previously met him. But Jack, after looking through the maiden speeches of the newly elected Labour MPs, said that here was someone who thought along the same lines as me politically and that I should link up with him. From then on, Gordon was firmly on my radar.

Gordon and Tony shared a room in the House of Commons and there was a more or less continuous discussion between them about how to get Labour into government and how to get the party back in touch with a public which kept on rejecting us. Working with them as part of John Smith's Shadow Cabinet, I had the strong sense with both of them that it was never about power for themselves, or for its own sake; it was about getting Labour into power so we could put our principles into practice, rather than just commenting from the sidelines. It didn't seem that we were sacrificing our principles to reform our party and our policies in order to win electoral support. On the contrary, it was us forever languishing in opposition, leaving people to suffer under a Tory government, that was a betrayal of our principles.

Tony's starting point was always the public. The public were worried about high interest rates and their ability to buy their own home. Why did we never say anything about that? Why did we talk about the poor and the super-rich but never show any interest in the hard-working people in the middle? The car workers and the office administrators and the self-employed weren't on the breadline, but we wanted to govern in their interests, too. These people didn't think we understood or spoke for them. This was brought home to us in every opinion poll and on countless doorsteps. We needed their support to get into government or we'd remain powerless to help the poor. Gordon, in his acute analysis of the electorate, held the same view, and, in addition, he had a deep connection with the party activists, which Tony lacked at that time. Gordon was more party-facing and Tony more public-facing. Between them they formed a political alliance which was to prove historic. But it was clearly going to be a long haul back to electability. At times, Tony would despair of Labour ever getting into government and pronounce that he had half a mind to go back to his work as a barrister. I'd remonstrate with him that if we all did that our party was doomed; we had to stay and fight.

As Gordon's deputy, and someone who saw things very much as they did, I was involved in many of Tony and Gordon's discussions in their offices at 1 Parliament Street, where Labour's Shadow Cabinet members had their offices. What I saw was a relationship that was highly productive and mutually supportive. Together, they built on Neil's work to broaden Labour's appeal. Tony and Gordon were very different, and so much more than the sum of their parts: Tony, with his unerring instinct for 'middle England', Gordon with his connections to the party and the trade unions; Tony keeping things relaxed, Gordon in relentless overdrive; Tony prepared to front up any resistance within the party, Gordon reaching out and bringing people on board. And between the two, even before the days of text or email, there was a 24/7 dialogue. One weekend,

Jack, the children and I were staying with Tony and Cherie and their children in their constituency home in Sedgefield. We were all about to sit down to a traditional Sunday lunch when the phone rang. Cherie, a tray of roast potatoes in her hand, said with cheerful resignation that we'd better get on and start without Tony, as it would be bound to be Gordon on the phone and it wouldn't be a quick call. Neither was it the first, nor would it be the last that day.

They always talked to each other about every new idea, plan or event. They sought and relied on each other's judgement. In any discussion I had with Gordon, he would always add, 'But Tony thinks . . .' And it was the same in any discussion I had with Tony: 'What does Gordon say?' It wasn't that they accepted each other's views unquestioningly, it was simply a highly productive dialogue. They fought each other's battles and always backed each other up.

Every junior Shadow minister will have moments of friction with their Shadow Secretary of State. Gordon was unswervingly loyal to junior members of his team but, despite the efforts of his head of office, Sue Nye, his working methods often made it hard to be his deputy. I had no disagreement with him on where we needed to take the party economically or politically. He was supportive of my arguments on women. But he would cancel meetings at the last minute or rearrange my meetings without telling me, he would task me to do something and then do it himself, again without telling me, or agree to speak at a major meeting but then pull out at a moment's notice and tell the organizers I would be going in his place. Such things prevented me from doing my job as well as I wanted to. Every team leader does it to an extent, but I found it really hard with Gordon. On a couple of occasions, I complained to Tony. I felt able to do this because it didn't feel disloyal – no one was more supportive of Gordon than Tony. Once, I said to Tony that I was going to stop being Gordon's deputy and move to being the Shadow Women's Minister instead. Tony was sympathetic to my complaints but insisted I stay as Gordon's deputy, and promised that he'd talk to him. The closeness and productiveness of Tony and Gordon's relationship, right at the heart of the Labour party,

was our greatest asset. And that's why it was so destructive and disappointing when their relationship later ruptured over the issue of
who should stand for leader after John Smith died in 1994.

On 11 May 1994, Labour leader John Smith and his wife, Elizabeth,
hosted a drinks party for some of the frontbenchers in their flat in
one of the tower blocks in the Barbican. Labour was riding high in
the polls. John Smith was, unusually for a politician, trusted and
respected by the public. The party had put behind it the bloodletting of sectarian division and we'd reformed our policies. It seemed
as if we were all set to make it into government at the next election.
That night, it felt as if we were in the presence of the man who
would be our first Labour prime minister since Jim Callaghan in
the seventies. Everyone was in high spirits as we looked out over
the spectacular views.

John sought me out to say that he remembered my promise to
repay his trust in me as Shadow Chief Secretary to the Treasury.
He said that, with the tax campaign, I had more than done that and
that he could not be more pleased with my work. After the problems that had beset me, I was so gratified, and very aware of how
much I owed him for having had such confidence in me. After the
drinks, John and Elizabeth went off to a Labour fundraising dinner
and I, as usual, hurried home to the kids.

The next morning, I was driving into the House of Commons
when I heard on the radio that a senior Labour figure had been
taken to hospital. When John's name was mentioned, and it was
reported that his condition was serious, I just couldn't take it in.
John had seemed in robust good health only the night before. I sped
into the House of Commons, turning up the volume on the car
radio. Abandoning the car outside the entrance, I ran into the members' cloakroom, where I came across Ian McCartney MP, who was
completely distraught. He was the Shadow Health Minister responsible for the ambulance service and, that morning, he had been in a
meeting with some of the ambulance trade unions when the news
had come through from their colleagues. They told him that John,

to whom Ian was devoted, had died. I asked the police on duty in the House to open a small sideroom and took Ian in to sit down. The police officer told us that the news had now been confirmed. Ian regained his composure, but his face was grey. We were all devastated. John was only fifty-five years old. I thought of his three lovely daughters and, of course, of Elizabeth. The man who had been carrying Labour's hopes and who we had been confident was going to be the country's next prime minister was dead. It was as if the lights had gone out.

Tributes poured in from all parts of the country, from the top of the establishment to the man and woman in the street. They all said the same thing: that he was a beacon of integrity and they felt the country had been robbed of a man who would have been a prime minister the country could be proud of. It was one of those times where the broadcasters accurately report an 'outpouring of public grief', and this was all the more remarkable given that he was an Opposition politician, not even in government. In the Labour party we felt the loss incredibly keenly and, along with this, such a sense of pride that he'd been our leader.

Still in a daze, later that day I was walking with Peter Mandelson from the Commons to 4 Millbank, where the Shadow Cabinet economic teams now had their offices. We talked of our shock and sadness at John's death. Peter asked me who I thought should take over as leader, which struck me as odd, as he didn't usually seek my opinion. I said it had to be Tony. We needed to communicate to those who weren't involved in politics and didn't readily identify with Labour. While Gordon was the master of the rousing speech at Labour gatherings in our heartlands, Tony's relaxed, conversational style worked well where we needed it to, for example on the TV sofas of breakfast television. While Gordon was quintessentially Scottish, Tony was quintessentially English (despite having spent some time at school in Scotland), and we needed to win over voters in the south. The overriding priority, as far as I was concerned, was winning the next election. Many people said that we were already in such a strong position that we were bound to win and therefore electability was not the main issue in choosing the leader. But scarred by seeing my constituents suffer from two decades of Tory rule and knowing that only with a Labour government would we make any progress for women, I was not prepared to take any risks.

I said to Peter that, as Tony and Gordon had both been working on the modernization of Labour, we shouldn't risk splitting the vote by having both of them stand for leader. Either Tony or Gordon should stand, not both, and we had to win the General Election, so it had to be Tony. What did he think? He said he couldn't decide. 'It's so hard. I love them both,' he said. I thought that was odder still. If it was blindingly obvious to me that it should be Tony, I could not believe that it wasn't evident to Peter, who was never usually slow in coming to a view.

I called Anji Hunter, Tony's head of office, and told her I was on my way over to see him. Arriving in his outer office in 1 Parliament Street, I found the place abuzz, phones ringing, people rushing in and out. I was ushered into Tony's room and he shut the door behind me and asked what I thought. I said that there should be only one 'modernizing' candidate and that it should be him. He started saying something along the lines of what a heavy burden it would be to be leader of the Labour party and that he 'didn't need to do it'. I said, 'For God's sake, if you're going to do it, you can't be half-hearted about it.' He said, 'Believe me, if I decide to do something, I don't ever do it half-heartedly,' and he said it with such blazing eyes and such steely determination I was astonished. I'd never seen him like that before. It was the first time I saw him show the resolve that became such a defining characteristic of his leadership of the Labour party over the following fifteen years.

I'd known Cherie and Tony when they were living in Islington. Cherie Booth was a barrister much sought after by radical solicitors to take on their cases. She was Labour, a feminist, and I thought she was terrific – a real mover and shaker. Our paths had crossed in many campaigns on progressive causes over the years, including on the Labour Co-ordinating Committee. I'd met Tony at mutual friends' homes, because he was her husband, but I hadn't taken much notice of him; in contrast to Cherie, who was a real dynamo, he was pretty laid-back. I'd been surprised when he was selected to fight the Beaconsfield by-election in 1982. It was a Tory stronghold but, even so, I felt we should have fielded a stronger candidate and I remarked to Jack that I thought this was another sign that Labour was going from bad to worse. But my surprise then was nothing compared to the amazement I felt when I heard later that year that Tony, a north London barrister, had been selected as the candidate for the constituency of Sedgefield, a mining area and a Labour stronghold in Durham. I wondered what on earth could have happened in the selection contest. Clearly, others saw qualities in Tony that remained hidden to me. Something similar happened when he was first in the Shadow Cabinet. Prior to one of our meetings, Neil and I had been having a discussion in the old Shadow Cabinet Room, just down the corridor from the House of Commons Chamber. The Shadow Cabinet members started to arrive, including Robin Cook, Gordon and Jack Straw. As Tony drifted in, late, Neil whispered to me, 'Here he comes, the future leader of the Labour party.' I chuckled, thinking it must be a joke. But then I saw from his face that Neil was completely serious. This was, at that time, such a bizarre proposition that it stuck in my mind. Evidently, Neil had seen something in Tony that I hadn't.

Over the years that followed I realized it doesn't necessarily become apparent what leadership qualities someone has until the mantle of responsibility falls on their shoulders. When Tony decided to stand for leader it was like one of those TV cartoons where a cat peels back his skin and a tiger jumps out.

The day John died, I left Tony's office and went back to my own, which was next to Gordon's. In contrast to Tony's, Gordon's office was eerily quiet, the phones silent. The only people there were his staff and members of his Treasury team, his staunch allies Nick Brown and Andrew Smith. They looked sombre. Gordon had been much closer to John Smith, a fellow Scot, than Tony had been and had worked as John's deputy in the Shadow Treasury team, so it was inevitable that John's death would hit him harder than it had Tony. But the sombre atmosphere was not just about John's death, it was also the absence of any sign of political clamour for Gordon to stand for leader. I put my head around Gordon's door and said I'd like to see him. A few minutes later he swept down the corridor past my office, coat and briefcase in hand, saying that he was dashing to the airport to catch a plane up to Scotland and that we'd talk later. I said I needed to speak to him now but he said he was in a hurry and that I shouldn't worry as I 'would have a central role to play'. I took this to refer to my role in his leadership election; he was obviously assuming that I'd be backing him. I couldn't let him leave for Scotland under the impression that he would have my support for leader. I blurted out that I felt there should only be one modernizing candidate standing. He agreed enthusiastically. But then I said it had to be Tony. It was an awful moment. I, his deputy, to whom he'd given unstinting support over the years, had just said I wouldn't back him. He said nothing and rushed off to catch his plane.

After that, Gordon couldn't bring himself to speak to me. But I hoped that, however unlikely it seemed, in time, he would come to recognize that I'd made the decision in the best interests of the party and, moreover, that I'd been completely open and honest with him from the outset. It took years, rather than months, but in due course our relationship did get back on track.

Along with the rest of the Shadow Cabinet, I flew up to Scotland for John Smith's funeral. It was a huge occasion, and took place in the darkly impressive Cluny parish church near John's Edinburgh home. The mourners, led by Elizabeth Smith and their three daughters, included politicians from across Europe and people from all walks of life and all over the UK. In addition to the nine hundred mourners inside the church, another two thousand stood in silence outside in the biting east wind, listening to the service, which was being broadcast through loudspeakers.

John Smith's death was a tragedy for his family, and it was a tragedy for Labour. I was seated in the pew in the front row, next to Lord Derry Irvine, another of John's fellow Scots, and who was later to be the Labour government's first Lord Chancellor. As he waited for his turn to give his tribute from the lectern, he was shaking so much I feared he wouldn't be able to do it. All eyes were on Elizabeth and her daughters, who bore themselves with such dignity. Politically, with a newly created vacancy for the leadership of the party, all eyes were on Tony and Gordon.

A couple of weeks after John Smith's burial on the Hebridean island of Iona, Gordon announced on 1 June 1994 that he wouldn't stand and would back Tony, and the leadership election got underway. John Prescott and Margaret Beckett both ran for the positions of both leader and deputy. Wanting to see a woman in our top leadership team, I backed Margaret for deputy, but I felt that by running for leader as well she had reduced her chances of becoming deputy. Tony's campaign was unstoppable. Even party members and trade unionists who didn't support his New Labour politics backed him. He looked and sounded like a winner and, after all the years of losing in General Elections, that's what the party was desperate for. The National Executives of the unions, whose members held a third of the votes in the electoral college, nominated and backed John Prescott for leader. But after John Smith's reforms, it was one member one vote for each trade unionist, and even in unions such as the TGWU, which most vigorously opposed Tony, individual members rejected the advice of their leaders and gave him their support. He won the vote of the majority of the MPs, the majority of party members and the majority of trade unionists, which gave him a rock-solid mandate to modernize the party and move forward to get us into government. John Prescott was elected deputy and Gordon remained Shadow Chancellor.

If Tony and Gordon couldn't sort out their differences over the succession to John Smith when they were Leader of the Opposition and Shadow Chancellor, they were never going to be able to do so once we were in government. The positions of prime minister and chancellor are the two most powerful in government. Being prime minister is of course the top job, but the chancellor has what the prime minister doesn't – a department that can implement changes in the most important of all areas: the raising and spending of public money. The prime minister has to work through other Cabinet ministers and cannot do things directly and, although the prime minister appoints and is the head of the Cabinet and in overall charge of all policy for every department, the chancellor's control of each department's budget gives them a major lever of policy control over their Cabinet colleagues. These competing zones are enough in themselves to have ruined the relationship between most prime ministers and chancellors.

For Tony and Gordon, I felt that, in addition to the usual structural tensions, there were two further nails driven into the coffin of their relationship: the bitter legacy of the leadership election and the role of Peter Mandelson. From 1983, when they were both elected to the House of Commons for the first time, the general perception was that Gordon was the senior one in the partnership. It couldn't have been anything other than galling for Gordon to see the man who'd always been seen as junior to him overtake him and seize the leadership, and he would not have been human if he hadn't felt some continuing resentment about it.

And then, Peter Mandelson. Senior political colleagues, whether in opposition or in government, will always have disputes. It's important that their advisers help build bridges and heal the rifts, and certainly it's important that they don't stir things up and exacerbate tensions. But there's a risk for a special adviser who tries to bring ministers or Shadow ministers together by arguing the virtues of the one they don't work for to the one they do. They can find themself looking as though they're arguing on behalf of the rival and are therefore not a loyal member of the team. But though it sometimes creates tension between the boss and the adviser, it's generally the right thing for an adviser to do. My senior advisers when I later became deputy leader, Anna Healy and Ayesha Hazarika, always extolled the virtues of any colleague I was complaining about, sometimes much to my annoyance. The more I was falling out with someone, the friendlier they'd be to them and their advisers. And that is the way it should be.

Sometimes, there's a genuine reason to fall out with someone and issues have to be thrashed out, but simmering disputes, grudges and petty wars are needlessly destructive. While good advisers smooth over arguments, some foment tensions in order to enhance their own power.

In the face of the inherent friction between the positions of Leader and Shadow Chancellor, and the acrimonious legacy of the leadership succession, Peter Mandelson could have tried to bring Tony and Gordon together. He was close to and had the confidence of both. If he had worked to heal the wounds, he might have succeeded and, to whatever extent he managed it, it would have greatly benefited the government and the party. But from what I saw and experienced, he didn't. When Tony's relationship with Gordon was at its strongest, before the leadership election, Peter's position was marginal. With Tony and Gordon's partnership ruptured and the two men at loggerheads, it seemed to me that there was space for Peter's power and influence to grow. It was in the interests of the country, and the party, for Tony and Gordon to work together, but perhaps it wasn't in Peter's personal interests. In 2010, in the title of his autobiography, Peter described himself as 'the third man'. Back in 1994, with Tony and Gordon at odds with each other and Tony likely to be elected Prime Minister, Peter placed himself firmly at Tony's side and sought to be 'the second man'. But I mourned the days when Tony and Gordon had been such a great team.

With Tony as Leader and Gordon as Shadow Chancellor, the PLP became increasingly divided into two 'camps', the Blairites and the Brownites, and this divide only widened when we got into government in 1997. To an extent, the arguments were about the direction the government should be taking, with Tony being seen as politically more to the right and Gordon more to the left. But it was more about the formation and development of two tribes around two powerful men, defined in opposition to each other because one was the current prime minister and the other the next prime minister. Because I was supportive of them both, I fitted into neither tribe. I would never say anything to either camp that could be interpreted as a criticism of the other. And neither was I prepared to listen to members of one complaining about the other.

Towards the end of Tony's time as Prime Minister, when the divisions between them were at their deepest, each believed that I was on the other one's side. Tony even came to think that, in 2007, in a plot with Jack and Gordon, I had sought to damage him by unleashing the 'loans for peerages' investigation. I had had nothing to do with it. The truth was that I was on neither's side, and against neither, but I don't think either could see that there was any position other than to be either for or against them. They didn't see that there was scope for supporting each of them in their respective roles. Ultimately, having been close to both of them, I became close to neither. I was sad about the deterioration of their relationship, not only on a personal level, but above all because of its detrimental effect on the party, on politics and on the country. They had been two towering figures and had achieved so much together, in a way they couldn't have individually. I mourned the loss of the close working relationship I'd had with each of them. I'd relished the momentum their relationship had created in Labour politics, and I had been a part of, though not central to it. And now, with Gordon and Tony, and the PLP, divided and me in neither camp, I experienced a return of the political isolation I'd not felt since the PLP in the eighties.

As newly elected leader, in 1994 Tony Blair took the bull by the horns and carried on with the project of the modernization of the Labour party. It was in this year that the project was named New Labour, in order to leave no one in any doubt that Labour had changed. New Labour challenged the notion that the country had to choose between economic prosperity and social justice. We argued that a strong economy and a fair society went hand in hand. Good education was not just important for the life chances of the individual, it was essential for a modern economy to have an educated workforce. Tackling unemployment was vital to help individuals without jobs, but to have so many people unemployed was also an inefficient use of the pool of labour. Services provided by the NHS were not only crucial for the individual but also contributed to the economy by keeping the workforce healthy and therefore productive. Since the founding of the Labour party, we'd had Clause 4 in our constitution, committing the party to 'the common ownership of the means of production, distribution and exchange', so ditching it, which we did in 1995, signalled to the British people the extent to which New Labour represented a break with Labour's past. It was a measure of our determination to deal with every obstacle that prevented us getting into government. We'd always hated News International, but if making peace with them would get Murdoch off our backs, so be it. We wanted a progressive tax system and to invest in the NHS, in schools, in housing and in all the public services that were then on their knees. But if sticking with Tory tax rates and their spending limits for our first two years in power meant we would get into power, then we were prepared to do it. There'd been a joke about the Labour party that we would stand for 'no compromise with the electorate'. But if you don't listen to the electorate, they don't listen to you, and why should they?

In the mid-nineties, New Labour transcended the old divisions between the right, the centre and the left of the party. It was an alliance between all those who believed that the ultimate betrayal of our values was our failure to get elected. There were still those who took what they saw as the 'correct' political positions and who were comfortable presiding over the party's decline but, for me, there was nothing progressive about sitting in my advice surgery on a Friday after a Thursday General Election defeat knowing that my constituents' problems were only set to get worse and that there was precious little I could do to help them. I believed that the country, and the lives of my constituents, would be transformed for the better when we won, when we were able finally to put into practice policies we could only dream of in our eighteen long years of opposition. And I still believe in this, and see the positive effects of this transformation.

As well as residual resistance to New Labour, there was also the institutional resistance to change which is to be found in any organization. When a policy has been in place for a long time, it becomes embedded in the party's identity, and many in the party, particularly on the left, felt that any change represented an abandonment of our principles and values.

PART TWO

Transformation: Changing Politics to Match Women's Changing Lives

4.

Pressing Forward for Women

Slowly and painfully, over the course of the period between 1982 and 1997, Labour overcame its internal divisions and we bridged the gap between our party and the voters. When we had discussed our policy in the early eighties, there had been too much focus on what the different factions in the party thought and too little on what the public thought. One of the foundations for our later success was putting people's concerns at the centre of our politics. So, from 1988 onwards, we ran a 'Labour Listens' programme. Labour 'listened' to anyone and everyone, in all regions: to women, to the elderly, to young people, to business, to workers. It wasn't because we didn't know what we thought – we retained our core values – but we needed to re-engage with the public and an important way to do that was to show that we were listening to their concerns.

New Labour was a change in the way Labour ran its politics – in shifting the emphasis to listening to people rather than shouting at them. 'Labour Listens' was about exposing party activists to what the public was thinking rather than the party's internal concerns. Too much of our debate had been about issues which, though important, were not people's priorities in their daily lives. The arguments in Labour had grown more heated, but they weren't about the issues faced by people who were not involved in politics and just wanted to get on in their lives.

Looking at the monthly editions of *Peckham Labour News* from the eighties, they are full of debate about Polaris. But though the voting public wanted us to be strong on defence, Polaris was never something my constituents raised with me. Their concerns were about housing, jobs, living standards, schools, childcare and their local health service. One of the things which Tony took forward as Leader was to shift the party's focus from 'what are we concerned about?' to 'what is the public concerned about?'

There was a widely held view in the party that the reason people didn't vote for us was because they, the public, were too right-wing. Instead of those in the party seeing that we had a problem and needed to change, many blamed the public and thought *they* should change. This focus on where it was thought the public were getting it wrong allowed the party to avoid facing up to where *we* were getting it wrong. A party which sees the public as the problem is not in the right place to get itself elected.

While it had never been top of the internal Labour policy agenda, people were profoundly concerned about interest rates and inflation. New Labour showed them that we understood this and developed policies to tackle both. People were worried that we would tax them too much and then simply throw their money away. We needed to prove that we wouldn't. Too many in the party believed that, if people became sufficiently dissatisfied and angry with the Tories, they would vote for us, and that all it required for us to be elected was for us to highlight the failures and unfairness of Tory government policy. But this wasn't the case. Throughout the eighties, there was plenty of evidence that there was hostility towards the Tories. People could see that their hospitals and schools were crumbling and that crime rates were rising, we ran dynamic campaigns against growing hospital waiting lists, and hundreds demonstrated against increasing unemployment and inequality. But, however much people despaired of the Tories and worried about the future, they didn't trust Labour, so they wouldn't vote for us. Labour's failure to get into government was less about the success of the Tories and more about our failure as a party.

'Taking the fight to the Tories' is undoubtedly an important role for Labour in opposition. But an opposition party that has little public support is in no position to be effective in opposing the government. The effectiveness of your opposition depends on the credibility you have with the voters as well as the coherence of your critique. If people are not listening to you because you are not credible, there's no need for the government to worry about you. However forensic your arguments, you won't be heard and you won't be an effective Opposition, let alone a government-in-waiting. An unpopular Opposition shouting angrily at a more popular government just alienates voters and bolsters the government's support.

Another reason for Labour's lack of popularity in the polls was that our leadership team was not sufficiently diverse. Too many people in too many parts of the country could not see anyone in the leadership of the party who they could believe had an understanding of their lives. For example, Margaret Thatcher, a woman at the very top of the Tory party, was very visible, but women in the Labour party in the eighties and early nineties were not. And we were out of touch with the south, with people in suburban and rural areas. We had no leading figures in the party who looked or sounded like the millions of people who lived in the areas we needed to win over. We had to make a determined effort to ensure that, in addition to the representatives of Labour's heartlands, we had men and women speaking for Labour who came from the south, from suburban areas and England's small towns, and understood them. We had to make sure that whether you were old or young, a man or a woman, from the north or from the south, you would be able to see and hear leading Labour people who looked and sounded like you. The transformation of the party thus saw us striving to change our public face so that we had a more diverse team at the top. And it also meant changing our policies.

For me, in my work, there were three big policy areas in which I was to lead this change to focus on the people and not on internal politics.

After Tony was elected Leader on 21 July 1994, I was re-elected to the Shadow Cabinet and Tony promoted me from being Gordon's deputy in the Treasury to Shadow Secretary of State for Employment. One of the policies we needed to work on was our policy on the national minimum wage (NMW). There was no minimum wage at that time and low pay was a major problem, with hundreds of thousands of people earning less than £1.50 an hour – and women were the worst affected, as they often worked in low-paid service jobs, as hospital cleaners or school dinner ladies (as they were then called), for example. In the private sector, women tended to find jobs in workplaces where pay rates did not benefit from strong union organization. And even when they were working somewhere that was unionized, the negotiated agreements that helped the men too often left the women behind. Even when the women were highly skilled, the traditional undervaluing of women's work condemned them to low pay, and this problem was compounded by the fact that they more frequently worked part-time, due to responsibilities at home. Women were working and working hard but they were firmly stuck at the bottom of the labour market. The Equal Pay Act had been in force for nearly twenty years by this time and had banned overt pay discrimination, but to claim equal pay a woman had to show that a man doing the same or similar work was being paid more than she was, and most women worked in 'segregated employment', where women and men did different jobs. And even where there was overt pay discrimination, it was daunting for a woman individually to take a case against her employer (which could last for years), even if she had the support of her union. In 1993, the official statistics from the Family Expenditure Survey recorded that there was still a gap between women's and men's hourly pay of 29 per cent.

Low pay was endemic in my constituency. I remember one man who came into my surgery for help because he was deep in debt and now, in rent arrears, feared eviction. He assured me that, far from being on benefits, he was working all hours. He reached into a carrier bag full of papers, pulled out his latest payslip and handed it to me. He was earning £1.60 an hour. His wages were stagnant and had been eroded by rising inflation. He wept as he said that he'd never had a day out of work in his life but he was starting to think that he'd be better off, and it would be fairer for his family, if he, like many others, gave up his job and went on benefits. Financially, he was worse off in work.

Our policy on the minimum wage had been the same since the early nineties. In response to the Tory dismantling of the Wages Councils, we made a commitment that when we were in government, we would make it illegal for anyone to be paid less than 'half male median earnings', which, at that time, was around £3.70 an hour. Just before the 1992 General Election, Tony had been Shadow Secretary of State for Employment and had become convinced that we couldn't go ahead with this policy. He had gone on *Election Call*, a daily BBC radio phone-in programme. A woman who ran a private nursery rang in and told him that, as a woman running a small business, she provided vital childcare services to working mothers, that she employed people, that she trained her staff, that the mothers of the children at the nursery were low-paid and she needed to keep the fees down. How could she continue to run her business with an NMW of half male median earnings? She'd have to sack staff and throw them out of work, put up fees to a level parents wouldn't be able to afford and the nursery would probably close, meaning that the mothers, in turn, would have to give up their jobs. We simply had no answer to this. This phone-in stuck in Tony's mind and he made it clear when he appointed me Shadow Employment Secretary that this was the one policy that he was not going ahead with. For all that there was a problem of low pay, we couldn't be seen as anti-jobs and anti-small business, and the policy on a national minimum wage, as it stood, was just that. It would cause businesses to cut back on the number of their employees or, worse, fold, and so it would increase unemployment.

I agreed with Tony that our policy, as it was, couldn't stand. The reality was not just that employers would oppose it but that there was a real danger it would cause job losses, and, as they were the lowest paid, women's jobs would be the first to go. But I was determined that we shouldn't drop our commitment to a national minimum wage and set about finding a different way to formulate it. I looked at other European countries; some of them had 'social partnership' arrangements whereby the employers and the unions got together to propose to government the minimum wage that should be set in different sectors and different regions. (We used to have similar arrangements with the Wages Councils for sectors from retailing and catering to textiles and agriculture, but by 1993 the Tory government had abolished all of them except the Agricultural Wages Board.)

It seemed to me that the best way to achieve something like a national minimum wage would be to put a floor under pay but to do so in a way which would not increase unemployment – by setting up something like a National Wages Council (as I developed the policy, I renamed it the Low Pay Commission, or LPC). The council would include employers and economists as well as the unions.

I floated this idea with the trade unions and all hell broke loose. The union leaders protested that abandoning the policy of half male median earnings was a betrayal. Their views were crucial not just because they represented working people but because they made up half Labour's National Executive Committee and held 70 per cent of the votes at the annual conference. I remonstrated with the public sector union leaders that the proposal of half male median earnings was all well and good for their sector, as the public purse would pick up the increased wages bill. And I complained to union leaders in the private sector that an NMW set at half male median earnings might work for their high-paid, well-organized members, but that private sector workers – particularly women – would lose their jobs. But their backing for half male median earnings had become an article of faith in the unions and on the left. The trade union executive committees were already protesting that Tony had made too many changes and decided they were going to draw the line on this one. They turned on me. The row kicked off, and the newspapers were full of trade union general secretaries denouncing me for betraying Labour's principles.

It was horrible to find myself made a pariah in the press by those on our own side – no previous attacks had challenged my commitment to Labour principles – but I pressed on, building up the evidence we needed to change our policy and producing a series of working papers called the 'Low Pay Map of Britain' which showed just how low pay at the bottom had fallen and pinpointed the groups that were hardest hit. My first report, in March 1995, showed that there were over a million people in the country earning less than £2.50 an hour, and that over half of these were women. There were over 300,000 people earning less than £1.50 an hour; Yorkshire and Humberside and the northern region were the regions worst affected. 'The Low Pay Map of Britain: Women' showed the number of women in each region who were earning less than £1.50 an hour. I produced maps for ethnic minorities and for young people. The front page of each was a map of Britain with numbers for each region and, inside, I laid out all the arguments against low pay.

In preparation for the discussion on low pay at our annual conference in 1995, I produced another paper, showing the similarity of what I was proposing to the social partnership arrangements of other socialist European countries. I hoped that would give me some cover and protect me from criticisms from the left, but it precipitated a front-page splash in the *Daily Express*: the General Secretary of the GMB union, John Edmonds, criticized me for betraying the workers. I went to see Bill Morris, General Secretary of the TGWU, to try to persuade him. I'd known him well for years and we were on good terms, but he wouldn't budge.

So I arranged for the TGWU members of the Agricultural Wages Board to come to meet me and my deputy, Wigan MP Ian McCartney, in my office at 8 Millbank to tell us how their social partnership worked in practice. I was encouraged by their account of how well it functioned. But Ian said, whatever the evidence, the unions wanted to draw a line in the sand against the New Labour modernization of our policy and this was to be it.

It was, I felt, a depressing example of male union leaders, who represented organized and better paid male workers, insisting on a policy which was unpopular with the public and which, if we implemented it, would hit low-paid women without union organization behind them the hardest.

As we approached the 1995 conference, Tony and I went for a meeting at TUC HQ of the TUC/Labour liaison committee to discuss the national minimum wage and I set out all my arguments. The trade unions knew them all only too well and sat there in stony-faced silence. Unable to reach agreement, we had an adjournment for the two sides to discuss the issue among ourselves. There wasn't really anything for Tony and me to discuss, so we sat and waited until the trade union side returned, half an hour later. They came back even more adamantly against, but said that we could fudge our disagreement with a 'form of words' which appeared to show consensus. I was in despair. We needed a proper policy. A 'form of words' would not survive a radio phone-in. Tony would just ditch the NMW altogether if we couldn't reform it; there would be a ruckus if we persisted. The trade unions said that unless we agreed to a 'form of words', there'd be a public row. I held my breath, wondering what Tony would do. He asserted that we would press on with the Low Pay Commission, saying, 'If it's a choice between a row and a fudge, I'd rather have a row.' There was no one better to have on your side than Tony, and not just because he was Leader but because he was clear in his arguments and not afraid to stand up to people when necessary. However, although Tony had said he was happy to have a row, with the conference fast approaching, it was my job to try to get it sorted out without one.

The newspapers which supported Labour were against the Low Pay Commission because of the opposition of the unions. Those which supported the Tories were against it because of the opposition from employers. The Federation of Small Businesses, led by Stephen Alambritis, was the exception, backing it on the grounds that they didn't want good employers undercut by bad ones who were driving down wages. But the leading employers and employers' organizations, such as the CBI and the Institute of Directors, having supported the abolition of the Wages Councils, didn't want a new wage-fixing mechanism, which they saw as unwarranted government interference in the labour market. They were not even slightly assuaged by my reassurance that they'd have nothing to fear because, as members of the Low Pay Commission, they'd be involved in setting the rate. I went to countless meetings with employers' and business organizations. It was nerve-wracking to face such hostility. They argued that any national minimum wage could cause businesses to close and throw millions of people on the dole.

The one ray of light was the National Union of Knitwear, Footwear and Apparel Trades (KFAT), which represented low-paid workers in the private sector, many of whom were women. John Mann (now MP for Bassetlaw and then working as trade union liaison officer at Labour HQ) suggested I meet them. They were affiliated to the Labour party and firmly focused on the concerns of their members. If their general secretary supported the Low Pay Commission, John said, it would give me a trade union ally and transform the debate.

John arranged for us to meet up with KFAT General Secretary Paul Gates and the union's president, Helen McGrath. Paul was the best of trade unionists, deeply committed to his members, hugely knowledgeable about his industry and with no time for any political manoeuvring. It wasn't only some of his members who were low paid; they all were. Working as they did in knitwear, footwear and textiles, low pay was the norm. They stood to benefit from a pay increase through a national minimum wage, but an NMW set at too high a rate would cost them their jobs and their industries. This was a time when the big UK textile employers like Courtaulds, Coats Viyella and Burberry were moving their operations to India and South-east Asia. A big hike in pay for UK employees would accelerate this trend. And that wouldn't just be bad for the individuals KFAT represented, it would be terminal for the industry because, once those jobs had left the country, they would never come back. It wouldn't be like retail, where too high an NMW might cause job losses and restructuring but the sector would survive. The UK textile industry would be gone and, with it, all the jobs in the industry and the union, too. After all the problems I'd had with the other general secretaries, Paul was, as John had predicted, a breath of fresh air. He gave me all the pay data for his members and information about their industries moving abroad and agreed to speak to the other general secretaries. He agreed to submit a motion to the Labour Party conference backing the Low Pay Commission and promised to speak at it. It helped that at that time one of the big unions that was leading the objection to the Low Pay Commission, the GMB, wanted to amalgamate with KFAT and take over their membership. While the GMB weren't inclined to listen to me, they had to take account of the situation of thousands of workers who might become members of their union.

KFAT's involvement transformed the situation. I'd worked out the policy and was on top of every detail. I'd put forward the case without flinching at the hostility from employers' organizations and so many trade union general secretaries. I could always take arguments head-on, but the lateral thinking needed to craft a political strategy to work around opposition was not my strong point. Fortunately, it was John Mann's.

Paul Gates, leader of one of the smallest unions, true to his word, broke ranks with the giants and, when we got to the conference, took to the podium. The unions always stuck together at the Labour conference, so it was extraordinary when he got up on the stage and urged the big unions with members in high-paid industries not to vote to put thousands of women and men out of work. In the face of such an overwhelming case based on the reality of the problems of his members and their industry, the resolution to change our policy to having our national minimum wage set by the Low Pay Commission was passed unanimously.

The Low Pay Commission went on to be a highlight of our 1997 manifesto, and Ian McCartney, who became the Labour government's employment minister, introduced the National Minimum Wage Bill as one of our first in government. It came into effect in 1999 and ensured pay rises for more than a million low-paid workers. With the boost it gave to low-paid women, it caused the biggest narrowing of the pay gap since the institution of the Equal Pay Act.

Despite predictions, unemployment did not rise after the

national minimum wage was brought into force. The level of employment, rather than falling, grew. The union general secretaries had now become vociferous in their support of the NMW and posed as its champions. The Tories, who'd opposed it, ultimately accepted it, and it is one of the measures the Labour government introduced which they dare not dismantle, so it looks set to be a permanent feature of employment protection for people in this country. For all the problems of low pay that still remain for too many people, the poverty pay rate of £1.50 per hour has long since disappeared from my advice surgeries and across the country. While I carried the political scars of the battles I had on the NMW, they were more than outweighed by how pleased I was that we were able to help people like that man on £1.60 an hour who wept in my advice surgery. And one of the many thousands of women who got a pay increase when the national minimum wage was introduced was John Mann's sister, a veterinary nurse.

I became Shadow Secretary of State for Social Security in 1996, and there were also battles to fight to modernize our policy in this area, particularly in bringing about change for women while at the same time remaining popular and being seen as practical and ready to govern.

In 1996, the largest number of people in poverty were the elderly, and most of them, and an overwhelming majority of the very poorest, were women. They had worked fewer years than men, were less likely to have an occupational pension from their work and, if they did, it was lower because of their lower pay. Most women took years out of the labour market caring for children or older relatives and then worked part-time, so they didn't pay 'the stamp' on which entitlement to the basic state pension was built. We talked about 'women pensioners', but most of them, though retired, were not pensioners but had to live on benefits.

While it was evident that pensioner poverty was a huge problem and one that we wanted to address when we got into government, it was equally evident that we wouldn't be able to tackle it by 'throwing money at it', because we had pledged that, in our first two years in power, we would spend no more than the Tories had planned to spend. But our pensions policy was perhaps the most iconic for the party, representing as it did the struggle against the indignity of poverty in retirement. The starting point was that any change to it would be a betrayal of Labour principles.

Traditionally, the centrepiece of Labour's policy on pensions was to increase the basic state pension, but this would cost a huge amount of public money and do nothing to help the poorest, especially the women who didn't qualify for it. I wanted to change our policy to target public money for the elderly initially on the poorest pensioners. This immediately set me at loggerheads with all the Labour pensioners' organizations, the trade union Retired Members Associations and the hard left of the party. Though women, in general, live longer than men, and the majority of over-sixties were women, the pensioners organizations were – and still are – dominated by men. The men, having worked full-time all their lives, did qualify for the basic state pension, so, unsurprisingly, that was the focus of their campaign. Many of them also had occupational pensions and, therefore, an increase targeted on the pensioners on the lowest income would be of no help to them.

I had angry meetings with pensioners' groups, including my local Southwark Pensioners Action Group (SPAG). As in most areas, the overwhelming majority of the over-sixties in my constituency were women, yet the leaders of SPAG – like the other pensioners' organizations – were men. SPAG regarded themselves as radical and to the left of the Labour party. I asked them what they thought was progressive about a policy that missed out the poorest and discriminated against women, but while I saw such a policy as a way of giving most help to those in greatest need, they saw it as the dreaded 'means testing', something reminiscent of the time when people who'd worked hard all their lives had to endure the indignity of proving they were poor to get any help in their old age. They were, I felt, resistant partly because they would stand to gain nothing if we gave better pension provision to the poorest, but I also understood the deep, long-standing hostility they felt to targeting the poorest. Some complained that giving most to the poorest would reward those who they felt hadn't worked hard all their lives and saved, at the expense of those who had.

I persisted, and Tony and Gordon both strongly agreed with me that the first call on public money when we got into government should be those pensioners who were in poverty. I thought the strength and clarity of our argument and their backing would be enough to get the policy through but, once again, I underestimated the need for a political strategy. It wasn't just that the Labour and trade union culture of commitment to the basic state pension ran deep, their standard-bearers were two legendary Labour figures: former Cabinet minister and Labour heroine Barbara Castle and former TGWU General Secretary and pensioners' champion Jack Jones. It was going to be very hard to be at odds with them. As it was a big-ticket item for a future government, Gordon, as Shadow Chancellor, got involved. He had long-standing, strong relationships with both Jack Jones and Barbara Castle and argued that we should sort it out with them behind the scenes, meaning that I should hold fire on making my arguments too public, as that would only whip up the row and make the task of reaching agreement harder. He suggested a review including terms of reference which would give reassurance to all sides, though I thought this just a fudge and wished to take the argument into the open. In any event, Jack Jones and Barbara Castle refused to be 'squared', even by Gordon, and publicly denounced me and any notion that we should change the policy. With Gordon busy with many other issues, Jack Jones and Barbara Castle refusing to budge and my arguments kept under wraps, we went into the debate at the Labour party conference of 1996 having come to no agreement.

Things came to a head during my conference speech. Liz Kendall, who was my special adviser and later became MP for Leicester, and I crafted a speech which contained the reasons why we had to start off with a targeted rather than a 'universal' approach. With some extra input from Ed Miliband, who was by then Gordon's special adviser, we put the final touches to it and it went on to the autocue before I went up on to the conference platform to listen to the debate on the issue before making my speech.

I knew I would have to be very persuasive and I sat apprehensively on the platform waiting for my turn to speak. But when I went to the podium and started to read out the speech as it scrolled up through the autocue, I realized to my horror that the words appearing weren't those I had prepared. I kept going, but when I got to the end of it I realized that much of the most important section – why we needed to go for targeting rather than the universal basic state pension – had been replaced by flattering words about Jack Jones and Barbara Castle and the proposal for a review.

Barbara Castle, who was at the conference as a Member of the European Parliament, was then called up to the stage and, to the rapturous cheers of delegates, argued against the targeted approach. There was nothing for it but for me to grit my teeth and clap along with everyone else.

When that conference session closed and I was able to leave the platform, I rushed backstage, demanding to know what on earth had happened to my speech. Liz told me that, while I was sitting on the platform waiting to speak, Gordon had gone through it and typed in alterations. Gordon's authority was such that there was no way special advisers, even two of them, could hold out against him. Liz knew how important that section of the speech was for me and later told me that, while I was waiting to speak, she had tried to pass up some notes of the deleted paragraphs for me to read out, but I hadn't seen her. But even if she had got them up to me, you can't simply deviate from the autocue and start reading something else, then go back to the autocue, so her efforts were in vain. Gordon's only intention was to be helpful. He'd always been supportive of me and argued my corner. We didn't disagree on the policy change that was needed. But it was exasperating that, even though I was Shadow Secretary of State, I didn't yet appear to have any autonomy as far as he was concerned. The pattern had been set during those years of my being his deputy and it was never to change.

I ended up with the worst of all possible worlds, having a huge row with the pensioners' movement without even properly making my case to the party. And I got a battering in the press. However, when we got into government, we did, with Gordon's support as Chancellor, implement the policy I'd argued for, tackling pensioner poverty by means of focusing a new Minimum Income Guarantee on the poorest pensioners. Pensioners, having been the poorest group in society, saw the fastest increase in their income of any group and, by our second term of government, were the least likely group to be in poverty.

However, although I had crafted a policy which was effective for that group, it was never popular in Labour circles and cast a shadow which was to hang over me when we got into government. Though I put a lot of thought into analysing the problem and identifying the solution, it was foolhardy to embark on pushing a policy through without a robust political strategy. I thought it was enough that my motive was good, that I knew the policy would work and that Tony and Gordon were backing it. It wasn't. I didn't pay sufficient attention to mobilizing potential support and protecting my back. And it was doubly painful that I ended up on the other side of the argument from Barbara Castle, who was the iconic Labour woman politician and who'd always been so supportive of me. Later, when I was sacked from the Cabinet, we became united again. Suffering at the hands of a prime minister was something she could identify with. She invited me to have tea with her in the House of Lords. 'You just have to remember one thing,' she said gleefully: 'All prime ministers are bastards.'

The third big area on which I was working was to reflect the huge change in women's aspirations for their working lives. This was what I had come into politics to do, and it was immensely satisfying to see the changes for which we had so long pressed at last becoming popular Labour policy as we drew towards 1997. The

Tories' policies were based on the notion that the man in the family was the breadwinner and the woman's place was in the home. This, they believed, made the Conservatives the party of the family. Labour's policy had largely been to argue for higher benefits for women, such as child benefit and lone parent benefits, in order to help families.

But the message that was coming through loud and clear from women in my constituency was that they wanted to work. And this was the case among lone mothers, too. Whether they were divorced or had never been married, the last thing they wanted was to bring their children up on benefits. They wanted to work, something married mothers were increasingly doing.

The Tories denigrated lone parents as feckless women who'd had babies in order to get a council house, but most were lone parents because of divorce, rather than having started out as 'unmarried mothers'. By 1997, there were 1.5 million lone parent families in Britain, and child poverty was concentrated in workless, lone-parent households. In 1994, 47 per cent of lone mothers were living on less than £100 a week, compared to only 4 per cent of married couples. Yet there was no government help for lone mothers to get into work. Job Centres helped the 'unemployed' with advice, with searching for a job and training as well as benefits, but lone parents were not classed as unemployed, so they couldn't set foot in a Job Centre; they were regarded as not 'available for work' until their youngest child turned sixteen. If a lone mother had more than one child, it might be twenty years before they would be called into the Job Centre and, after so long not working, it was usually impossible for them to find work. So while their benefit may have changed from Income Support to Job Seeker's Allowance, they continued to live on benefits.

In Collyer Place, in my constituency, the Job Centre was next door to the social security office. The men went into the Job Centre to register as unemployed, get help to find a job and, if not, to pick up their unemployment benefit. The women went into the social security office to register for their benefit. And the system was divisive, contributing to a rift between mothers who were married and those who weren't. Married women couldn't claim benefits if they wanted to stay at home until their youngest child was sixteen, and many married mothers who had to work for financial reasons resented the fact that, if they had been lone mothers, they would have been entitled to benefits, enabling them to stay at home. If a lone mother did find a job and then it didn't work out after a short period, for whatever reason, she would have to reapply for benefits. The money could take many weeks to come through, leaving her and her children with nothing to live on in the interim. Most lone mothers didn't dare risk the security of a regular benefit payment for the insecurity of a new job. I felt we had to take the risk out of going back to work.

However, the biggest problem was lack of childcare, which is why Labour developed the first ever policy of a National Childcare Strategy. Instead of providing nursery places only for the children of 'problem' families, Labour wanted there to be affordable, accessible, quality childcare for every child whose parent wanted it. This was one of the first demands formulated by the women's movement.

Yvette Cooper, now Gordon's special adviser, helped him to develop the policy of the New Deal for the young unemployed and for the long-term unemployed, and I developed the policy of the New Deal for Lone Parents. Yvette had previously been my special adviser until she, like Ed Miliband, was lured away by Gordon. She went on to become MP for Pontefract and Castleford and a major force for women in Labour and in Parliament.

With polls showing that 90 per cent of lone mothers wanted to work, our pledge was to give them a 'hand up not a handout', but this was resisted by those on the traditional right of politics who still thought a mother's place, whether married or unmarried, was in the home. It was also resisted by the traditional left, who wanted to defend the right of a lone mother to stay at home on benefit until her youngest reached the age of sixteen. Even our proposal just to invite lone mothers with children over twelve to an interview at the Job Centre to discuss a voluntary return to work met with fierce resistance and was characterized as an 'attack' on motherhood.

The New Deal for Lone Parents consisted of four elements: childcare for working mothers; the right to ask for flexible working hours; advice and support in looking for work from lone parent advisers at the Job Centre; and tax credits to top up their income so that, even if they were working part-time, they'd be better off in work than on benefits, and changes to the benefit system so that when a lone mother got a job, she would continue to receive benefits until she got her first pay cheque and, if she lost the job, her benefits would recommence straight away.

With the polls predicting that the Tories would lose the next election, Tony, in addition to planning our election campaign, was preparing for the business of government. With no experience of being in power since 1979, we needed to be able to cope with being catapulted into the highest offices in the land. Tony devoted a great deal of attention to this, not just in terms of himself as future prime minister but also in terms of how things were going to work for the machinery of government: all the different departments, his Cabinet, the ministers and the special advisers. I wasn't involved in these discussions and, superstitiously, I felt that the more we planned for success in the next General Election, seeing it as a certainty, the less likely it was to happen. But I must have been the only person in the country who still harboured the slightest fear that Labour could lose as, by this point, it was an inevitability that we were going to get in.

Early in 1997, Tony's office arranged a day's training at Templeton College, Oxford, for all his Shadow ministers. Aside from Jack Cunningham and Michael Meacher, who I didn't feel could be role models for me, I didn't know any former ministers or any current civil servants. And I certainly wouldn't be talking to any current Tory ministers about the do's and don'ts of government or about anything at all. I knew I was going to be doing it differently, I just hadn't worked out how. At Templeton, former Labour ministers who'd been in government nearly two decades earlier were brought out of retirement to speak to us. They seemed like creatures from a different planet. These were the Labour MPs who had taken the party into Opposition, and we were the ones who were going to bring the party back into government.

The former ministers talked about what sounded to me like irrelevant, ancient history and the academics spoke as if they'd studied politics but never been part of it. Former civil servants spoke in jargon about a world which seemed so alien I couldn't take it in. One of the former civil servants struggled as he tried to explain to us the difference between a minister's relationship with his private office and his relationship with his department. As we looked blankly at him, he tried again. It's like this, he said, 'When you have an affair, the civil servants in your private office will have to know, but you can rely on them to keep it secret from the civil servants in the rest of your department.' It just underlined to me that, whatever they were expecting a Secretary of State to be, it wasn't me. I left the day's training none the wiser. I regret not realizing at the time how much I could have learned from the people there.

If I could only have seen past the differences between me and them, I might have gained some important insights which might have helped me when I came, sorely lacking, into government. My focus remained on getting us into government rather than on what I'd do when I got there. When you move from the Opposition front bench into ministerial office, you move into a different world. I, for example, would go from leading a team of four to heading up a department that employed 93,000 and had an annual budget of over £80 billion. Relationships change beyond recognition. Instead of colleagues working together, we would now face each other as the heads of different, and sometimes conflicting, government departments. Instead of being a team, we'd be a rigid hierarchy with the prime minister at the top. I understand now that I should have started getting my head out of Opposition mode and into government mode well in advance. My failure to do so meant I was woefully unprepared when we came into government.

At this crucial point, in the run-up to getting into government, my efforts to protect my children's privacy met with spectacular failure. Many years earlier, when my eldest started primary school, I'd made sure they were never in any public photographs and, though I talked endlessly about my personal quest to balance my parental responsibilities with my work, I didn't talk about my children as individuals. I'd refused to join the front-bench education team in 1987 precisely to avoid the personal and political spheres overlapping. But, in 1996, our choice of a grammar school for our second son, rather than any of the local schools, made headline news. His closest friends from primary school were going to go there but, despite the fact that it was a state school, not a private, fee-paying one, the pupils were selected on the basis of an entrance exam. Labour's policy on grammar schools was that we were against selection and that we were not going to open any new grammar schools. We weren't going to close existing ones, but the parents of children at them could hold a ballot to choose to change an individual school into a comprehensive. Our choice of school for our son caused controversy in the party and put my family in the front line of politics, where no politician's family would want to be. It caused a storm in the newspapers, which predicted that it would finish me off politically, starting with being knocked off the NEC in the next elections, in September 1996. Luckily, whatever the Labour party thought about my choice, members voted for me to remain on the NEC and I was re-elected. But it was a reminder that, as we neared government, we were in the spotlight as never before.

In April 1997, the General Election campaign got under way. We started receiving reports from our candidates in the Tory marginals that they were certain they were going to win – and comfortably. Our candidates in constituencies where we had thought we'd have no chance began to report that they, too, were heading for victory. And so it happened, on 1 May 1997. It is hard to overstate the euphoria of winning that election. After having been the losers for so long, at last we were the winners. No longer confined to protesting about life for our constituents becoming harder, we were going to be able to do something about it.

The public wanted a Labour government. It was time to set about putting our principles into action. A beautiful dawn broke on the South Bank, where thousands of party members and supporters had been all night as Labour's victory unfolded. As the final results came in, it was a perfect cue for Tony to announce, 'A new day has dawned, has it not?' Many of the Shadow Cabinet were there, and it was surreal to hear my name being chanted as I walked through the crowds. It would have been easy to lose our heads, but Tony was adamant that we shouldn't be too triumphant. The very scale of our win meant that we had to be magnanimous, or we'd be condemned for being arrogant. So we had to repress our natural instincts and be gracious instead. I was ecstatic not just that we had won with a landslide but that, thanks to the huge swings to Labour in the marginal constituencies where we had all-women shortlists, the PLP and British politics were to be transformed by the election of 101 Labour women MPs.

These were women from all parts of the country, of all ages, from all walks of life. With Labour making gains across the nation, every region had a new cadre of Labour women MPs. In the south-west, we had not only Candy Atherton in Cornwall but Tess Kingham in Gloucester and Diana Organ, a former Jaeger executive, in the Forest of Dean. The south-east, for so long a no-go area for Labour, elected Laura Moffatt, a nurse working in Crawley Hospital, and Milton Keynes elected Phyllis Starkey, a local government leader. Among the Welsh contingent was my feminist friend Julie Morgan. Barbara Follett was elected in Stevenage, Patricia Hewitt in Leicester. These new Labour women MPs weren't just a breath of fresh air, they were the wind of change. Just by their very presence they embodied the notion that politics, and our government, was now going to represent women as well as men. Their presence changed the other parties, too. Faced with a government made up of both men and women, the overwhelmingly male Tory line-up looked old-fashioned, and they began to look for more women to put up in the next election.

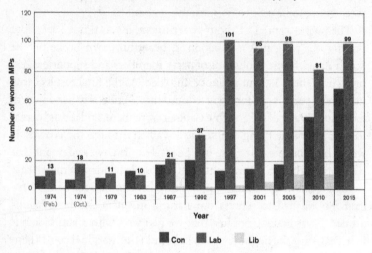

Women Members of Parliament 1974–2015 by party

The arrival of 101 Labour women in Parliament made a key difference, right from the outset, to our ability to help drive through progress for women on childcare, maternity rights and equal pay. And, in some instances, the new Labour women MPs stopped the government from doing things which would make things worse for women. When the Treasury suggested paying child tax credits to the man of the family rather than to the woman, it was stopped by an alliance of women MPs led by the new MP for Rochdale and PLP Women's Committee Chair Lorna Fitzsimons and Yvette Cooper, now MP for Pontefract and Castleford.

The arrival of all these women in Parliament changed not just the face of Parliament but also the political agenda. We were still outnumbered by men by over three to one in the PLP but now there were enough of us to make a difference; we formed a 'critical mass'. From having been one of only eleven Labour women MPs in 1982, I was now one of over a hundred. Women in the country saw us proudly thronging the government benches, some colour now among the grey suits. And with the new Labour women, issues which had hitherto always struggled even to be seen as political were now aired in Parliament. There were now so many more women MPs who could be counted on to give vigorous support to Labour's plans for childcare and maternity rights and to tackle domestic violence, it transformed the political dynamic in the PLP. It's never just a question of the strength of your argument, it's about how much support you have for it, too. And I knew all these women and had become good friends with them when I'd joined them in their campaigns for their marginal seats. Suddenly, instead of being one in a beleaguered handful of women, there were, everywhere I looked, women with the same political agenda as me.

I wanted to have a photo taken of all the new Labour women MPs. Women in the country would, we knew, be delighted to see us all together. We told Number Ten but, to our dismay, found that they had automatically assumed Tony would be in it. Our intention had been to take a photograph of powerful women in Parliament. Tony's presence would turn it into a photograph of a powerful man surrounded by a large group of women – the very opposite of what we intended. However, it isn't the done thing to tell the new, hugely popular prime minister, that he's not wanted, and especially when his popularity had contributed to so many of these women winning highly marginal seats. I ventured to Number Ten the no doubt unwelcome suggestion that it should be a women-only photo-call, but the nuance was lost on them.

There were too many of us to be photographed in any room in Parliament so we all lined up on the steps of Church House, and into the front of the gathering strode Tony. The picture hit the front pages of all the papers. But, as I'd feared, instead of a powerful picture of female solidarity, it was a photograph of a hundred-plus women gathered adoringly around one man. I was reminded of the phrase from the musical *The King and I* – 'a flock of sheep and you're the only ram'. This was the cue for the press, disparagingly, to label us 'Blair's Babes'. But the massive media coverage meant that the photo was seen by women all over the country. Deborah Mattinson reported back from focus groups that women loved it; they felt that women MPs had finally arrived in Westminster in significant numbers and that we were going to speak up for them and improve their lives.

Though the arrival of 101 Labour women in Parliament was a historic breakthrough, it was only the beginning. Because most of them were newly elected, it took time for them to settle into Parliament, to get up to speed and into the junior and then the senior ranks of government. The senior members of the government in 1997 were still men. But at least the women were there in Parliament and starting to gain the experience which could see them progress up the ladder. Women from that intake, many from all-women shortlists, later went on to play a major role in government. Estelle Morris became Education Secretary, Jacqui Smith was the first ever woman to be Home Secretary and Yvette Cooper became Secretary of State for Social Security.

Their presence represented a sea change for women, who expressed their excitement about this to us wherever we went, from political meetings to supermarket checkouts. There was a sense of euphoria among women about our breakthrough into Parliament. But the overwhelmingly male political reporters took a different view. While lauding the new government, they characterized the new women MPs as substandard, nothing more than mindless groupies of the Prime Minister who'd got in only because there had been discrimination against men candidates. While the government as a whole enjoyed a honeymoon, the new women MPs were, from the outset, embattled.

The day after the election, Tony was planning his new Cabinet, and I went home, with one ear out for the expected phone call from Number Ten. I presumed he'd told the 'big beasts' of the Shadow Cabinet – Gordon, Robin Cook, Jack Straw and David Blunkett – what job he would give them, but he'd said nothing to me before the election and I hadn't asked. The call duly came and I was sum-moned to Number Ten.

I walked along Downing Street in the sunshine with Liz, past the waiting press photographers. I'd only ever been to Downing Street before to deliver protest letters and petitions. It was so excit-ing to go over the threshold and into Number Ten, a moment to remember and savour. I was ushered into the Cabinet Room, in which Tony was sitting at the huge table. Brushing aside my con-gratulations to him on winning the election for us, he said, 'It's Social Security,' and looked down at his papers. He didn't seem very happy about this appointment, and in his memoirs, *A Journey*, published in 2010, he writes that he had wanted Frank Field to be the Secretary of State for Social Security but Gordon had blocked it, insisting that it should be me. Presumably, Gordon had been concerned that Frank would have plans which would involve big, upfront spending, when our manifesto committed us to two years of sticking to the Tories' projected budget spend. 'I've asked Frank Field to lead on welfare reform,' Tony added, 'and I want you to work with him on it.' I promised I would, though noth-ing Frank had been arguing for had been in our manifesto. The welfare agenda I had been working on was all about helping the poorest pensioners and helping get people off benefits by getting them into work – the New Deals. Rights and responsibilities were to go hand in hand. Our mantras were 'The best form of welfare is work,' 'A hand up not a handout' and 'Work for those who can, security for those who can't.' The depiction of this, which I had been deeply involved in shaping as somehow being not welfare reform, and the struggle to meet the expectation that there was some new, much higher-level programme of welfare reform in the Department of Social Security (DSS) which Frank would promul-gate was to be one of the things that blighted my period as Secretary of State.

I was an experienced constituency MP and had been on the front bench for thirteen years. I was a tried and tested election cam-paigner. I had played a key role in getting women to view Labour as their party. I'd helped transform the place of women in the party. I'd helped Labour reach out beyond our northern heartlands into the south. I had formulated policy and campaigned successfully to get it adopted. But the fact remained that I was wholly unprepared for being a Cabinet minister. I knew everything there was to know about Opposition but nothing that I needed to know about government. I didn't realize at the beginning that, although when you're in Opposition, you could be 'all in it together', once in government, colleagues default to departmental defensiveness.

Having previously had two members of staff in my constituency office and two political advisers, I hadn't a clue how to lead a department of 93,000 people. I felt disorientated, as not only my working relationships but all my day-to-day arrangements had changed. Instead of driving myself into the office, listening to the radio and thinking things over for the day ahead, my driver would be sitting in the government car outside my home waiting for me. I went from my cosy office in Millbank to one that was half the size of a tennis court, with a well-stocked drinks cabinet. I no longer simply picked up the phone to make a call; my private office dialled the number and put me on the line, then listened in and took notes. With the change in my relationships with my colleagues and the complete absence of any 'headspace' in which to think about things uninterrupted, I lost my bearings. Others, like Gordon, Jack Straw, David Blunkett and Alistair Darling, seemed to move effortlessly from Opposition to government. But I didn't, only finding out the hard way.

I was delighted when, the day after my appointment as Secretary of State for Social Security, I was made Labour's first Minister for Women and Equality. Under the Tories it had been a junior front-bench role. But we'd argued in Opposition that the Minister for Women must have the strength of being in a Cabinet role. I hadn't been expecting to be offered it, as this role had been done in Opposition by Janet Anderson and she had been highly effective, among other things having run a campaign which ultimately led to stalking being made a criminal offence. But after the General Election, she was appointed to our Whips' Office and, as such, she wasn't in the Cabinet.

While I was extremely pleased to take up a post so close to my heart, I felt resistance from my department. My top team of civil servants in the DSS saw my additional role in Equality as unimportant and as a distraction from my departmental responsibilities. They thought it was going to be hard enough to lead the DSS, the biggest-spending department in government, through the two-year period we'd promised to implement the Tories' spending cuts. They felt that the DSS already had enough problems with other departments, including the Home Office, Communities and Local Government, Health and the Treasury, without opening up whole new areas of potential conflict between Equality and other departments.

But I was never going to let the Equality role be swept under the carpet and so I had to expend effort and energy arguing with the DSS about the fact that I needed my time and their help to be able to perform it effectively. Because it was hard to combine with the huge responsibilities of the DSS, I really needed more support for Equality, not less. The less they did on it, the more I had to do. And the reality is that to solve many of the problems the DSS was grappling with – child poverty, pensioner poverty, joblessness – an understanding of women's lives was required, so really, my role in Equality should have been seen as contributing to the work of the DSS.

I also needed a junior minister to work with me on it. I couldn't expect one of my DSS team to do it and, anyway, the Commons junior ministers Tony had appointed were men. That meant a struggle with Number Ten, because, for the twenty-five or so departments, there is an overall limit of ninety-five on the number of ministers and, no doubt, many of the other Cabinet ministers were pleading for additional support. Eventually, I won agreement to have a Minister for Women. My immediate choice was Joan Ruddock. She was a feminist, hugely able and had been overlooked in the ministerial appointments, despite having been a leading light on our front bench in opposition. But even after a lot of wrangling, I managed to get Joan only on the basis that she would not be paid as a minister. It was mortifying that the Minister for Women was not going to receive a ministerial salary – and of course, it wasn't just about the money for its own sake, it was simply no way to set an example on equality. But an unpaid minister was the only offer on the table, so I took it, grateful for Joan's forbearance in brushing over the embarrassment of being in a role where she had to fight for equal pay for women at a time when her own role was not deemed worthy of being paid at all.

Joan and I then had to work hard to get a proper team to staff her private office and to move the Women and Equality team of civil servants over from the Cabinet Office, where it had been. I pressed for a special adviser for our Equality brief and appointed Anna Coote. After all her years in the women's movement, Anna immediately set out our priorities as childcare, tackling domestic violence and increasing women's representation. It was thrilling to see the objectives we had shaped in the NCCL and toiled for in opposition suddenly appear in writing in a document under a government logo.

Though we quickly gained backing for these as our priorities, it was difficult to deliver on them because all the other government departments were also busy with their own new priorities and didn't want us interfering in their work. The Home Office thought domestic violence was their responsibility, and they didn't want us butting in on their territory. The Department of Education had the lead on children, and neither David Blunkett, the new Secretary of State, nor his civil servants thought childcare was any of our business. For them, it was purely about a child's education and wellbeing and nothing at all to do with women wanting to go out to work.

Our childcare manifesto commitment had been about helping the hundreds of thousands of mothers who wanted to work, like those I'd heard from in my constituency. In opposition, I'd pushed our commitment to childcare as part of changing our policies to reflect women's lives, and it had been accepted by the party on that basis. David hadn't been particularly involved in that policy development but was now responsible for its implementation. We had an awkward meeting with him, during which he asserted that childcare was not a 'women's issue, it was a children's issue'. Of course it was a children's issue, but it was also very much a women's issue because it was women who were demanding childcare for their children. Of course, it was crucial that the childcare was high quality; a mother wanted that for her own children more than any government minister did. We'd won our commitments within the party to childcare precisely by arguing the economic and welfare case of enabling women to work. I felt that, at a time when the economy and cutting unemployment were the priorities, we'd make greater progress if it was presented in this way and not simply as an issue of child welfare. It wasn't that the government was telling women to put their children into childcare because it was intrinsically good for them. Had we argued for childcare purely from the child development point of view, it would have looked as if we believed that nurseries were better at caring for children than their mothers, which would have inflamed yet more resistance from the supporters of the 'stay-at-home mothers' and, anyway, it was not what we were saying at all. In any case, I don't think women like men politicians telling them what's good for their children. But David didn't see us as the helpful allies we wanted to be, and his department wanted us out of the way.

The minister responsible for childcare within the Department for Education was Alan Howarth MP, a Tory who'd defected to Labour in the previous Parliament. He was progressive and courteous but had never had any involvement in the movement towards childcare for all. Margaret Hodge, who had done a great deal to develop childcare in Islington when she was council leader, was a new backbencher and a friend of Alan, so I took her to our meetings to back me up. But it was an uphill struggle.

It's no easy task trying to persuade other government departments to do something they don't want to do, so it was a huge advance when Margaret Hodge was appointed to the new post of Minister for Children within the Department for Education in 2003, with responsibility for the National Childcare Strategy. She made the case for quality childcare as something that was good for children, as something that mothers wanted and as something the economy needed. She drove the expansion of childcare, which led to children's centres being opened in every community around the country.

As well as trying to persuade the Department of Education and the Home Office to move forward with our priorities for women, Joan and I also had to keep an eye out for anything that other departments were doing which might undermine our agenda. I had the policy responsibility for women but 'family policy' had been with the Home Office, reflecting the fact that, hitherto, the government perspective was focused on clamping down on 'problem families' rather than helping all families. I was deeply apprehensive when I heard that Jack Straw, the new Home Secretary, had agreed with Tony that Labour was going to set up a new 'parenting' institute.

As far as I was concerned, parents didn't need an institute set up by the Home Office to tell them what to do. Parents needed the Labour government, having listened to their concerns, to act upon them. Parents had already told us what they wanted, which was childcare, better maternity pay and leave and new rights to paternity leave and pay. When I heard that this new institute was going to be launched with the backing of the Archbishop of Canterbury and the Chief Rabbi, I was appalled: the male heads of patriarchal institutions were going to set the tone on this. I protested to Jack and to Tony that, as much as they wouldn't want a government institute to tell them how to be a parent, why would anyone else? And Labour had got into government to support women's liberation and progress, not to support patriarchy and reaction. We needed practical action, not psychobabble. Parents feel guilty enough as it is; they don't need the government to make them feel even worse. But the parenting institute was well on the way to being launched and, as Ministers for Women, we weren't strong enough to halt the plans of the new Home Secretary and new Prime Minister. The institute came into being in 1997 but, thanks in no small part to the director, Mary McLeod, it moved on from its inauspicious start and generated a stream of research underlining the need for families to have high-quality childcare, enough money coming in to live on and decent housing.

The argument ahead of the institute's launch was only one of many highlighting the challenge for the Ministers for Women as we tried to prompt or restrain juggernaut government departments to ensure that they carried out policies which would improve the lives of women, in the areas women had asked us to.

Joan and I also forged links with women in other European countries in order to network, to encourage each other and share ideas about how to make progress.

In 1998 it was the UK's turn to hold the presidency of the European Union (a role which is carried out in rotation by the different countries of the EU). During every presidency, there are summits at which ministers meet – security ministers, ministers for finance, for the environment, and so on. Now, however, countries in the EU were starting to have Equality Ministers, and Joan and I proposed a summit of all the EU Equality Ministers so we could establish this as part of every future presidency. Inevitably, this met with opposition from the civil servants. They were busy enough organizing all the meetings of ministers as it was, they couldn't see the point of our coming together as Equality Ministers and thought it would be a waste of money, but my civil servants came up with a way of winning support for the proposition.

The presidency ministerial meetings are held all around the host country, to give more than just the capital city the benefit of holding the position. Ministerial meetings were already booked for Glasgow, Manchester and Birmingham. Cities with good transport connections, either close to London or with their own airports, were always popular. We were in the middle of the peace process in

Northern Ireland and the government wanted to show it was making Belfast a priority city. But none of our ministers who had presidency meetings would agree to hold their meeting there, so we jumped in and said we would. It was also a great advantage that, at that time, the Secretary of State for Northern Ireland was Mo Mowlam. Mo had already established close relations with the women's movement in Northern Ireland and ensured that our summit enjoyed the welcome characteristic of her great warmth.

I had put on the agenda equal pay, childcare, maternity rights, domestic violence and women's representation, but the Ministers for Women and Equality, particularly those from Italy and Greece, were insistent that we talk about the scourge of the trafficking of women and children across Europe for sex. This was the first time I ever heard the term 'human trafficking'. I was horrified, and at the time had no idea that Britain would soon become a destination for this evil trade and that tackling it would become a major part of my work when I later became Solicitor General.

On women's issues, things were progressing, but my work as Secretary of State was going from bad to worse. In addition to my own unpreparedness, there were two problems in particular: the cuts to lone parent benefits and having Frank as my deputy.

Tony's decision to appoint me with Frank as my deputy turned out to be disastrous for both of us. Just fifteen months later, I was sacked and Frank resigned, never to return to government. There were fundamental problems in putting the two of us together. Frank, as a former director of the Child Poverty Action Group (CPAG), was regarded as the expert and I was not, and I don't think he ever accepted being deputy to someone who he felt knew less than he did. In addition, as a long-standing backbencher, he was not used to the idea of ministerial line management. He'd earned respect for being prepared to 'think the unthinkable' on welfare, such as transforming the system into one based on contribution rather than need, while I was seen as a predictable Blairite loyalist. Though not particularly popular in the PLP, Frank was the darling of the media commentators and respected by the welfare stakeholders. I, still bruised by my battle with the pensioners organizations, was neither.

Another difficulty was that there was a difference in the policies we wanted to pursue. His vision for a universal welfare system based on entitlement through contributions would, in my view, work against women, who, often spending fewer years at work, were able to contribute less. But I think the worst problem was something I heard from the Permanent Secretary of the department, Ann Bowtell. She came into my vast office, shutting the door behind her. When the Permanent Secretary shuts the door between you and your private office, you know it's serious. She said that, although she was reluctant to raise this with me, she had to because it was causing major problems for the department. Frank was saying to her, and others, that I was going to be Secretary of State only for a short while and then he'd be taking over, and they should therefore take their strategic direction for the department from him rather than from me. I said that this was ridiculous and that we should ignore it, but she said it was destabilizing and had to be tackled. The department needed to know whether what Frank was saying was true because they needed to know who they were working for; I should sort the matter out once and for all with Number Ten.

So, reluctantly, because I didn't like running to Tony, I insisted on a meeting and told him about the mounting problems with Frank. When I reported that Frank was telling people that Tony had said he would be Secretary of State within the year, Tony didn't deny it. He just groaned and appealed to me to press on, to try to make things work and keep things calm. It seemed clear to me that Tony had been so keen to persuade Frank to come into government that he'd allowed him to go away with the impression that being my deputy would be a stepping stone to becoming Secretary of State. I should have told Tony that, as this was a problem of his making, he should solve it. But ever ready to help solve rather than cause problems, I left having agreed to do what I could to make the situation work. But nothing could do that.

In the meantime, we got on with implementing the New Deal for Lone Parents. It had turned out to be controversial even to ask lone mothers if they wanted help with finding a job, so I wanted to hear feedback about the New Deal from the lone parent advisers themselves rather than wait for written reports from my civil servants. They were the ones on the front line and they would know what the lone parents were saying when they were invited into the Job Centre, and whether they welcomed the contact or resented it. Their reports were wholly positive. Most lone mothers were keen to go into the Job Centres and, as the programme developed, some who'd been helped by lone parent advisers became advisers themselves, which meant the programme became ever more attuned to the needs of those it was helping. I was so proud of the advisers; they were such committed pioneers and were breaking new ground. The lone mothers who found jobs through the New Deal were evangelical about it, saying it had changed their lives and, even more importantly for them, those of their children.

I wanted to do everything we could to prevent the New Deal for Lone Parents looking and feeling like what people usually expected in their dealings with the DSS. Many of my constituents told me that when they saw a buff-coloured window envelope from the department their heart sank and they often couldn't bring themselves to open it. So I commissioned an advertising agency to give our communications a completely new look. They proposed that instead of such envelopes we used lilac ones. Many of the civil servants thought this was flaky, but it was all part of our taking a completely new approach, and it worked: there was never any shortage of lone parents in the Job Centre seeking advice.

However, despite the progress that we were making on the ground, the hostility of those on the right of politics to our promotion of work for mothers and that of those on the left of politics to our challenge to a life on benefits ensured that the New Deal for Lone Parents was in for a rough ride.

We'd got into government with a manifesto commitment to spend no more than the Tories had planned within each department for the first two years, and they, of course, had planned to make cuts in the DSS. There was a general, albeit grudging, acceptance in the party of this overall commitment, as people recognized that it had been necessary to reassure the voters. But it was a different matter when it came to putting it into practice in my department. All the other Secretaries of State who made cuts in their departments in order to stay below the spending ceiling set by the Tories had some room for manoeuvre, perhaps deferring projects or freezing vacancies. They didn't need to come to the House of Commons and fight for support for new legislation to do these things, but I did, because the spending in my department was the direct payment of benefits to individuals, and these were laid down by law. Benefit entitlements could only be changed by a vote in Parliament. I was the only Cabinet member who would have to spell out and push through Parliament the cuts the Tories had specified and which we'd agreed to follow through. If we didn't want to cut the benefits of those unable to work because they were in retirement or disabled, keeping our promise would mean cutting the benefit for new claims by lone parents by about £6 per week. It caused uproar in the Labour party and, even though we intended to reinstate and increase the benefit levels for lone parents in subsequent years – and did so – I was pilloried. It was not as if lone parents on benefits were well off, far from it. There was no argument in favour of it; it was only that we'd promised to stick to the Tory spending cuts. I hated being put in a position in which I felt desperately uncomfortable. But Gordon was adamant I had to go ahead with it, as was the Chief Secretary to the Treasury, Alistair Darling, although he did subsequently, after he was promoted into my job when I was sacked, observe to me that it was a mistake to go ahead with the cuts.

The opposition to the cuts built up and I went to see Gordon to spell out the problems. But he said it was a manifesto commitment and that it would have to be carried out. If we didn't, it would send a signal that we weren't going to be financially prudent in the way we'd promised, it would cause instability in the money markets, there would be a loss of confidence, the government would fall, and I would be responsible for bringing down the first Labour government for eighteen years. After Labour had struggled in opposition since 1979, largely under a cloud of our perceived economic incompetence, it seemed impossible to countenance doing something which would plunge us into economic chaos. The Tories were vanquished and we'd won by a landslide, but I'd clearly not adjusted to this being the new reality. Our government still felt fragile to me. I couldn't do anything to threaten it. And it was certain that our Tory opponents and the right-wing elements of the press were waiting to pounce on any breach of our foremost manifesto promise. Gordon believed that, as changing the benefits for new claimants was a change in regulations, a shorter parliamentary procedure than amending an Act of Parliament, the rebellion would be short-lived. But it wasn't fair on lone parents and the rebellion only grew.

I should have refused to make the cuts and insisted that Gordon and Alistair help me find a way out without breaking our manifesto commitment on spending. I should have taken it to the Cabinet as a whole to ensure they understood what was happening and asked them either to back me up or to help me get it changed. But Gordon didn't want me to take it to Cabinet, saying it would cause a split. I knew he was wrong to think it could all be done under the radar, and I didn't agree with it, but Gordon had been so pivotal in reshaping our economic policy to get us into government, I didn't feel able to second-guess him on what the money markets would do.

With the hostility to the lone parent benefit cuts and the instability resulting from Frank and I being yoked together in the department, the newspapers began to fill up with reports that I was to be sacked in the first reshuffle, due in 1998. I hated seeing the reports, but I didn't believe them. Tony and I had worked together through thick and thin for fifteen years. He wouldn't sack me. But the reports made it impossible for me to lead the department. If I was to be gone by the summer, there was no point in the civil servants planning anything or developing any policies, as there'd be a new Secretary of State, who, inevitably, would want to change it all. I could even sense my diary secretary hesitating to schedule appointments.

In the early summer of 1998, I took the ministers and the top team of our department's civil servants away for an overnight brainstorming and strategy session, something Secretaries of State often did. We went to the beautiful stately home of Chevening. We'd arrived the night before and started the discussion over dinner. When we came down the next morning, alongside the sumptuous breakfast laid out on the gleaming mahogany table were all the newspapers. The huge front-page headline of the *Daily Mail* was 'HARMAN TO FACE AXE'. All the ministers and civil servants saw it. I abandoned any idea of talking to the team over breakfast, rushed back to my room, rang Number Ten, protested and asked them to set the record straight at the press briefing later that morning. When they didn't, I could only conclude it was because they had been the source of the story.

The politics of my department, both internally and externally, had got badly out of control, and I should have taken a firm grip on the situation. I should have told Tony that the partnership with Frank was not workable and insisted that he reshuffle the team. I should have told Gordon that the lone parent cuts were a bridge too far, that I was refusing to do them, and I should have insisted he found the money from somewhere else. But the idea of standing up against either Tony or Gordon was anathema to me. For so many years, we'd worked so closely together; I shared their politics and admired their judgement. I felt they'd find a way through it. Little did I realize that the way they found through it was to pitch me out of government. I should have listened when I was warned that it was naive to believe that it would all be sorted out because Tony was 'my friend'. 'He's not your friend,' was the riposte, 'he's the Prime Minister, and the Prime Minister has no friends.'

Speculation about the reshuffle gathered pace, with my name always at the top of the list for the chop. It's the ministerial equivalent of being on death row. You know your days are numbered; you just don't know how long you've got. Then the press started to give a date and I took the precaution of booking a flight to France on that day to go and stay on a French mountainside with my schoolfriend Kate Wilson. If I was going to be sacked, at least I wouldn't have to watch the media reporting my downfall.

Number Ten rang the night before the reshuffle and asked me to come to meet the Prime Minister at 8 a.m. at the House of Commons. That was not a good sign. If you're going to be moved or promoted, you get to walk down Downing Street and through the front door of Number Ten. Sackings are done in the House of Commons, away from the press pack assembled in Downing Street. I went into the Prime Minister's suite of offices. The atmosphere was funereal. Tony was sitting on the sofa, grey-faced. 'I'll have to let you go,' he said. There are few occasions which are so grim there is nothing to be said, but that was certainly one of them. Tony looked even more miserable than I felt, so I thought there was no point in prolonging the agony with any political small talk. The usually gregarious Anji Hunter was uncharacteristically silent as I hurried out. I got back into my ministerial car and was driven the short distance to my department, past the bank of waiting camera crews.

Number Ten had called my private office to say that I must not leave my department until the reshuffle announcements had finished. Doing so would confirm the fact that I had been sacked to the press, and Number Ten wanted the TV news to lead with all the positive stories about new appointments. They didn't want my sacking to spoil the good-news story of the reshuffle. It felt bizarre to cooperate in such a strategy. But despite the obvious discomfort of my private office, who felt it would have been much better if I could have just got out of there and gone home, I agreed, and dutifully sat in my office, watching the TV news reporters speculating about the reshuffle, while, with the door firmly shut to the adjoining room, the staff of my private office, embarrassed, were busy preparing for the arrival of my successor, Alistair Darling. I phoned Gordon, who said he knew I'd been sacked and told me how dismayed he was. I phoned my family and then just carried on waiting, with Anna Coote and Liz Kendall sitting with me in solidarity. Margaret Hodge and Patricia Hewitt also came to sit with us. I popped upstairs to see Tessa Jowell, who was at the time a minister in the Department of Health. She was thrilled to have been appointed Minister for Women, in place of Joan Ruddock, who'd been sacked along with me. John Reid, who was then Minister of State for Transport, dropped in to commiserate. I appreciated that. Most ministers seemed to be afraid that, if they showed me any sympathy, the Prime Minister would interpret it as disloyalty. A dismissal is contagious, and most colleagues steer well clear.

For my constituents, things were looking up, so the last thing I was going to do was turn against the government when we'd only just started working on all the things we wanted to do.

My private secretary assumed that, commensurate with my thorough humiliation, I'd leave by the back door, but I didn't feel that I should hide away, going out like a convict leaving the Old Bailey in the back of a car with a blanket over their head. So I went calmly out through the front door, and stopped and spoke to the press, saying I was proud of the work I'd done over fifteen years to get Labour into government and of what I'd been able to achieve in my fifteen months in the Cabinet, and that I'd fully support the government from the back benches.

Then I went home, grabbed my suitcase and set off for Heathrow. As I sat in the departure lounge, the TV news showed film of me leaving the DSS over the strapline 'SACKED', and the other passengers threw sideways glances at me. But, later that evening, I was in France. It's hard to feel bad when you're on a French hillside with a dear and supportive friend, sitting outside on a warm evening eating a leg of lamb and drinking red wine. I knew it would be a struggle when I returned to my new role as a backbencher, but at least I could postpone it for a few days.

Awaiting me on my return from France was a letter that had been delivered to my home from Number Ten. Four days after he'd sacked me, Tony had written saying that, although he thought I might not believe it, he 'felt more emotion over [me] than anything else [he had] since becoming PM', and that he recognized only too well his own personal responsibility in the difficulties I had had in the Department of Social Security. I appreciated the fact that he'd written and that he'd trusted me in writing such a heartfelt letter to a sacked Cabinet minister. I realized then that, just because you're Prime Minister, it doesn't mean things always turn out how you want them to. But the fact that Tony had admitted that he had contributed to my 'difficulties' didn't make me any the less frustrated with my own inability to have avoided those difficulties.

My diary, usually packed with Cabinet meetings and committees, was suddenly empty. My phone, which had buzzed with constant messages from my private office, was silent. The only person who didn't cancel on me was Tessa Blackstone, a Labour peer and former Number Ten adviser to the Callaghan government, and I was grateful for that. Only a year previously, it had felt daunting to go into a department as a minister. Now it felt daunting to go into one as a sacked Cabinet minister.

Some weeks later, I was in the south London kitchen of Anna Coote, saying that I'd messed things up and let everyone down and lamenting the fact that I would be setting my children an example of failure. She said, on the contrary, that now was the chance for me to show my children the most important life lesson a parent can teach – that when you suffer a massive setback you pick yourself up and carry on. So, instead of my task being performing the role of Secretary of State, I set myself the task of doing 'defeat' well. I'd seen so many MPs from all parties become bitter and twisted after being sacked. The only people who value them is the opposing party, which is able to use their comments to attack the other side. It was no mean feat to avoid the throng of false sympathizers determined to encourage me into public or private criticism, urging me to agree that Tony was a bastard, for example. Having never been supportive of me before, they were now eager to suggest that I'd been a brilliant Secretary of State and that my sacking was unjust. But even though I felt upset and humiliated, I couldn't console myself with the belief that my sacking was everyone else's fault except mine.

Faulty though my judgement proved about my vulnerability in government, it was flawless in the decision about how I should cope with being sacked. I could still recognize that no one is interested in someone who is bitter. No one is interested in the self-interested, and especially not in the Labour party, where you are supposed to be in politics for the sake of other people, not for your own career. There were plenty of role models of how not to behave after you have been sacked, and I was going to do the opposite.

When you are sacked from a ministerial job, you don't become unemployed. You still have your role as member of Parliament representing your constituency. And I reminded myself – and Jack reminded me – that it was a great privilege to be an MP. Jack, from the outset, was convinced that I would be back in government one day. I didn't believe him, but it was comforting. I bought a Delia Smith cookbook and, having only ever cooked meals I'd seen my mother cooking, without a recipe, I cooked my way through *Delia's Complete Illustrated Cookery Course*.

I was, once again, out of synch with the Labour women I'd worked alongside. In the early years, I'd been in Parliament and they'd been on the outside. Then, when they got into Parliament, I was in the Cabinet and they were backbenchers. Then they were starting to make their way up the ministerial ladder in government but I was sacked. Margaret Hodge rang me when I was in France for those few days after I'd been sacked. She was calling to commiserate with me but she herself was celebrating being put in government, as Minister for Disabled People. I was delighted for her but envious that she was in government when I wasn't. Patricia Hewitt was appointed Treasury Minister. After all the support she'd given me when I was on the way up and she was facing adversity, I couldn't begrudge her her delight. There's a different rhythm to being a backbencher than there is to being a minister and, inevitably, some discussions between ministers can't be shared outside the ranks of government. I'd often come upon the two of them in the Division Lobby and find them deep in some discussion which I was excluded from. That was painful, but I was hugely supportive of what they were doing and got on with my work on the back benches and at local level.

I sought advice from Deborah Mattinson and Scarlett MccGwire, a feminist friend and long-standing Labour activist who works in broadcasting and communications. When Deborah established Opinion Leader Research, she'd developed a new method of polling which involved setting up a panel of people at the top of their profession – business bosses, trade union leaders, permanent secretaries in the civil service, the media and academia – and seeking their views at regular intervals on a wide range of issues. To help her in giving advice to me she added to one such survey that she was undertaking for other clients a couple of questions about what the perception of me was. The judgement of me by these 'opinion leaders' was as grim as it could be. There were two firmly entrenched views: I was hopeless and I was not a 'team player'. Deborah was completely open about it and didn't try to soften the blow. I laughed wryly when she said that, as my reputation among opinion formers was at rock bottom, the only way was up. This was to be the baseline, and we would be able to look at how their views changed in the future and so chart my progress.

Scarlett advised that, for the foreseeable future, I should turn down all press requests and have a complete media blackout. There was no point trying to justify the way I had run the Department of Social Security. I couldn't turn over a new page if I was still talking about the old story. What I should do, she said, was to get on with some good work that I could do well. It would be work that would be important for its own sake, and it might – just might – at some point in the future allow me to restore my reputation. It felt strange turning down radio and TV requests and not returning calls from newspapers (except the *South London Press*, which I kept in contact with on constituency issues). For more than two decades, I had been living in the public domain. Every week – usually, every day – I had talked to the press. The media, for their part, couldn't believe that I wasn't going to speak to them and called day and night. But Deborah and Scarlett were right: the only things the media wanted from me was to admit what a failure I'd been, or to criticize Tony for sacking me, or both. A resentful sacked Cabinet minister spilling the beans on former ministerial colleagues makes excellent copy, especially when they lash out at their successor and the Prime Minister. As I wasn't going to do that, all I could do was drop out of the picture altogether, but the worst thing to do would be to announce that to the press and thereby create a story. 'Just do it,' said Deborah. 'Don't talk about it.' She said I had nothing to lose because the media slant on me was wholly negative now but, because my media profile had been high for so long, if and when I felt in a position to re-enter the fray, they wouldn't have forgotten me. If a story is negative, the natural political instinct is to keep returning to it to try to put it right. If people have a hostile view of you, the temptation is to keep trying to change their mind. It's hard to accept but, sometimes, it is just so negative it can't be done.

After a few months, when the initial relief of being out of the media firing line had worn off, I was tempted to go back on the airwaves, but Scarlett was adamant that I shouldn't even think about it, that I shouldn't even review the decision for at least six months. After this period of time, we continued to keep away from the press, though I'd often call Scarlett suggesting some contact with them because some new and exciting press request had come in. She patiently reminded me of the reasons for our decision and was resolute that I hold firm.

The Labour government continued to enjoy its honeymoon, unemployment started to fall and the investment began to flow into our hospitals and schools. One day in 1998 I went to see Gordon in the Treasury. I'd hit upon the idea of being Chair of the Employment Select Committee. At that time, Select Committee chairs were not elected by MPs, as they are now, but appointed by the party Whips. Knowing Gordon hadn't wanted me to be sacked and that Tony felt badly about having done so, I thought it would be straightforward. But Gordon was not impressed by my request, making the obvious, but unwelcome, point that there was no vacancy. Raw from my sacking, I had been sure Gordon would arrange for me to replace former Labour Chief Whip, Bishop Auckland MP Derek Foster. But Gordon, though sympathetic to me, was, rightly, loyal to Derek. He pointed out that, just because I'd been sacked, it didn't mean that Derek Foster should be turfed out. I protested limply; what was I going to do? He asked what I cared about, which was clearly a rhetorical question as, after more than a decade and a half of working together, he knew only too well. But I went over the issues that lay close to my heart once more: women, equality, childcare, maternity leave, tackling domestic violence, and so on. He said that this, then, was what I should do. It should have been obvious to me, but my mind was still fogged in post-sacking confusion. I felt a moment of clarity and left the Treasury with a restored sense of purpose. I didn't need to struggle against the demon of bitterness because, by the time the relief of being out of the firing line wore off, I was once again hard at work.

In 1998, I got together with Ann Longfield, who ran 4Children, to set up the Childcare Commission, which I went on to chair. The commission published its report in January 2001, calling for there to be children's centres in every area. We submitted it to government and Ann Longfield worked with the Prime Minister's Strategy Unit to put its proposals into practice. She worked on the plans from autumn 2001 to summer 2002, when the first children's centres were opened.

No longer hemmed in by the boundaries of a particular government department, I was, through the commission, able to look at the whole picture, not just at childcare but also at maternity and paternity leave, time off work and flexible working – issues which, in government, were separated into a number of different departments, from the DTI, to the Education and Employment Department, the Department of Social Security and the Treasury. In government, rather than joined-up working on policies, a great

deal of energy is wasted in territorial disputes between departments and, in those day-to-day struggles, it's sometimes hard to
step back and see the bigger picture. But from the back benches,
with an expert team assembled and supported by Ann, we were
able to map out what we felt the government should be doing
across the piece.

I worked on it at a local level, too, taking over the chair of Southwark Early Years Partnership. The Early Years Partnerships (EYP)
were new bodies which the Labour government had set up in every
borough to coordinate the roll-out of childcare. Having initiated
the National Childcare Strategy in government, it was great to be
able to make it work in practice in my constituency. The Southwark EYP looked at what childcare was available and what was
still needed. Having mapped out the childcare in the borough, we
set about increasing the number of childcare places, improving the
quality of the buildings and staff qualifications and offering parents
more choice and flexibility. We generated an incredible expansion
of childcare. New children's centres were built, existing nurseries
were expanded, the hours on offer were extended and there was a
major programme to recruit and train staff. Our aim was that
childcare should be there not only for vulnerable children from
chaotic homes but also for the children of working parents in stable
households. The idea was twofold: working parents needed good
childcare and it was also good for vulnerable children to play and
learn alongside children from more stable backgrounds as well as
those who, like themselves, had problems. By 2007, I was able to tell
the local party in my annual report to them that the number of
childcare places in Southwark had risen from under five thousand
in 2001 to more than eleven thousand in 2006 and that a further
eight children's centres were to be opened in Southwark over the
following twelve months.

Gordon was committed to this agenda and his door at the Treasury continued to be as open to me as it had been when I was a
minister. In fact, if anything, our dealings became easier and more
productive. I no longer had to have those difficult conversations

with him about cutting numbers of civil servants and staying within budget. I pressed Gordon to double maternity pay and leave (which, when we came into government, was than less than £60 per week for a maximum of fourteen weeks). I also pressed him to use the new system of tax credits to help low-income working families with the cost of childcare and to send money down to council level to have children's centres built. Tax credits were important not only to top up the income of parents with young children but also to enable them to reduce the number of hours they worked while their children were young. It was always about helping parents to get childcare they could afford but it was also about helping them be able to afford to spend time with their children.

When the time came for Gordon to deliver the 1999 Budget, the House of Commons was so overcrowded that I went to sit right up in the gallery, overlooking the front bench and the Cabinet of which I was no longer part. It felt strange to be looking down on them, rather than on the front bench next to them, but I felt so pleased when our benches cheered at the announcements of more money for maternity leave, more childcare and more tax credits. It might have seemed unlikely to be celebrating when I was out of the Cabinet, but the project which was the driving aim of my life in politics, and which I had put so much into, was at last under way and gaining momentum.

I had thought that, after I was sacked, the outside world would see me completely differently than they had when I was a Cabinet minister. But my constituents' view of me hardly changed. My political demotion, which felt so massive to me, meant nothing to them. Although the official position was that my star had fallen, strangely, as far as they were concerned, nothing had changed. One day shortly after I was sacked from the Cabinet, I was doing my usual constituency activity of walking along a street with a team of local Labour members, knocking on each door and saying hello to people, when a man exclaimed how amazed he was to see me on his very own doorstep in view of 'how busy I was in the Cabinet'. I reminded him that I'd been sacked and was no longer in the Cabinet. He said, of course, he'd seen it in the papers, but 'you know what I mean'. What I think he meant was that they knew me for what I did rather than any office I held. Ultimately, people judge you by what they see you doing, not just as inhabiting a position you've been appointed to. So, even though I was no longer in the Cabinet, much remained the same. Labour was still in government, I got on with my work on women and families, my constituents still saw me as a national figure for the Labour party, I was often in the Treasury working with Gordon, and Tony invited me and Jack to lunch at Chequers.

Although there are common concerns for mothers bringing up young children, I wanted to engage with women in different parts of the country and in different sectors. I was completely familiar with the working experiences of mothers in shops, offices and public services in my own patch, but I felt it would strengthen the case for more support for parents with young children if I widened the focus to include the experience of mothers across the country. Also, this would be a way of addressing the accusation that I was just pushing childcare as a middle-class Londoner. From the back benches, I once again had the opportunity, which you lose in government, to just get out and about and put your ear to the ground elsewhere. In 2000 I went to talk to Paul Gates, the General Secretary of KFAT, at his Leicester HQ. I'd worked with him when I was formulating our policy on the national minimum wage. KFAT represented men and women working in the leather and textile factories of the East Midlands. He arranged for me to meet his executive, and I explained that I wanted to hear from their women members about their experiences of being mothers in manufacturing, and to then write a report and use it to press for policies which would help them. They agreed, and I went to six factories – R. Griggs and Co. and Loake Shoemakers in Kettering, Courtaulds Underwear Ltd in Chesterfield, Pretty Polly in Sutton-in-Ashfield, Coats Viyella in Huthwaite and Burberry in Leicester – and sat down at each one with a group of between eight and twelve women and listened to them tell me how they coped with the twin responsibilities of work and children. They poured their hearts out to me. It was nothing like the usual political or trade union meeting. They needed to earn money for their families. Their husbands were not high earners. The industry was insecure. They didn't dare give up their own job in case their husband then lost his. Some of them were lone parents. They were all working for the sake of their children but felt that working took its toll on their children, on their relationship with their husbands and on their own parents. Many of them had, because of the inadequacy of maternity pay and leave, gone back to work when their baby was only ten weeks old. Without affordable childcare and with inflexible shift patterns, they struggled through with a patchwork of arrangements which all too often left them exhausted, knocked their maternal self-esteem and undermined their marriage. And they gave heartbreaking accounts of all the tears they had shed on leaving their babies and returning to work, driven back by lack of money.

'I'm dreading fourteen weeks at £60. I haven't earned that little since I left school,' said Heather at Burberry, and Jane, of Coats Viyella, who went back to work when her son was eleven weeks old, told me, 'He cries every day when I go to work. It's not fair on him or me, or on my mum. He's still bonding at such a young age.' These women felt that going back to work so early undermined the development of their parenting skills. 'At the mother and baby club, you see how other children of the same age are doing. You exchange ideas of how to solve daily problems – but I can't now I'm back at work,' said Stacey at Courtaulds. And it also harmed the relationship between the two parents. 'We exchange the baby in the car park when he's going in to work and I'm leaving,' said Linda at Coats Viyella, describing it as 'shift parenting'. 'Shifting the baby from place to place shifted our marriage from place to place as well. It was a vicious circle,' said Deborah of Courtaulds. 'When I get in from work, he's not there. When he gets in, I'm asleep. We leave each other notes on the kitchen table,' said Joan from Coats Viyella.

One woman had arrangements which involved her looking after her sister's children one day a week, her sister looking after her child one day and her sister's husband looking after the child a third day. When her sister had a prolonged bout of flu, three people's work patterns were thrown into disarray. Another said that if she could start her shift just twenty minutes later than she did at the moment, she could drop her daughter at school before work and wouldn't need to pay a childminder. But though she, and her union, had asked the manager, he wouldn't give her even that little bit of flexibility. Yet another told me that she took her baby to the childminder on her way to work, passing, on the way, her mother's house. Every day the toddler would lean out of the pram, stretch out his arms and call, 'Nanna!' and then scream as she took him up the path to the childminder's house a few doors down. Her mother worked; she needed the money. She longed to give up her work in the local supermarket and care for her beloved grandchild, but she couldn't afford to. The childminder's fees could be claimed in tax credits, but the mother couldn't claim to pay her own mother to give up her work and care for her grandchild. That was the very care – family care – which she wanted for her child. She told me that both she and her mother resented the fact that the government would give her money to pay a childminder, with whom the child was unhappy, but not the grandmother, whom the child loved. They felt that the government had no understanding of their family life and valued the care of a child by 'a stranger' over that by a loving grandparent. Their situation was making them and the child miserable and had convinced them that the government was out of touch by dictating, through the rules on qualification for tax credits, what sort of care the child had to have. To them, it felt almost worse than if the government gave no help for childcare at all.

I wrote their experiences up in a report entitled 'Mothers in Manufacturing', in which I recommended that maternity leave should be extended to a year and maternity pay increased to make this possible, that women should have the right to go back to work part-time after maternity leave and that tax credits should be available to help pay relatives who care for the children of working mothers. In 2001 the government extended maternity leave to twenty-six weeks and increased maternity pay to £100 a week.

We implemented a 'right to request' shorter hours and flexible work but, to this day, public policy still doesn't recognize or support the role that grandparents – mostly grandmothers – play in the lives of working mothers and their children. At the outset, the argument I met when I pressed for this was that it would involve paying grandparents who were now retired. My counter-argument that we could make it conditional on the grandmother proving she had given up her work in order to look after the child fell on deaf ears. Then the argument against was made that childminders, as registered childcare professionals, were better for the child than grandparents, who could be of 'varying quality'. This incensed me. It should be for the mother to choose, not us. And anyway, I reminded them, childminders themselves were of 'varying quality'. Then someone made the case that grandparents who wanted to care for a grandchild could register as a childminder. The proposition that a grandmother should have to be authorized by government to care for her own grandchild led – justifiably – to fury. More than ten years later, when I was still unsuccessfully pushing for support for grandparents, I came up against the argument from some newer women MPs and male policy advisers that paying grandparents would entrench women's role in the home and 'let the fathers off the hook', thus reinforcing the expectation that, if not the mother, then the grandmother would care for the child. But the reality is that, even leaving aside any expectation of the different role of men and women in the family, most fathers earn more than grandmothers and therefore the grandmother giving up work or reducing her hours is often an option for them in the way it isn't for the father. Over the years, I have failed to win this argument within the Labour party in the face of these counter-arguments, none of which I have any time for.

After decades of listening to my constituents, and to women all around the country, as well as drawing on my own experience of motherhood, my view is that government policy should provide a year's maternity leave, paid at a rate which makes it affordable for mothers to stay off, give paid leave to fathers, give parents a right to flexible working and a right to work part-time, ensure high-quality free childcare in all areas, and give financial support to grandparents who provide childcare. We want and need parents to be able to work – mothers as well as fathers. But we must make sure that the parenting role is not an afterthought, consigned to be 'fitted in' around the work role. It's a cliché, but true nonetheless, that today's children are tomorrow's workers and we all have a stake in the next generation.

There's a compelling democratic argument for this, too. If it's what parents want, then the presumption should be that it is what the government does. It's not for government to dictate to parents but instead to facilitate their choices. Different families will want and should be able to do things differently. At different times a family might want to have different arrangements and, even within the same family, different children often need different sorts of care. And this is another strong argument for equal pay for men and women. Against a background of unequal pay, it is, in practice, not possible for many men to take much time off to look after the children because of the drop it would cause in the family income. Things are very different today in that, now, women have qualifications equal to those of men, the workplace has changed a lot from how it was thirty years ago and technology has moved on so much, both in and outside work, but the fundamental difficulties of reconciling work and family responsibilities remain as entrenched as ever. Despite there being much greater equality between young men and women now, things change as soon as a couple has children. And one of the main ways to tackle the problems working women face is to address the problem of women's pay being so much lower than men's.

The decisions that have such a profound effect on families' lives were, and to a large extent still are, taken by the men who run the companies. I felt that male domination at the highest levels of business was a problem not just for the women who wanted to join them at the top but had an effect throughout the organization. In 2000, from my position as a backbencher, I set out to count the number of women on every board in the FTSE Top 100 to expose the exclusion of women from the decision-making which affects women's lives at work. Alan Hayes was my parliamentary researcher at the time, a Liverpudlian and a graduate of John Moores University. One of the projects we set to work on was the FTSE Female Index.

Men-only boards send the message to women working in a company that they are not good enough to be the ones making the decisions at the top. It's sex discrimination, without a doubt. It can't be that the women in the company are just not good enough to be on the board. You'll never get the impetus to push ahead with family-friendly working arrangements from a board of men who've delegated their family responsibilities to their wives. The changes in recruitment, in training and in pay structures necessary to tackle unequal pay will never be led by such a board.

All-male boards are not diverse, and a homogeneous board suffers from 'group think': its members merely reinforce each other and do not spot potential problems. This certainly proved to be the case at the higher echelons of the financial services sector prior to the banking crisis.

To compile our FTSE Female Index Alan went through the company reports for each of the FTSE Top 100 companies, counting the number of men and women on each board. Some listed directors called, for example, Hilary or Jo, names which could be for a woman or for a man. So Alan rang them up saying that Harriet Harman would like to know whether a certain Jo was a man or a woman. This question was greeted with suspicion and annoyance, but we got the numbers and put together a league table. It showed that, in 2000, half the boards in the FTSE Top 100 were men-only. Alan's inquiries had alarmed the companies, and just before I was due to publish the index I got a call from the

Financial Times Stock Exchange Group telling me that I couldn't publish the league table under my intended title, as FTSE was a trademark and, if I used the name, they'd take me to court.

I decided to go ahead anyway. I published FTSE Female Indexes the following two years as well, and then, when their publication had become a fixture on the calendar, I handed over the responsibility for compiling the list to Susan Vinnicombe at Cranfield School of Management, who'd joined me in working on the indexes for 2001 and 2002.

When later, in 2007, I became Minister for Women and Equality, together with the Department for Business I commissioned Mervyn Davies to put together a report on women on boards and make proposals. I argued for quotas, like they have in Norway, but was told this was impossible because our Company Law framework was different. I didn't accept that this would be a show-stopper, and Mervyn took his work forward under the 2010 Tory-led coalition government. However, while the Tory government maintain that they are committed to progress, they are not prepared to intervene in any way to ensure that progress happens, so meanwhile, although more women are coming on to executive boards, this change is happening only at snail's pace. As was the case with the drive for more women MPs, unless you impose quotas, progress is unacceptably slow.

While one impetus behind the provision of more nursery care was to help lone mothers trapped with their energetic toddlers in high-rise blocks, the need for after-school care was also of particular importance for Peckham's growing African community. They came largely from West Africa, and were initially those fleeing the terror of the civil war in Sierra Leone, and then from Nigeria. The parents tended to work long hours, partly because, despite having professional qualifications, they found themselves starting at the bottom of the labour market. You will find Nigerians with degrees in accountancy driving minicabs and teachers from Sierra Leone working as cleaners or car-park attendants. Often, even on their low pay, they are providing for family members back in Africa as well as for their immediate family members here. By sending money back for living expenses, schooling and health care, my African constituents are the welfare state for many villages back in their country. As great value is placed on education and professional qualifications, many of the African parents study as well as working, either to get a new degree or professional qualification or update existing qualifications and have them recognized here. This means that many of them are not home at 3.30 p.m. when primary school finishes for the day. Often only one parent would come to the UK with the children while the other stayed behind, possibly with other children, until further arrangements could be made for them to come, too. And as most West African families are keen that their children should work hard and do well at school, studying after school is common. So with hard-working parents, no grandparents on hand and a strong commitment to education, after-school clubs, which we had strongly argued for over many years as part of the National Childcare Strategy, are essential for the African community in Peckham, as well as, of course, for many others.

The Labour government was offering funding to develop a comprehensive after-school-care service and, with the massive public investment going into extending and rebuilding primary schools, it seemed a waste of resources that children had to be off school premises after 3.30 p.m. and before 8.30 a.m., so as there was a high level of need locally and government funds were available, the Early Years Partnership in Southwark drove forward to get more after-school clubs. But many of the heads of the primary schools resisted. They felt they already had enough of a challenge teaching the children during the school day, and they didn't want the extra responsibility of running an after-school club or allowing an outside organization on to the premises to do so.

By late 2000, most children in Peckham primary schools still didn't have access to after-school clubs. And this was also the case at Oliver Goldsmith Primary School, among whose pupils was ten-year-old Damilola Taylor.

Gloria Taylor had brought her three children to Peckham while her husband Richard travelled back and forth between Peckham and Lagos prior to settling here permanently with his family. On the afternoon of 27 November Damilola left Oliver Goldsmith School and walked to Peckham Library. After a while he left to walk the short distance home.

I was in my office when, later that day, I started getting calls from people in Peckham and from the press. The reports were unclear. A teenager had been shot and killed, or a young boy was in hospital with stab wounds. While the details of the reports varied, they all came with a sense of urgency and some foreboding that something terrible had happened, and the community was bracing itself for what it was about to find out. Hearing that the crime had taken place on the North Peckham Estate, I rang Maria Williams, a tenants' activist who knew everyone in the area, and said I was on my way down to meet her. By the time I got there, twenty minutes later, Maria had found out the shocking facts. Damilola Taylor had been found dead from stab wounds in a stairwell in a semi-derelict part of the estate.

Damilola's tragic death was devastating for his parents and siblings, whom I grew to know well over the following years, and it hit the local community hard. As an MP, I wanted to show Richard and Gloria my sympathy for their terrible loss and give them any practical support they needed. They'd lost their beloved son in terrible circumstances in a country where they were still only new arrivals. I urged the local community to do everything they could to help the police investigation, and was aware that I needed to support the local community, too. Rumours were circulating that Damilola had been killed by a Jamaican criminal gang who were terrorizing the Nigerian community. With the upsurge of sympathy for Damilola's family there came the potential for the different communities in Peckham to fall out and seek revenge. Peckham was already struggling to shake off a poor reputation. A horrific crime would cast a further cloud over the neighbourhood and all the good people in it.

Richard Taylor flew in from Nigeria. There was both national and international media attention. Both he and Gloria reacted with such strength and dignity that they drew admiration not only from me and those who knew them but the wider community and the press. In their grief and anguish, they could have provoked a storm of division in the area but instead they argued for everyone to help find the killer and for all different communities in Peckham to work together to do so.

In the Queen's Speech debate following Damilola's death, I quoted Kemi, a Nigerian woman in my constituency, who summed up the feeling that Damilola's murder had engendered when she said, 'We have lost an African boy, but it could have been an English boy, it could have been a Turkish boy, it could have been a Jamaican boy. We all have lost a son.' I spoke about the grief in the local community that such a crime had taken place in it, and of the community's deep resentment at the description of the community as one riven by warfare between gangs, between those who had recently arrived from Africa and those whose families had come from the Caribbean.

As I visited the Taylors' friends and neighbours, attended church services for Damilola and had meetings with the police and the council, I took with me one of our local Labour party members who was a leading light in the Nigerian community and subsequently became our mayor: Tayo Situ. His connection with the Nigerian community in Peckham and the respect in which he was held helped me perform my sad but important role as MP after this horrific local crime.

Together with Tayo, I called on local people to cooperate with the police inquiries. In the early years of my being an MP, the relationship between the police and the local community in Peckham was bad, especially among young people. People didn't cooperate with the police either because they feared reprisals or out of downright hostility towards them. One of my earliest memories of being in Peckham is driving behind a police car under a footbridge between the Camden and North Peckham estates. There was a row of youths on the footbridge with petrol-filled bottles ready to be thrown down on to any passing police car. The police told me that they would never leave a police car unattended or they'd return to find its tyres slashed. However, the soul-searching in the Metropolitan Police precipitated by the public inquiry into their investigation of the murder of Stephen Lawrence, launched in 1997 by Jack Straw, the first Labour Home Secretary, transformed the way the police worked with black communities and had made a big difference in Peckham. The Metropolitan Police had worked hard to improve relations and, although they were still far from perfect, they did at least have a more solid base in the community when it came to investigating the killing of Damilola. When they did house-to-house inquiries, they were met with a degree of cooperation that would have been unthinkable in earlier years.

Richard and Gloria moved out of Peckham into the Eltham constituency, but I stayed closely in touch with them, particularly as the police investigation progressed. The Taylors had to endure seeing suspects arrested, then released, and go through two trials, a retrial and an appeal before Damilola's killers were finally jailed in 2006. In the years since Damilola died, the estate where he was murdered has been demolished and rebuilt, and the entire area is being regenerated. Damilola is still remembered locally with great sadness. There is a sculpture in his memory outside Oliver Goldsmith Primary School and a new centre for youth and community activities just yards from where he died called the Damilola Taylor Centre – and there is now an after-school club at Oliver Goldsmith primary.

When you become an MP, you can't foresee what will happen in your constituency but, whatever your role in your party or in government, if tragedy strikes in your constituency, that has to take priority. When you ask people to vote for you and win an election, it's as if you've made a very solemn promise that, whatever happens in your constituency, you will be there, doing what you can. As a family and a community struggles in the aftermath of a tragedy, you have to abandon your other commitments and just be there.

5.
Making the Law Work for Women

In 2000, I held a party for my fiftieth birthday in our garden at home. It was for close friends and family, and Patricia Hewitt, Margaret Hodge, Deborah Mattinson, Polly Toynbee, Anna Coote, Amanda Jordan and Scarlett MccGwire were all there. There weren't many MPs, but Gordon came, which greatly impressed my friends and family, particularly my mother, who he took time to talk to. I walked him out to his car when he was leaving and he said I was doing great work and would be back in government in due course. I couldn't see that happening, but his continued support was very encouraging.

By 2001, I had done three years hard work locally and nationally from the back benches. The press – particularly women like the *Guardian*'s Polly Toynbee and the *Observer*'s Yvonne Roberts – were supportive of my work in their reports and the tabloid press had largely given up hounding me. You're of less interest after you've been sacked because you can't be toppled. But I began to feel a sense of frustration that I would be able to do more if I had a ministerial role. Even though things were happening, on childcare and maternity rights, and so on, it was galling to have to tell male colleagues what I wanted them to do instead of doing it myself. I told Sally Morgan, Tony's political secretary, and Carey Oppenheim, a leading member of his Number Ten policy team, that I wanted to come back into government. Like many women at work, I found it hard to ask for what I wanted. It felt awkward and a bit supplicatory, but I knew I had to overcome my normal reluctance to ask for something on my own behalf. And it was not difficult to talk to Sally and Carey.

Every time there was a rumour of a reshuffle or a sacking, I hoped that I might get a call. Reshuffles came and went, but my phone didn't ring. Disappointed, but not surprised, I didn't take it personally. No one before had come back into the Cabinet after a high-profile sacking. But I knew Gordon supported my return and, as we approached the 2001 General Election, I knew there'd be a vacancy in either the Law Offices or the Ministry of Justice (then Constitutional Affairs) coming up and I thought, if I could get one of those, it would be a safe way to perform the tricky task of re-entry.

The 2001 election was the first time since 1984 that I hadn't been a key campaigner, and it felt strange to watch the national campaign on TV. I campaigned hard in my own constituency, and with my friends in theirs, and on election night I watched the results with my constituency team in a local pub, cheering every Labour candidate elected and jeering the Tories. We were jubilant to see Labour elected for a precious second term. Afterwards, I went home, hoping the phone might ring with a call from Number Ten.

The day after the election I watched the TV reports as Tony appointed his Cabinet. Then, that weekend, a call came in from the Number Ten switchboard. Tony wanted to speak to me. I was over the moon. This could only mean that, three years after sacking me, he was going to bring me back into government. When Tony came on the line I congratulated him on what an amazing achievement it was to win us the prized second term. He asked, rather apologetically, whether I would consider being Solicitor General, saying that he knew it was only an obscure and lowly post. I assured him that, whatever anyone else thought, to me it was a great job and, as a lawyer, I respected the role of the Law Officers. I said I'd be delighted.

If I'd gone straight back into the Cabinet, I'd have been bound to get a repeat of the press mauling I'd suffered before, and I couldn't face that. A Cabinet position would have involved me running a giant department, and I still didn't have the confidence to do that. Though it was not high profile, the role of Solicitor General was important nonetheless. It was the perfect way for me to take my first step back into government. I felt sure that, of all the ministerial roles that Tony handed out that day, I was the happiest recipient. It was ironic that I was, if anything, even more pleased about my appointment to the role of Solicitor General than I had been when I was appointed Secretary of State. A second chance is even more precious than the first.

I hadn't known it at the time, but the previous Solicitor General, Ross Cranston, MP for Dudley North, had been sacked to make way for my return. I called him and he told me ruefully that he'd only agreed to go quietly because Tony told him he was being 'let go' to make way for 'new blood'. When he found out it was me, the very opposite of 'new blood', he was less sanguine. Nevertheless, to his credit, he was always helpful when I called on him for advice.

The formal appointment of Solicitor General is full of tradition and ceremony. I was fitted with a wig and gown, and the 'full-bottomed' wig made of grey horsehair reached down to my shoulders. I had to go out and buy black patent shoes on which to clip the traditional buckles that were part of my outfit before appearing in front of the Lord Chief Justice and the Lord Chancellor and receiving a sealed parchment appointing me to the office and, at the same time, making me a QC. What made the occasion complete was that my mother, whose own legal career had not had the opportunity to flourish, and who I knew had suffered on my behalf, reading the abuse the press had thrown at me over the years before I was sacked from the Cabinet, joined me and Jack in the Lord Chancellor's chambers in the House of Lords for the ceremony. I'd come such a long way since the time when, as a radical lawyer twenty years earlier, the government was prosecuting me for contempt and the Law Society was trying to strike me off. Now I was in government and at the top of the legal profession. And it would be me who would have the responsibility of deciding whether to launch prosecutions for contempt of court. Having been on the other side, I exercised it with the utmost care.

After the awful time I'd had at the Department of Social Security and three years of being on the back benches, I was determined not to squander this opportunity. I'd been given a second chance – I wouldn't get a third. It was wonderful to be back as part of the team. Tony had broken with convention by appointing an Attorney General in the Lords and leaving the Commons with only the deputy Law Officer post of Solicitor General, and I was the first Law Officer who wasn't a practising barrister. So I had to win the confidence of both the House of Commons and the legal profession in my new role. This was my chance to finally banish the bad reputation I had left the DSS with and to confound my former critics by being totally competent and utterly teamly.

This was complicated by the fact that, although the Law Officers are government ministers, there is much in the role that has to be done in 'the public interest', in a non-partisan way. The Society of Labour lawyers, whom I had known well from as far back as my days in the law centre, were supportive of my appointment. But the legal fraternity generally were more guarded. They and the Tories had known me only as a rampantly partisan Labour campaigner, so I had to go out of my way to reassure them that I knew where the boundaries were and that I would not overstep them.

I asked to see all the former Law Officers – Tory as well as Labour – to hear their reflections on the role and learn from their advice. They all had a commitment to the office and so were more than willing to come and advise me. I instituted a 'former Law Officers' lunch', inviting former Labour Attorneys Peter Archer and John Morris, Labour former Solicitor General Ross Cranston and Tory former Secretary of State for Northern Ireland and Attorney General Patrick Mayhew. I learnt a lot from them but, even more importantly for me, I was sending the message through them to the legal fraternity that they could trust me in the significant and constitutionally delicate role of Law Officer.

I also had a huge, elegant office with floor-to-ceiling windows in a Georgian building overlooking Buckingham Palace. It was early summer when I was appointed, and I felt how fortunate I was as I walked from my new office through the blossoms of St James's Park down to the House of Commons. Few people knew what the Solicitor General did and even most MPs had never heard of the position. But I knew what I was going to do with it.

As Deputy to the Attorney, the Solicitor General, as well as giving advice to other government ministers, is responsible for the Crown Prosecution Service (CPS). The women's movement had long campaigned for domestic violence to be treated seriously in the criminal justice system and, in my new role, I was now perfectly placed to make that happen.

Over the decades, progress on tackling domestic violence and sexual offences had been evolving, but only very slowly, and there was still such a long way to go. The problem of domestic violence being perceived as a private matter, or the woman's fault, or something that nothing could or should be done about remained entrenched. This contributed to a situation where most victims didn't report incidents of domestic violence. If they did, few cases got as far as court, and even fewer as far as a verdict, and where the perpetrator was found guilty he usually got off with a lenient sentence. And, worst of all, in domestic homicide cases, the woman victim was usually blamed by the man, and sometimes by the judge, for provoking him to kill her.

Since the seventies, there had been an active movement in support of tackling domestic violence. And in every police force in the country, at all levels of seniority, there were officers striving within their organization to change the culture of 'it's only a domestic' and to protect women. There were some inspiring, experienced prosecutors committed to issues of domestic violence. There were women running refuges and working in family law, and women working in local councils and in voluntary groups. But hitherto, they had never had anyone in government to bring it all together and single-mindedly take their cause forward. But now I'd been appointed and was there on the inside, I could make changes throughout the system, support victims, deter perpetrators and challenge embedded attitudes.

I established a specialist team of domestic violence prosecutors in the CPS so that the preparation of every case would be carried out by a prosecutor who was specially trained and fully committed and understood how vulnerable victims feel as the trial draws near. Unlike much of the rest of the barrister profession, there were many highly qualified women in the Crown Prosecution Service. A government service, by that time it offered part-time working and proper maternity leave, benefits which women did not get as a private barrister. I went to CPS offices around the country and was inspired and encouraged to meet so many dedicated women lawyers, many of whom were from minority ethnic backgrounds and were strongly committed to improving the prosecution of domestic violence.

However, the criminal justice system still badly let down women suffering domestic violence. Women who did report domestic violence would find it took months before their case got to court, during which time the perpetrator, and often his family, would cajole, threaten and pressurize the victim to drop the case. Unsurprisingly, often, she would retract her statement. We speeded up the process so the delay between court hearings did not erode the woman's ability to give evidence.

If the case got to court, the victim would usually meet the prosecuting barrister for the first time only on the day of the trial. Victims often found that the barrister showed no empathy towards them. We changed things so that the CPS would only select barristers from a list of those who'd been specially trained.

The trial was horribly intimidating for the victim. She would have to give evidence with her attacker glaring threateningly at her from the dock and his relatives menacing her from the public gallery. We had the rules changed so that a woman could give her evidence in court from behind a screen. The judge, jury and the barristers would be able to see her, but she'd be out of sight of the defendant and the public. We won agreement that some of the woman's evidence could be given on video, so she'd have to be in the witness box only for the cross-examination. We also secured improvements in the training of judges, so that they would understand how incredibly hard it was for a woman to have the courage to report a violent husband.

In addition to all this, we also worked with children's charities to highlight that it's never just the woman who suffers when there is domestic violence taking place in a family. It always affects the children, too. The assumption that the children didn't know that their mother was being assaulted was almost invariably wrong. Even when the perpetrator wasn't beating their mother, the children would live in fear of his violence. And often the children would themselves be caught in the crossfire, being hit or sometimes even killed.

If the case did make it through to a conviction, too often the sentence would be a 'slap on the wrist' – a suspended sentence or community service – and the victim would walk out of the court with him emboldened, only to be jostled and jeered at by him and his relatives. If she wanted to get an injunction to stop the man harassing her, she would have to apply for Legal Aid, go to another court and start proceedings for an injunction. The criminal court could punish him, but it didn't protect her. I had new court rules introduced which allowed the criminal courts to protect the victim as well as punishing the perpetrator, and by appealing sentences to the Court of Appeal, and through the Sentencing Guidelines Council, I had the sentences handed out for domestic violence increased. The court should also, we argued, always take into account the damage to the children in the family when sentencing in cases of domestic violence.

I challenged the notion that we had to be 'culturally sensitive' about domestic violence, that we shouldn't interfere if it was 'part of the culture', say, in an Asian or an African household, for a man to beat his wife. I worked with Southall Black Sisters to highlight how much more difficult it was for an Asian woman to report violence in the home if she was newly arrived in this country, didn't speak English or go out to work, had no friends and was living with her husband's family. I worked with men's groups such as the men's subcommittee of the South London African Women's

Organization, which brought men together to challenge the attitude that you weren't a proper man if you didn't keep your wife in order by beating her.

The problem with domestic violence is the degree of impunity for the man. He hits the woman but promises he won't do it again. She doesn't report it because she hopes he won't or because she fears that, if she does, he'll only hit her harder next time. I worked to make it clear that domestic violence never happens just once. It is invariably a 'repeat offence' and always escalates, which is why it's imperative to tackle it from the outset, before the woman ends up enduring life-changing injuries or being killed.

One of the issues which was controversial within the women's movement right from the seventies was who should make the decisions in domestic violence cases, particularly the decision on whether to continue or drop the case. Many in the movement argued that it should be the victim's choice. They argued that domestic violence disempowered the victim and it disempowered her still further if decisions in the case were taken by prosecutors rather than by her. Some of us, including me, believed that if it was her decision whether to continue or drop the case it made her even more vulnerable. And tackling the crime was important not just for her but also because it might protect the woman who could otherwise become the perpetrator's next victim, and send out the message that domestic violence was not a private matter between a husband and wife but a public safety issue. When someone is assaulted in the street, the police don't ask the victim's permission to prosecute. They know they have to prosecute in order to protect others.

Some in the radical wing of the anti-domestic-violence movement argued that because the police, prosecutors and judges so often let them down, it was wrong to urge women to report domestic violence. But I believed that this attitude merely served to guarantee impunity for the perpetrator, make the victim likely to suffer more in the long run and sent out a terrible message that domestic violence could not be stopped. I was emphatically pro-prosecution. Giving up on the criminal justice system would get us nowhere. What we had to do was change it.

Working with the CPS and the Home Office, we brought in a new role of Independent Domestic Violence Advocates (IDVA). These were people, mostly women, trained to support women through a prosecution, to keep her informed of progress, advise her about safety, tell her what would happen in court and sit with her through the trial. In arguing our case for funds for these IDVAs with the Department of Public Prosecutions (DPP), the Treasury, the Home Office and the Court Service, we produced a calculation that their cost to the public purse was more than outweighed by the cost of failed prosecutions or the cost of social service support for children damaged by domestic violence.

In addition, I wanted a proper review by all the agencies whenever a woman was killed in a domestic homicide. It had long been the case that if a child who is on the books of the social services dies, there is, as well as an inquest, what is called a Part 8 Review. All the agencies – the school, social services, the local hospital, police – sit down together, go through their records and work out whether it could have been foreseen so they can learn lessons from what went wrong and alter the way they work in the future.

In autumn 2001, the year I became Solicitor General, I initiated the first CPS-led multi-agency domestic-violence review, into the murder of a woman and two of her four children. This was the case of Jill Bluestone. In their home in Dartford, her husband, Karl, a police officer in his thirties, bludgeoned her to death with a hammer, killed their two younger children and then hanged himself. He'd been arrested twice after previous attacks on Jill but had never been charged or even disciplined. There had been so many warning signs of his escalating violence, but they were never acted upon. Because children had been killed, there was to be a Part 8 Review, but I asked the CPS to review their case files, too, and to join in this multi-agency review, to ensure that previously unheeded lessons were learned. They did, and it was led by a senior prosecutor, a CPS special casework lawyer.

By June the next year, two further domestic homicide reviews had been completed and two more were under way. I discovered that the Metropolitan Police were thinking along the same lines, so we arranged that London domestic homicide reviews would be led by them and, outside of London, the CPS would lead on multi-agency reviews. The idea was not only that the local agencies could learn lessons by sitting down together and reviewing what had happened in a non-blaming way, but also that we, in government, could identify any changes in procedures and the law which might be necessary.

These domestic homicide reviews were all being done by the CPS and the police at my request, but to ensure it continued in the future after I stopped being Solicitor General, I wanted to put it into law that there had to be a review after every domestic homicide, in the same way that Part 8 Reviews on a child's death are a legal obligation. I had begun, by this time, to argue for a new bill for all the changes I wanted to see on domestic violence, and added domestic homicide reviews to the list of measures I wanted in a new Domestic Violence Crime and Victims Bill.

I visited, learned from and highlighted the ground-breaking work which was going on all around the country at a local level. Julie Morgan, MP for Cardiff North, invited me to meet Cardiff Women's Safety, run by the remarkable Jan Pickles, which provides support for women who are experiencing domestic violence. They also led the argument about how to improve the justice system for women. Jan pointed out that a family suffering domestic violence had to go to two different courts. The County Court dealt with child custody, access and injunctions, and then the same set of facts had to be produced in evidence all over again, quite separately, in the criminal court, which would decide the verdict on any criminal charges and the sentence. Cardiff Women's Safety and the local police and prosecutors were exasperated at how difficult this made things. They told me about one case where the magistrates' court found the accused guilty of assault and gave him a non-custodial sentence. As his victim walked out of court, he chased after her and threatened her for giving evidence against him. The magistrates' court had sentenced him, but it had no powers to protect her. Cardiff Women's Safety rushed her into the County Court and applied for an emergency injunction against him, whereupon she had to go through the ordeal of giving the same evidence all over again. She got an injunction but, when he breached it by threatening her and she called the police, they could do nothing. He'd breached the injunction, but it was the order of a civil court and therefore the breach was not a criminal offence. Cardiff Women's Safety developed the argument that the jurisdictions of the two courts should be brought together. The criminal court should be able to give a protective order, something like a civil court injunction. If a civil court had imposed a non-molestation order, breach of it should be a criminal offence. Separately, I also found out that, in Northern Ireland, for some years, breach of an injunction imposed by the civil court had been a criminal offence, so when the police were called they could arrest the man, charge him and take him to a criminal court. That's what we needed in England and Wales.

I added this to my growing list of laws to go into a new Domestic Violence Bill. The Law Officers advise other departments on their bills, but they don't take bills through Parliament themselves so, if I wanted a bill, I'd have to persuade the Home Office to do it. Like all departments, they don't like other ministers trampling on their territory and always have a full agenda of bills, generally to do with immigration, terrorism and crime. But the idea of a bill had the active backing of the PLP Women's Committee and the new All-party Parliamentary Women's Group started by Margaret Moran. And there were now women as ministers and special advisers in the Home Office. The Domestic Violence Crime and Victims Bill would probably never have happened without the support from within the Home Office of Baroness Patricia Scotland, then a junior minister, and Kath Raymond, then David Blunkett's special adviser. Kath steered the bill through the maze of the vast Home Office civil service empire. With her intelligence, commitment and political skills, she defused any incipient arguments that brewed up between me and David, born out of my frustration at having to deliver progress on domestic violence through a department headed by a man and wanting everything to be done faster.

So much of what needed to be done on domestic violence stretched across different government departments: the Justice Department (then the Lord Chancellor's Department), because of their responsibility for the courts and the criminal law; the Home Office, because of their responsibility for the police; the Health Department, because of the need to involve general practitioners and Accident and Emergency departments in identifying domestic violence; the Local Government Department, because of the funding of refuges; and, in addition, the Minister for Women. In the autumn of 2001, I won agreement for the establishment of a Cross-departmental Committee on Domestic Violence. Of course, I was keen to chair it, but I realized it was best if I didn't. The Law Officers are in such a tiny department, and huge departments such as the Home Office and the Health Department would just ignore the committee if I was the chair. So, gritting my teeth, I proposed that a Home Office minister should chair it. The first was Southampton MP John Denham (who'd been one of my junior ministers in the DSS), and after him it was Harrow MP Tony McNulty. They both chaired the committee highly successfully, and worked in close conjunction with me on it but, most important of all, the committee had the clout of their heavyweight department behind it, so we made progress on all fronts.

Sentencing is the responsibility of the judges, under the guidance of the non-political Sentencing Guidelines Council. Usually, it's only the offender who can appeal against a sentence, but one of the powers I knew that the Solicitor General and the Attorney General had was that they can refer a case to the Court of Appeal and ask it to review a sentence if they think it is 'unduly lenient'. And this has consequences not just for the case in hand but for future cases, because when the Court of Appeal pronounces on a sentence it sets a precedent for other cases in the future. I knew about this power to refer unduly lenient sentences (ULS) because I'd been an

MP when the Tories introduced it and Labour had voted against it, arguing that it could allow political interference in sentencing in through the back door. But now I was Solicitor General, this was exactly what I wanted to do on overly lenient sentences handed out in cases of domestic violence.

Inadequate sentencing in such cases not only denied the victim justice, it sent out the message to other perpetrators that the criminal justice system didn't treat these cases with the seriousness they did other crimes of violence, and this served to demotivate the police and the prosecutors. I sent out a memo to the Crown Prosecutors, saying that they could send up to me any domestic violence case where they thought the sentence was too lenient and I would consider sympathetically whether to refer it up to the Court of Appeal.

The CPS prosecutor would send me all the statements taken by the police, all the medical reports, the transcript of the barristers' closing speeches and the judge's summing-up and sentencing comments. As part of my feminist beliefs, I'd always taken the view that domestic violence was appalling, but here in the bulging files that covered my desk was the heartbreaking evidence of the true horror of it: the broken ribs, the black eyes, the terrorized children. The files laid bare the way in which the beatings escalated, and the growing fear and misery that was unfolding behind closed doors. Working late into the night, I would read every word in these files, growing ever more determined that I would do everything I could to get justice for these victims and to deter future perpetrators of domestic violence.

In order to set off the process of ULS, I would brief a barrister, who would draft an application to the Court of Appeal for the sentence to be reviewed. At the hearing, my barrister would make my case for the sentence to be increased and the offender's barrister would make the case for it to remain as it was. The cases were heard in the dark, oak-panelled courts in the Strand, with three judges in full-bottomed wigs and purple gowns sitting at a bench placed fifteen feet above the level of everyone else in the court. It was where I'd taken cases when I was at Knapp-Fisher, Brent Law Centre and the NCCL; it was like coming home. I discovered that, previously, it had not been the practice of the CPS or the Law Officers to tell the victim that the prosecution had appealed against the sentence until after the ULS case had been heard. Technically, they were not party to the case; it was between the Law Officer and the offender. But I ensured that the victim was told as soon as I had decided to refer a case, and that they could attend if they wanted. Often I would go myself, hoping my presence would show the judges the importance I placed on the case, and I would always make a point of talking to the victim and her relatives. Frequently, the local prosecutor who had referred the sentence to me would come and sit in the court with the victim and it would be a chance for me to meet them in person.

I looked out for cases which highlighted particular problems so that important issues could be addressed and precedents established. I suspected that the courts gave lighter sentences if they thought domestic violence was part of the perpetrator's culture. One such was that of the young woman who was brought to west London from Pakistan for an arranged marriage, to the younger brother of a large family in whose home she would live. She spoke no English, did not go out to work and had no friends in London. Shortly after the marriage, she had two children. Her young husband was well down the pecking order in the power structure of the family, and his older brother started making sexual advances to her. She tried to avoid him, but when the rest of the family was at the mosque on a Friday he would beat and rape her. She didn't dare report him to anyone, she was so trapped in the family, but when he started eyeing up her elder daughter she went to the police and he was convicted. He was given a sentence of only two years.

I referred the case to the Court of Appeal, arguing that the sentence should be higher, to reflect the fact that he'd taken advantage of the victim's vulnerability. The court duly increased it, and stated that the law would deal severely with any man who took advantage of a young, isolated woman in his home.

There was also a common classist misconception that domestic violence was committed by unemployed drunks living on council estates who beat their wives. And, paradoxically, if ever a middle-class perpetrator was convicted, the court would accept the argument that he should have a lighter sentence because the shame for him was greater.

A case which illustrated this arrived on my desk in 2002. An eminent doctor employed in a major teaching hospital had married one of his brightest students. She was twenty years younger than him and they went on to have two children. However, while, over the years, her career went from strength to strength, his began to fade, and he became angry and resentful. He started treating her roughly at home, shouting at her, and pushing and shoving her. Her efforts to placate him didn't work. But there was no question of her complaining about him to anyone. He was her husband, and they both had professional reputations to maintain. One night when she came home from work and he'd been drinking he attacked her. He punched her in the head, blackened both her eyes, broke two of her ribs, tore off her clothes and ripped out her tampon. He then fell, semi-conscious, into an armchair, and she fled up to her bedroom. As a doctor, she realized that one of her lungs was punctured but she was terrified that if she tried to leave the house he'd wake up and start attacking her again. When she heard her son come home from a night out in the small hours of the morning, she called to him. He rushed his mother, who was barefoot and wearing only a nightdress, into the street, and she was hospitalized for four days. Her husband pleaded guilty but the judge was impressed by the evidence offered in mitigation. In his sentencing, the judge described the husband as a man with an outstanding record of public service, of high professional standing, who, finding it hard to cope with the prospect of retirement, had grown depressed. He was admired by his colleagues, was a popular figure in the hospital and every year played the part of Santa Claus at the hospital nursery Christmas party. So despite being convicted of grievous bodily harm and indecent assault for committing a terrifying attack on his wife in her own home that left her seriously injured, he was not sent to prison but given a community rehabilitation order.

I referred the sentence to the Court of Appeal. I briefed the barrister to argue that it was a travesty to minimize the violence this woman had suffered because her husband was outwardly jovial and well-liked at work. The fact that he was a role model to younger professional colleagues made his behaviour worse, not better. And however welcome his appearances as Father Christmas, they were irrelevant and shouldn't be a reason to keep him from serving a custodial sentence. The Court of Appeal agreed. He wasn't in court so a warrant was issued for him to be arrested, and he was taken straight to prison.

In this way, a body of Court of Appeal judgements was building up and the lower courts were starting to sentence the perpetrators of domestic violence more robustly. However, even though this progress was evolving, case by case, I wanted a step change in sentencing across all courts, and for that I needed the Sentencing Guidelines Council to tell the courts to increase sentences for domestic violence. It is they who set the 'tariffs' by which the courts have to abide. By 2003, I had persuaded the Home Office to ask the council to conduct a review. I compiled my ULS cases into a dossier, submitted it to the council and went to see them. At the end of the process, three years later, they set the tariffs higher, which, together with the precedents set by the ULS cases, was a major step forward in tackling lenient sentences for wife-beaters.

I wasn't in the Cabinet. In the official pecking order of government ministers, I was at the bottom. But that was immaterial because, with strong support from the women's movement, the active backing of Labour women MPs and my work with women ministers and special advisers in other departments, I was making progress in leaps and bounds in my work on domestic violence.

However, there were always cases of domestic homicides appearing on my desk, and I'd see the same pattern in them again and again. The man would start to be violent. The woman would leave him, or threaten to leave. The violence would escalate, and he would kill her. Sometimes he'd kill one of the children, too. He'd admit the killing but say that it was the woman's fault because she'd provoked him. Then, using the defence of 'provocation', the charge would have to be reduced from murder to manslaughter and the perpetrator would be handed a sentence of only a few years, which would then be suspended and, often, he'd walk free from court. The defence of provocation, colloquially known in the legal profession as the 'nagging and shagging' defence, was something the women's movement had been protesting about for decades, but we had made no progress. There needed to be a change in the law.

Though the pattern was all too familiar, each case was a personal tragedy. In one case the victim had called her sister in terror, begging her to come over because her estranged husband had said he was on his way to her home and she was afraid. The sister rushed there and, not finding her sister in, sat down to wait for her in the front room. The man came downstairs, greeted her breezily, then left. The woman's body was found locked in the wardrobe in her bedroom. He said she'd provoked him by saying she wouldn't let him see their child.

In Rotherham, a solicitor killed his wife in front of their four children but escaped a murder charge by arguing that she'd provoked him; she had said she 'had feelings for her karate instructor' and was threatening to leave him.

The perpetrator, usually having no option but to admit that he'd killed the victim, would say in the witness box that it was her fault: she'd driven him to it, she'd belittled him, she'd nagged him, she was unfaithful. And of course the woman could not contest any of this because she was dead. Her relatives were condemned to sit in silent misery in the public gallery while the killer blamed the victim for her own death, listening to the killer turn himself into the victim as he told the court how she'd made him suffer. And the proof of this was that he'd been driven to kill her. Why, otherwise, would he have done it, when he loved her so much? I felt it was so unfair that, while everyone else had their say, the people who cared most, the victim's family, were condemned to tortured silence. The first time they'd have the opportunity to say anything would be outside, on the steps of the court, when it was all over. So as well as working to get the provocation defence abolished for cases of sexual infidelity, I worked with groups of victims' relatives to have the rules changed so that, after a conviction but before the sentence, the relatives would have the chance to speak in court about the victim.

In 2007, when, for the first time, relatives were allowed to speak in court and that first court statement, so heartfelt yet so dignified, was reported, it seemed completely appropriate and the very least we could do for people whose lives had been devastated by crime. The judges had fought against it tooth and nail when I first proposed it, and continued to grumble about it for some time, but it's now an accepted part of the court process.

Yet I still felt the whole basis of the defence of provocation was wrong. And it was grotesque that the legal test that the prosecutor and the court had to apply to decide whether it was provocation was whether, in those circumstances, a 'reasonable man' would have been driven to kill. There's never any justification, no matter how badly someone behaves in a relationship, for resorting to violence, let alone killing. It's never 'reasonable'. The overwhelming majority of homicides in which the killer and the victim know each other are domestic homicides, and the overwhelming majority of those are men killing women. The defence of provocation effectively allowed a man to get away with murdering his wife. It was the ultimate in the culture of excuses. My quest to abolish 'provocation' as a defence caused controversy within the anti-domestic-violence women's organizations, and among defence barristers, who are always wary about ever limiting a form of defence. Some women argued that, rather than trying to abolish the provocation defence, we should extend it so that it could also be a defence for women who kill a violent husband. But I didn't agree; the defence didn't fit the cases in which a woman kills her violent husband. Provocation is based on the notion of anger, not fear, but while men kill their wives out of anger, women kill their husbands out of fear. I didn't think provocation could be turned into a defence for those who are fearful. In addition, allowing the many men who kill their wife a defence for the sake of the tiny number of women who kill their husband didn't make sense. And rather than excusing the wife who kills her husband out of fear, I wanted us to tackle the cause of that fear by ensuring that we stepped up our efforts to protect victims of domestic violence.

As well as having arguments with women's organizations about this, I also had many revealing arguments with my male colleagues. I sought support from fellow ministers in the Home Office and the Justice Department and with those who were likely to be influential in helping me get the law changed. I'd learned the importance of having a political strategy from my previous time in government. But I was taken aback by how many, having listened carefully to the case I was making, said things like 'But what if she's been unfaithful? What if she's wound him up? What if he's really upset and he loved her?' In the end, in 2009, thanks to the help of two influential women lawyers, Elish Angiolini and Vera Baird, the law was changed so that violent husbands can no longer escape a murder charge by using the victim's infidelity as an excuse.

Elish had became Solicitor General in Scotland at the same time I became the UK Solicitor General and, like me, was the first woman and the first solicitor (rather than barrister) to hold the office. She is tremendously bright, comes from a working-class background and is very much a 'sister'. Unlike me, she'd become Solicitor General after a career as a front-line prosecutor and had the serious legal and prosecution credibility I lacked. Vera Baird was also a formidable ally. Newly elected in 2001 as MP for Redcar, and another working-class woman who'd become a highly respected criminal QC, Vera had defended a number of women charged with murder for having killed their violent husbands, including the seminal case of Emma Humphreys in 1995. So though some of my colleagues felt able to brush aside my arguments as being genuinely felt but legally unsound, they found it harder to dismiss the arguments being made by these two leading woman QCs, one a prosecutor and one a defender.

I was even more determined, now I was making progress back in government, not to mess it up again. I relied on Scarlett as a one-woman conflict-resolution agency, advising me how to deal with the rows I inevitably had with the judges, the attorneys, fellow ministers or civil servants. She continued to give me unfailingly good advice, for example saying that I shouldn't do any interviews in the media until I'd settled into the role and had some good initiatives under way. As Deborah Mattinson had put it, 'Just do it. Don't talk about it.' So I turned down the flood of interview requests, particularly as this wasn't just the usual press interest in any new minister; journalists specifically wanted to interview me about what it was like coming back into government, having been sacked. I didn't want simply to be labelled as the political equivalent of Lazarus, I wanted to get on with the job at hand. The stories had to be about things that I was succeeding in doing, and not about what I'd failed to do in my last ministerial job in the Department of Social Security. So, just as I had after I'd been sacked from the Cabinet, I once again turned the press down.

A year after I'd been appointed Solicitor General, having already got a great many projects going, I agreed, on Scarlett's advice, to do an interview, but she advised me to bypass my old foes, the political journalists, and go instead to the veteran *Guardian* legal editor Clare Dyer. In the resulting piece, Clare referred to my sacking from the DSS only briefly, focusing instead on what I was doing in my current position with the headline: 'Harman wants to make sure not only that men who beat up their partners are brought to court, but that when they are convicted they go to jail.' After this, it seemed, I was once again able to discuss my current and future work and have it reported in the newspapers. I felt I was really moving on from the debacle of my time at the DSS.

More and more reports started appearing in the media about my work on domestic violence. When I managed to have the sentence increased in the tragic case of the domestic homicide of a young Liverpool woman, the *Echo* wrote a big story about it. When I visited the Manchester HQ of the CPS I publicized the statistics on domestic violence in the city, and the *Manchester Evening News* covered it. I'd appear on local radio interviews to highlight domestic violence, for example BBC West Midlands' *Ed Doolan Show*, which drew a huge audience.

These media reports re-energized the strong bond I'd had with the grass roots of the Labour party. I was inundated once more with invitations to Labour party meetings and dinners. At literally every occasion I attended, anywhere in the country, women would come up to me, catch hold of my arm, draw me aside and, with tears in their eyes, say, 'Keep up what you're doing.' They'd whisper that they, or their daughter, or their mother, had been subjected to violence in the home. They said they felt that I was speaking up for them personally and against what they had suffered and how much that mattered to them. These were young women, older women, professional women, working-class women, women from every ethnic background, women members and councillors. They inspired me to press on, and I knew, when I was battling with other government ministers over women's issues, that there was massive, heartfelt backing for it.

It takes years to drive change through government, so it was fortunate that I could continue my work on domestic violence when Tony moved me in 2005 from the position of Solicitor General to the Ministry of Justice, and then, when I was elected Deputy Leader and moved back into the Cabinet as Leader of the House of Commons and Minister for Women in 2007, I was able to lend the issue even more impetus across government. Once, worried that I was focusing too much on domestic violence, and that people might be fed up that I was 'banging on about it', I asked Scarlett whether she thought I should scale down my work in this area. She obviously thought this was a ridiculous proposition. 'Is the problem solved?' she asked. 'Well, if it isn't, you had better get on with it.'

By the time Labour lost the election in 2010, so much had changed on domestic violence. There was specialist training for judges and prosecuting barristers, a specialist squad of domestic violence prosecutors, victims were allowed to give their evidence from behind a screen, police could make an arrest for breach of an injunction, sentences were increased, magistrates could issue protective injunctions, victims' relatives could speak in court, the provocation defence was abolished for jealous husbands, domestic homicides were reviewed and work across government became joined up through an inter-ministerial committee on domestic violence. However, although we made a great deal of progress, there is a lot more to be done.

In 2011, when we were back in Opposition, I was called for jury service at Southwark Crown Court. I was advised that, as Labour Deputy Leader, I could apply to be excused, but as, when I was Justice Minister I had brought in new laws to make everyone, including lawyers and MPs, do jury service, I felt I could hardly apply myself to be let off. I was called on to the jury for the trial of two Lithuanian men charged with raping a young woman prostitute. As well as changing the law and processes for domestic violence, I'd done the same on sexual offences when I was Solicitor General, so I was intrigued to see whether all the processes on rape that I'd put in place as Solicitor General and Justice Minister were working in the way we'd intended.

To encourage victims to report rape, we'd changed the law so that their previous sexual history couldn't be used in evidence and so that the victim would be able to give evidence from behind a screen, and we had set up sexual assault referral centres, where victims could not only be treated for their injuries but where forensic evidence would be sensitively gathered. The incidence of reporting on rape was definitely increasing. There's a strict rule which prevents jurors reporting on the jury's deliberation on the verdict, so I say nothing of that. But what was clear for me and anyone else to see in the public court hearings of this particular case at least was that as soon as the victim reported the rape she was seen by a specialist woman police officer from Operation Sapphire, the Metropolitan Police specialist sexual offences unit. She was taken to hospital to one of the new sexual assault referral centres and the specialist clinician gave evidence to the court. She'd not only treated her but had recorded the victim's bruises and carried out forensic tests on the evidence that had been taken. The victim was shielded from public view when she gave her evidence, and the police testified how they had caught the suspects by working with their EU counterparts in Lithuania. A woman barrister, acting for the CPS, was completely in command of her brief. The men were convicted and the judge passed a heavy custodial sentence, in so doing reminding the court and the offenders that, just because a woman was a prostitute, it didn't mean men could rape her and get away with it. I was sure that not every case ran quite so smoothly, but it was remarkable to see, from the jury box, the changes I had made when I was a minister being applied.

6.

External Challenges and Inner Turbulence

Our first term of Labour government had been devoted to taking forward important issues which were already under way, like getting a peace deal in Northern Ireland, finding strategies to alleviate the problems we'd inherited, such as long hospital waiting lists, crumbling schools, pensioner and child poverty, and also trying to re-set the political culture of the country to be more progressive, democratic and inclusive. Examples of this are the Human Rights Act (1998), the Freedom of Information Act (2000), the setting up of a Scottish Parliament and a Welsh Assembly in 1999, the repeal of the homophobic Clause 28 in 2003 and legislating for civil partnerships in 2004. The government had enjoyed a longer 'honeymoon' of popularity than we could ever have expected, and we'd won that precious second term in 2001. But the path of government never runs smooth and, of the problems that emerged, some were solved and others proved intractable. The decision to use force in Iraq was most emphatically the latter.

On 11 September 2001, the Attorney General, Peter Goldsmith, and I, together with our civil servants, stood in the private office we shared, watching in disbelief as the TV showed jets flying into the World Trade Center. While I was transfixed in horror, Peter instantly understood the geopolitical significance of what was happening, saying that nothing would ever be the same again. Tony, who had gone down to Brighton for the TUC Congress, left without making his speech and the conference was abandoned. Almost three thousand people in the US had been killed by a terrorist force that was using Afghanistan as a safe haven, and further attacks were threatened. Diplomatic efforts were made to root Al-Qaeda out of Afghanistan, but when these failed the Cabinet agreed to join the attack on Al-Qaeda there. Though the post-war handling of Afghanistan proved problematic, there was a widespread belief, both inside and outside the Labour party, that there was no alternative other than to use military force.

It was to be an altogether different story in Iraq. However, it's important to remember the awful years before we invaded the country in 2003. Iraqi trade unionists would regularly come to Labour party and trade union meetings with horrific stories of torture, executions and the crushing of workers' protests. Iraq's war with Iran saw over a million people killed, and Iraq's invasion of Kuwait caused global outrage and yet more regional instability. Saddam Hussein's brutal suppression of the Marsh Arabs in the south and the Kurds in the north, including with the use of chemical weapons, cemented his reputation as a tyrant and saw hundreds of thousands killed and fleeing their homes. He boasted that he still had those weapons of mass destruction (WMDs), and there was every reason to believe he had. However, ultimately, that belief was proved to be wrong and, with it, the legal justification for the invasion of Iraq.

The Attorney General was becoming more and more deeply involved in giving legal advice to Number Ten as reports from Iraq grew increasingly disturbing and concerns about Saddam Hussein grew. As deputy to the Attorney General, I usually knew about everything that was happening in the office: I was routinely copied in on all correspondence and internal memos, attended key meetings and took part in telephone conference calls. But it was to be different with Iraq. Peter made it clear that I was not to attend any of the meetings, and neither was I to see any of the papers. It was going to be a very difficult time for him, and I thought it would help him to have me by his side, which I couldn't be if I knew nothing about it. I felt it was odd that I was being excluded; it implied that he didn't trust me or was concerned that I might go behind his back. Yet, without ever saying why, the Attorney General was resolute that he should handle things on his own, so I got on with all the other issues I was dealing with, while he grew increasingly tense as the controversy over the legality of the war started to emerge, and then rage, in the press. It wasn't until he made a written statement to Parliament on 17 March 2003 that I saw the Attorney General's argument for the legality of war in Iraq.

On 18 March 2003, Tony put to the House the proposition that we use military force in Iraq, and I voted in support of it. The basis for my decision was not that we needed to get rid of Saddam Hussein, that is, effect 'regime change', despite the years of heartfelt pleas from those who suffered under his oppression. My decision, though in the face of obvious opposition in the party and from many of the public, was based on the belief that, if Saddam Hussein did have weapons of mass destruction, it was right to go in and destroy them before he used them again.

In the days following the invasion of Iraq, Peter seemed increasingly anxious. About three days afterwards, he despairingly exclaimed, 'They still haven't found any weapons of mass destruction! Where are they?' The belief that Saddam had these weapons was the political underpinning of our decision to invade. Without them, the justification was not there. If WMDs had been found, there would still have been controversy, but it would have been muted. As it was, Tony was accused of deliberately misleading the public, telling us there were WMDs when he knew there weren't in order to pressurize us to back the invasion. You have to make your own judgements about people's character, but I never believed, and I still don't, that Tony would have been capable of urging us all to support the use of force, and to put our troops in a position where many risked and lost their lives, and which cost the lives of thousands in Iraq, on the basis of a deliberate lie. For him to have done that would have been monstrous. I've been dismayed that so many of his erstwhile friends and colleagues have been prepared to go along with the 'Bliar' version of events. If they thought he was that sort of person, they should never have supported him or been prepared to serve in his government. Casual acceptance of the worst criticism imaginable is a common feature of politics. If I'd have known there were no WMD in Iraq, I wouldn't have voted for the use of force. But no one knew for sure.

After the invasion, as the months and years unfolded, Iraq experienced not peace and democracy but chaos and division. The lives of 179 British service personnel were lost, and thousands of Iraqi lives. Our failure in Iraq, documented in the report of the Chilcot Inquiry in 2016, came to define our government's role in foreign policy, eclipsing successful interventions in Sierra Leone and Kosovo and the lives that were saved and changed by our leadership of the movement to end poverty in the developing world. And this failure came to define Tony's premiership, throwing a shadow over his remarkable achievement of getting, and keeping, Labour in power so we could make Britain a better, more prosperous and fairer country.

Despite the controversy over Iraq, we went on to win the 2005 General Election and an unprecedented third term of Labour government. But the longer Tony remained as Prime Minister, the more the relationship between him and Gordon seemed to deteriorate. Relations between those MPs who regarded themselves as supporters of Tony and those who were in Gordon's camp became increasingly tense. Tony announced before the 2005 General Election, his third as Leader, that he would not fight a fourth. This was the culmination of mounting internal criticism and destabilization, attributed in the newspapers to those who wanted Gordon to take over. A flashpoint was reached when, in September 2006, a letter signed by seventeen Labour MPs, including one minister and four PPSs, was sent to Tony, urging him to stand down. And after this, the atmosphere among ministers and in the PLP became increasingly one of mutual suspicion and hostility.

As a minister, but one who was in neither the Blair nor the Brown camp, I watched all this unfold with mixed feelings. Tony had led us to three election victories, but he was coming towards the end of a decade as Prime Minister and we'd lost over a million of the voters we had won in 1997. Perhaps we would get a boost with a new prime minister, and with Gordon, do the unthinkable by winning a fourth term.

In 2007, shortly after Tony's announcement that he would stand down later that year, he held a policy seminar in Number Ten to do some 'blue-sky' brainstorming for the future. Ministers from across government were there. There were presentations from special advisers and we broke into groups for further discussion. But though we were in Downing Street, at the heart of government, the exercise felt pointless. Tony held the highest office in the land, he was Prime Minister and would be for some time, but we were there to discuss the future and Tony was not going to be part of it. His power and influence had dematerialized. Authority had already seamlessly transferred to Gordon, in the settled expectation that he was to be the next prime minister. Gordon's advisers were walking tall; Tony's were looking for their next job. Ministers and civil servants alike were preoccupied by what Gordon thought about all the issues; what the current prime minister thought no longer mattered. The handover was set for June 2007.

As soon as Tony said he'd be standing down, there was discussion in the newspapers about some Blairites meeting up to agree on a candidate; also, some who, though not Blairites, wanted there to be another candidate, because they thought the competition would be good for the party and good for Gordon. After all, we hadn't had a leadership contest since 1994 and there would, in any event, have to be an election for the position of deputy leader, as John Prescott had said he would be standing down at the same time as Tony. The party generally prefers democratic elections to unopposed 'coronations', but – unsurprisingly, in view of Gordon's popularity – no one came forward to challenge him. Gordon's supporters were jubilant and his detractors – those who blamed him for Tony leaving office – could do no more than fume in silence.

With Gordon's succession to the party leadership and to the office of prime minister assured, attention focused on the position that would be contested, the deputy leadership. MPs started to talk about who would run and who they would back. Names of Cabinet ministers who might stand started to appear in the press: Peter Hain, Alan Johnson, Hilary Benn. The only names being canvassed for deputy were those of men. The sole candidate for leader was a man. After campaigning for over thirty years for a woman to be in Labour's leadership team, I was appalled that we were heading into a leader and deputy leader campaign where we didn't even have a woman among the candidates. We had made a Labour party for the twenty-first century. We were in government, we had 127 women Labour MPs, yet we were about to embark upon a men-only 'beauty contest'. What message would this send to all the women in the party? What would it say about our women ministers and Cabinet members? We'd be relegated to being invisible and irrelevant, simply admiring the qualities of these men. Women MPs started to be concerned about this, resentment grew and it became accepted that we needed a woman candidate and, to do justice to all the women in the party, she would need not only to run but to do well.

I wasn't going to run. I still bore the scars from being sacked from the Cabinet. And I was at last feeling secure and confident in my junior ministerial role. I couldn't even countenance the idea that I would once again put myself right back into the front line and subject myself to all the denigration that would invariably come from the press. As far back as 2005, when Tony announced he'd stand down, Martin Kettle had written in the *Guardian* that I wouldn't be a candidate in any future deputy contest as the prospect evoked 'incredulity' from both the Brownites and the Blairites. Yet Scarlett and Jack were both pressing me to run. Scarlett arranged to come to our house so she and Jack could ambush me. Margaret Hodge started telling me and any woman within earshot that I should run. Women in the party were starting to urge me to run and, though it was gratifying, it seemed inconceivable that I should. I had been downwardly mobile in government. This hardly seemed an auspicious base from which to challenge the big and popular men in the Cabinet. And it would do nothing to advance the cause of women in the party if my candidature attracted derision. I would have undone all the good work I'd done to rehabilitate myself in the ten years since my sacking.

However, the complaints about the looming men-only contest and the encouragement for me to stand grew and, as can often happen when people start talking about something, I started getting used to the idea and it began not to seem so preposterous after all. The idea of running in order to stop it being an all-male race made it feel as if I would be doing it not just out of an inflated sense of my own importance but for women as a whole. As when I ran to be Labour's parliamentary candidate in Fulham, I would be doing it for the cause. And with that thought in my mind, a certain readiness to do it began to take shape. Objectively, it was still a ludicrous prospect. I was an outsider contesting with insiders, a junior minister challenging the Cabinet big beasts. I hadn't yet decided I would run but I was now at least firmly sitting on the fence.

In September, before our 2006 party conference, speculation about who would go for Deputy was swirling through the press. No one had yet declared themselves, but my name had started to be mentioned. On the 14th of that month, I was waiting for a 7 p.m. vote in my office in the lower ministerial corridor of the House of Commons with my constituency team, which was led by Charlotte Montague. She had taken a call from Rosa Prince, a lobby journalist for the *Daily Mirror*, asking whether the rumours that I was going to run were true, and she was pressing for an answer. I had been quite comfortable sitting on that fence. It was flattering to have my name in the frame and easy to allow speculation to build without having to take the risk of committing. I still feared I might get no support and end up looking ridiculous. I'd made such progress since being sacked ten years earlier, and I was doing well in my ministerial work – why put that all at risk? But with a young woman journalist at the *Mirror* waiting for a reply, it seemed like the moment had come to decide one way or the other. I called Jack, and Margaret Hodge, and both they and Charlotte strongly urged me to have Charlotte make the call to the *Mirror* to say I was going for it. In the moment that I decided to do it, I wondered why I always had to take on a challenge and couldn't just for once opt for a quiet life. But it was a thrilling and terrifying decision, like leaping out of a plane to skydive, being uncertain if your parachute will open. People can't rally in your support if you don't put your head above the parapet and say you're running. You have to stick your neck out, and that means taking a leap of faith in yourself.

The newspapers were universally awful and jeered at me. The bookies had me as the rank outsider. Alan Swales, a TGWU officer from Plymouth who was a friend of both Jack and me, put a bet on me to win at 100:1. But, of all the candidates, I had the clearest pitch. I was a woman, and the party needed a woman in the leadership team alongside Gordon. I was from London, and someone from the south would counterbalance a leader from Scotland. Having both a man and a woman, a Scot and a southerner, right at the top of the party would broaden our reach. The party needed stability at the top, and I'd worked well with Gordon and would not undermine him. I wouldn't be seen as an alternative leader, so I wouldn't threaten him. After years of Blair/Brown rivalry, the party yearned for this stability. And after years of campaigning with them all over the country, all the party members knew me and could be confident that I was energetic and committed. I began to feel not only that I should run but that my candidature would have a simple, clear and true message. And there was one further factor that made it possible for me to be a candidate: the children had left home. I could risk the massive press exposure, the constant travelling around the country being a candidate would involve, and the heavy responsibility of doing the job in a way I couldn't even have contemplated doing when the children were young. For once, the timing was right for me.

I told Gordon I was running, but I didn't ask his view on it, or for his support. For all his support would be massively helpful because of the strong position he was in in the party, I was not going to be his candidate. I had to do it as my own woman, even if that meant losing. I didn't want to owe my position to him; I wanted to be accountable to the women throughout the party, not the man at the top. I wanted to be a deputy leader who would be able to give the leader frank and independent advice, and a deputy who is beholden to the leader cannot do that. I wanted to win the deputy leadership in my own right. I didn't want to be seen as doing it on Gordon's coat-tails. I wanted to decide everything about my own campaign. I didn't want Gordon to be dictating it, or even having a say in it. I needed to do it completely on my own terms. I didn't want him rewriting my speeches. If he was in any way involved on my side, he wouldn't be able to help himself, he'd dominate my campaign. I didn't want him to be able to say, in the unlikely event that I did win, that I owed my position to him. And if, and this was more likely, he said he didn't want me to run, it would be awkward, because I'd already made up my mind I was going to.

The media carried differing accounts of who Gordon was supporting. I didn't know whether he was genuinely staying out of it and letting the election take its course or whether he was trying to give everyone who might have a chance of winning the idea that he backed them. He didn't need to intervene, as there was no one in the race who he couldn't have worked with as his deputy. But when it came to positions in the party, it was unlike Gordon to sit back and let events take their course. Among his key allies, the picture was mixed. Nick Brown and Yvette Cooper nominated me; Ed Balls nominated Alan Johnson.

I was in the Portcullis House café with Hastings MP Michael Foster when he asked 'if there were still space on the campaign team'. Hastings had been staunchly Tory and we'd won it off them for the first time in 1997. Michael said he thought that, as part of Labour's leadership, I could connect with his south of England voters and his Labour members. I admitted that not only was there a space, there was, as yet, officially no campaign team, and I invited him to lead it.

From there, we put together a great team, including Deborah Mattinson, the consummate pollster, Scarlett MccGwire, with her long-standing connections in the party, and Joe Calouri, who was working in the Local Government Association and subsequently became an Islington councillor. After the first couple of months, Mike Foster had to go to the USA with his Select Committee and the lead was then taken by my friend and ally of many years Joan Ruddock MP, who ran the campaign with a combination of flair and forensic attention to detail. Our pitch was first and foremost about the partnership between leader and deputy leader. As well as us being man/woman and Scot/southerner, Gordon was Radio 4, I was Radio 2. We would work together in harmony and, between us, we'd have everything covered. It was so simple and it was true. I knew and had worked with so many people in the party and, more to the point, they all knew me. They knew I'd campaigned hard for a Labour government and had remained solidly in support of it. I was in no doubt about the value of a Labour government and could quote evidence of the good Labour had done in my own constituency.

As it turned out, the largely dismissive press coverage of the announcement of my candidacy made no impact. Having known me for as many as twenty years, the party members had long since formed their own views about me and, as it turned out, they were not going to be deterred by what the political commentators said. Even so, I was still the outsider in the contest, so we knew we would have to be the best organized campaign team.

I felt a big responsibility to do well and, above all, to avoid a derisory vote. So from the outset our team worked incredibly hard, morning, noon and night. I was fully prepared for every meeting. I was (at Joan's insistence) smartly dressed and made-up for every appearance. With the children grown up, I felt for the first time the exhilaration of being able to throw myself into a campaign without that gravitational force pulling me home.

This was, however, tested midway through the campaign. One of the hustings for all the candidates clashed with a concert in which my daughter was going to perform. Normally, I would have prioritized the concert without a second thought. I broached the idea of missing the hustings with Joan. She was characteristically steely. She has a father, doesn't she? Joan asked. Yes, I agreed, she did. Can he go? Yes, I knew he could. Would she perform in other concerts I could go to in the future? Of course! Imagine, said Joan, that you lost by five hundred votes, votes you could have garnered at that hustings. How would you feel about it then? You would have let down all those who'd stuck their neck out to support you and all who were working so hard for you. She was determined that I had to be single-minded and put my heart and soul into our campaign for the deputy leadership. And I did.

Alan Johnson was, justifiably, the clear favourite. A popular former General Secretary of the Communications Workers Union (CWU), he'd led the successful campaign against the Tories' attempt to privatize the Royal Mail. He'd been outstanding in a number of ministerial posts and was universally liked and admired, not only in the party but by the political commentators, too. Politically, he was a Blairite, but he had never been seen as anti-Gordon. From a working-class background, he had overcome extraordinarily difficult family circumstances to make it all the way into the Cabinet, where he was Secretary of State for Education. A Londoner, he represented a Hull seat so, while he sounded like the south, he had a base in the north. John Cruddas had now joined the other nominees, Peter Hain and Hilary Benn.

Later on, Hazel Blears, who was in the Cabinet as Secretary of State for Communities and Local Government, and whom Tony had appointed Chair of the Party, threw her hat into the ring, but although I was no longer the only woman in the contest, for once, being the person who'd made the argument for women's representation over the years counted in my favour rather than against me. I benefited from the growing feeling that there needed to be what came to be seen as a 'balanced' leadership team. Hazel's message was that she, unlike me, was not running 'just because she was a woman'. But women members wanted exactly that: a woman who was running for women.

Throughout the campaign, I was phoning MPs asking them personally to consider supporting me. If they are going to support you, that's fine, but it's an uncomfortable call if they aren't because you still have to work together in the future. Yet you can't expect people to support you if you don't ask. Even those who didn't support me appreciated the fact that I'd made time to call them personally rather than getting a member of my campaign team to do it. And those who were already going to support me appreciated the call too, as it showed I valued their vote and was not taking them for granted. I hoped it sent the signal that, if I was to become Deputy Leader, I'd call them directly rather than asking someone on my team to. I even called those who were reported in the newspapers to be supporting one of the other candidates. I'd say that, although the papers had them down as supporting someone else, I didn't want to assume what the newspapers had said was in fact the case, and I did want to do them the courtesy of speaking to them myself. It's good to be on speaking terms with all the voters, even if they're not going to vote for you. The Deputy Leader election is done on a preferential voting system, where the voters rank the candidates in order and, if your first choice has the lowest vote and drops out, your vote goes to your next preference. So second preferences are as important as the first preferences to candidates who stay in the race after the votes of MPs, party members and trade unionists are counted in each round. If an MP said they would not make me their first choice, Joan would call them to ask them to give me as their second preference.

I went to every hustings, even the unofficial ones which drew only a few party members, never sending a stand-in, as some of the other candidates did. My team decided that I should accept every invitation. People give you credit if you are prepared to get out and meet them, because that's what they would want of their deputy leader when elected. They can't believe you think members are important if, while they take the time to give up an evening, you can't be bothered to show up. It was enjoyable going all around the country, making my pitch, catching up with members I'd known over the years and meeting new ones.

I would show them I'd made the effort to prepare in advance, make as good a speech as possible, turn up on time, look my best and embrace the opportunity of meeting them. The temptation is to focus on Labour strongholds or areas in which there is a large membership, but I felt that, even if there was only a small group of Labour members in a Tory area, visiting them was every bit as important as taking up an invitation from a Labour city stronghold. Every individual member of the party matters equally; they all pay the same membership fee. And as it's harder to carry the flag for Labour in Tory areas, I wanted to show my respect to members there for doing just that. Although the party didn't publish the membership figures at the time – let alone by regions – I suspected that the areas which delivered a strong vote for Labour were not always the ones with the largest membership, so I went everywhere. If it was a huge event, that was obviously good, as I'd get to see and be seen by lots of members. If it was a small event, with just a dozen members, I'd be able to have a much deeper discussion with them and, as often turned out, they'd be grateful that I'd visited and spent time with so few and would become fervent supporters of me and organize the support of others.

I visited every corner of Scotland, Wales and England. One night, Jack and I went to Newcastle for a local party dinner which I'd been invited to by Nick Brown, who was one of my nominators. I made a speech, although it was not one of my best, and it was fascinating to talk to all the people there – members, councillors and supporters – as I walked around, sitting at each of the tables. I'd seen Cherie Blair do this at Labour dinners and was struck by how much members appreciated it. The women, especially, were always happy to chat to me. They knew about me, so they wanted to tell me about their lives, and I was, as always, keen to hear. The next morning we took the train home. We felt pleased with ourselves to be travelling in the comfort of First Class, having upgraded our tickets for a Weekend First for only £5, and we read the Sunday papers as the sun streamed through the train's windows and the beautiful countryside sped past. I felt that, whatever the outcome, it was amazing to be able to talk to so many members, to be part of a Labour leadership election and to go to every corner of the country. And as it turned out, I was gaining the knowledge and connections I'd need when I became deputy leader of the whole party.

Jack came to all the official party hustings, and would sit in the front row, looking enthusiastic. Often, especially in the early weeks of the campaign, I'd be anxious and self-critical afterwards. Jack would go over all the points I'd made and assert that I'd done terrifically well, giving me crucial reassurance, even when I didn't believe him. At one point, I'd been invited to a dinner in Blackpool which my campaign team said was important, but which I would have to turn down because of a campaign event in London the following morning. Jack was adamant I should go and insisted that he'd collect me from Blackpool and drive me home, so we accepted the Blackpool engagement (which turned out to be a very big occasion). On the day, Jack, who'd already driven from London to Bristol for a union meeting, then drove from Bristol to Blackpool, arriving as the dinner finished, to drive me back through the night, home to London. It dealt with an otherwise insoluble transport problem but, above all, it was affirming to have such support.

Travelling up to Aberdeen, Frank Doran MP's constituency, I found it hard to work on the train because of the stunning scenery and townscapes on the East Coast line up past Berwick and Stonehaven. I travelled to North Wales on the line that runs where the mountains of Snowdonia sweep down to the sea. I went from the north-east to the north-west along Hadrian's Wall and then back from Lancashire to Yorkshire through the enchanting villages of the Dales. I was determined to savour everything I saw. In Redcar, at dusk, the red lights glittering at the top of all the rigs high above the steelworks looked beautiful to me, and we ate the best fish and chips. Candy Atherton hosted a lunch for Labour members in Cornwall to come and meet me. She picked me up from the station and what was an everyday drive for her was a treat for me, passing villages tucked into valleys along the breathtaking Cornish coast. I was driven through the dense greenery of the Forest of Dean on my way to Stroud. And, for the first time, I could enjoy all this without wanting to be at home with the children.

I'm sure my enjoyment rubbed off on those I met. For all the candidates, it was the biggest personal campaign we'd been involved in. But for me it was the first time in more than twenty years that I'd done it free from the worry of childcare responsibilities, and I had a fresh enthusiasm for the opportunity the campaign gave me to see every part of Britain and meet all the Labour members who support the party through thick and thin.

A couple of Scottish Labour MPs voiced doubts that I'd ever get any support in Scotland because I was 'too London and too posh', but I was running to be Deputy Leader of the UK Labour party and had to show I could win backing in Scotland and Wales as well as in England. Scottish Labour had a proud, traditional, working-class male base, but I had for years worked with women in Scotland, such as those in Strathclyde Regional Council, as they pioneered the development of childcare, and with the ground-breaking Edinburgh 'Zero Tolerance' movement against domestic violence. And I'd knocked on doors with Labour members all around Scotland in countless election and by-election campaigns, so I was sure there'd be some support for me up there.

Nonetheless, it was a surprise, and a great boost to my campaign, when a majority of the Labour members of the Scottish Parliament came out and publicly backed me. Unlike MPs, MSPs could not nominate candidates. MSP votes counted the same as that of an individual member, but the backing of the MSPs was politically significant. Rallied for me by Margaret Curran MSP, a strong working-class feminist from East Glasgow (later MP for Glasgow East), it enabled me to say that I could win the support of Labour people in a traditional Labour heartland as far away from London as you could get.

Finally – and paradoxically – the fact that no one saw me as a potential leader or prime minister worked in my favour. Some of Gordon's supporters backed me because they feared that Alan

Johnson was so popular and effective that, should Gordon ever hit problems, Alan would be seen as a prime minister-in-waiting. They were concerned that he'd attract, even unwittingly, support from those who wanted to undermine Gordon. With me, however, they felt certain not just of my loyalty but that I'd never be deemed good enough to challenge Gordon. For years, being a woman, not being from one of the Labour strongholds of Scotland, Wales or the north and not being seen as 'leadership material' had held me back. Now they were my trump cards. My perceived weaknesses were now my strengths.

Aside from Hilary Benn, I was the candidate with the least funds. Hazel, as Chair of the Party, had worked with Labour donors, so was well placed to reach out to get funds from them for her campaign, and, as a Greater Manchester MP, she had been able to secure funds from the Union of Shop, Distributive and Allied Workers (USDAW), whose headquarters were near her constituency. Peter Hain had funds from his former employer, the UCW, raising £200,000. John Cruddas had funds from a number of the unions, including the TGWU (later Unite), and raised £143,000. Even by the end of my campaign, I'd raised only £46,000. The TGWU, of which I was a member and with whom I had always worked closely, pledged £5,000, but when I, complying with the Whip as a government minister, didn't vote the way they wanted me to on a Private Member's Bill, they renegued. I strongly disapproved of using the offer of members' funds in a Labour election that way, but I was not overly worried about the money. I could pay my own travel expenses and, though I was never going to be able to afford to pay staff, I had many brilliant young volunteers. However, the issue of campaign finances did subsequently become a major problem.

As we got to the concluding stages of the deputy leadership election, the Labour party discovered that some of the candidates seemed to have got hold of membership lists that were supposed to be confidential. So, in an effort to make it fair to every candidate, it was decided to allow access to them to all the candidates so we could all write to every member. I was dismayed. I couldn't afford to pay for printing, envelopes and postage to over a hundred thousand members. The decision was an attempt to be even-handed, but it wasn't fair on me because I didn't have the money to follow it through. Joan said she wanted to come and see me at home and she wanted Jack to be there as well, which was an unusual request. When she arrived she said that we both needed to sit down. The party was going to send out the ballots in a few days' time, and if there was to be a mailing to all members it needed to go within a week. It had to drop on the mat at the same time as the ballot and the letters from the other candidates.

To print the letters and send them first class would cost £40,000. To pay the printer and the postage upfront, we'd need the cash within twenty-four hours. Joan said not doing this mail-out would cost us the contest. She said we couldn't have it that members would receive letters from every candidate other than me. Many MPs had gone out on a limb to nominate me, and it would be letting them down if we didn't do this mailshot. She asked if there was any way we could find the money, and I said there was absolutely no chance. To my astonishment, however, Jack said that, although we didn't have it, we would find it; we could take out a second mortgage. This was a remarkable response, since I was firmly expected not to win and it would therefore be taking on a huge debt for a doomed campaign. But Jack was resolute that, having put in for it, I should 'give it all I'd got' – or, in this case, 'all we didn't have but could borrow'. It was 2007 and before the global financial crisis, but even in those days of easy borrowing no bank or building society would give us access to funds that quickly, so we decided to ask my sister Sarah, who at that time ran her own firm of solicitors, if she would lend us the funds for a week while we tried to set up the second mortgage on our home. So we borrowed the money from her, got the second mortgage, paid Sarah back, and the mailing went out in the nick of time. So, when the ballots dropped through the letterboxes of all the Labour members, so did my letter.

It was typical of Joan that she instantly understood how crucial that mailing was. It was typical of Jack to offer to mortgage our house for a campaign in which I was predicted to come last and it was typical of Sarah that she, without blinking, was prepared to lend me such a large sum of money. But you shouldn't need to have a husband and a sister prepared to help raise tens of thousands of pounds in order to stay in a Labour leadership election. And, in any case, party members don't like to see hundreds of thousands of pounds being raised and spent on internal elections.

The result of the deputy leadership election was to be announced on 27 June 2007 at a conference in Manchester, and I, Jack and Joan went to stay the night before in the Stockport home of my friend and ally local MP Ann Coffey. I felt buoyed up by the warmth of the support I'd received all around the country and confident that we'd run a great campaign but I did not think, for one moment, that we'd win. On the radio, we heard various announcements from Gordon about the role he planned for the new deputy leader. We suspected that the votes had already been counted and he'd been told who'd won but, as the candidates didn't know as yet, he used that time as a window of opportunity to make the announcements without having to negotiate with the person who was going to take on the role.

The Labour party had told each of the candidates to write a five-minute speech in case of victory, to put it on a disk and hand it in to Labour party staff first thing in the morning. This was intended to be a practical arrangement to ensure that the winner's speech could be safely uploaded on to an autocue, ready to be read out, printed and instantly available to the waiting press. But it's uncomfortable, especially for the candidates who don't win, for the party to have in their possession a victory speech which the candidate will never get to make and, in fact, for that reason, it's no longer done in this way.

I rehearsed and honed my 'victory' speech, with Ann, Joan and Jack squeezed together on to a sofa playing the role of a conference audience of five thousand. Starting off with a ringing greeting of 'Conference!' in front of their enthusiastic and supportive faces made me crease up with hysterical laughter. Joan told me to take it seriously and get on with it. In the end, we drafted a short and simple speech, but our lack of computer skills meant that saving it on to one of Ann's disks took us longer than it took to write.

The next morning, Joan took the disk to the party staff and I went into the conference centre. I mingled in the coffee area with the party members who had travelled to the conference from all around the country, and you could feel the excitement build as we waited for the proceedings to start. I bumped into Yvette Cooper and, full of excitement, babbled about who might have won. Yvette had been a great supporter of mine from the start of the campaign, but now she fixed me with an uncharacteristically disapproving eye and, in unusually directive tones, said that, instead of dizzily speculating about who had won, the only purposeful thing I could do was to imagine how I would behave if I *had* won, and that I needed to get my head together. If I hadn't won, nothing would be lost, she said, but in the unlikely event I had, at least my head would be in the right place. It was such obvious and sensible advice that I stopped buzzing around the gathering members and switched my head out of 'excited' mode into serious 'ready to step up' mode.

Jack and Ann had, along with the rest of the team, taken their places in the hall in the second row from the front. As Joan and I went into a back room before going to be told the result, Joan pronounced that I looked too pale and accosted me with a huge make-up brush full of shimmering bronzer. I worried that I might look orange, and there was no mirror to check. It turned out that, after such a long, intense campaign, I'd built up such a level of trust that I'd become happy for the team to decide even the colour of my face.

Candidates are told the results before they go out into the conference hall, so each of us, together with our agents, were ushered into a small room, at the centre of which was a grand piano. The General Secretary, Peter Watt, stepped forward and said, 'We now have the result. Congratulations . . . Harriet.' Because, thanks to Yvette, I'd clicked my brain into 'step-up mode', I didn't blink. I moved seamlessly into my role as Deputy Leader, thanking the other candidates for being part of such a comradely campaign and the General Secretary for presiding over a well-organized series of hustings. That advice from Yvette has stood me in good stead in the years since, reminding me that, rather than getting carried away by what you feel about something, you have to remember what you are actually going to have to do and how others will be feeling. I couldn't indulge myself in my delight, especially in front of those I'd just beaten. I was no longer one of the candidates, I was now the winner and had to reach out to the other candidates for their support which, to their credit, they all gave in the months and years ahead.

I was ushered out of the room and found Gordon waiting for me behind the stage. He congratulated me, but I couldn't detect whether he was pleased or disappointed that I had been elected rather than one of the others. He'd been looking over my acceptance speech on the disk Ann had handed into the party staff and started pointing out some changes that he wanted me to make. But when I looked at the draft he was holding, I realized, to my horror, that I must have saved the wrong version. All I had in preparation for my first public moment as deputy Labour leader was our first, and very primitive, draft. The party staff were telling me I had only a few moments before I had to go on stage on live TV in front of five thousand party members, and I had the wrong version of my acceptance speech, and Gordon was telling me to say a whole load of things I hadn't planned to say.

I went to sit on my own in a tiny room with a computer and wrote a few simple messages, thanking the other candidates and the party staff, praising Gordon and saying I'd support him, vowing to listen to party members and to stand up for women. The temptation is, the bigger the audience, the more you feel you have to say. But, although this was a huge occasion, it really called only for a handful of simple, clear and heartfelt points. I didn't have time suddenly to change it in the way Gordon wanted, and the spontaneous brief speech I ended up making after the results of the deputy leadership election were announced to conference was much better than the one I'd prepared the night before. The conference just wanted me to show them how pleased I was, to thank them and to remind them why they'd voted for me.

Although we candidates now knew the result, the members at the conference did not. We walked out into the hall and took our seats at the front of a cheering and expectant crowd. The party had arranged slides which showed on a giant screen the results in each voting round for each section of the three sections of the electoral college (trade unions, MPs and party members). The candidate with the lowest vote, Hazel Blears, dropped out, then Peter and Hilary and, with each round and each elimination, the tension in the hall mounted. John Cruddas came third, leaving Alan Johnson and me head to head in the final round. The announcement of his percentage of the vote came first. He had won 49.56 per cent of the total vote. There was a gasp in the conference hall as they worked out that I had won, and by less than one per cent, a ridiculously narrow margin.

The senior figures in the party were lined up in a row at the foot of the stage to congratulate the winner. Among them was John Prescott, looking grim-faced. I reached out and, as I shook his hand, I said, 'I'll need all your advice and support. I hope you'll help me?' 'No,' he replied. 'I won't.' He had never liked or approved of me, but I was taken aback that he would put personal antagonism above the interests of helping his successor do a good job, and I was disappointed I was not going to enjoy the benefit of his advice and his thirteen years' experience as Deputy Leader. Worse, it signalled that he'd be muttering against me to the press and to anyone in the party who'd listen. I thought it was sad for him to end his highly successful period as Deputy Leader on such a sour note. But I was resolute: I would be undeterred. I'd won the election, I had a vital job to do and I was going to get on with it.

I also felt that the party members who had voted for me had

placed such faith in me that I was determined to do them proud. There's such a connection between expectation and ability. They expected me to justify the faith they'd placed in me, because of that I was now Deputy Leader, and that in turn drew forth my ability to perform the role.

Reporters swarmed around Alan Johnson, asking for his response to my victory. In the clearest and most generous of messages, with his characteristic wit and a self-effacement which is almost unique in politics, he said of the result, 'I was the best man, but as is so often the case, along came a better woman.' In saying this, he was signalling to his supporters that he accepted the result and that they should rally behind me as the new Deputy. If he'd been resentful about the result, it would, in conjunction with my wafer-thin margin of victory and John Prescott's opposition to my election, have made life impossible for me. But Alan, steeped in the collectivist culture of the trade union movement, was the ultimate team player and looked to the interests of the party and the government. His magnanimity gave me the chance to succeed. And it also served to increase his standing in the party. Gordon promoted him and he went on to be successful in the Cabinet as Health Secretary and then Home Secretary.

After the results conference, I, with Joan, Scarlett, Charlotte, Deborah, Jack and my team of supporters got on the train to go back to London. It was only then that I was able to relish my victory. Suddenly, champagne corks were popping as the packed post-conference train swayed back down south. It seemed that everyone was coming up to me, congratulating me, wishing me well. My supporters were jubilant; Alan's supporters, following his lead, were magnanimous. Neil Kinnock, who, together with Glenys, had backed me strongly, hugged me so hard I was gasping for breath.

I now seemed to be on the invitation list for every party event. I felt that it would be wrong if, having been prepared to go to such events to win their votes, I turned the invitations down once I'd been elected, so my office rule was that I would agree to do now anything I would have been prepared to do in the campaign. I couldn't turn down those local parties who'd voted for me and to whom I owed my victory. And I couldn't turn down those who hadn't voted for me, needing to reach out to them to win their confidence now that I had the job.

So, the years that followed my becoming Deputy Leader were every bit as demanding as the deputy leadership election campaign, but I no longer had to depend on volunteers to trek around the country with me. The party paid for my travel; Sophie Wingfield or Mabel McKeown, my excellent team of party staff, would come with me; and party staff locally would help make the arrangements. Instead of asking for members to give me their votes, I was giving them my time. And our long-standing agenda of demands for women in the party, policy change and more women MPs now saw another piece of the jigsaw in place – a woman in the leadership team once again. I also brought in rules for campaign spending caps for leadership elections and for the selection of MPs. Candidates have to show that they can raise money, but it's against Labour's ethos that the candidate who has the most money should get ahead.

Having been elected at the end of June, the 2007 annual Labour party conference, barely three months later, was to be my first big official duty. And it was daunting. John Prescott, having been Deputy for the previous thirteen years, had defined the role. I was to replace him, but I had won by only the narrowest of margins. The party doesn't, for the most part, hold meetings in August, so there was not much I could do to build support between the end of June and mid-September. Each of the regions and Scotland and Wales hold receptions at conference at which both the Leader and the Deputy Leader speak. Every time I walked on to the platform and looked into the hundreds of faces of party members, I saw many of them staring back at me with what I feared were guarded or resentful gazes. They were used to John Prescott and now they had to listen to me instead. Many had backed one of the other candidates.

I felt that, although winning had not been easy, the work that lay ahead would be even harder. I was daunted at the prospect of attending one of the high points of the conference circuit, the traditional Welsh Night. But as I arrived, a group of women in their fifties sitting together at a table called me over and, beaming, announced themselves to me as 'Caerphilly Girl Power!'

7.

Through the Glass Ceiling?

At the same time as Tony was elected Leader in 1994, John Prescott had been elected Deputy Leader, and it was taken as read that if we won the next election he would be made Deputy Prime Minister. When we won in 1997 he duly was, and he remained Deputy Prime Minister throughout the time Tony was Prime Minister. During the deputy leadership election in 2007, everyone assumed, including the candidates, that whoever won and became Labour Deputy Leader would be appointed Deputy Prime Minister. During the hustings, we spoke of what we would, and wouldn't, do 'as Deputy Prime Minister'. Indeed, the thing that had made John Prescott particularly angry with me was that I had said that, if I won, I wouldn't use the 'grace and favour' stately home of Dorneywood, as he had. However, the day before the results of the deputy leadership election were announced, a briefing appeared in the papers that Gordon was not going to appoint a deputy prime minister.

Once I'd been elected, Gordon confirmed this to me. My supporters were indignant. Charlotte Montague kept getting calls from the media and party members asking what was going on. I'd won the deputy leadership – why wasn't I going to be Deputy Prime Minister? But, having never expected to win the deputy leadership, I found that I was not properly prepared. Just as when I was first appointed to the Cabinet in 1997, once again I hadn't considered all the scenarios that might play out. I should have challenged Gordon on his decision not to make me Deputy Prime Minister, but I didn't. The Tories had had the first and, until then, only woman prime minister, Margaret Thatcher. Labour had more women MPs than all the other parties put together and had fought to become the party for

women. Yet not only had Labour never had a woman prime minister, we'd never even had a woman as deputy prime minister. Me
winning the deputy leadership was a golden opportunity for Gordon to put that right and, if it had been any other woman in the
position of Deputy Labour Leader, I would have recognized that in
an instant. I'd have fought for her to be deputy prime minister and
I'm sure I would have succeeded. But it feels self-serving if you're
fighting on your own behalf.

Looking back, I can see why I didn't raise it with Gordon. He'd
already made the announcement publicly, and he'd be unlikely to
do a U-turn on a decision made in the first twenty-four hours of his
premiership. If I'd made a fuss, it might have caused a row, which
would distract from Gordon making a flying start as new prime
minister, and it could have caused bad relations between us. The
government had already been scarred by one bad relationship at
the top; the last thing they would have wanted was for that to be
immediately replicated in another. Transitioning between one
prime minister and another was always a nervous time. And I'd
won the election on a unity ticket, promising to support Gordon.
While all this might have been so, it was also the case that, if Alan
Johnson had won, I'm sure Gordon would have felt that he had no
option but to appoint him Deputy Prime Minister. I don't think he
would have dared not appoint the popular front-runner. But it was
just all too easy not to appoint me.

The worst of it was that, as women in the party looked to me to
lead the protest, instead of galvanizing them in support of my being
made Deputy Prime Minister, I played it down. I smoothed over
the concerns of the angry women members and resisted press
attempts to provoke me into complaining. But even though I didn't
raise it at the time, I should have returned to it once Gordon had
settled into being Prime Minister. I should have found an early
moment to press upon him privately that it would be good for the
party and for the government for him to appoint me. However,
with Gordon leading the country through a summer of floods and
Bluetongue disease, and then the start of his slide in the polls after

the 'election that never was', the onset of the MPs' expenses scandal and the global financial crisis, it was one thing after another and the time never seemed right. Even though many people assumed I was in fact Deputy Prime Minister, my failure to challenge Gordon deprived Labour of having our first woman in that position. At the time, I was dismayed with and disappointed in Gordon. Now I'm annoyed with myself for letting it happen. My motives might have been worthy but my judgement was wrong. And it added insult to injury when, in 2009, Gordon decided that he wanted to have a deputy prime minister after all, but that it should be Peter Mandelson rather than me.

Many years later, in my Speaker's Lecture of 2014 on the subject of women in Parliament, with Labour out of government and Gordon no longer Prime Minister, I ventured for the first time to address the issue publicly. There was a fair amount of sympathetic indignation on my behalf, but there were also a good number of colleagues who protested to me that I should have kept quiet about it, that it was hard for Gordon to have lost the election and that I was making him 'look bad'. There's never a right time for a woman to complain about a man; the woman is blamed and the man becomes the 'victim'. And, ironically, the worse the complaint makes the man look, the more the woman is criticized for making it. Having missed the opportunity to take up the position of Deputy Prime Minister during Gordon's term, I made it clear to Ed Miliband when later he became leader that he'd have to make me his Deputy Prime Minister if we won in 2015, and I'm sure he would have. But that was well and truly shutting the stable door after the horse had bolted. We didn't win the election, so it never happened. I was to be Shadow Deputy Prime Minister but never the real thing. I hope I'm the first and last woman Deputy Leader in a Labour government not to be Deputy Prime Minister.

Having won the deputy leadership, I was clearly going to be back in the Cabinet. Even though it had been ten years since I had been sacked from it, I was apprehensive after my bad experience in the

Department of Social Security and didn't want to return to heading up a big operational department. Additionally, I needed a Cabinet role which wouldn't be so all-consuming that it would prevent me carrying out my duties to the party as Deputy Leader. So I asked Gordon for the role of Leader of the House. That would give me a central role in getting all the legislation of other government departments through the House of Commons and would be relatively uncontroversial publicly. As the Leader of the House duties are performed only when the House is sitting, it would leave me free to carry out my responsibilities as Deputy Leader at the weekend and in the recess. I knew that Jack Straw, who was Leader of the House at the time, wanted to move on, so there was the added advantage that Gordon wouldn't have to sack someone to give me the position.

Gordon agreed. It was a delight to be back in the Cabinet and I inherited a terrific private office team. Des McCartan, our press secretary, was the most experienced in government and totally level-headed. I would have the reliable civil service advice and guidance on dealing with the press which I had lacked at the Department of Social Security ten years earlier. Mike Winter, the assistant private secretary, knew everything there was to know about the legislative programme and the foibles of all the other government departments we'd have to deal with.

Stephen Hillcoat was the private secretary. On the day I was appointed Leader of the House, and after we had met for the first time, he called me when I was in my ministerial car being driven off to a meeting to say that he'd had a call from Number Ten and they wanted me to be Minister for Women and Equality in the Cabinet as well as Leader of the House. He said I should do it, because even if I wasn't in the official role as Minister for Women, now that I was back in the Cabinet I'd inevitably end up shouldering the responsibility for it, but without the benefit of the civil servants and the official role. He said I'd go mad watching anyone else in the Cabinet doing it. This was unusually forthright, coming as it did from a private secretary with whom I had not worked before. But if that's how it looked to him, I thought I'd better take it, so said he should call Number Ten back and say I'd be delighted to take on the role. And I'd clearly have, within my private office, the civil service backing for my Equality role which I had lacked when I was first in the Cabinet, combining the Women and Equality role with that of Secretary of State for the Department of Social Security. So, at the same time as becoming Deputy Labour Leader and Leader of the House of Commons and rejoining the Cabinet, I also became Minister for Women and Equality.

The position proved more than fruitful. Had I not taken the role, we wouldn't have got the strong new Equality Act through in 2010 which toughened the law on equal pay and brought in new laws, including ones against disability and age discrimination. I was only able to do it by using the authority I had as Deputy Leader combined with the crucial role in legislative gatekeeping I had as Leader of the House. Even then, because we had so many fights within government about it, we only managed to get it through at the eleventh hour. I became Minister for Women and Equality at the end of 2007, and the Equality Act was the very last government bill to be passed into law before we lost the General Election in May 2010.

Now that I was back in the Cabinet, and with two Cabinet positions, I needed two special advisers. I'd worked with Anna Healy when she was in the press team in Labour HQ in the eighties. She knew every corner of government and every aspect of the Labour party but she was the very opposite of a machinating spin doctor. She had an improving effect on whoever she worked with, keeping people calm, focusing on the bigger picture, utterly loyal to the party and committed always to doing the right and honest thing. She'd stopped being a special adviser when Tony stepped down, but I begged her to return to the role for me. Having her advice and support from 2007 through to September 2010 was critical to my successful re-entry to Cabinet-level politics but also to the very challenging period when I had to lead the Labour party after our 2010 election defeat.

I recruited Ayesha Hazarika to be Anna's deputy, with lead responsibility for the Equality brief. Ayesha had been working in the private sector for the music business EMI but had been a civil servant in the Department of Trade and Industry press office before that, and had impressed Patricia Hewitt, who was then the Secretary of State. Ayesha was completely different from all the other special advisers in Whitehall, not just because she was a woman and a Muslim but because she's a stand-up comedian as well as being a completely serious Labour loyalist. I'd never used humour in parliament or in speeches, being afraid that it would deepen the problem of my not being taken seriously. But Ayesha showed me how to use it politically, in a way that would help me put our case, cheer up our supporters and diminish our opponents. From Prime Minister's Questions through party conference speeches to the Trade Union Congress, my speeches were laced with humour, thanks to Ayesha. But it was always with a political purpose. And she was a consummate networker and media strategist.

If you want to know who's important in government, you only have to look at the Cabinet seating plan; the arrangement is significant both symbolically and practically. Power radiates out from the Prime Minister's seat in the middle of the huge table in front of the marble mantelpiece. The key Cabinet ministers – Chancellor, Foreign Secretary, Home Secretary – sit directly opposite, in the Prime Minister's line of vision. On one side of the Prime Minister sits the Cabinet Secretary and on his other the Deputy Prime Minister. And they both whisper in the Prime Minister's ear during the meetings. Gordon had reshuffled the Cabinet. Alistair Darling was the new Chancellor, David Miliband the new Foreign Secretary.

At Gordon's first Cabinet meeting after becoming Prime Minister, my first as Deputy Leader, there were name cards in each of the places. I noticed that the card in what I had assumed would be my place next to the Prime Minister had Jack Straw's name on it. Of all the things I had to think about when I became Deputy Leader, I hadn't considered the Cabinet seating plan. While it might seem petty to worry about who sits next to the boss, in reality, it is politically significant in the unwritten codes of government power. But Gordon had clearly decided on the seating plan, all the Number Ten civil servants would have known about it, and Jack was sitting there.

As Gordon prepared to open the meeting and welcome his new Cabinet, I could hardly start protesting about the seating arrangements. I couldn't let it seem as if I thought where I sat in Cabinet was the biggest issue facing the government. I wanted Gordon's first Cabinet meeting as Prime Minister to go well, for him, for Labour and for our government. So, once again, I didn't make a fuss, saying nothing about it, to Jack, to Gordon or to anyone else. But it was the continuation of a pattern. Gordon could assume that I would put the interests of the party and the government first, that I would look at the bigger picture and that he would never have to worry about me making any trouble. In general, this is the right way to go about it. But while Cabinet colleagues who threaten to throw their weight around lose the goodwill that's necessary to work effectively across government, sometimes the menace of a public fallout means that they are treated more respectfully. While all the Cabinet members and civil servants at that first meeting were preoccupied with the agenda for the next phase of government under Gordon's leadership, no one could have failed to notice that, as we all took our seats in our new roles, I slunk down to the end of the table. Our line-up for the formal photograph of Gordon's first Cabinet tells the same story: far from being central, I'm almost out of sight, at the end of the row.

In early March 2008, news started to circulate that Gordon was going to be away the following Wednesday and there would have to be a stand-in for him at Prime Minister's Questions, the biggest political and parliamentary event of the week. There was controlled hysteria in my office. Usually, it would be the job of the Deputy Prime Minister, but there wasn't one. If Gordon asked someone else to do it, I'd be humiliated, having to sit next to them. If Gordon asked me to do it, I'd be humiliated if I couldn't pull it off.

I suspected Jack Straw would be given the task of doing PMQs, but the message came through to my office that it was to be me. My private office staff were delighted and apprehensive in equal measure. Anna Healy became calmer and more purposeful than ever.

This was going to be a key test of whether I was 'up to the job' of Deputy Leader. I'd sat in the House for Prime Minister's Questions for twenty-five years and I'd asked Prime Minister's Questions from the Opposition countless times. I'd sat next to Gordon every Wednesday, supporting him as he answered PMQs and I'd always thanked my lucky stars that it wasn't me in the hot seat. But now it was.

With Gordon away, David Cameron wouldn't be asking the questions as Leader of the Opposition but would arrange a stand-in, and we had heard that it was to be William Hague. Having himself been Leader of the Opposition, Hague was an old hand at PMQs and, with his witty and knowledgeable repartee, had often got the better of Tony. Since Hague had given up the leadership, and after a spell off the front bench, he'd grown in stature, becoming Shadow Foreign Secretary and David Cameron's deputy. He was someone who was universally regarded as being able to 'command the House' and I, most definitely, was not. The press lobby was buzzing about my first appearance, eagerly anticipating what they unanimously predicted would be a bloodbath.

It's hard to overstate the atmosphere in the House of Commons for PMQs. All the MPs, most of whom are men, cram on to the benches on both sides of the House. MPs who can't find anywhere to sit gather in a throng and stand at 'the bar' opposite the Speaker or crowd around the sides and the back of the Speaker's Chair. Up above the Chamber, in the press gallery, the lobby journalists lean forward in their seats, and the public gallery is packed.

No woman had answered Prime Minister's Questions since Margaret Thatcher had for the last time eighteen years earlier. As the days and hours ticked away, my dread and fear grew and the tension in my office mounted. I wasn't worried on behalf of the government; it wasn't going to stand or fall on my performance as Gordon's understudy. But the party would hate it if their deputy was publicly vanquished. And I knew there would be women all over the country, watching PMQs on television, who would be crestfallen if I, a woman, fell flat on my face on this big parliamentary occasion. I thought the predictions were right and that Hague would wipe the floor with me. I knew that if I flopped it would be a field day for all my detractors in the press and that the parliamentary sketch writers would dip their pens in my blood.

The Monday before the dreaded PMQs Wednesday, I went out, as part of my usual constituency activities, with the police on a patrol through Peckham. It's routine for a local MP to sit down with the Borough Commander, the head of the local police, for a meeting and then join the police at work in a police car or on foot patrol. As the police put on their stab-proof vests, they handed over one for me and one for Charlotte, my constituency assistant, to wear. For more than twenty years, I'd walked around Peckham, never once taking any security precautions, and Charlotte and I had gone into the police station together unprotected half an hour earlier. But I put on the proffered vest and out we went, on to the streets with the patrol. As she did routinely for every constituency visit, Charlotte took a picture of us and uploaded it on to my website later in the day, reporting that I'd been out on the streets with the police and praising the work they do in Peckham. It joined other pictures of me wearing the gear of the people I was visiting: a hairnet in a food factory, a visor in an engineering factory, a hard hat on a building site. I wasn't expecting anyone to think I was actually preparing the food, operating the machinery or laying the bricks, any more than they would think I was fighting crime, but I'd always politely donned the outfits I was given without a second thought. But later in the afternoon Ayesha got a call from the *Daily Mail* telling her that their front-page story was me wearing a stab vest in Peckham. The picture apparently proved how violent London had become under Labour and how unpopular I was in my own constituency.

The story was at one and the same time both malicious and trivial, and I thought it would go nowhere beyond the *Mail*, but it became a lead item on Radio 4's *Today* programme on the Tuesday.

I was so angry that the BBC were promulgating a misrepresentation that I rang up and protested, which only made it worse. The 'story' raged through the other newspapers, on television and on radio all Tuesday and into the Wednesday of my PMQs. I was furious that, once again, the media had made Peckham look like a bad place, but also that this time, unwittingly, I'd precipitated the bad coverage. And my sense of trepidation about the PMQs grew. I could just imagine William Hague rubbing his hands with glee at the terrible publicity I was getting the day before I was to face him. As well as doing my normal work as Leader of the House and Equality Minister and preparing for PMQs, now I was also having to fight the national press.

Gordon's PMQs prep team of Number Ten civil servants came to my office on Monday night. I recognized them immediately from having seen them sitting, poker-faced, in a row every Wednesday in the civil servants' box under the press gallery. James Bowler and Nicholas Houghton were total professionals. They each had two enormous files, bristling with brightly coloured flag markers, and there was also a set for me. The PMQs prep file is like a vast political encyclopaedia. There are over six hundred MPs and they can ask anything they choose, from demanding that a new drug be made available on the NHS, through the prospects for interest rates, to the effect of climate change on the Brazilian rainforest or the cost of housing in the West Midlands. I would need to be sufficiently on top of every issue to understand what the question was about, what the key facts were, what the government's view was, what action we were taking, if any, and what the potential criticisms of us might be. James and his team were calmly determined to equip me to perform this impossible feat. Anna and Ayesha joined us, together with Des McCartan and Mike Winter from my private office and my witty and Commons-savvy Deputy Leader of the House, Rhonnda MP Chris Bryant. We spent an hour or so scoping out all the issues that could possibly come up in the thirty minutes which awaited me. My immediate instinct was to think that I didn't know anything. But as I went through the files over and over again, I realized that, after so many years immersed in all the issues affecting people in this country, it was all familiar to me.

We met again in my office on Tuesday afternoon, and on Wednesday, at 8 a.m., we began our preparation for what lay ahead around the enormous table in the Prime Minister's grand room in the Commons, complete with gilded mirrors and plushly upholstered furniture. The last time I had been in that room was ten years earlier, when I'd been sacked by Tony. This time, I was preparing for my 'execution' by William Hague. Prime Minister's Questions is not just about your government's policies, it's about your performance as well. PMQs is like taking an exam, in public, where the syllabus is the whole world.

Instead of 'attack is the best means of defence', we decided on a 'no first strike' rule. We anticipated that Hague would make a snide reference to Labour never having had a woman leader. We wrestled with how to deal with the ridicule that he would heap on me because of the story about the stab vest. My initial suggestion was that I should treat any jibe with disdain and try to 'rise above it', but Ayesha said this wouldn't work, and that I'd have to fight back. She came up with the idea that, if he tried to make fun of the stab vest, we should remind the House of how ludicrous he'd looked wearing a baseball cap in a recent photo. We decided to reference, in my response, the then-current television show hosted by Trinny Woodall and Susannah Constantine, *What Not to Wear*.

Usually, when it's the understudies doing PMQs, it's less well attended, but when I walked in my heart sank to see that it was every bit as packed as usual, with every seat taken, MPs sitting on the floor in the aisles and standing twelve deep behind the 'bar' at the end of the House opposite the Speaker. Remembering how often Hague had beaten Tony at PMQs, the Tories were clearly anticipating a Hague triumph. They cheered him in, and cheered again, ironically, when I took my place opposite him. The atmosphere on our side was uneasy, but I was grateful for their supportive, though muted, cheers as I took my seat. I looked up at the press gallery, jammed with journalists, pens poised to report my drubbing, and then up at the visitors' gallery opposite me, where Jack and our children were beaming down encouragingly. I'd always been keen to keep the children out of the public eye and this was the first time they'd ever come to see me speak in the House of Commons. I suddenly thought I must have been mad to bring them to witness my biggest public challenge and the moment of my probable humiliation.

William Hague started out with a back-handed compliment to me for being the first Labour woman to answer PMQs and reminded everyone that it was the Tories who had had, with Margaret Thatcher, Britain's first, and only, woman prime minister. Sitting next to him, no doubt to emphasize the Tories' female credentials, were two of the women in the Shadow Cabinet, Theresa Villiers and my opposite number, Shadow Leader of the House Theresa May. But it wasn't wise for him, a man, to attack me, a woman, on the issue of gender. I was ready with my opening rejoinder, and challenged him as to why it was he who was asking the questions at PMQs while Theresa May, who should have been doing it, was sitting next to him in silence. I asked him if it was now the role of women in the Tory party to be seen but not heard. Suddenly, it looked like they'd made a mistake putting William Hague up against me. The Labour benches were astonished to see him floundering and the apprehensive quiet from our benches turned into noisy cheers.

Hague pressed on with his next question, making reference both to my not being taken seriously in the Cabinet and the stab-vest photo, saying that, because I dressed for each occasion, I probably went to the Cabinet in a clown's suit. I rejoined by saying that, when it came to deciding what to wear or what not to wear, the last person I'd take advice from was the man in the baseball cap. By this time, our side were cheering loudly. And as they grew louder, the Tories fell silent. Hague went through the motions for his remaining four questions to me, but it was clear that I was not only going to get through PMQs, I was going to come out on top.

I answered questions from all sides on a multiplicity of issues.

That week, Gordon's abolition of the ten-pence tax rate he'd brought in in 1999 came into effect. It was deeply unpopular and had made many people worse off, particularly women between the ages of sixty and sixty-five. Gordon subsequently recognized that abolishing it was a mistake, but at that point we were still defending it. Given that it hit women hard, it should have been the key attack from Hague, but his mistaken decision to attack me personally, rather than to attack this one policy which was a genuine weakness, deprived him of the chance to challenge us on an issue of substance and delivered me a wholly unexpected Commons 'moment'. I'd been worried there would be questions about the abolition of the ten-pence tax rate, but no one asked about it.

As soon as the thirty minutes were up, I squeezed past my fellow Cabinet members on the front bench, getting congratulatory thumps on the back. I met up with Jack and the children and we walked together through the Central Lobby to the Pugin Room, where we had tea, with Anna and Ayesha. It took us quite a while to get there, as Labour MPs who'd backed me for Deputy in 2007 bounced up to congratulate me, happy and relieved that today, at least, their decision had been vindicated. Labour colleagues who hadn't backed me came up and said they had thought I wouldn't be up to the job and were surprised but pleased to discover they had been wrong. Even Tories came up and said how well I'd done. We were on the main television news that night and all the papers the next day declared me the winner. The following morning I received a package containing a DVD which the Number Ten civil service team had made of the occasion in a case emblazoned with the complimentary newspaper headlines. After all the years of feeling like the underdog in the Commons, it felt like a moment of triumph.

At one level, PMQs is just half an hour on a Wednesday with lots of shouting and jeering. Many regard it as a ludicrous spectacle which demeans our democracy. It is particularly criticized, as it is seen to be bullying and to replace reasoned argument with taunting. But for all my criticism of PMQs over the years, I couldn't, as the 'stand-in', seek to redefine it on this one occasion and therefore my only option had been to try to succeed on its own terms. Gordon was delighted with how well it had gone and texted me enthusiastically. The Labour members were happy to have a moment of pride at a time when the government was being buffeted on so many fronts. Every Labour dinner or meeting I went to thereafter, I was always introduced as not only the Deputy Leader but as the woman who had slayed the Tories at PMQs. What PMQs does is not only show whether the government has a robust position on the issues raised, it also exposes whether or not the individual can command the confidence and backing of their own side and win in a trial of strength. My PMQs appearance was an important enhancement of my standing and strengthened my arm for what I was trying to do in government.

Later that week, I was in Washington for an official visit to talk to people in the White House about equality legislation, and we stayed with my long-term friend, Democrat feminist Judy Lichtman. She switched on her television, as she always did, to watch the weekly round-up of UK news, which included PMQs. The US has nothing like it and, like many Americans, Judy was fascinated by it. It seemed an even more bizarre parliamentary event when I watched it on television on the other side of the Atlantic.

It was a joy to take on the role of Women and Equality Minister, and so different from when I had first been in the Cabinet ten years earlier. This time I was in my new incarnation as Deputy Leader, with seven other women now in Cabinet, including Yvette Cooper and Patricia Scotland. Plus, the women MPs who had arrived in 1997 and who supported the equality agenda were by now seasoned parliamentarians. In every government department there were women junior ministers who were our allies and who helped us fight our corner, and there was a cadre of women civil servants and special advisers committed to feminism who'd risen up the ladder to senior positions, like Francine Bates in the Education Department, Kath Raymond in the Home Office and Maeve Sherlock in the Treasury.

In addition, our arguments on women had gained much wider political acceptance.

A priority for me was to get a new Equality Act passed. Patricia Hewitt, when she was Minister for Women and Equality, had fought to get a commitment to a new Equality Act in our manifesto for 2005. She succeeded, but it was only the very last sentence on the very last page and, two years later, preparations for it had yet to begin in earnest. The manifesto said we would introduce a single Equality Act to modernize and simplify equality legislation and, while it was obviously a good idea to bring together all the law on discrimination into one Act, I wanted to take the opportunity to do much more than consolidate and simplify. I wanted to use a new bill to make a quantum leap forward on equality, to strengthen and extend legal backing for and the promotion of equality on gender and race but also on disability, age, sexual orientation and class.

With the Equality brief, there arrived a new team of civil servants, headed by Lise-Anne Boissière in my private office and later joined by Vicky Francis as press officer and Melanie Field as lead civil servant. They were a new generation of civil servants who were committed to equality and proud of their work in the Government Equality Office (GEO), a world away from those I'd met in 1997, who had felt that being in the GEO was some form of punishment.

I called together the key equality organizations, among them Stonewall, Operation Black Vote, the TUC, the Fawcett Society, the Equality and Human Rights Commission, Scope and Age Concern. We met around the vast table in the grand dining room downstairs from my office in Admiralty House, surrounded by portraits of admirals and enormous oil paintings depicting naval conquests. I asked them what they wanted in the Equality Bill, hoping for a long and radical list. But I was disappointed: they had no specific demands. They all seemed to have accepted that the bill would be just a consolidation exercise. They'd been working consensually and productively with our government and the agenda had been progressing steadily for so many years that their subversive 'outsider' identities had been dissipated, their demands muted. With women coming into government as MPs and special advisers, the government commitment to equality had grown stronger but, outside, the movement for equality had grown weaker. They'd become supporters of and partners with the government, but now, if I was to make progress in the teeth of resistance from other government departments, I needed them once more to be 'outsiders', challenging the government and making radical demands of us. The temptation is for an outside organization to support a government which is sympathetic to their agenda. But these organizations need at the same time to keep some distance and their independence. They need to set the agenda and maintain the ideological lead. That can't be left to the government, and yet that's what had happened.

I pressed them, asking if they could have anything they wanted in the bill, what would it be. I said that modest demands were not what I was looking for here and urged them to spell out their 'unreasonable demands'. I emphasized to them that I'd fight within government for as much progress as we could possibly make but that, to get it through, I'd need their backing and their insistence that, whatever we did, it wasn't enough.

After that meeting it became an office joke that I would always ask people for their 'unreasonable demands'. Every demand I've ever made has been denounced as unreasonable, but so many of them have then been implemented and become generally accepted. My experience is that, when it comes to equality, today's heresy is tomorrow's orthodoxy. And it has an energizing effect to ask people what they really want rather than having them ask just for what they think they might get. Our office mantra became 'Remember: today's unreasonable demand is tomorrow's conventional wisdom.'

That summer of 2007, as soon as I was in my new role as Minister for Women and Equality, I had a meeting with the civil service team who were going to be leading on the bill. They were bright and professional but, despite the enthusiasm and high quality of the civil servants in it, the GEO was still seen by other government departments as marginal and inferior. Around Whitehall, the prestige lay with civil servants in the big-delivery departments, such as Health and Defence, the big-spending departments, like the Department of Social Security, historic departments such as the Foreign Office, and the department that holds the purse strings, the Treasury. At our first meeting, the team seemed able to tell me only what other government departments would stop us from doing. I explained that I wanted an Equality Bill which would break new ground and be truly radical and that, together, we would make a step change in equality law. They looked intrigued but unconvinced.

The first equality laws had been brought in by a Labour government more than forty years earlier. Progress had been made to outlaw overt discrimination, but it couldn't be denied that inequality and discrimination persisted. Men working full-time still earned 40 per cent more per hour than women who worked part-time. Although more disabled people were working than ever before, a disabled person was still two and a half times more likely than someone without a disability to be out of work. If someone is black or Asian, they are less likely to be in work and, if they are in work, they are more likely to be earning less than would be expected for someone with their level of qualifications. Homophobic bullying still blighted the lives of most lesbian and gay young people and it was still perfectly lawful to say to someone, 'I'm sorry, but you're too old,' and deny them anything, from health care to insurance.

My belief, drawn from the women's movement, was that everyone had the right to be treated fairly and to have the opportunity to fulfil their potential, and in order to progress towards that the government had to take an active role. Equality is necessary for the individual: it is a basic right to be free from prejudice and discrimination. It is necessary for society: an unequal society can't be at ease with itself; an equal society generates greater social cohesion. And it is necessary for the economy: a modern economy thrives in a culture which offers employers the broadest labour pool, makes sure that everyone of working age who is able to participates in the labour market, rather than some being marginalized or excluded, and recognizes that diversity makes us outward facing as a country, helping us to compete in a global economy.

We began to develop the agenda for change over the next few months. And the following June, I announced to the House of Commons the first outline of the proposed contents of the Equality Bill. It would no longer be enough for public authorities not to discriminate; every part of the public sector would have a new duty to promote equality. We would ban all discrimination on the grounds of age. We would make employers publish their gender pay gap. Men-only clubs, golf clubs and working men's clubs alike would have to open their membership up to women on equal terms with the men. We would extend the law to allow the continuation of all-women shortlists for Parliament. We would change the law to allow for positive action so that where an employer – for example, the police service – had valid reasons to increase their percentage of black and Asian recruits, they would be allowed to discriminate positively to do so without breaking the law. Every action would have to be judged against the test of whether it would narrow the gap between rich and poor, and this would be policed by the Equality and Human Rights Commission.

A major cause of inequality is class background, and this had never previously been included in the responsibilities of the Minister for Women and Equality. But one of the most fundamental principles of Labour, and one which had led me and most other Labour members to join the party, was a hatred of the unfairness of life chances being limited because an individual is born into a poor family or privileged because they are born into a wealthy one. The Labour party is about giving everyone an equal chance and, as well as tackling all the other forms of discrimination, I saw the Equality Act as an opportunity to make a decisive intervention in tackling inequality rooted in social class.

Knowing that there'd be resistance to this from those in government who would think it too radical and therefore likely to frighten off voters in the centre ground of politics, I thought the best approach would be to lay the basis for this legislation with a Royal Commission on income inequality, following in the footsteps of the 1979 Royal Commission on the Distribution of Income and Wealth. It could set out the facts and figures about class inequality in twenty-first-century Britain. But Number Ten wouldn't wear it, and neither would the DSS or the Treasury. They were concerned about highlighting the fact that, despite more than ten years of Labour government, there was still a problem of socio-economic inequality in the UK. They didn't want attention drawn to it and then to be forced to pursue radical policies to attempt to remedy it. My view was that we should be proud of the progress we had made on tackling the widening gap we had inherited from the Tory government but that we should not hesitate to acknowledge that there was still more to do. It was better to face up to the intractability of class inequality and show we were stepping up our action to tackle it, rather than sweep it under the carpet.

In the end, I managed to get agreement to commission John Hills, Director of the Centre for Analysis of Social Exclusion, Professor of Social Policy at the London School of Economics and a long-standing analyst of inequality, to establish and chair a National Equality Panel and to produce a report on socio-economic inequality for us. In January 2010, with the General Election a few months away, and despite many misgivings from, and wrangling with, other departments, we published the National Equality Panel's seminal report 'An Anatomy of Economic Inequality in the UK'. It showed that, while the gap between rich and poor had stopped growing since Labour came into government, it remained wide. It demonstrated, also having looked at other countries, that the bigger the gap between the top and the bottom, the further apart the rungs on the ladder and therefore the harder it is to climb. Inequality is the enemy of social mobility.

This was the analytical basis I needed to place a duty on all public sector bodies to take active steps to narrow the gap between rich and poor. The Equality Bill would oblige them, by law, to consider, when they took any action, whether it would narrow or widen the income divide. This became Clause One of the bill. It was sup-ported by Labour councillors, MPs, the TUC and anti-poverty campaigning organizations, but in addition, Trevor Phillips, who'd been appointed to the chair of the Equality and Human Rights Commission (EHRC) some years earlier, proved a crucial and out-spoken ally. Undeterred by it being outside the remit of the EHRC, Trevor enthusiastically backed the 'socio-economic duty' in Clause One, and we met up frequently to plan how to get it past the host of nervous ministers and on to the statute book. When the press got hold of it, it was decried, in a parody of the discredited Stalinist notion of 'socialism in one country' which had underpinned the Soviet Union, as 'socialism in one clause'. But this was exactly what I wanted: it would take the drive for socio-economic equality into every council, quango and government department.

Getting the Equality Bill through entailed tussles with many other government departments. The Health Department was wor-ried about the impact on the NHS of a new law on age discrimination. The Communities and Local Government Department was wor-ried about the impact on council finances of their new duties to promote equality. But our biggest foe was the Department of Busi-ness, which opposed the proposition to make employers publish gender pay gaps in their business and argued that, with the econ-omy reeling under the impact of the global financial crisis, all progress on equality would have to be put on hold. And just about all the departments were worried about the big change that Clause One, that on socio-economic duty, would bring about.

We got bogged down by all the objections to the bill. No matter how hard the team worked, my special advisers, junior ministers and civil servants were rebuffed on all fronts. We were coming up against a brick wall. There's a convention in government that a department can't proceed with a bill without the agreement of every other department its implementation would affect. Some-times, it's an outright 'no'; sometimes more consultations and pilot schemes are suggested before the bill is kicked into the long grass. But with the next General Election on the horizon, this kind of delaying tactic would have killed the bill as surely as any out-right 'no'.

However, while internal resistance was hardening, word had started to spread that there was the possibility of a genuinely rad-ical Equality Bill, and the demand for it from outside organizations and from the wider Labour party took off. A far-reaching network of organizations that backed the bill was building up. Age Concern was pressing for the age-discrimination provisions, the TUC and women's organizations wanted pay transparency, the police wanted the positive-action provisions implemented, the disability lobby and the LGBT organizations wanted the public sector duty, and party members backed the whole thing, as it showed that their gov-ernment had a strong commitment to equality. As well as strong support from our backbench MPs, the bill had crucial backing from Labour peers. It was the old network – experienced trade unionists and committed feminists like Margaret Prosser and Glenys Thornton, Jan Royall, who was now our Leader in the Lords, and Anita Gayle, former Women's Officer and General Secretary for Wales – women with whom I'd worked for decades and who were now, fortunately for our quest for the Equality Bill, in the House of Lords. The Labour peers were crucial in ensuring that the bill made it through the Lords before we ran out of time.

Vera Baird, the Solicitor General, later joined our equalities min-isterial team for the bill, and she and Barbara Keeley, a feminist Greater Manchester MP and my parliamentary aide, together with Ayesha and the civil servants, pressed on, determined not to take no for an answer. But other departments still blocked the bill and pre-vented it getting over its final hurdle. And it was not as if we could count on the support of sympathetic Tory women either. Far from helping us to get the Equality Bill through, Theresa May, who was at that time Shadow Minister for Women and Equality, was set to vote against it in its crucial first vote in the House of Commons.

As Deputy Leader, I had fortnightly one-to-one meetings with Gordon. As the months wore on, with the global financial crisis, his poll ratings sliding and the press becoming full of bitter briefings between him and Cabinet ministers, I spent most of these trying to prop up his morale. When all the problems of the world were on his shoulders and bearing down on the Labour government, I was reluctant to bring him yet another by asking him to get involved in my battles on the Equality Bill. And I didn't want to admit that, even though I was Deputy Leader, I was incapable of winning my own battles.

But the weeks and days were counting down to the dissolution of parliament for the General Election and the bill was in danger of failing through lack of time. I needed Gordon's backing, and Ayesha was adamant that, on this occasion, I should pile on the pressure and insist on getting the bill passed.

I used one of my last bilateral meetings with Gordon as Prime Minister to demand that he take my side in the row on the bill. He said he'd back me but was a little vague, so I wasn't sure whether I had really managed to nail it down. But the next time I passed Jeremy Heywood, the Cabinet Secretary, in Number Ten, on my way to a meeting, he asked me what I needed him to do. After all the obstruction and trench warfare that had beset the bill for the best part of two years, this was a huge relief. With Number Ten on our side, the Department of Trade and Industry would 'do business' with us, we could resolve the remaining issues in sensible discussion and the Equality Bill could go through into law.

The Commons agreed the final stage of the Equality Bill on 6 April 2010, the very day that Gordon called the General Election. At the eleventh hour, the Equality Bill, which Patricia Hewitt had crowbarred into our 2005 manifesto as our very last promise, was the last Labour bill to pass through all its parliamentary stages and into law.

I celebrated with Vera, Ayesha, my private office, and Melanie and her team of civil servants from the GEO. It felt like a triumph over the odds to have got the bill through. But now the shadow of the impending General Election was hanging over us. We dreaded the thought that, within just a few weeks, the Tories could be in government and that we would have to retreat to the impotence of opposition, unable to use the bill to drive forward progress on equal pay, on tackling discrimination and in bringing in the new socio-economic equality duty. And it did look increasingly likely that we were going to lose.

A bill which becomes an Act of Parliament doesn't come into effect until Parliament agrees a 'commencement order' to implement it. Because we got the Equality Act into law only in the last days of the Labour government, we were not able to 'commence' any of its provisions and it would be the responsibility of whoever became the government after the General Election to decide whether and which bits of the Act to bring into effect. As soon as the new Conservative-led government was formed, the new Equality Minister, Theresa May, announced that, despite the fact that she and the Tories had voted against it, they would implement much of it – but not Clause One. So, while Clause One remains on the statute book, it has never been brought into effect.

All inequality undermines community and national cohesion. When some are so much more disadvantaged than others, it's impossible for people to believe that we are 'all in it together'. The length of time it took me to get the Equality Act on to the statute book meant that, while our government had implemented many policies which helped redress class inequality, we lacked the unique powers that would have been put into place by Clause One – a lever across every public organization to bear down on inequality in everything they do and a high-profile, totemic symbol of our commitment to tackling class inequality.

Had we implemented the Equality Act in 2007, it would, I believe, have had two important political effects. It would have countered the sense among white working-class communities that the government is an elite which is never, even when it's Labour, on their side. It was this sense of alienation that was overwhelmingly in evidence when it came to the vote to leave the European Union. And it would have made it harder for the ultra-left in the Labour party to promulgate the view that our government didn't care about class inequality.

Clause One remains unfinished business. Despite declaring herself committed to equality, Theresa May is still refusing to implement it. And I've watched with mixed feelings as the Tories put the clauses on equal pay into action, pleased that it will help women make progress but frustrated that it should ever have been such a long, hard battle for a Labour minister to have the clauses put into law.

One effect of the global financial crisis was to plunge the government into work to rescue the banks and to do what it could to protect jobs. It sucked the oxygen out of any radical political impetus on equality. Most ministers thought we needed to tackle what they regarded as the basics rather than develop new horizons on equality. And those who had never agreed with the equality agenda in the first place had a ready excuse. Gordon had done so much on equality when he was Chancellor, from tax credits to global anti-poverty targets. But when he was Prime Minister there was to be no new progressive agenda, just a struggle with the global markets and a slide into political unpopularity. And Labour's loss of office meant that our anti-poverty agenda is now slowly but surely being eroded by the Tories.

It would all have been so different if Gordon had called an election in 2007, won it and then had five years to develop and implement progressive measures. He had started off as Prime Minister in 2007 riding high in the opinion polls. That summer, the country was hit by flooding and then an epidemic of Bluetongue disease. Gordon cancelled his family holiday, returning to Number Ten to lead the government response, and his poll ratings climbed still further as he was seen to seize the helm in difficult times. In early autumn he convened a political meeting of the Cabinet at Chequers. A political Cabinet is where the Cabinet meets without civil servants and discusses party political matters as well as government business. It was a sunny day and, from the beautiful oak-panelled room where we were gathered, you could see the idyllic rolling Buckinghamshire countryside, dotted with sheep and the shadowy figures of police marksmen. Everyone was in high spirits. Deborah Mattinson reported to the meeting that the polls showed that Labour was ahead of the Tories, and that Gordon was even more popular than the party and way ahead of Cameron. The question in everyone's mind was, how long would it last? Should Gordon go for the election now, or leave it and try to consolidate his position yet further? We discussed it at the meeting but nothing was formally concluded. This was a political judgement rather than an exact science and, ultimately, the question of when to call a General Election was for the Prime Minister alone to decide.

Over the following days the newspapers were full of speculation about whether Gordon would call an election. He didn't involve me in these Downing Street discussions, but assuming that I was party to them, Labour MPs and party members lobbied me. They were evenly divided, some wanting to wait, worried about campaigning for a November election on dark evenings when people don't want to stand on their doorstep chatting. Others said it would be looking a gift horse in the mouth not to have an election when our poll position was so strong. Speculation mounted and contradictory briefings continued to appear in the papers.

Our September Labour party conference and the newspaper briefings from inside Number Ten aroused an expectation that Gordon would call an election. So we were nonplussed when the briefings in early October reported that he was about to announce that he'd decided against it. As it turned out, the decision he made was the wrong one. It seemed as if he'd hovered on the brink but then run away from the electorate. A prime minister must always look decisive, and it's fatal to appear to fear the voters. It was dubbed the 'election that never was' and Gordon's poll ratings plunged. His honeymoon with the public ended overnight. If the speculation hadn't been allowed to run in the first place, there probably would have been no public clamour for an early election but, once it had, Gordon had to explain why he wasn't calling an election. He said there should be more time for the public to see the changes that he would bring in as Prime Minister before they voted. But it wasn't entirely clear what those changes would be, or exactly how his government would be different from Tony's, in which he'd played such a prominent part.

So, politically, after barely three months, Gordon was under siege. And in Parliament he came under fire not only from the Tories but also from those Blairites who continued to smoulder about what they believed was Gordon's part in pushing Tony out. Gordon seemed to think that everyone was against him. Satirical cartoons started to appear; in one, even I was depicted stabbing him in the back.

I'd seen Gordon's work, with Tony, to make Labour electable. I'd worked closely with him over so many years and had a deep admiration for his intellect. Though working relations between us were not always smooth, I, unlike some other ministers, never briefed against him in the press. My chief special adviser, Anna Healy, was implacably opposed to malicious briefings against anyone, let alone the Prime Minister. And that was the tone she set for the office. She wouldn't even engage in retaliatory briefing, where you 'set the record straight' by having your own say when a journalist tells you something nasty that a colleague, or their advisers, is saying about you. Her view, rightly, was that the first briefing didn't justify the second and that the party didn't want either to be happening. I strongly disapproved of off-the-record briefings against Gordon, regarding them as cowardly and counter-productive.

However, this wasn't the case across the board. No sooner had Gordon become Prime Minister, on a promise of 'no more briefings and spin', than the newspapers filled up with briefings from Number Ten against ministers and complaints from unnamed senior ministers that Gordon's 'people', and, in particular, Damian McBride, his adviser, were briefing against them.

Ministers, seeing malicious insider reports about them appearing in the papers, and suspecting Gordon's adviser, McBride, complained to Gordon. But Gordon would always say that McBride denied it. There was no proof, and the nasty briefings continued unabated. Ever since I'd become Deputy, MPs had warned me that

Gordon's people were briefing against me. I hoped that wasn't the case. It would be so destructive, and what on earth would be the point?

In the baking-hot last days of September 2008, with the storm of the global financial crisis growing stronger and the press full of malicious briefings and counter-briefings, we headed up to Manchester for our annual conference. The conference hotel, where I, the Cabinet, the NEC and senior party staff were all staying was the new, luxury Radisson Blu.

As usual, it was to be my task as Deputy Leader to make the closing speech to the conference. It's not something you can prepare for much in advance, because you have to pick up on the themes of the conference in it. As always, conference was frantically busy for me; I would speak at receptions held by all the regions, meet and greet countless party members from all over the UK and then rush back to my room to join my staff team and Chris Bryant to work on the next speech for the next reception. On the Monday afternoon, we were working on a first draft of my closing speech, due to be given on Wednesday. The room was hot and, feeling that my head was about to burst with the pressure, I stepped out on to the balcony for a breath of air. As I stood there for a few moments, I heard a man talking on a balcony a couple of floors up. I couldn't see who it was but I could hear him clearly and heard my name. The man was telling a story, and I was at the centre of it. It was total fiction. It sounded like some sort of radio drama, with me as a character in it. Bewildered, I beckoned my staff to come out on to the balcony. Suddenly, as we stood out there listening, we all recognized the voice of the man who was talking. It was Damian McBride.

Since we could hear no response to what he was saying, it was clear that he was talking on the phone. What we heard McBride say was that there'd been a big row between me and Sarah Brown, Gordon's wife, and that I, trying to muscle my way in, was insisting on introducing Gordon before he gave his Leader's speech at conference the next day. But, McBride chortled, Sarah had slapped me down, insisting that she, not I, was going to introduce Gordon. She had really put me in my place – and how I had fumed! This was a pack of lies. The Deputy never introduces the Leader's speech, and it had never crossed my mind that I should do it and the idea had never even been floated by me or by anyone else. But McBride veritably purred as he described how Sarah had cut me down to size. I was horrified at the suggestion that I was in any way rivalrous with Sarah. She was Gordon's wife and I was his deputy. The idea that I would be arguing with her over Gordon was demeaning and the idea that she'd slapped me down was humiliating. It wasn't just that it wasn't true, it is the worst thing for men to set women against each other. And it was frightening to hear the Prime Minister's special adviser briefing against me, his loyal Deputy. It was impossible to comprehend what purpose it could serve.

I dialled McBride's number and, as soon as he was off the call, he picked up. I said something along the lines of 'What on earth are you saying? It's all a pack of lies, you've got to stop it.' He said not to worry, that he'd sort it out right away, and the call ended. I was too shaken to carry on preparing my speech and wanted to storm off to Gordon there and then. But Anna insisted that I must focus on my busy schedule for the rest of the conference, let Gordon get on with his own conference duties, including his all-important Leader's speech, and that we'd sort it out with him when we got back to London. A short while later, we left my room to go off to another engagement. We called the lift and, as the doors opened, who should we see standing there in the crowded lift but McBride. He muttered to me, 'I've dealt with it.' He must have called around all the journalists and asked them not to run the 'story'. However, it did appear in one newspaper, which carried a fictitious account of a story on the bottom of its front page. Gordon was introduced by Sarah for his conference speech and in it paid a warm tribute to me.

Having worked in the Cabinet Office and being familiar with the Ministerial Code, Anna Healy knew that McBride had breached it in numerous ways. Under the code, a special adviser must not brief against another member of the government and must not tell a lie. The code requires the employing minister to take responsibility for the special adviser's compliance. The weekend we got back from conference, I rang to tell both Ed Miliband and Alistair Darling what we'd heard. I knew they had both complained to Gordon about McBride and I wanted to discuss what had happened with them before I saw Gordon. It was awful that McBride had been lying about me to the press but at least, this time, Gordon would have to put a stop to it. There were witnesses, so there could be no denials; and there could be no excuses, as it had not even the remotest connection to the truth. I asked to see Gordon on the Monday after the conference and went into his study at Number Ten. I told him what we'd heard McBride say and protested about it vehemently, saying it had to stop and McBride had to go. Gordon looked beleaguered and drained but expressed none of the outrage I'd expected, or even sympathy about what McBride had done to me. He said that he hadn't asked him to say what he did. But I hadn't alleged that he'd told him to say it. What I'd said was that he needed to stop it.

I said how angry this sort of thing made ministers, how unfair it was, how much it destabilized government, how bad it was for Gordon. I warned him that McBride couldn't continue in his job, as he'd carry on doing such things, and it was wrong and would rebound on Gordon and ruin his reputation. He said that he'd deal with it. I said that the best way to approach it was for me to make a formal complaint to the Cabinet Secretary, which is the procedure for any breach of the Ministerial Code. He was emphatic that I shouldn't, insisting again that he would deal with it. I left his study, muttering that he 'better had'.

But I was worried about what I'd discovered. The authority the Prime Minister's special adviser derives from their position gives them a hotline to the nation's media. Lives can be ruined by the media, and I was concerned about what McBride might invent next. I was dismayed by Gordon's failure to apologize for it or to make him apologize. And, of course, in the end, nothing changed.

Gordon didn't come back to me, but in the papers a few days later it was reported, with no explanation, that McBride was no longer going to be dealing directly with the press and would instead be head of 'strategy and planning'. But that meant he was still going to be in Number Ten and, inevitably, talking to the press. I was convinced that, from there, and knowing I'd complained, he'd step up his efforts to undermine me. All I'd succeeded in doing was making him an even bigger enemy. Perhaps I should have made a formal complaint. But we were in the grip of the global financial crisis, and Gordon was trying to steer the country through it. I knew it would give Gordon's enemies a field day if it became public that McBride had been caught lying about me and, once again, I didn't want to add to the difficulties Gordon and Labour were already facing.

Six months later, in April 2009, the press got hold of some emails Damian had written in which he was planning a smear campaign. In the first, sent on 13 January, Damian writes: 'Gents, a few ideas I have been working on for RedRag [a proposed new website]. For ease, I've written all the below as I'd write them for the site.' The ideas set out included spreading fabricated rumours about David Cameron and George Osborne, and making allegations of a sexual nature about the Tory backbencher Nadine Dorries, which she vigorously denied.

The fact that the Prime Minister's Head of Strategy and Planning could be doing this caused public outrage. I was disgusted. The Tories are our political opponents, but we should beat them with arguments, not smear them with lies. It was all in the public domain, so Gordon had no option but to sack McBride. And Gordon himself was badly tarnished as having been responsible for someone who, while being paid out of public funds, did such harmful, dishonest things. I hadn't put my foot down about McBride when I'd had the chance, feeling that, in the great scheme of things, a special adviser briefing against me wouldn't be seen as the biggest problem facing the country. But the reality was that it wasn't just about me. McBride undermining Cabinet ministers was a major problem for the government. It alienated Cabinet ministers from Gordon and made them guarded and resentful, just when we all needed to be pulling together. It made it impossible for there to be a genuine sense that we were working as a team and prevented Gordon from getting the backing that a prime minister needs even at the best of times. And when it became public for all to see, it blew out of the water Gordon's promise that, when he became Prime Minister after Tony, there'd be 'no more spin', and it undermined the sense that Labour was a party of principle and our leader a man with a 'moral compass'. And I hated the very thought that someone in Labour's team could feel that he could unleash havoc and misery in the lives of others.

With the collapse of Lehman Brothers in September 2008, the global financial crisis had gathered pace, hitting the economy, businesses, jobs and living standards. No one could be in any doubt about the gravity of what was an unprecedented crisis. The following year, it was the UK's turn to host the G20 summit, and the leaders of the world's developed economies descended on Downing Street. At the reception before the main G20 dinner, I was struck by the authority Gordon commanded in the room. It was more than just the fact that he was the host. All the attendees were shocked by the threat to their economies, and from their body language and the conversations they were having, it looked to me like they were turning to Gordon for guidance on how they should respond as the markets, like a *machine infernale*, stripped the value out of the banking system. They knew him from his ten years as Chancellor of the Exchequer, and he had a clear idea about what had to be done. What every government, and the global banking institutions, had to do was to leap ahead of the markets and, using however many billions it took, stand behind the banks, preventing them from failing, not because the banks deserved it but because to let them go under would turn a banking crisis and a recession into a global depression.

Though I was at the reception, I was not at the G20 summit dinner. Instead, I was invited to join the G20 wives' dinner, hosted by Sarah Brown. My office were aghast when the invitation came in, and we had an earnest discussion about how I should respond to it.

Should I refuse to go, reminding them that, although I am a woman, that did not make me a G20 wife? Or would that be an insult to all the women who were there and make it look as if I thought I was somehow above them? Should I therefore go and show sisterly solidarity? In the end, we decided that there was nothing for it but for me to go, and with good grace. I sat next to the wife of the Conservative Prime Minister of Canada and there was a lively discussion at the table about a new diet.

Despite Gordon's historic role in preventing a recession turning into a global economic depression, the jaundiced public perception of him after the 'election that never was', combined with the loss of jobs and the squeeze on living standards, obscured his highly significant role in and deft handling of the global financial crisis. Instead of seeing him as the country's best protection against a global problem, the perception became that he had caused an economic problem while he was Chancellor to which the country had now fallen victim. His custodianship of the economy, which had been his great strength, was now the cause of his unpopularity.

Throughout 2008, reports had been appearing in the press that there was going to be a 'coup' to depose Gordon and replace him with David Miliband. David began looking more prime ministerial, his shirts gleaming whiter – he even seemed to be growing taller; while Gordon was looking increasingly crushed and rumpled.

MPs, peers and party members started to ask to see me, but they would refuse to tell my office what it was about, which was a sure sign they were coming to complain about Gordon. Their complaints were not about policy, or the political direction of the party or the government, they were about Gordon's leadership style and his unpopularity with the public. Ministers complained that he was 'impossible' to work with, that he kept them in the dark, did things behind their back, agreed to something and then changed his mind, that he briefed against them, that they couldn't get in to see him and, when they did, it was pointless because he'd just fob them off and the problem would persist. MPs complained that their constituents had turned against him and those in marginal seats feared that, at the next General Election, they'd lose because of him. I listened to them, as I felt it was my job to do so. I couldn't argue with what they were saying, because it was obviously true, but I couldn't see that their complaints were going anywhere.

In the first week of June 2009 and in the week of the council elections, the government was rocked by the resignation from the Cabinet of Hazel Blears. She'd accused him of a lamentable inability to get Labour's message across. We were braced for poor results in the council elections and Jack and I were discussing the instability in government as we hurried to get to a concert in Hanover Square. Peter Mandelson had been calling on all ministers to stay loyal to the government, and suddenly I became convinced that Gordon was going to make him Deputy Prime Minister. Gordon's position was becoming increasingly destabilized, and Peter, who was Secretary of State for the Department of Business, was manoeuvring himself further and further into Number Ten. Jack said that this was inconceivable. It just wouldn't happen. It couldn't, as I was the elected Deputy Leader. We rushed into the concert as the conductor raised his baton and, much to the annoyance of the man sitting next to me, my phone started to rumble incessantly. I saw texts saying that James Purnell had resigned from the Cabinet, that it was expected that David Miliband would follow. And with Hazel Blears' resignation the previous day, it looked like a full-blown coup against Gordon was under way. The man sitting next to me protested about the light emanating from my phone, and I switched it off.

By the time we left the concert, it was clear that the coup had been abortive. David Miliband had come out and said he was staying in government. Gordon would do a reshuffle to replace the two Cabinet ministers and Number Ten called and asked me to come into Downing Street at eight o'clock the following morning. I told Anna Healy that I feared Gordon was preparing to make Peter Deputy Prime Minister. Anna always sought to reach agreement and to find a way around a problem, but this time she was adamant. I was Deputy Leader; I could not let it happen; it would show disrespect for the party which had elected me. To make it worse, Peter was not even an MP but an unelected appointee to the House of Lords. It would be a slap in the face for me personally to give the role to a man when it should have been mine, and a slap in the face for women. It was one thing my not being Deputy Prime Minister because there wasn't one; it was quite another for there to be one and for it not to be me. As I was in the car on my way to Downing Street, Anna called and told me that as Caroline Flint had just resigned, saying that Gordon treated women as window dressing, Number Ten wanted me to do interviews to defend him. The global financial crisis was rocking the economy and the government was being shaken by a potential coup. As Deputy Leader, it had always been my role to help stabilize things, so we agreed that I'd do the interviews, as soon as I'd seen Gordon himself.

I was ushered into the Prime Minister's study and Gordon beamed at me and said, 'I've got a great new role for you, which will be crucial for the party and for the General Election – Health Secretary.' I realized at once that my suspicions of the night before had been justified. I said, 'You're going to appoint Peter to be Deputy Prime Minister, aren't you?' Gordon had clearly planned not to tell me and looked shocked to be confronted. 'But things are so bad, I need him to help me,' he said. I pointed out that he'd put Peter in the Lords, he'd made him Business Secretary, and so of course Peter would help him. But as for him being Deputy Prime Minister, it would be 'over my dead body'. He started on again about how much he needed Peter and how difficult everything was, but I said I didn't have time to listen as I had to go and defend him against Caroline's accusations that he treated women as 'window dressing'. I pointed out how ironic this was. Just as he was trying to appoint a man over my head, he needed me to stand up and defend his treatment of women! He begged me to come back in after the interviews but I said it was pointless; my attitude would not change. He said I should anyway.

In the interviews I gave outside Parliament, I said that, although I could understand Caroline's frustrations, because we all wanted to make more progress and faster, the reality was that, with Gordon as Chancellor and then Prime Minister, the government had done so many things that had improved women's lives, bringing in the national minimum wage, the provision of universal childcare, and so on. I defended Gordon's record but didn't criticize Caroline, and then I went back to Number Ten. On the way, Anna called and said there were yet more requests for me to go on air to defend Gordon against Caroline's accusations, and we agreed that I'd do them once I'd seen him again.

For the second time, I was ushered in. It was a repeat of the first. He was pleading for me to agree to Peter being Deputy Prime Minister and I was adamant I wouldn't have it. I asked him how on earth he thought I'd be able to defend the decision when interviewers asked me what I thought. 'Over my dead body,' I repeated. We were going around in circles and I said there was no point continuing to talk about it as I wasn't going to change my view and, anyway, I had more interviews lined up to say, once more, that he didn't treat women as window dressing. Again, the irony! He insisted I come back, which I again said was pointless and again agreed to anyway. After more interviews, I returned. Gordon seemed calmer and said that he wouldn't make Peter Deputy Prime Minister. I was pleased but suspicious and, as I left, my parting shot was 'Okay, but you'd better not be going to double-cross me and do it by the back door.'

Later that afternoon the news broke that Gordon had appointed Peter Mandelson to be First Secretary of State. I, like most people, had never heard of the title before, but discovered it was an office which puts the holder above all other Cabinet ministers and is always held by the Deputy Prime Minister. It had previously been held by John Prescott when he was Deputy Prime Minister and was subsequently held by Nick Clegg when he was Deputy Prime Minister. Just in case anyone was to miss the point, Number Ten briefed the media that Peter Mandelson was now 'Deputy Prime Minister in all but name'. Rumours circulated that this was the price Peter had demanded for persuading David Miliband not to resign from the Cabinet. It was an affront to me, but one born out of Gordon's weakness. Peter had manipulated him into believing that he held the key to Gordon's re-election. He didn't; the only person who held the key to the election was Gordon and, with the 'election that never was', that ship had sailed. And even after Peter became 'Deputy Prime Minister in all but name' and moved into a large office with an adjoining door to Number Ten, old habits died hard with him and he still rolled his eyes behind Gordon's back in meetings.

I was furious with Gordon but, once again, I gritted my teeth and got on with my job, and for the same reasons I always did. I wanted us to win the election, so I didn't want to rock the boat. I wanted to live to fight another day, to remain in the team so I could push for the things I cared about. Resignation gives you fifteen minutes of fame and then you are impotent. Threats to resign aren't believed if they're not carried out but they certainly infuriate everyone. And though I was angry with him, I also felt sorry for Gordon. He'd wanted so long to be Prime Minister, and it was all turning to ashes in his hands. The judgement about how much fuss to kick up and how much to compromise had always kept me awake at night. I never thought about it strategically but, looking back, I can see that staying just the right side of remaining on the inside meant not only that I stayed loyal to the Labour cause but also that I could stay to do my job. It also meant that, while I saw countless other women MPs fall by the wayside, I was still there on Labour's front line, fighting the cause for women, surviving (except for those three years after I'd been sacked in 1998) a record thirty-one years on the front bench.

Despite his growing unpopularity with the public and the ministerial resentment against him, Gordon was not pushed out. There were many reasons for this. The economy was only just being pulled back from the brink of the financial precipice. Gordon had been the one to come up with the strategy that saw governments around the world stepping in and saving not just our but the world economy from total collapse. The global financial crisis had become the dominant issue of his prime ministership and there was no disagreement within the party about how he'd handled it. Deposing the Prime Minister would inevitably destabilize the government and threaten the economy, causing more businesses to fold and even more people to lose their jobs.

And there was the deep loyalty so many in the party felt towards him; he'd earned it over decades. Unlike Tony, he'd cultivated the party activists and was very much a 'party man'. The party's support for him was based not just on his years of working and campaigning with them but also on a recognition that Gordon was the architect of the modernization of our economic policy, which had been key to us getting out of opposition and into government. Party members were, justifiably, grateful to him.

He also had a bedrock of support in the PLP. In every section of it, and in every region, there were Labour people whom Gordon had personally helped, to whom he'd given advice, support, jobs. In Scotland, which had thirty-nine Labour MPs, Gordon was loved as a national icon of the party and was highly popular with the public, and still is today. Party members knew he'd been waiting for years to be Prime Minister, and they sympathized with the great personal grief he'd suffered with the tragic loss of his and Sarah's first child, Jennifer Jane.

While David Miliband was evidently keen to be Prime Minister, he couldn't declare that he'd run against Gordon and risk being seen as splitting the party at a difficult time for the government and the country. Given that 'he who wields the dagger never wears the crown', there was no declared alternative candidate to rally around.

And Gordon showed no signs of being prepared to stand down. He survived the resignation of James Purnell, Hazel Blears and Caroline Flint from the Cabinet, and the calls in January 2010 by former Cabinet ministers Patricia Hewitt and Geoff Hoon for him to go. If he did have any doubts about staying on as Prime Minister, he certainly never shared them with me, or anyone else that I heard of. This meant he could only be deposed in what would be a bloody, destabilizing coup. The personal loyalty and sympathy the party felt for Gordon and the admiration for what he'd done for decades meant that they wouldn't force him out against his will. Loyalty to our leader trumped the party's survival instinct.

Labour MPs have sometimes looked back enviously at how easily the Tory party ditched Margaret Thatcher when she became unpopular. The Tories seem to have such a deep instinct for getting and staying in power, remaining loyal to their leader when they're popular but ditching them without hesitation when they fall from public favour. Sometimes it seemed to me that Labour was the opposite. Labour members criticized Tony even when he was popular with the public and stuck with Gordon even when it seemed certain he would lead us to defeat. In any case, Labour's rules mean that it requires a vote of the whole membership to depose a leader, and the odds are always against that.

As the General Election campaign got under way in the spring of 2010, the polls predicted that Labour would lose. We had been in power for thirteen years and seemed to have run out of steam. And people were saying to us quite openly on the doorsteps and on the high streets that they wouldn't vote Labour because they didn't want Gordon as Prime Minister.

One day in the run-up to the election, I was canvassing in the Whitchurch suburb of Cardiff with the popular and energetic MP Julie Morgan. Everyone in the local high street greeted her warmly and spoke about the good work she'd done for them and their area. But then they declared that they weren't going to vote Labour this time. They were vehement. One man summed it up by declaring that he would vote Labour if anyone – literally anyone – else was Leader. They didn't like the Tories, and they knew it was they who would win the seat if Julie lost. But they weren't going to vote Labour so long as Gordon was Prime Minister, so they weren't going to vote for Julie. They'd never vote Tory, they just wouldn't vote at all. And I was hearing the same thing all around the country, except in Scotland, where loyalty to Gordon was strengthened by their sense that one of their finest was being attacked by the

English. Looking back at our General Election manifesto, it seems unsurprising that we lost. There was no fresh vision for the future, no new ideas of any scale or ambition, and the government had grown increasingly remote from the party's grass roots.

Whatever Gordon did or said, no one was listening any more. I was reminded of the time when, in the run-up to the 1997 election, I bumped into Tory Cabinet minister Virginia Bottomley in the Lady Members' Room behind the Speaker's Chair in the House of Commons. We exchanged 'how's it going?'s. She said that it didn't matter what the Tories did or said, no one wanted to see them or hear them. She added wryly, 'One day it will happen to you, too, you know.' And it did. But when the General Election results came in, although it was clear we hadn't won an overall majority, neither had the Tories. There'd have to be either some sort of coalition or a new election. After an election, a prime minister remains in post until a new government is formed, so Gordon was in the excruciating position of having been rejected by the voters but still being Prime Minister. I went into Downing Street to see him. He'd clearly been having lots of meetings, but he didn't say much to me except that he'd have to leave Downing Street immediately because, even though he was still Prime Minister, the public wouldn't like to see him still 'squatting' there after we'd lost the election.

Coalition talks were getting under way between Labour and the Liberal Democrats. We had what felt like very perfunctory planning sessions to go through the papers that had been prepared for the meeting and to commission further work. I assumed there must have been much more work done which I'd not been involved in. The meeting with the Lib Dems took place in Portcullis House. Labour's side consisted of Ed Miliband, Peter Mandelson, Lord Andrew Adonis, Ed Balls and me. For the Lib Dems, there were Danny Alexander, David Laws, Chris Huhne and Andrew Stunnell. It was a bizarre occasion. Though each party has its own manifesto, coalition talks take the form of discussing which of your election pledges you'd be prepared to ditch, which of the promises you'd just made you'd be prepared to break. Peter Mandelson seemed to be contemplating us changing the Westminster voting system for MPs from 'first past the post' to proportional representation by bringing a bill straight into Parliament without having a referendum first. I thought that was impossible. David Laws's body language was disengaged, bordering on hostile. He seemed to be pushing for even more austerity than the Tories. Ed Balls looked like he was going to explode. All in all, it felt like we were just going through the motions.

The Lib Dems were clearly putting the final touches to their coalition talks with the Tories. With them they could form a majority government. The combination of Labour and Lib Dem MPs wouldn't constitute a majority. Even in coalition with the Lib Dems, we'd still only be a minority government and we'd struggle to win every vote in the House of Commons. I wanted anything other than a Tory-led government and felt that a Labour–Lib Dem coalition, even though it would be unstable, would be infinitely preferable to a Tory-led coalition. I couldn't have disagreed more strongly with those commentators who argued that 'Labour needed a period in opposition'. That ignored the inevitability that any Tory-led government would undermine the progress we had been able to make. As night follows day, the NHS always suffers under the Tories, as do people on the lowest incomes. Although it was a long time ago, the effect of the Tory governments of the eighties and nineties on the country as a whole, and to my particular knowledge on my constituency, was still fresh in my mind.

However, whatever any of us felt about it, the numbers meant that the Lib Dems were never going into coalition with us. The electoral arithmetic dictated a coalition between the Lib Dems and the Tories. While the Lib Dems have a markedly different political character in different parts of the country, in London they fought us from the left. It was extraordinary for me to see my neighbouring MP Liberal Democrat Simon Hughes, who had criticized us relentlessly when we were in government for being insufficiently left-wing, backing a Tory government.

Gordon had said that he would resign as Leader of the Labour party, handing over to a new leader, in September. When the announcement came on 11 May that the Lib Dems were indeed going into coalition with the Tories, Gordon called me to say that he was going into Labour HQ in Victoria Street and that I was to go there with him. In the car, he told me that he was resigning as Leader. As he'd said he'd stay as Leader until September, this came as a shock. It suddenly dawned on me that, within a few minutes, we would be at Labour HQ and, with his resignation, I would be Leader of the Labour Party. I was thunderstruck. Sarah was encouraging Gordon and reminding him what he was going to say to the staff.

We swept into the basement car park and went up to the offices, where all the staff were assembled, crestfallen and exhausted. Gordon was grey in the face. He spoke only briefly, thanking them for all their work, telling them that he was resigning and that I was now the Leader of the Labour Party. They looked shell-shocked. I was, too, but I felt that, after the despair of the election defeat and the blow of losing their leader, the last thing they needed was me dithering and looking overwhelmed. I knew I had to show them I was going to step up to the challenge and do my absolute, purposeful best. I looked at the staff's anxious faces and, stepping forward, said how much we owed Gordon for all he'd done. All the families who now lived in decent homes, all the people at work who now had proper pay, all the children playing in nurseries as their mothers worked, all the lives saved in developing countries – that, and so much more, was Gordon's legacy, and it was Tony's, too. I thanked the staff for their work in the General Election and said that, with them, I'd take the party forward and rebuild, that we were now the official Opposition and we had to get on and do that important role to the best of our ability.

This was an hour of great nervousness for the party. We'd lost the election and, with Gordon going, we'd lost the second of the two great leaders of that generation who'd dominated the party for a decade and a half. It was now down to me, and I was going to have to do my absolute best and then some. It had been a turbulent period, we had been defeated in the election and now I was to be Leader of the Opposition.

Three things happen when you become leader of a party. People in the party who might have been dismissive of you in the past suddenly, out of party loyalty, become helpful; your allies redouble their efforts to support you; and you find out what you are made of. It was traumatic, after thirteen years, to be back in opposition once again. And I was in shock at suddenly finding myself Leader – something I had never expected. But I quickly determined that I would not allow myself to feel intimidated by the responsibility. It would have been self-indulgent and pointless to worry about whether I could do it. There was no choice; I was doing it. The effect of everyone looking to me to lead them helped. Anna Healy set a tone of calm determination. She worked through the weekend to assemble my team. Charlotte Montague, who'd run my constituency office, moved over to become my diary organizer, and Mabel McKeown worked to set up the office in what had been David Cameron's suite of rooms in the Norman Shaw South Building overlooking the Thames. It's not an attractive proposition to work in a Leader's office after an election defeat, even less so when it's only for a period of four months. Highly experienced people who've been advisers in government look for permanent jobs. But my loyal Deputy Leader's team stepped up a gear, and additional people were brought in. Over the weekend, Anna, persuading and cajoling, brought together a brilliant team who worked 24/7, sustained the party and enabled me to do the very best job I could as interim Leader.

Charlotte made sure, with total professionalism and dedication, that whether it was going to Buckingham Palace or to the Peckham CLP General Committee, Westminster Cathedral or visiting a factory, I was there where and when I was supposed to be, accompanied by the right staff members and properly prepared. Ayesha Hazarika headed up our work on the media, on writing speeches and preparing for PMQs, which was now going to be a weekly ordeal.

On my first day, I called all the former Cabinet ministers, urging them to join the Shadow Cabinet for the months until a new Leader was elected. They were all exhausted after the election campaign, disappointed we had lost and far from keen to take up a position in the Shadow Cabinet. Many of them, like Jack Straw and Alistair Darling, had done their time in opposition before we were elected in 1997 and had served many long years in government. The Opposition front bench held no attraction for them. But out of a sense of duty to the party, and greatly to their credit, they all agreed to stay until the new Leader was elected and the new Shadow Cabinet formed. The only one I did not invite to stay on was Peter Mandelson. I suspected that he might be a force for instability, and I needed the support of a Shadow Cabinet I could trust. So Pat McFadden, who'd been Peter's deputy, took his place.

Our first Shadow Cabinet meeting – back in the dreaded Shadow Cabinet room – felt surreal. Around my table were people who had held high office – Home Secretary, Foreign Secretary, Lord Chancellor. The last time they had sat together had been around the Cabinet table in Number Ten, to which they'd come in their ministerial cars, from their respective government departments, carrying their red boxes of official papers. Now they were all just shadows.

I decided to forgo the usual photo of a new Leader and Shadow Cabinet. This was one photo I would have been in the centre of, but it was not going to happen. I feared that the gloating tabloid captions would be 'How have the mighty fallen'.

Immediately, I was on what felt like a vertical learning curve. I'd never held an economic or foreign affairs portfolio in government. Now I had to respond to any prime ministerial statement, whether it was on Europe or defence, and challenge the Prime Minister at PMQs on everything from health to housing. My team made sure things all ran seamlessly, with the help of the former Cabinet ministers, their researchers and the party staff. We'd often get hardly any notice that the Prime Minister was coming to the House to make a statement. Sometimes we'd hear the night before, or even that morning. We'd get an advance copy of what he planned to say, but usually with less than an hour's notice, or none at all. I responded to prime ministerial statements on Afghanistan, on the report on the sex offences committed by Jimmy Savile, on European Council meetings, on international G8 and G20 summits, as well as on the government's programme for legislation (the Queen's Speech) and the Budget. Whatever the subject, whatever the event, I had to be on top of it. I couldn't go in there with a quavery, uncertain voice, or get the facts wrong, or make a mistake in the tone or position I took. Beside me on the front bench would be all my Shadow Cabinet colleagues – former Cabinet ministers – behind me were the Labour backbenchers. They'd all be watching, hoping I'd get our argument off to a good start so that they could then come in strongly with their own speeches and comments. I was determined to deprive our opponents of the satisfaction of seeing us follow up our defeat at the polls with humiliation in the Chamber. But I had the full support of my colleagues. It spurred me on to do the very best I could, and more. It was an extraordinary feeling no longer to be looking over my shoulder.

If we knew there was going to be a statement, all morning meetings would be postponed, my team would assemble at 8 a.m. and start work on what I was going to say. For my response to European statements, my team would need to talk to the leader of our Members of the European Parliament, Glenis Wilmott, our MPs who were particularly involved in Europe and our Foreign Affairs team in the Lords, as well as in the Commons, among others. On defence, we'd need to talk to former defence secretaries to draw on as much expertise as we could. We needed to be sure that I'd looked around every corner of the issue. Everyone who could feed in important views had to be called; no one would want to be taken by surprise by what I was going to say. And, above all, it needed to be clear, confident and correct. As interim Leader, I had to hold the fort for Labour and to keep our argument visible in the country while steering clear of making any new policies. That would be for the new Leader. As interim Leader, you don't have the power of a

Leader, who, by making appointments or sacking people, can make or break someone's career. As an interim Leader of the Opposition, all you have is the support that you can build among your colleagues. Around the Shadow Cabinet table were people who'd been much higher up in the government hierarchy than I had. And now I was the Leader. Again, it was to their credit that, out of loyalty to the party, they rallied round and helped me.

The reality of our loss of power hit home as the Tories took up the places on the government benches that had been ours for the last thirteen years. Instead of us doing things and them commenting, they were going to be doing things and all we could do was comment. With the Lib Dems joining the Tories, the government had a big enough majority to ensure that we were never going to win any votes. We were going to be voting, night after night, and we'd lose every one. It was utterly demoralizing, as being in opposition always is. Most of our MPs had never been in opposition before. They had been backbenchers in government, and many had served as government ministers, but being in opposition is completely different and they didn't know where to begin.

PART THREE

Challenge: No Slipping Back

8.

'Uneasy Lies the Head that Wears the Crown'

My long years in Parliament before we got into government meant that I knew only too well how grim it was to be in opposition. The Tories took up their places on the government benches, grinning from ear to ear. After thirteen years in the wilderness they were running the country again. They were jubilant, and our MPs were miserable, although I did hear many say that it felt terrible now but when they got down to work they'd feel better about things. I didn't have the heart to tell them that, as time went on and their constituents began to suffer, it wouldn't feel better, it would feel even worse.

We'd not only lost power, we'd lost friends and colleagues with whom we'd worked closely. Vera Baird lost Redcar to the Lib Dems; Julie Morgan lost Cardiff North to the Tories; Barbara Follett lost Stevenage to the Tories. The advances we'd made in the south in 1997 were all but wiped out. We lost Michael Foster in Hastings, Howard Stoate in Dartford and Ann Snelgrove in Swindon. Even though they'd been hard-working, conscientious MPs, when your party nationally falls in the polls, most fall with it. The sixty-four newly elected Labour MPs who'd replaced retiring MPs, though pleased to have made their way into Parliament, joined a demoralized PLP. They needed to be given confidence and welcomed as part of Labour's team. I felt such a responsibility towards the new Labour MPs to ensure that they felt some hope and sense of purpose for the future. I met and talked to many of them individually and put a great deal of thought and effort into what I said to them at the PLP meetings on Monday evenings, above all when it met for the first time after the election, in Committee Room 14 on Wednesday 12 May.

I felt it was important that the disappointment of our defeat and the concerted attack on us by the Tories and in the media should not shake our pride in being Labour or our confidence in what we had achieved in government. Plenty of our opponents were saying we'd been a terrible government; the last thing we should do was agree with them. When a party wins, they dominate the 'media discourse', and I knew that the Tories would try to use their victory to denigrate everything about our period in government in order to make it even harder for us at the next election. It was a dangerous moment and one in which we needed to fight for our version of the history of the previous Labour government so, in my speech to that first PLP after the election defeat, I said that we should be proud of our legacy and that it would endure. Every child who, instead of being cooped up in a small flat, is playing in a brand-new children's centre, every patient who is treated promptly in a new hospital instead of suffering on a waiting list, every person in an African village whose life has been transformed by the cancellation of world debt – that is Labour's legacy.

I reinforced the importance of defending our government's record once again at the meeting of the PLP on 18 May, as well as reminding our MPs that, with more than double the number of women MPs than the Conservatives, and more women members than all the other parties put together, Labour was still the voice for women in politics and that we should defend childcare and tax credits, which are so important to so many women. It was what they wanted and needed to hear. They were generous in their support of me; they could see that I was going to give it my all until their new leader was chosen.

The party leader usually attends the PLP meetings only when they are to speak, but because it was such a fragile time I went to every PLP meeting. I needed to listen to what the front-bench speaker was saying, I had to hear what the PLP were saying and see the expressions on their faces. And above all, I needed to show my face and look confident and determined. Labour MPs told me they really appreciated this. There was not one single negative briefing about me in the newspapers. Everyone was friendly and helpful. Thirty years earlier, going through the Division Lobby to vote had felt like running the gauntlet. Now, it was a pleasure to go through feeling part of a team – and not just part of it, leading it. I had no time to grieve for the fall in the Labour party's fortunes: I was too busy. And I was buoyed up by the approbation I was receiving.

To my surprise, I also found myself the centre of attraction for some of the newly elected Tory MPs. I was invited to speak as part of the induction process for all the MPs who'd been elected for the first time in 2010. There'd been a huge turnover, not just because Labour had lost seats but because so many MPs on all sides had stood down after the parliamentary expenses scandal that had come to light the previous year. Out of a Commons of 650 MPs, over two hundred of them were new to the House. The 147 new Tory MPs and our 63 new Labour members gathered in the Chamber to hear me and Sir George Young, Leader of the House, speak to them. Seeing them all there, keen and eager, I remembered so well how I had felt when I was a new MP. Remembering the lack of encouragement I was given, I urged them to be bold, telling them to ignore Whips and senior members, who would inevitably tell them to keep their heads down, that they had to learn the ropes for at least ten years. I said that they, having been elected, were not apprentice MPs or trainee MPs but the real thing. As the one and only MP for their constituency, they counted every bit as much as an MP who might have been there for decades; they had to blaze a trail so their constituents could see them fighting on their behalf. I told them there was no right or wrong way to be an MP. They would do it differently from the way in which we'd done it in the past and each of them had to do it in the way they felt was best. They should not get too worried about the complex rules of speaking in the Chamber; the important thing was to get their own voice heard, in their own way.

I underlined the importance of everything they now did, telling them that, although we send out hundreds of letters every week, for the recipient, it is anything but routine. Every person who receives a letter in a House of Commons franked envelope on House of Commons crested paper feels it's important. I recounted the tale of a constituent I had once visited who told me I'd written to him some years earlier. From a metal box on his mantelpiece he took out his two most precious documents: his will and my letter! I urged the new MPs to be high profile – there is no point in being an anonymous MP: everyone would be keen to see what they were doing and everything they did would matter. I told them that the previous week in my constituency I'd met a young woman coming out of the supermarket with a child in a buggy. She stopped me to tell me that I'd helped her mother when she was a child. I could see her own child listening to this tale of me helping her granny. One action, taken three decades ago, was still valued and had been passed on to a third generation. I warned the new MPs that they were not 'only a backbencher'; as an MP, they held a public office and everything they did would be scrutinized. I said it was a noble thing to be an MP, something to be proud of, and they should remember to enjoy it. No doubt because of the excitement of being newly elected, they cheered wildly.

Thereafter, as I went around the House I found myself accompanied by a posse of new Tory MPs. The Prime Minister was holed up in Downing Street and the other senior members of their party who'd been made ministers had all gone off to work in their government departments, so they weren't around in the House of Commons to mingle with the new MPs. They wouldn't even bump into them on the Underground, as the new ministers were now all sweeping past in government cars. Having no government department to go to, I was very much around, and they, being new, had not yet been allocated an office or put on any committees. The fact that I was walking along corridors with new Tory MPs, or chatting with them as we waited for a vote, caused me some consternation. I worried what Labour's new MPs would think, seeing me at the centre of a throng of Tories. I remembered how appalled I was in the eighties when I'd just arrived in

Parliament and would see the Labour grandee MPs chumming up, laughing and joking with the enemy Thatcherite Cabinet ministers. But I couldn't sustain this inclination now. The new Tory MPs were so unguarded and friendly I felt it would be churlish to shun them, so I acquiesced in what became a very strange new role as Parliamentary 'mum'. This lasted until the summer recess, by which time they had all been given their offices, had made friends in their own party and found their feet. Despite myself, I warmed to some of the new Tory women, for example Tracey Crouch, and even to some of the men Tory MPs, like Sam Gyimah, and I hoped they would not face barriers in their party similar to those I'd faced decades earlier in mine.

At the National Executive meeting in May 2010 we had to set about the process of electing a new leader, which would take four months. I told the party that I would be scrupulously neutral in overseeing the election. It had become clear that David Miliband was going to run, as well as Ed Balls and Andy Burnham. Diane Abbott threw her hat into the ring, sparing us the embarrassment of a men-only leadership contest. Everyone thought it was a foregone conclusion that David would win, including, I suspect, David himself, but rumours started to circulate that his brother, Ed, was going to run. I thought it was idle speculation. I couldn't believe that two brothers would compete to become Leader. They had such a close relationship; Ed had been David's best man at his wedding. But the rumours gathered in strength and, finally, the announcement came that Ed would indeed be joining the race. I was staggered. I couldn't imagine how it would work out. We were still scarred by the rivalry of the political 'brothers' Blair and Brown, but these were real brothers. What would that be like at the hustings? What would happen to the one who won? And to the one who lost? And what must their mother be feeling about it? At one level, it was perfectly straightforward: anyone who got enough nominations could run; no one had the right to exclude anyone else. Just because David was older and had been more senior in government didn't mean that he had the right to exclude Ed. And yet it felt so strange to have two Milibands in one leadership contest. It gripped the public imagination. Only a minority of people take a close interest in politics, but everyone is interested in families.

I had been very close to Ed when he was my special adviser, and we had worked together when he was first advising Gordon, but when he went off to Harvard for two years our paths diverged and so, while I retained an admiration and affection for him, we hadn't been close for eight years. In any event, I was resolute that I would be completely impartial. My role was not to get the Labour party to support any particular candidate but to make sure that the election contest ran properly. The first issue was the timing of the election. Some argued that it should be done quickly so that we could have a new leader in place and up and running before the House broke for the summer recess. They said that after the shock of our defeat it was a dangerous time to be left with only an acting Leader. But it would take some time to work out what sort of person they wanted to lead them in the new and difficult task ahead. The party was disorientated at finding itself in opposition again. Labour hadn't had a leadership election since 1994, sixteen years earlier, so it seemed wrong to rush it through in a few weeks and deprive the party of the time it needed to discuss and debate.

Although there were good arguments on both sides, I favoured giving the party time to consider the candidates. Except for Diane, they'd all been senior figures in government but, even so, they had all been in the shadow of the giant figures of Tony and Gordon. We needed time to see them in the new context, standing on their own two feet, operating as Opposition politicians setting out a new direction for the party and landing blows on the Tories. The Tories, when they went into opposition in 1997, had initially chosen leaders who failed. The election of the new Labour leader was an important decision and it needed to be made carefully, without additional pressure of time. However, as it turned out, it didn't matter what I thought because it became clear that the NEC was determined that there would be a longer campaign so the party could watch all the candidates and put them through their paces over the months to September. David Miliband's supporters took this to be a hostile act on my part, designed to help Ed Miliband, and they were suspicious that I was somehow rigging things. Their suspicions were bolstered by Jack's active support for Ed. I remained steadfast in my neutrality, resolute that it was for the party to choose, not me, but I privately thought that, if David was the front runner in July, there was no reason he wouldn't win in September.

There was no election for the position of Deputy, as I'd made it clear I wanted to stay on, and there was, gratifyingly, not so much as a whisper of a suggestion that anyone would stand against me. The leadership election got underway and it became the fashion for the candidates to claim not that they were 'heirs to Blair/Brown' but instead to distance themselves from both of them. The criticism of our thirteen years in government by the Tories and the media was echoed in the campaigns of those who were running for Leader of the party. My vocal support for and belief in what we had achieved during our period in government was drowned out. I genuinely believed – and still do – that, for all our imperfections, the country had massively improved in those years. It seemed to me – and still seems – wrong to join with those who said we were hopeless. If that was the case, then why should anyone vote for us next time?

While we reshape our future, we must be careful not to misrepresent our past. We fought to get into government so that we could work on the problems caused by the Tories. Labour tackled pensioner and child poverty, modernized the health service and our schools, trebled the number of young people going into higher education, repaired council homes and introduced the National Minimum Wage, the Human Rights Act, the Equality Act and the Civil Partnerships Act. Denigrating our past denies those achievements, strengthens the position of our opponents and pushes further into the future the day when Labour gets into office again. While we have to be honest in recognizing that we could have done more when we were in government and we have to acknowledge our mistakes, we must not be so critical that we hand our political opponents a stick with which to beat us. And we should never say that there was no difference between our Labour government between 1997 and 2010 and the previous and subsequent Tory ones, because that is simply not the case. I only have to go to a children's centre anywhere in the country or walk down any street in my constituency to see that.

As Leader of the Opposition, I had to make the reply in the House of Commons to the Queen's Speech of 25 May 2010. That's when David Cameron, as Prime Minister, set out the government's programme of laws for the next session of Parliament. The first Queen's Speech after an election defeat is perilous for the Opposition because, while you are full of resentment at the government, you have to show some recognition that they were elected and you weren't. And however strongly you believe it, you can't say the voters got it wrong. At the same time, you have to sustain your party's confidence and pride. It's a tricky balance, acknowledging the other party's victory but not bending the knee. I congratulated David Cameron with as much grace as I could muster. I said we wouldn't oppose him for the sake of it, but where we could see that the government were getting it wrong we would criticize it fearlessly. And I tore into the Lib Dems, who'd opposed us from the left and who were now, unbelievably, sitting as ministers in a Tory Cabinet.

In June, the government introduced their first Budget and I had to reply to the Budget statement. This is renowned for being a difficult parliamentary occasion at the best of times. The Chancellor makes all his big announcements and the Opposition leader has to say what they accept and what they reject without having been given any advance notice. It was, that year, even harder, as it was the first Budget of a confident, newly elected government, and we had just been kicked out, largely because of our perceived weakness on the economy. But, as ever, my excellent team prepared me well. And Yvette Cooper, who was sitting next to me, spotted all the problems hidden in the columns of the Budget figures.

All this led to a change in fortune for me. When I took over the leadership on a temporary basis after Gordon's resignation, some party members suggested that I should run for Leader. However, these were only muted voices and I took them as speaking out of politeness and solidarity rather than genuine commitment to my running. The decades of denigration at the hands of the press had taken their toll on me. It's hard to be exposed to such criticism for so many years and not be affected by it. I thought I'd done a good job as acting Leader but I didn't think I was up to being party leader.

Yet towards the end of my leadership, in September 2010, everywhere I went members said I should have run for Leader and, now, I felt they genuinely meant it. It was so gratifying – and not just the general tide of affirmation but in particular the pride of the women members, who told me that they'd always supported me and felt vindicated that I'd done well as interim Leader. Labour MPs with whom I'd crossed swords in the past and who'd been openly hostile reached out to be friendly. Even Frank Field generously offered to bury the hatchet, a full thirteen years after we'd fallen out when we were thrown together as ministers in the Department of Social Security. MPs who'd been junior ministers and Cabinet ministers encouraged me, saying, often ruefully, that they felt they'd underrated me for years. Having attracted so much flak for so long, I no longer had to steel myself to walk down the corridors of the House, into meetings and into the Chamber. Instead, I was surrounded by good will and support. After decades of feeling such an outsider, it was extraordinary to feel accepted.

I did a better job than I thought I would be able to do. I stoutly defended our record and was effective in parliament against the new government. The party grew by over 32,000 members and I worked to bring into our membership disaffected Lib Dem voters. All around the country we were winning council by-elections with swings to us from the Tories. I welcomed, and bound into the PLP, the new MPs, and generally kept the show on the road, despite the body blow of our ejection from government.

While I was buoyed up by all this, I had no regrets that I didn't run for Leader. I was relieved to be handing over the enormous responsibility of leading the party and hopeful that Ed Miliband, who was elected on 25 September 2010, would be a success.

I'd always held David Miliband in high regard, and it had never bothered me that this didn't seem to be reciprocated, but I was disappointed at his response to his brother beating him in the leadership election. Though it was a close result, he needed to accept it and adjust to the new reality. In the small room in the conference centre in Manchester when Labour General Secretary Ray Collins announced to the candidates that Ed had won, beating David by 1.3 per cent, Ed looked surprised, but David looked both shocked and furious. He'd obviously expected, and felt entitled, to win. I congratulated Ed and commiserated with the other candidates, but I should have urged David to give his full support to Ed. After such a narrow win, Ed needed it. I regret that I didn't. Somehow, I expected that David would do what Alan Johnson had done when he lost out to me in the deputy leadership election, which was, for the sake of the party, to lead his supporters to back the winner. But the bitterness of David's supporters hung over the conference and the press stoked the divisions.

It boiled over during the no doubt excruciating, for David, occasion of his brother's first Labour Party Conference speech as Leader. David and I had been allocated seats next to each other in the front row of the Shadow Cabinet section of the hall. Ed got to the point in his speech where he was talking about Iraq and, as he started to say that our intervention had been a mistake, the conference burst into applause. Although I'd voted for the war and had done so in good faith, the premise on which we went into war – depriving Saddam Hussein of WMDs – was undoubtedly mistaken. And I was Deputy Leader, so I was hardly going to sit on my hands, expressing disapproval of the newly elected Leader while everyone else clapped. But as I joined in the applause, David Miliband hissed at me. Because of the noise, I couldn't hear clearly what he was saying, but it sounded as if he was challenging me as to why I was clapping.

I should have just kept my mouth shut, kept smiling and applauding, but instead I irritably encouraged him to join in with it, whispering to him, 'Because he's the Leader and we've all got to support him.' Although we could hardly hear each other speak, the TV and radio microphones with their acute sound-sensitivity picked up every word and aired our spat on all the news programmes.

David, and his team, seemed to be of the view that I'd backed Ed, which I hadn't, and that I'd fixed the election for him, which, again, I hadn't. The reality is that the election was David's to lose. He had a fair wind in the press, plenty of campaign funding, an outstanding record in government and a great deal of support in the party. Whatever the reason he lost, it would have helped the party if he'd thrown his weight behind his brother. It would have been the right thing to do and would have increased the esteem in which the party held David.

Being Deputy in 2010 was very different to how it had been in 2007. In 2007, we were in government; in 2010, we were consigned to be the Opposition. In 2007, I was Deputy to Prime Minister Gordon Brown, who'd been a towering presence in British politics for over a decade; in 2010, I was Deputy to Ed, who was largely unknown. In 2007, I'd been elected by a whisker; by 2010, I was well embedded and unchallenged. With Gordon, I'd always been the junior partner, but the last time I'd worked with Ed I had been his boss.

Many people wondered whether it would be difficult for me. But it wasn't. Ed pitched into the difficult task of leadership with commitment and energy and, surrounding himself with a new team and doing things his own way, he wasn't looking to me to tell him what to do. And I hadn't run for leadership and didn't want his job, so I supported him to get on with it in his own way.

I had an important role steadying the party's nerves, and they had a vital task winning as many new council seats as possible to build up our electoral strength, especially in those areas where we wanted to gain seats at the next General Election. So although it was in very different circumstances, I enthusiastically got on with my task of going around the country, to regional Labour party conferences, to Scottish and Welsh conferences, and campaigning in every by-election and in council and European Elections, elections for the Scottish Parliament and for the Welsh Assembly.

But it was depressing to feel, once again, the impotence of Opposition. If there was a problem in my constituency, I couldn't just have a word with one of my colleagues in government and get it sorted. I could no longer make plans to put our demands for women into action. We had to watch the Tories enjoying themselves in government. All we could do was work, and wait, in the hope that, next time, we would win. The coalition, an unlikely partnership between Tories on the right of politics and Lib Dems, who'd been on the left of politics, proved robust, as I had feared it would. There was no prospect of a government collapse precipitating an early General Election. We were stuck with them for five years.

I took heart, though, that the election had brought in more new, young Labour women MPs, a different generation as well as a different gender to those they had replaced. Catherine McKinnell, a lawyer from Newcastle, took over from Doug Henderson in Newcastle North. Gloria De Piero, a high-profile TV presenter from a working-class background in Bradford, took over from former Cabinet minister Geoff Hoon in Ashfield. Ali McGovern, who'd been active in the party in my own constituency of Camberwell and Peckham and a Southwark councillor, won her hometown seat of Wirral South off the Tories at the age of thirty. Lucy Powell came to run Ed's office in 2010 but then in 2012 left to take over the constituency of Withenshaw in a by-election which was to see her join the Commons as the only Labour woman MP to represent a Manchester constituency. Pat Glass, a former director of education from a mining area, took over the constituency of North West Durham. Bridget Phillipson, a leading campaigner in the north-east against domestic violence, replaced Fraser Kemp as MP for Houghton and Washington East. Liz Kendall, formerly my special adviser in the DSS, took on the Leicester constituency which Patricia Hewitt had represented.

Gloria became Shadow Minister for Women and Equalities and pressed forward on equal pay. Lucy became Shadow Minister for Children. Bridget championed the fight against domestic violence and Liz took on the issue of care of the elderly. I was pleased to see the women in the 2010 cohort throw themselves into their work. It became normal for one or more of them to be pregnant.

With the new women Labour MPs taking forward the agenda on childcare, maternity rights and domestic violence, I took up the suggestion of Fiona Mactaggart MP that we should work together to highlight a different issue. Once again, I'd be looking at families, work, caring for children and the elderly, but this time through the perspective of older women.

We set up Labour's Commission on Older Women and embarked on a programme of going all around the country meeting and listening to groups of older women. I met women working in the tourist industry in Cornwall and women in Croydon working in supermarkets. Pat Glass brought together a group of older women for discussions in a former mining village in Durham. I met older women in the north-west and in North Wales. And wherever I went, older women were bursting to talk about their lives – they had not got together before to discuss what it is to be a woman of their age in twenty-first-century Britain. The meetings had the dynamism of those of the women's movement in the seventies.

This is a new generation of older women, in their fifties and sixties, and their lives continue to be very different from those of their mothers' generation. Their health is markedly better, they have had fewer children and had them later, have much higher educational qualifications and have done much more in the world of work. They are the generation who turned their back on the old ideas that women should be subservient to men and have instead an expectation that women should be treated as equals. Though no longer in their youthful child-rearing years, they are not frail and elderly.

It is often said that different women lead very different lives and that you shouldn't generalize, but whether it was Wales, Cornwall, Durham or London, although the women's accents were different, the stories from older women were the same.

Over the years, they had invested a lot of themselves in their work, were committed to it and believed that, with their long experience, they were better at it than they had been when they were younger. Despite having taken the main responsibility for caring for their children when they were young, this generation makes a big contribution to the world of work. Their income and their work is important to them and their family. With the age at which women can receive their basic state pension having been postponed and with them being less likely than men to have built up a good occupational pension, many cannot afford to retire, even if they want to. These women seethed with resentment that, far from that being recognized, they were the least valued at work and the first in line when it came to redundancies. The pay gap between women and men is twice as large for those between the ages of fifty and fifty-nine as it is overall. It's 11 per cent for those under the age of thirty-five, but 30 per cent for those aged fifty. A teacher who'd dropped down to part-time hours to enable her to care for her grandchildren described her position in the school as 'nearest to the exit'. A woman who worked in a supermarket 'local' complained of the irony that she was always asked to train the new young staff, only to see them promoted to be her managers. Older women who work part-time, sometimes because they are playing the vital role of supporting their husband through a period of illness, are the least valued of all in the workforce.

We heard shocking accounts of harassment by younger male colleagues. Harassment of younger women at work is challenged, and rightly so, but harassment of women because they are older – with jibes about the menopause – is not. Those who would now recognize that it would be totally out of order to joke that a woman had done something wrong at work because it was 'that time of the month' think nothing of daily taunts about hot flushes. One woman even found a 'jokey' picture of an ancient crone on her computer screen one morning – this in a workplace where there would be no question of the acceptability of sending suggestive sexual pictures to younger women.

These women play a vital role in the family, too. They have grown-up daughters and daughters-in-law who are now working and who, with high-quality childcare still unaffordable for many, depend on them to help care for their children. They feel that, although there is now a better understanding among employers of the issues of work/family balance for mothers with young children, there is no sign of any such recognition of the role of older women. Typically, they take or collect the grandchildren from school, or care for the baby a couple of days a week, help without which their daughter or daughter-in-law wouldn't be able to keep her job, let alone her foothold on the career ladder. These women are keen to help with childcare for the love of their grandchildren but also to help the women in the next generation have the opportunities which they didn't have. They don't want to see them, having worked hard at school and college, have to give up their work or rein in their ambitions. Their childcare help is essential for the family finances of the next generation, for many of whom it wouldn't be worth working if they had to pay for school pick-ups or the care of a baby. Mothers of young women who had to go back to work when their baby was only a few weeks old explained that their daughter couldn't afford to pay for care but, even if they could, they wouldn't want to entrust their baby at such a young age to the care of 'strangers'. This echoed what I'd heard expressed so strongly when I was preparing my Mothers in Manufacturing Report back in 2000. Some employers who employ a large number of women of all ages recognize that the childcare done by their older employees helps keep their younger employees in the workforce, but most do not.

As I went all around the country, listening to women aged over fifty, they also talked about their struggle to combine their work with support for an ageing parent. The years of frailty for the very elderly are much longer now and, however good the care services, there is still a great deal of vital care and support which falls on this generation of older women. This raises the issue of rights at work – flexible working or leave for care of the elderly – and the inadequacy, in quality and quantity, of public support services, but also the question of housing. If they live nearby, it's easier for families to provide the support they want to give, and which is needed by, the older generation. But this issue has not, as yet, taken its place on the housing policy agenda. The consideration of school places, nurseries and play spaces is rightly required when a decision is being made on a new housing development. But there is no similar requirement to consider the building of a new day centre for the elderly, or to ensure that a certain number of the homes have granny flats instead of a double garage, or to make sure that there is access to the new shopping parade for those with walking difficulties. Families who are well off have choices, as they can afford to pay for an older relative to move near to them, or build an extension for them to live in. But for the sake of the majority who don't have these resources, this issue needs to be on the agenda not just for councils considering planning applications for new developments but also for the management, building and allocation of council housing and for housing associations. The reality is that if public policy can help families to support their older relatives, that is not only doing what many families want, and many older relatives want, it is also ensuring that those older relatives can stay active and independent for longer. Loneliness and inadequate support are not only miserable, they also accelerate the ageing process.

At the conclusion of each of these heartfelt discussions, I'd ask the women to name someone in the public domain who understood their lives and was speaking up for them. At that point, there would be a total silence. On one occasion, after a long pause, they did come up with two names: Ann Widdecombe and Joan Bakewell. It was revealing that they couldn't see any current politician, in government or in opposition, or even any organization, who was speaking up on the issues that dominated their lives. They can hear, at last, a discussion of the issues which affect younger women who want to have a family and make progress at work, and there is a long-standing and well-established lobby for the frail elderly. But this generation of active older women, playing a key role both in the family and in the workforce, remains invisible.

One of the most obvious signs of discrimination against older women is in television. There have been plenty of older men in broadcasting – John Simpson, John Humphrys, David Dimbleby, Jonathan Dimbleby, Jon Snow, Andrew Neil or Bruce Forsyth, among many others. They are respected for their experience and maturity. And there are now many young women in broadcasting. But where are the older women on TV? Under the auspices of the Older Women's Commission, in 2013 I carried out a survey of the percentage of older women in broadcasting, asking the six main UK broadcasters how many women over the age of fifty they employed either as an on-screen presence or behind the camera. I had expected that many of them would simply refuse to reveal the information but, to their credit, they replied carefully and fully. I chased up one late responder, only to be told that they were delaying because they had one woman who was about to turn fifty and they were waiting until her birthday so they didn't have to file a 'nil' return on their employment of older women. As we expected, the survey showed that, while a minority of the over-fifties in the country are men, the overwhelming majority – 82 per cent – of TV presenters who are over the age of fifty are men. While TV presenters are broadly representative of age in the general population (30 per cent of TV presenters are over the age of fifty, nearly matching the 34 per cent of the general population), they are wholly unrepresentative in terms of older women. While the situation for TV presenters under the age of fifty is broadly representative of the gender balance in the population (48 per cent of TV presenters under the age of fifty are women, compared to 49.7 per cent of women in the general population), when they get older, women vanish from the screen. Only 7 per cent of the total TV workforce (on- and offscreen) are women over the age of fifty. So it seems you can be on TV if you are a younger woman but once you are part of the majority of the population who are older women you have to be removed from the screen.

Women broadcasters were delighted that the survey had been done and the pledges from the broadcasters to mend their ways. Those who were approaching fifty and had feared their days were numbered felt that the publicity was going to give them many more years in their career and that perhaps they wouldn't need to struggle so hard to look younger than they were. And younger women who had felt they would have to pack their career into the years before they reached the age of fifty said they felt they could now pace themselves more easily, because perhaps they would not now be 'culled'. Simply putting the spotlight on this issue promised to give women broadcasters a decade more in their career and offered older women viewers the prospect of seeing women like themselves on their screens. The industry appeared to take the findings of the commission seriously and the Broadcasting Diversity and Equality network committed to continue the monitoring themselves. They certainly need to do this, because there remains a degree of denial. When questioned about the lack of older women in the corporation, the then Director General of the BBC George Entwistle said that they realized it was a problem and, to solve it, they'd go out and look for some older women. But there is no need for them to go outside to look for them, they just need to stop pushing out the ones they've got.

This invisibility of older women is pervasive. I was amazed when I calculated that, in the PLP, out of eighty-one women, more than fifty were over the age of fifty. Somehow, we'd all assumed that most of the women in the PLP were young. They weren't; it was just that only the younger women were visible. Often, as older women, we are invisible even to ourselves.

By the end of our work on the Older Women's Commission a clear set of policy objectives had emerged. Eligibility for tax credits should be extended so that, as well as being able to claim for a nursery place or childminder, a working parent should be able to claim in order to pay a grandparent who is giving up work, or reducing their hours, to care for a child. There should be the option of sharing the year's maternity leave entitlement, which the mother is now able to share with the father, with a grandparent. Alongside the focus on tackling sexual harassment of younger women at work, there needs to be a drive against the harassment of older women at work. The Equality Act provision which outlaws dual discrimination (that is, discrimination which is based not just on gender or on age but on a combination of both) should be brought into immediate effect. There should be a right for an employee to alter work hours to care for an older relative, not just a 'right to request' the change. Planning guidelines should change to insist that the need for accommodation for older people is taken into account in new developments.

All these concerns are so universal and so pressing, but they weren't – and still aren't – anywhere on the political agenda. I felt Labour should put these policy objectives in our 2015 manifesto, and I still think it's imperative. It's important for the Labour party politically, too. We need to regain the electoral support of older women, which has fallen back sharply. Just as we had, decades earlier, started to press forward on the changes that were being demanded by younger women, now Labour should push for the changes needed by this new generation of older women. As it was then, it was not only right in principle but it makes perfect political sense. Labour has no electoral 'offer' for this new generation of older women, yet their votes are electorally critical for us. They constitute the majority of the older population who, unlike younger people, invariably turn out to vote. Our work on young people, particularly on apprenticeships and financial support for school and university, was given a high profile in the 2015 election. Young people knew they were on our agenda. But even with Liz Kendall, as Shadow Minister for Social Care, doing sterling work, older people appeared to be nowhere on our radar.

However, despite the fact that most of the younger parents in the PLP or working in the Labour party, like everyone else, relied on their grandparents for help with their children, Ed and his office didn't embrace this agenda. They were worried that business would see it as another burden Labour was imposing on them. They worried that extending child tax credits to care by grandparents would be too costly for the public purse or that it would look as if we were giving up on nurseries and falling back on family care for the children of working parents. They thought that letting mothers share their maternity leave with grandparents would somehow 'let fathers off the hook' and thereby entrench the idea that the family is still the woman's domain.

Ultimately, despite my best endeavours and many heated arguments, all I could get into our manifesto was the very general statement 'We will take a whole-family approach to policy making, supporting relationships, and the involvement of fathers, grandparents and relatives in the care, education and health of children' and a non-specific promise to 'support grandparents in caring for their grandchildren'. There were, in our 2015 manifesto, stronger commitments on football and on animal rights. It was galling, after all the work of the Older Women's Commission and all that older women had told us, but it remains, in my view, a further frontier of progress that women are aiming for. I hope that we can do it in less time than it took us to make progress on our agenda for younger women.

As the date of the election approached, Ed asked Douglas Alexander and Spencer Livermore to run the General Election campaign. After my experience with the manifesto, I was doubly determined that we should not repeat the experience of our 2010 campaign (run by Peter Mandelson and Douglas Alexander), in which women had been invisible. I strongly believed that in our party of men and women the women members who were so important to campaigning to get the vote out at local level were entitled to see women included in their national election campaign. And I knew it would make it less likely for women to vote for us if they could see only men at the top of our party.

It was expected that, as Deputy Leader, I would do the usual General Election tour of the country, but I thought my best contribution to the campaign would be to mobilize the women members and make sure that voters knew that Labour was concerned to improve prospects for women. I decided to go around workplaces, meeting women at work, to support our new women candidates, and to mobilize our women members to become active in the campaign, whether their Labour candidate was a man or a woman. Instead of the usual red 'battle bus' (which had last been on the road during the referendum campaign in Scotland), I wanted a vehicle that was eye-catching and would shout 'Women!', so I chose a bright pink mini-bus.

The aim of the pink bus was to be a rallying point for Labour women members and to encourage women to vote. We knew that if women did cast their vote, they'd be more likely to vote Labour, but over the last three elections women's participation in voting had slipped behind that of men.

My choice of pink for a Labour campaign on women was controversial, attracting derision among many women as well as many men, who condemned it as 'patronizing'. But the aim was not to appeal to women who were already politically involved, or to the commentariat, but to grab the attention of the more than 9 million women who didn't vote at all, and the millions more who did vote but not for Labour. Wherever it went, Labour's pink bus was instantly recognized as Labour's call-out to women to vote. Labour women MPs, candidates and activists joined me to go in it to call centres, shopping centres, care homes and factories, to hear from women about their working lives. As the bus headed over the Severn Bridge to Wales, the woman taking the toll money leant out smiling and said how much she loved it. Rather than a huge coach, it was a fourteen-seater, so we could park up in local shopping parades. Women came out to talk to us, to ask us questions and tell us their concerns. The pink bus never failed to make the front page of the local papers, highlighting our election pledges for women and putting the spotlight on our women candidates.

We met women Labour members up and down the country. The criticism the bus attracted from the political commentators had helped us achieve our objective of ensuring that women weren't invisible in our campaign. But too often the women we met raised deep concerns about Labour. Could they trust us with the economy? Would we put up their taxes and be wasteful in how we spent the money? Would we be too soft on people who could work but just didn't want to? Why did we want more immigration when they couldn't get a pay rise as immigrants were prepared to work for less? And they couldn't see Ed as Prime Minister. They didn't love the Tories and there was no warmth towards David Cameron, but they weren't ready to trust us. In English constituencies, they feared that, if we didn't win an overall majority, we'd end up in a coalition with the Scottish National Party (SNP) and that Nicola Sturgeon would dominate Ed, pushing him into an unwelcome anti-austerity binge in public spending. In Scottish constituencies, the concerns expressed were less about anti-austerity; they simply thought the SNP would be stronger in standing up for Scotland. The criticisms were deep-seated, and I could see that our campaign was not even beginning to address them. But as the 2015 election campaign got under way, the opinion polls showed we were neck and neck with the Tories, and I put my concerns down to my usual anxiety about Labour's electoral prospects.

The political commentators and our opponents, as well as the opinion polls, all predicted that the 2015 election would see us back in government – not as a Labour administration with an overall majority but at least leading some sort of coalition. It was, as it turned out, a seriously wrong collective misjudgement. All the signs were there, if we had but seen them. The opinion polls told us that people didn't trust us on the economy; that we were out of touch with their concerns about immigration; that we were weak on welfare; and that Ed Miliband was not seen as Prime Minister material. Our campaign on the cost of living crisis that was hitting middle- and lower-income families was successful in picking up their resentment that, although they were working harder, prices

were rising while their pay was stagnating. We'd correctly identified the problem but we were not regarded as the solution. Worse,
many blamed us, and the global financial crisis, for causing their
increasing difficulties in keeping up with the cost of living. It was
the Tories, rather than us, they looked to as more likely to solve the
problem we were successfully highlighting.

Although the opinion polls correctly identified the concerns voters had about us, their electoral forecasts were inaccurate, and, by the
time we came to the election, our problems were probably too
entrenched for any election campaign, however brilliant, to dig us
out of. We'd failed to embark on a persistent and dogged exposition
of our achievements in government, which served to assist those
who wanted to denigrate our record and lend passive support to
the highly successful Tory mantra 'Why give the car keys back to
the people who crashed it?' Our sympathy for Ed in the face of the
media denigration of him and our hostility to his detractors ren-
dered us unwilling to face up to the fact that his leadership, from
the doorstep feedback we'd been given, was an evident problem for
many. The fact that the Tories, even after thirteen years in opposition, had failed to win an outright majority and were only in
coalition made us feel we were in touching distance of victory this
time, when we were nothing of the sort. And this sense of likely
victory acted as a disincentive to have the arguments and do the
hard work of changing the party that we had done in the eighties.

Ed was up in his constituency of Doncaster on polling day, and I
divided my day between campaigning in Peckham and meetings at
Labour's HQ off Victoria Street, with Ayesha, Labour peer and constitutional expert Charlie Falconer and party staff. As the polls
closed, I went off to the Millbank TV studios to go live on the BBC's
News at Ten. Our line was to be that the Tories had lost support, that
they no longer had a mandate to govern and that it was our right
and responsibility to set about forming a government. Our objective, which we'd discussed exhaustively, was that, in the expectation
of there being no outright winner, we would challenge the Tories'
right to govern and assert ours. The exit poll was due a few minutes

after ten, but the BBC pressed me to be on camera at the top of the news. We needed to get in ahead of the Tories, but as the minutes ticked towards ten o'clock Ayesha decided it was a bad idea for me to be on camera when the news of the poll came through. And, as it turned out, that was just as well.

Ayesha told the BBC that I'd only go on once I'd seen the exit polls. We sat at a table in the deserted restaurant at 4 Milbank watching the BBC live on my iPhone, our hearts in our mouths as we waited for the report of the exit poll. We didn't have long to wait. The headlines were as bad as they could be. The exit polls called it for a Tory victory. The BBC reported that the Tories were seven points ahead of us and that Labour was set to lose every one of our seats in Scotland to the SNP. Paddy Ashdown came on, saying that the polls' prediction that the Lib Dems would be nearly wiped out was wrong and he'd eat his hat if it was right. Though we didn't want to believe the exit polls and still had to wait for the votes to be counted, Ayesha and I went back to our HQ, steeling ourselves for a night of utter defeat for Labour.

As the results rolled in, the atmosphere at our HQ became funereal and reports from party staff and campaigners grew ever bleaker. Douglas Alexander MP, former Cabinet minister and our General Election campaign organizer, was going to lose his Scottish seat to a twenty-one-year-old SNP student, Mhairi Black. Jim Murphy MP, our leader in Scotland, who a few months earlier had been hailed as a hero for helping rescue people from a burning pub, was going to lose his Glasgow constituency – and by a landslide. We abandoned hope of winning new seats outside of London, other than in big cities, and began to dread the loss of Labour seats in England. It seemed that things could hardly be worse – until they were, with news from Morley and Outhwaite. This was the constituency of Ed Balls, former Cabinet minister, Gordon's right-hand man, who'd travelled around the country to help our candidates win their seats off the Tories. Our Yorkshire regional staff reported to HQ that the result there was too close to call. There was a recount under way, but we were told not to hope for a miracle. Just a few hours earlier, we'd been planning for government, and now we'd lost every seat in Scotland and the man who was to be our Chancellor was no longer even an MP.

The loyal, dedicated party staff were downcast. Many were in tears. All holiday leave had been cancelled for months before the election and they were wrung out with exhaustion and, now, bitter disappointment. I felt it would only make things worse if I descended into a heap. The party members and supporters would sink even further into despondency if, having lost out on being in government, we collapsed as a party. We had to prepare, again, for Opposition. It wasn't the job we wanted, but it was the job we'd got. And, as Deputy Leader, I set about the duties of defeat, starting with the heartbreaking task of writing to all our MPs who had lost a seat. I knew they'd find it hard to get their next job, and to face their community and friends without the magic letters 'MP' after their name. Overnight, they'd become 'formers' – former Cabinet ministers, former Shadow ministers, former MPs. I thanked them for their long years of work for the party and commiserated with them on their defeat.

I wrote to the candidates in the seats we'd expected to win, men and women who I'd hoped would be alongside me in the PLP of a new Labour government. Many had sacrificed their jobs, their finances and time with their families not just for months but for years. And I felt the loss of those new candidates who would have been such great MPs, like Sophy Gardner, a former RAF wing commander who'd stood in Gloucester; Lara Norris, who'd built up a great Labour team but failed to win Great Yarmouth; Mari Williams in Cardiff North; and so many others I'd grown to admire and become friendly with over the years of campaigning. They hadn't lost it for us. We'd lost it for them. I was determined that we must learn the lessons from what was now our second defeat. It was obvious there would be a bitter post-mortem and much dispute about the reasons we had lost, but I thought it should be informed by the views not just of the MPs who'd returned to Parliament but also by those of the MPs who had lost their seats, of the candidates who hadn't won the chance to come to Parliament, of all the party members up and down the country who had worked so hard. I also commissioned Deborah Mattinson to put together focus groups. We needed to hear and face up to what the public said about why they had rejected us.

After the election count was completed in the small hours of the morning, Ed Miliband travelled down to London by car. I phoned him. There wasn't much I could say. He was a man of intelligence and principle who'd put his heart and soul into being Leader of the Labour Party, but it hadn't worked. We had never discussed what he'd do in the event of us losing. Would he be able, as Neil Kinnock had, to stand at the dispatch box for PMQs as the vanquished Labour leader facing the victorious mob of Tory MPs? Would he be able to face up to the triumphant ranks of new SNP MPs in front of the demoralized and diminished Labour ranks? Gordon had decided to go immediately after the election defeat, and I suspected that, like Gordon, Ed would want to resign as Leader right away. No one contacted me, urging me to press him to stay. When I went into Labour HQ the Friday morning after the election, he was in his office and asked his advisers to leave us on our own. It seemed as if he'd already made up his mind to go.

Ed called a press conference to announce that he was standing down with immediate effect and, once again in the aftermath of an election defeat, I took over as interim Leader. But this time, unwelcome though my new role was, at least I was ready. I made it clear right away that not only would I not stand as Leader but that I would be standing down from the position of Deputy which I'd held since 2007. I'd been on the front bench for twenty-eight years and Deputy Leader for eight. I'd served as Deputy under two leaders. It wouldn't feel right to go on to a third.

Rosie Winterton, the Chief Whip, was in the office first thing on Friday morning, together with Luke Sullivan, her chief adviser, and Charlie Falconer. Ayesha went from being my adviser as Deputy Leader to being my Chief of Staff, assembling and running my office as Labour Leader. With Parliament not yet reconvened, we based ourselves in the party HQ.

We worked solidly over the Friday and the first weekend. The lighting in the building was triggered by movement, and there were so few us there in the cavernous Labour offices we kept being plunged into darkness. Once we'd worked it out, we regularly jumped up and down, and waved our arms. The heating was off and we were freezing, so we kept our coats on. A team of builders came in and ripped off all the huge campaign panels, leaving the walls looking like those in a demolition site. The next-door building was in fact being demolished and the view out of our windows was of bulldozers and swinging wrecking balls. The building was echoing our fate.

I made Rosie Winterton my de facto deputy and we worked seamlessly as a team. Ayesha named us Cagney and Lacey, and there was a lot of humour, albeit of the gallows variety. Meanwhile, I had, once again, to lead the PLP into Prime Minister's Questions, the Queen's Speech debate and the Budget debate and decide how to respond to government statements on everything from the EU referendum, through the expansion of Heathrow, to Syria.

As the next leadership election got under way, there was a groundswell of demand for me to run for Leader, but I felt the moment had passed. It wasn't because, at sixty-five, I regarded myself as too old – Hillary Clinton was running for US President at the age of sixty-seven. I found it perplexing suddenly to be challenged to answer questions as to why I hadn't run for Leader – especially when they were from journalists who'd spent years saying I was useless and demanding that I resign from whatever post I was in at the time. For so many years when the children were young, in such an overwhelmingly male political world, it had been a huge effort just to keep going, let alone harbour ambitions to lead the party. And having been denigrated in the press and certainly not seen as leadership material, it's perhaps not surprising that this wasn't how I saw myself. Around many MPs there is a buzz that they could, at some stage, lead their party, but though I'd been in the front line for decades there'd never been that buzz around me. It was, nonetheless, gratifying when I was acting Leader, and before the focus shifted to the new candidates, to meet members and supporters all around the country who thanked me for stepping into the leadership and said they wished I was staying on as Leader. But while Jack and my friends had insisted I run for Deputy in 2007, there was nothing like the same urging from them for me to run as Leader now. It was more a case of 'we'll support you if you go for it.' But I wasn't going to go for it. Sometimes a decision seems to take itself. It wasn't a calculation. It was a gut feeling that this was it. But after so many years of being criticized, it felt strange to be getting supportive media coverage. The *Spectator*, for so long a media adversary, gave me a Lifetime Achievement award. By the end of July, despite the controversy over the Welfare Reform and Work Bill, an Ipsos MORI poll showed that I had a positive rating not only among Labour voters but also among Tory voters.

For the first time, the leader was to be elected under the new rules which Ed had established in 2014, abolishing the tripartite electoral college (a third each for MPs, unions and members) and replacing it with one member one vote for everyone. So instead of MPs having a third of the electoral college, which meant that each MP's vote was worth several thousand members', the votes of MPs were now the same as those of a new member. In addition, there was a new right for anyone who supported the party to pay £3 and sign up to choose our leader.

There had been tensions in the party since the start of the Blair years that we were not progressive enough, that we were too centrist and needed to be bolder, but our being in power and then, after 2010, our hoping to get back into power, had masked that. Once we lost the 2015 election, Jeremy Corbyn's candidature gave vent to those feelings.

The public had gone in one direction and the party was setting off in the opposite one. Our 'Learning the Lessons' election post-mortem review confirmed what we had heard on the doorstep in marginal seats and was hammered home in Deborah's polling.

People were concerned that we would tax and spend too much and were not sure whether they could trust us on the economy. However, while we had not reassured the voters in 'middle England', neither had we inspired party members with a new, progressive vision. This latter was the vacuum that Jeremy Corbyn filled. Although he'd been in Parliament since 1983, he was 'untarnished' by power. He hadn't campaigned to get Labour into government and had been a persistent critic of the Blair/Brown governments.

There was a heated argument over the eligibility to vote under the new leadership election rules. My phone buzzed with desperate MPs, councillors, NEC members and local activists protesting that the election process was being abused and that members of other parties, such as the Trade Union and Socialist Coalition (TUSC), were infiltrating Labour to capture it for the hard left. Meanwhile, Twitter was ablaze with protests that Labour HQ was rigging the election to exclude those who might vote for Jeremy Corbyn. The party was raw with the disappointed rage of defeat. In Greece, a left-wing party, Syriza, was surging on an anti-austerity programme. In the Commons, the SNP and the Tories were gloating victors and we were the miserable losers. I struggled to hold things together from May to July, but by the end of July things were straining at the seams. I had a week's holiday in Sicily. We took my ninety-seven-year-old mother, but I spent the whole time on calls, including one particular conference call with the NEC Procedure Committee where everyone on the call was shouting but I could hardly hear. There was a massive storm outside and at every crucial point there would be a huge thunderclap. Jeremy Corbyn had unstoppable momentum; the other three candidates lost their way. My embattled team and Labour HQ worked seven-day weeks right up until the announcement of the leadership election result and, on 12 September 2015, I handed over to the new Leader, Jeremy Corbyn. Although we'd both been in the PLP for more than thirty years and we were both London Labour MPs, I hardly knew him.

What is happening in the Labour party since Jeremy Corbyn's election is a painful echo of what happened in the eighties. Once again, our local party meetings are a bad-tempered battleground of procedural conflict. The public are dismayed to see us wrangling and, while our meetings and rallies grow larger, so does the Tories' lead in the opinion polls. And now we have the added dimension of the deep division which has cut through the country on the issue of our membership of the EU.

As is ever the case when there's a Tory government, with my constituents facing mounting problems, my constituency work-load grows. No longer on the front bench, I have taken the role of Chair of the Joint Committee on Human Rights, a cross-party Parliamentary Select Committee of members of the House of Lords and the Commons. The membership changes from time to time but currently includes Margaret Prosser, with whom I've worked since she backed my selection in Peckham in 1981; Karen Buck, who I first worked with when she was the Labour researcher to our health team in 1992; Doreen Lawrence; and two of the new Tory women MPs who were elected in 2015, Amanda Solway and Fiona Bruce, a new breed. Granted, they are Tories, but in their commit-ment to the advance of other women they bear no relation to Margaret Thatcher. Lord Woolf, who initiated the Woolf Reforms (1999) in the civil justice system, is a towering presence on the com-mittee. Having a Human Rights Act was a long-standing demand of the National Council for Civil Liberties when I was their legal officer. We introduced it when I was in government and, now, with us once again back in opposition, I'm chairing the Human Rights Committee at a time when the government is moving to repeal it.

I work, too, with the new Labour women MPs, playing an active but not, I hope, overbearing, role in the Women's PLP and support-ing our new Shadow Minister for Women and Equality, Sarah Champion, who was elected MP for Rotherham in 2012. I'm replete with experience from all my years of focusing on women's struggles since the seventies and am as committed to progress as ever I was in those early years. But I constantly remind myself that I mustn't tell the new Labour women MPs what to do. As they face new chal-lenges in their work in the Labour party and on women's issues, they have to work things out for themselves. I'll back them up, but it's for each generation of women to find their own way forward.

There is much talk nowadays about role models and mentors. But neither of these notions sits easily with the women's movement. For a start, a role model is an individualistic concept, while the women's movement is all about the team, the collective. In the women's movement, we work together on equal terms. We look to each other for support rather than looking up to a heroine. Looking up to someone can be disempowering, whereas working with others on equal terms always strengthens you. The notion of a role model is essentially a conservative one, about modelling what you do on someone who's already done it, but the point about the women's movement is that it must strive for more progress, not simply for new women to repeat the experience of those who've gone before. The notion of having a role model is about following in someone's footsteps, but the women's movement is about breaking new ground. Women need to be pioneers, not followers, even of other women. I've also had mixed feelings about training women in politics. What are we training them to be? They are supposed to be changing the political system, not being trained to be part of it. So I've always struggled when I've been asked to name my role model. I admire what Barbara Castle did. It was extraordinary. But I've gained strength from the women I've worked alongside rather than those who came before me. I'm always delighted if a woman says that, because of my encouragement, she's gone into politics and become a councillor or an MP. I'm glad to have been supportive but I'd never want to be a role model. I want the next generation to do far better than we in ours have.

After several decades of Labour women being the dominant women in UK politics, many in the party allowed themselves to believe that our battles for women had been won. Sadly, that is very far from the case. It was only with concerted effort over so many years that we made Labour into the party for women as well as for men, and we need to work to maintain that work. Without that, we will slip back, as we did when we were again in the position of having a men-only leadership team when I stood down as Deputy Leader in 2015. And there is nothing to stop women's policy concerns sliding down the agenda other than women in the party making sure they don't. Although it was hard for me in the PLP in many ways, it was at least straightforward: the resistance I encountered was active – so many men openly opposed progress for women and were eager to tell me to my face. It's difficult for the new women Labour MPs when men indignantly declare themselves to be feminists and every bit as much in support of women's equality as the women themselves and yet somehow still contrive to block change. This is the scourge of passive resistance. The reality is that unless Labour is, and is seen to be, the party for women, women's progress will stall and slip back, not just in the Labour party but more widely. The Conservatives have never advanced women's rights, and there's no reason to believe they'll do so now. Labour remains the only alternative government to the Tories, so if there's to be further government impetus for political progress it has to be from a future Labour government. And unless Labour is, and is seen to be, the party for women, we will not win women's votes, we will be unable to get into government again and so we will not be able to make changes for women.

The opportunities for my generation of women have been so much greater than for our mothers, for whom the domestic role was so dominant. But with our new opportunities have come difficult personal choices about how to balance work and home. Now, few would argue in favour of discrimination against women or say that they oppose women's equality, but there is still a failure to acknowledge the extent to which inequality still exists and how much more needs to change. The demands of the women's movement are now, in principle, accepted. And that is a great step forward from when they were seen as subversive or denounced as outlandish. But they have yet to be met in practice. Few would now seek to justify inequality between men and women. So it's time it ended.

Epilogue
Continuing the Cause

In 2005, the British Council, which works in all African countries and has a strong commitment to gender development, set up a programme to twin UK women MPs with African women MPs. This helps the women in Africa but it also strengthens relations between this country and those in African countries. I asked to be part of the scheme and was paired with a Tanzanian MP, Monica Mbega. It was not a case of either of us knowing how to do things right and telling the other, it was genuinely an exchange. First, she came to London to shadow my work. We immediately started to chat about our lives and the difficulty of combining being an MP with being a mother. I told Monica I had three children and asked her how many she had. Ten, she replied. Three were those of her and her husband and seven were children of close family members who'd died of AIDS she now cared for.

She joined me as I undertook my constituency work, coming to meetings and sitting with me at a busy advice surgery. She was interested in the form which I and my constituency team fill in for each constituent at the surgery which asks for their name, address and an outline of the problem, and which we use as the basis for our case file in the office. I took her to meetings I had with tenants' associations and pensioners' groups.

A few months later, I went out to the Western Highlands of Tanzania to shadow her. My constituency is fifteen minutes from Parliament; hers is eight hours away from the capital, along dangerous roads. A member of the British Council met me at Dar es Salaam airport and drove me to Iringa, where Monica was the MP. By UK standards, my advice surgeries, with up to sixty people attending each session, are very busy, but they are nothing compared to Monica's. As we arrived at her house there was a long queue in the road outside – hundreds of people. She held her advice surgeries at her home, there being no other suitable building. Her constituents had started queueing the night before. The pressure on her was immense: with so little in the way of health services, education or income support, Monica was expected to provide the services of the welfare state as well as being an adviser and problem-solver. She spent all that day seeing her constituents, each, it seemed, with a greater problem than the previous one. I was touched to see that she was writing notes on advice surgery forms identical to those she'd seen being used in my surgeries.

The following day, we drove for two hours to one of her regular meetings in a remote village in the countryside in her constituency. I felt shaken to my bones as our jeep took on pot holes, ruts and rocks in the road. When we arrived, the entire village was gathered, out in the open. Over five hundred men, women and children were sitting waiting for her. She made a speech which lasted more than an hour and a half. The village didn't have access to phones, television, radio or newspapers, and part of her speech was to bring the villagers up to date with regional and national events. She went on to tell them that she was continuing to press for a new road to their village, to report on when the rebuilding of the school would be complete and on her progress in getting a new maternity clinic. She then spoke to them about AIDS, and she didn't mince her words. She said that it was not the fault of the orphan children that their parents had died and that it was the duty of the whole village – every single one of the villagers – to care for the AIDS orphans and ensure that they were fed, looked after and went to school. She took the issue of the stigmatization of the children head on, lambasting those who shunned them. As I followed her doing her work as an MP, I saw her being the welfare state and the news media and providing moral leadership for her constituents.

I returned to London full of admiration for Monica and her work, and with a new perspective on my own. Monica worked so hard, I felt I should redouble my efforts. I promised myself I'd make my speeches more comprehensive and no longer take for granted the political expertise of my audience. I committed myself to working harder to support women MPs in Africa, and I promised myself that I'd never again complain about how hard it is to combine family and home. I did of course continue to moan, but always thereafter there was, in the back of my mind, the awareness that, whatever we as women MPs in the UK have to do to keep everything going, it is nothing compared to the heroic work of women MPs in Africa.

When we were back in opposition, I asked Ed to appoint me Shadow Secretary of State for International Development and for Rushanara Ali to be my deputy. I'd got to know Rushanara in 2007 when she was selected from an all-women shortlist to be our parliamentary candidate in Tower Hamlets. I'd gone to campaign for her in Brick Lane and was both appalled to see the older male Labour party members trying to push her out of the photos and impressed by her feisty determination to press on as the candidate. She was such an asset for us, and she was admired nationally. When I visited an Asian women's centre in 2013 during Emma Lewell-Buck's by-election in South Shields after David Miliband left Parliament, it was clear that they all knew of and admired Rushanara. She'd come to London with her family from Bangladesh when she was seven, speaking no English, and then, after going to the local school, won a place at Oxford. She brought a unique voice into our Parliament and, for all that I had decades more political experience, I had much to learn from her.

My opposite number was Andrew Mitchell, as Secretary of State for International Development. Unlike Justine Greening, who took over the post when Andrew was sacked, he'd worked for years on international development projects and was clearly committed to his brief. Most of the Tory backbenchers (and indeed many Labour voters) felt that, at a time of cuts in public spending, the development budget should be reduced and certainly not increased, but Andrew was determined that the Tory government stuck to their manifesto promise of increasing the budget of the Department for International Development (DFID) to 0.7 per cent of Gross National Income. At DFID questions in the House of Commons, I found myself in the position of supporting the government minister, against the objections of his own backbenchers. That was an odd role for an Opposition shadow, whose job is to challenge the government minister. And it was even stranger for me, for whom going into politics was all about getting the Tories out of government in order to pursue the policies that I felt, and still feel, are important. It's easy when you're in government to work cross-party; you want to assimilate the Opposition. But in opposition you want to show that you are distinct from the government, and your aim is to replace them, so the last thing you want to do is support them. It wasn't that I'd gone soft on the Tories, but Mitchell was trying to carry on work we had done in government and was up against it from his own side. I'd been disappointed when I was in government as Minister for Women and Equality and had been battling against some on my own side that Theresa May, who was Shadow minister at the time, chose to oppose me rather than back me up. So I was convinced that the right thing for me to do as Shadow International Development Minister was not to oppose Andrew for the sake of it, but to give him my support.

The women's movement, and left politics more generally, has always had a strong internationalist strand, and many of my constituents had come from Africa. However, though there are plenty of opportunities for MPs to go all over the world, in the eighties and nineties, with a busy constituency, a demanding front-bench role and young children, I felt I had too much on my plate already to go abroad for work. From 2004, though, I began to go abroad regularly: to the White House and the headquarters of the United Nations in the US; to Brussels and Strasbourg to visit EU institutions and to meet up with other members of the European Parliament and European Ministers for Women and Equality; and to Africa, the continent from which so many of my constituents had come.

Because new residents in the UK keep in close touch with their friends and family back home, as a constituency MP you get an inside track on what's going on in different parts of the world. I will often hear a compelling first-hand view from my constituents long before it appears on the news. I'd hear from Kurds what was happening in Iraq, from South Americans about their countries' struggles for democracy and from Nigerians about the over-mighty multinational oil companies.

In the nineties, even before the harrowing news reports of killings and amputations in the civil war in Sierra Leone began to appear on our TV screens, my Sierra Leonean constituents were telling me about the atrocities being committed there. One day in an advice surgery a constituent sat down and spread out on the table in front of me a series of photos. I was just admiring some colourful pictures of a neat and tidy cottage with, behind a little wall, a garden filled with flowers, when she showed me the next set of photos. I thought they had been taken on black-and-white film, but they were in colour: the home had been totally burnt out. To my horror, I realized that the objects I could see on the garden wall were body parts. She wept as she told me that the members of her family had been killed. The newspapers started to report the rebel atrocities and controversy arose over whether the use of our armed forces in 2000 had been properly authorized by the government. Robin Cook, as Foreign Secretary, came in for criticism about whether he'd seen and agreed some documents that civil servants had put in his Red Box proposing the use of our armed forces. But at every advice surgery, my Sierra Leonean constituents would urge me to thank Tony Blair for our intervention and say, whatever the process might have been, they were deeply grateful for our government's actions.

On polling day in the General Elections of 2002 and 2005, as I toured the polling stations in my constituency I met Sierra Leoneans who would tell me they'd just voted for Tony Blair. Although my name was on the ballot paper, it was Tony they were voting for. Tony Blair was a hero to them and remains, to this day, hugely popular in Sierra Leone and among my Sierra Leonean constituents in London.

As well as telling me about what is happening in their home countries, my constituents also gave me a world view of how our country was seen abroad. In 2002, at a meeting with one of the Ivory Coast community associations in Peckham, I was told that, in fleeing the violence and strife, their families had scattered all around the world, including France and Canada. They said that, despite being French speakers, they'd chosen England rather than France, as they felt more at ease with our multiculturalism and more able to keep a connection with their Ivorian culture. Above all, they wanted their children to grow up speaking English – the language of the whole world, they said. It's always frustrated me that, while we've faced shortages of foreign language teachers here in the UK, we have failed to draw on the many educated French-speaking Africans here.

To pay my respects to and learn more about my constituents of African origin, I visited Sierra Leone, Nigeria, Ghana, Tanzania, Ethiopia and Kenya. Prior to each visit I would call a local meeting of the community groups, party members and individuals I knew from that country to hear from them what I should be looking out for and to discuss my itinerary. I would get briefings from the House of Commons Library and the Foreign Office, but I wanted to hear from my constituents, what they thought was going on and where they suggested I should go. And if I was visiting their home country, the last thing they would want is to hear about it first from their relatives. Each pre-visit meeting generated a vibrant political discussion, as well as requests for me to divert miles from my planned route to go to their village. I held the meeting prior to my Nigerian visit in Southwark town hall on Peckham Road. As I parked my car a few streets away I heard the distant sound of African drums. Walking around the corner, I saw the town hall steps crowded with drummers in flowing, colourful robes. They were calling my Nigerian constituents to the meeting and welcoming me. It was the noisiest and most joyful greeting I've ever had there.

I've always supported the UK playing a full part in international efforts to tackle poverty, but travelling from Heathrow airport and arriving in a place where people cannot rely even on having the basics of clean water and enough to eat hammers home how vital it is. There's much – and justified – concern about waste and corruption bleeding resources from the aid which the UK government and individuals donate, but what always stayed with me when I visited places such as the Dadaab camp for Somali refugees in northern Kenya, where I went in 2010, was the huge difference local organizations make even with the smallest amounts of money. Our aid in Sierra Leone, Nigeria and Ghana, for example, pays for the training and work of midwives, enables children to go to school, and for people to be vaccinated and to sleep under bed nets protecting them from the malarial mosquito. This aid reaches from the cities to the smallest, most remote villages, where local organizations are transforming the prospects of their local communities. And the aid our government gives is matched by the 'remittances' my constituents and diaspora communities all around the UK send back to their villages out of their hard-earned wages.

Free from the responsibilities of having my children at home, I was able to do more to support and network with women internationally. I met women in the parliaments of Ghana, Nigeria, Tanzania and Ethiopia and I admired their determination and the progress they were making. I am certain that they are the best hope for the women in their countries. The international stage has always been dominated by men, but there are now women coming through in parliaments and governments in every country and on every continent and the international agenda must change to reflect that and to accelerate progress for women.

As a counterpart to my visits to women MPs in Africa, back in the UK I would always be happy to meet and sit down for a discussion with visiting delegations of these women. The issue of gender would inevitably be high on the agenda, with the women describing how they grapple with the patriarchal systems in place in their own countries. The women are usually highly critical of men, complaining that the women work hard and take care of the children but that the men don't pull their weight. And inevitably, as women getting together, we'd talk about our husbands. It's hard for a woman to be an MP in a patriarchal society, but it poses challenges for her husband, too. I frequently heard African women MPs tell me that their husband's family thought she was undermining him and that his friends lost respect for him: he must have 'lost control of her' or she wouldn't have become an MP. One woman explained that she didn't suffer the usual maternal anxieties when she was away from her children on her parliamentary duties because her husband was always there to look after them. He could do this because, as she described it, he had no 'peer group'. His family and friends shunned him, not regarding him as a real man because his wife was a prominent MP.

With the male domination of politics in Africa, it would fall to non-governmental organizations (NGOs) to lead on services, advocacy and support for women. I strongly support the work of NGOs like the British Council, which empower women in politics so that they can, in turn, improve the lives of women in their country. Far better this than to assume that politics will always remain predominantly male and that the advancement of women has to be the immediate responsibility of NGOs. Ultimately, the most sustainable way to ensure that girls have equal access to education, that women in remote villages have decent maternity care and that women can flourish as entrepreneurs is for women to be in politics. The women in the state and federal legislatures are the best champions for the women in their villages. Women should be able to rely on women in their own political system to understand and address their needs. They should not have to put up with a male political system and see their needs addressed only by foreign-aid-funded NGOs.

Certainly, many African women believe themselves to be the antidote to the pernicious corruption which enriches the men at the top of their societies while leaving ordinary people struggling in poverty. In patriarchal societies with men controlling the wealth, women are less likely to be wealth accumulators and there's therefore less pressure on them to distribute aid corruptly. Women politicians offer the prospect of a clean break with the currently endemic corruption. They echoed the women I met in the villages, who said that women worked hard and that any money they earned would be spent on the family. The expectation was that women politicians would spend money on the people, whereas men politicians would be more likely to spend it on themselves.

What is also striking about so many of the women African politicians is their overt determination to champion women. In 2011, I met a group of Kenyan women MPs who were visiting London. As part of their election campaigns, as well as their name and their party, they each give themselves a 'campaign name'. The campaign name of one woman, who represented one of the poorest areas of Nairobi, was Gender. Another, from a rural area, had chosen as her campaign name FGM. Even talking about FGM (female genital mutilation) is highly controversial but campaigning to end it was this woman's most compelling reason to be in politics, and she was going to make this clear to all the voters.

There is a well-established international network of male politicians. They are seen at every photo line-up at global summits, peace conferences and at gatherings at the UN and operate continuously behind the scenes. Because there are still few women political leaders, hardly any are involved in these powerful international networks. But women need to be equally involved in global politics and women politicians need to be able to meet up with others and to build networks so that they can be part of decision-making processes that affect women's lives. They also need these networks to share ideas and give each other support as they face the challenges which beset all women politicians in dealing with their constituency and their family as they try to break into a man's world. In my role as Mother of the House of Commons (the longest- serving woman MP) I am pressing for our Parliament to host a forum for women parliamentarians from all around the world. A gathering of women MPs from all the different continents would not only help strengthen them but would help us identify how we can support them further and enable us to learn from them. And the sight of women of all different ethnicities resplendent in their diverse costumes would provide a forceful visual reminder that there are women struggling on behalf of other women all around the world. I strongly believe that our government should use the influence of our Foreign Office and our substantial aid budget to support women moving into politics, ensuring that half of those in all our delegations to international meetings are women, and to insist that global summits and peace conferences include women as well as men. International organizations such as the UN, the World Bank, the World Trade Organisation and the Socialist International should also rule that the delegation from each country should be split equally between men and women representatives. And all international organizations should publish a positive action plan to support networks of women politicians as a central part of their work, including seizing the opportunity of using social media and the internet to build and sustain networks of women politicians.

The involvement of more women in politics helps politics in their own countries become more representative and less prone to corruption. And having more women involved in politics internationally will bring to those proceedings an understanding of and a voice for women which is currently lacking.

In the face of the deeply male nature of global leadership, in 2010 the UN, to advance its work on women, brought together the four different departments within the UN working on gender into a new agency, UN Women, something I'd pressed for as a government minister. Its first executive director was the highly successful former president of Chile, Michelle Bachelet. She was succeeded by Phumzile Mlambo-Ngcuka, former deputy president of South Africa. UN Women aims to ensure that both within their own countries and internationally women share in decision-making and that their concerns are given equal weight to those of men. In their local offices in countries around the world, they provide a vital point of coordination and focus for women.

I saw this myself in Cairo, where I met up with some women who'd been part of the Tahrir Square Arab Spring protests but were later pushed back out of politics, and in Ghana, where the local office of UN Women was supporting the justice system in tackling violence against women. Greater funding and recognition for UN Women is vital, offering as it does the prospect of further progress for women around the world. For women suffering poverty, violence and oppression, the fact that there is a UN agency that is on their side, knows what they are enduring and believes it to be wrong is of immense importance. The practical help they give to women is, of course, vital. But even more than that, UN Women legitimizes their struggle and empowers them to carry on the fight. A declaration against FGM, or against child marriage (or rape, as it should more accurately be called), from a major international agency such as UN Women greatly strengthens the arm of otherwise powerless women.

At home in the UK, the scorecard for our progress as women over the last thirty years is extraordinary. The lives we have been able to lead, and the opportunities we have, are so different from those that were possible for our mothers.

There has been great change in our politics. We have gone from a situation when women formed only a tiny minority in Parliament to being a 'critical mass'. John Major's first Cabinet had no women. Now, a men-only Cabinet would be unthinkable and we have our second woman prime minister. In business, men-only boards were the norm for FTSE companies. Now, though they remain male-dominated, those boards know they must change and are looking around for women to join them. The top echelons of medicine, the law, the arts and science used to be exclusively male. Now, there are pioneering women working their way up to the highest levels in every profession and enterprise. Work used to be divided into full-time and part-time. Now, there is a range of different working patterns: compressed hours, four-day weeks, remote working from home, among many others. Employers used to advertise and recruit for men's jobs and women's jobs and, even where men and women were doing the same work, men were paid more. Now, that is illegal. There is an erosion of the concept of the natural division of labour in the home, where it was assumed that it must always be the woman who takes day-to-day responsibility for the children while the man is the breadwinner. Men are more likely to want to take a greater role in the daily care of their children.

The 'public discourse' has changed. The argument that there is one role for men and a different one for women and that these are natural and must be adhered to has receded. But while that view is less likely to be expressed publicly, privately it is still held by many. Just as there is a general recognition of the abomination of racism yet racism persists, the public commitment to and genuine progress towards equality for women exists alongside deep sexism and discrimination.

Even though so much progress has been made, we remain far from equality, not least around the issue of the care of children, disabled people and older relatives. Although there has been change, there remains a marked division of labour in the home. The relationship between a mother and her work remains profoundly different from that between a father and his work. In the overwhelming majority of households, the woman shoulders the main responsibility for the home. And this is the case even where both parents are working full-time. The woman takes more time off around the birth of a child. During this time, when he's continuing to work and she isn't, she gets up in the night so he can sleep. If she's breastfeeding, she will be getting up in the night more frequently than he is. She therefore becomes more confident than he is in dealing with the baby. In the early years, her expertise and his lack of it create a vicious circle. The father helps but the mother remains responsible. And this both entrenches and is entrenched by unequal pay. If the father is earning more than the mother, then, for most families, there is no choice but for her to drop her hours to take care of the child. For him to do so at a time when the family finances are newly stretched by the costs of having a child would not be practical.

The commitment to men sharing parenting has advanced further than the reality. This sets up expectations among both men and women which create frustration when they are not met. On school visits in my constituency I always ask the teenage girls if they expect that the impact of a baby on their working lives will be different from the impact on the working life of the baby's father (assuming it's not a same-sex partnership). The universal answer is 'no'; they expect things to be equal. All the messages from school and more widely say that they should work hard, be ambitious and do more in their working lives, if possible, than previous generations of women. When I ask the boys in the same class the same question, the answer is different. They expect a baby to have a bigger impact on the mother and are perplexed by the idea that progress in their own work will need to be balanced against the needs of their child.

Most of these young women and men have been brought up in households where the mother takes the main responsibility for children, so, while the girls aspire to go further than previous generations of women have been able to in their work and therefore share domestic responsibilities, the boys see a model of home life with them as main breadwinner and head of the household. All the messages the boys receive from school and more widely are to foster their ambition, to work hard, to do well and better, if possible, than previous generations. They see their twenties and thirties as years when they will be advancing their career. For boys and girls to emerge into adult life with widely divergent views and expectations about parenting makes the process of resolving and negotiating the mutual responsibility of the care of a child more difficult.

Previously, the overwhelming majority of both men and women accepted that the home was 'woman's work'. Now, only a minority think this, but women are more likely to regard the unequal division of labour in the home as unfair. The British Social Attitudes

Survey reports that while, in the mid-eighties, close to half the public agreed that 'a man's job is to earn money, a woman's job is to look after the home and family', now, only around 10 per cent subscribe to that view. Yet the division of labour in the home remains. Women report spending thirty-six hours a week on housework and caring for family members. The equivalent figure for men is eighteen hours. Among women, 60 per cent report that they are doing more than their 'fair share' at home – but only 37 per cent of men think they are doing less than their fair share. This represents a major mismatch between what men and women expect of themselves and each other.

This persistent division of labour in the home feeds into attitudes of employers. While, under the Equality Act, women have the right not to be discriminated against on the grounds of pregnancy, this is still widespread. A report by the Equality and Human Rights Commission published in 2015 estimated that 54,000 new mothers are losing their jobs in Britain every year. The same report found that 10 per cent of pregnant women were discouraged from attending antenatal appointments and that one in nine women had been dismissed, made compulsorily redundant or treated so poorly that they had to resign from their jobs. Of those who did return to work, 10 per cent said that they were treated worse by their employer than they had been before. Even when mothers were given the chance to work flexibly when they went back to work, they felt they had fewer opportunities and that their work was less valued.

For most women, the reality is that the childbearing years are a time when they are likely to be struggling just to maintain their position at work rather than forging forward in their career. For many, asking their employer for flexible working arrangements seems hard enough. Asking for flexible working at the same time as applying for promotion seems impossible. And where being promoted requires putting in long hours at work and doing extra training, it is more difficult for women with young children who are also taking on the majority of the care on the home front.

There is a legal right that a sick employee can take time off work, but this is not the case for an employee whose child is ill. Many women say that when their child is ill and they have to stay at home to look after them, they tell their employer that it is they who are unwell. They don't like having to lie, but they can't tell the truth and risk dismissal; neither can they leave a sick child at home alone. Then they may be in the situation that, if they themselves are ill, they feel that, having had time off for a child's sickness, they can't afford to take any more, so they go into work when they should be at home recovering. Or they don't go into work, call in sick and get a poor sickness record. When a child of nursery or school age gets ill, they need someone to look after them. No one would want a young child who is unwell to be left at home on their own; indeed, it is an offence for a parent to leave a child at home alone if they are so young it places them at risk. Many parents don't have family nearby who can step in to help. The sick child of the working mother is an everyday occurrence but is completely invisible to the public policy agenda. There should be sick leave and statutory sick pay for the parent of a sick child, just as there is for the employee.

What we are striving for is freedom of choice and equality of opportunity. Women and men should not be constrained by expectations of what is appropriate for men and for women. That is unfair on the women and on the men who want to choose how they do things, but it is also bad for the family, for society and for our economy. Things work better if people can do what they want to and are best at, but in order to make space for those choices to be possible entrenched patterns have to be challenged organizationally. To enable women to become MPs, we had to change the expectation of what an MP was. That couldn't be done simply by argument when the reality people were faced with was that nearly all MPs were men. All-women shortlists discriminate against men but they do so with the objective of breaking the entrenched pattern of discrimination against women by ensuring that women get selected for Parliament. It was – and is – a transitional imperative. The imposition of quotas on the boards of FTSE companies is necessary to disrupt the prevailing old boys' network. Even though successive governments have committed to more women being appointed to public boards, without quotas the pace of change is so slow as to be almost imperceptible. Quotas are necessary here, too.

When a woman becomes the first in her field, she is breaking the mould just by being there. Her colleagues can become accustomed to working alongside a woman as well as alongside men. Other women can see her carrying out her work and recognize that the role can be performed by a woman and that they, as women, might do something similar; men also see and recognize this and come to understand that they can work alongside, and for, women as well as other men.

Many women who break into new roles try to do more. They speak out on the importance of women in their field, they encourage and support other women, they set up organizations to help open doors for other women. For example, the first woman to conduct the BBC's prestigious *Last Night of the Proms*, Marin Alsop, used the opportunity to encourage young women to become conductors. Jude Kelly, artistic director of London's South Bank, and one of the very few women leading one of the major arts organizations in the UK, organizes the Women of the World Festival. The Women's TUC brings women trade unionists together every year. There are countless organizations set up by women who have broken into male-dominated worlds to help other women, among them the Association of Women Solicitors (which I joined as an articled clerk in the seventies), Women in Advertising and Communications, and Women in Film and Television. The Union of Construction, Allied Trades and Technicians (UCATT) have undertaken a survey of women in construction to identify the issues they face, and Women in Engineering was established at Sheffield University in 2012. The political parties have their own women's organizations: the Labour Women's Network, the Conservative Women's Organization and Liberal Democrat Women.

However, although individual women have broken through in most fields, organizations to support women's progress have been set up and public sexism is greeted with opprobrium, there is much that still hasn't changed. We have to recognize this in order to progress further. The argument that women are different and that equality of opportunity is neither possible nor desirable has yet to be banished entirely from the public domain. Often it is couched in the form of 'tongue-in-cheek' or 'humorous' remarks. But while it is, quite rightly, unacceptable to engage in racial stigmatization, sexism is not off limits in the same way. It is important not to let these attitudes go unchallenged, even though it is never easy. Every time there is a challenge, there is a wave of sympathy for the transgressor and a backlash against the complainant. Barrister Charlotte Proudman was dubbed a 'Feminazi' for protesting about unsuitable comments made by a male solicitor. Caroline Criado-Perez was subjected to death and rape threats for complaining that no woman was depicted on UK banknotes. But behind any individual complaint there are hundreds of thousands of women who have had similar experiences and feel the same way.

In Parliament, as in society, there's still a long way to go. A woman MP is still defined by her marital status and reproductive record in a way that would be unthinkable for a man. This has been evident in the commentary on Hillary Clinton over the years. The Clinton conundrum is: bake cookies and you are a real woman, but you can't be a leader; fail to bake cookies and you can be a leader, but you're not a real woman.

This can be painfully divisive when it comes to the question of children. In any interview, a woman MP who doesn't have children is required to explain herself, something that doesn't happen to a male MP. A woman shouldn't have to explain to anyone whether having no children was a positive choice or whether she would have loved to have children but was unable to. If she explains that she took a positive decision in order to focus on her work, she's seen as inadvertently implying that women with children can't do their job properly. Women with children who explain that this is the reason why they are not putting themselves forward for advancement in the party are seen as inadvertently criticizing the mothers who do. Men aren't challenged, and don't challenge, each other in the same way. If a woman MP has children, she is either a devoted mother and a deficient MP who'll remain forever on the sidelines, or is she a dynamic and ambitious MP and therefore a deficient mother. An MP father who leaves a meeting to attend his child's school open evening and tells everyone about it in a loud voice is admired as heroic, but a woman MP had better not mention it because she'll be labelled as insufficiently committed to her work. And this is because the underlying reality, and the cultural expectation, is that, in most families, it's the mother who takes on the daily responsibility for young children, and indeed for older relatives.

Maria Miller MP, a Tory Cabinet minister in David Cameron's government, was criticized in 2013 for saying that she understood the need for controls on internet porn as she was the only mother in the Cabinet. This was taken as passing judgement on the other women in the Cabinet who didn't have children – but not on the men who didn't have children. Andrea Leadsom MP had to withdraw from the Tory leadership contest when she conveyed the impression in a *Times* interview that, because she has three children, she would be a better leader of the Conservative party than Theresa May, who has none.

In its early days in the seventies and eighties, feminism was unequivocally at odds with Conservatism. Feminism demanded change, and the Conservatives, as their name suggests, wanted the status quo to continue. Feminism demanded rights to equal pay and maternity leave; the Conservatives saw this as an unwarranted intervention in the labour market and as oppressive regulation on business. Feminists wanted the woman to be able go out to work and the father to share the daily care of the children; the Conservatives were for the traditional family, where the woman stayed at home and looked after the children and the man went out to work. Feminism demanded childcare, to expand the public services that women, in particular, rely on, such as nurseries and care for the elderly; the Tories wanted to 'shrink the state', with fewer, not more, public services and, in any case, thought that care of children and the elderly was the role and responsibility of the mother, rather than the state.

Feminism believed that a wife should be able to leave her husband and that, if he was beating her, divorce was a thoroughly good thing. We thought it was unfair to stigmatize lone mothers and at the same time offer no criticism of the child's father. We wanted to support rather than disapprove of lone mothers and make the fathers contribute financially to the upbringing of their child. The Tories were against divorce and disapproved of single parents. Feminism is a creed of collectivism and solidarity; the Conservatives are the party of individualism. We want strong trade unionism to advance women's rights at work; they are hostile to trade unionism. Feminism is an internationalist movement, in solidarity with women throughout the world; the Conservatives are inward-looking and nationalistic. While we were in politics as a vocation, and for the cause, Conservative women discussed being an MP as a career option so we disapproved of them as 'careerists'. Conservative women such as Margaret Thatcher wanted to beat the male politicians at their own game, while we wanted to change the game, to do politics differently.

So, if you were a feminist and wanted to be politically active, why on earth would you join the Conservatives? Labour, for all its drawbacks, was our political home. And the feminist women who came into Labour in the seventies and eighties brought feminism into mainstream politics, made Labour into the political wing of the women's movement and campaigned against the Tories.

One of the most basic tenets of feminism is solidarity among women, but we Labour women couldn't be in solidarity with Conservative women. They were opposing all that we were fighting for. The women who were politically active in the Tory party were a different species from us Labour activists and vehemently opposed our arguments for women's advancement. It was bad enough to have the Tory men and Labour men arguing against us; it was even worse when it was a woman, even if she was a Tory. Whenever I went on television or radio, the Tory party would put up one of their very few women MPs – often Theresa May – to argue against me. Their first Minister for Women was a man (David Hunt) but, even when they appointed a woman to that role, there was no question of any support from her for our objectives.

There was a lot of expectation that, as feminists, we Labour women MPs would work on a cross-party basis with Tory women MPs in order to support women in the country. I found it impossible to feel sisterly with women who were, in my view, MPs who backed a government that was making life so hard for my constituents and who were a drag anchor on our quest for progress for women. Tory women denounced all-women shortlists as patronizing and argued that it didn't matter that there were hardly any women MPs, because the only thing that mattered was 'merit'. They argued against proposals on greater maternity leave as a burden on business. They argued against childcare on the grounds that it subsidized women to go out to work when they should be at home looking after their children. If a woman wanted to go out to work, they argued, then that was her choice, but she should pay for the expenses incurred in doing so herself, not expect the public purse to foot the bill. It was bad enough facing the arguments of the tabloid press, but it was dispiriting to hear those arguments not just from Tory men but from Tory women as well, sadly, often echoing the complaints of Labour men.

So the answer to the question of whether I worked on a cross-party basis with Conservative women was a firm 'no'. More recently, some of the Tory women have changed their minds on certain issues and there's a new breed of Tory women MPs. Maria Miller voted against civil partnerships but now supports them. Theresa May criticized our moves towards greater representation of women but then became their champion in the Tory party. Many of the Tories, men as well as women, now support our demands for tougher laws on domestic violence. But I find it hard to forget how much the Tory women pulled us back in the long years of our hard struggle for progress, and I find it difficult to make common cause with those, even women, whose social and economic policies are the very ones I am in politics to fight against.

The paradox is that, ultimately, the Tories came to recognize that they had to have more women MPs. With, from 1997, Labour's ranks looking and sounding more like a modern team made up of both women and men, the male domination of the Tory party began to look downright old-fashioned. Photos of Labour looked as if they were taken in the twenty-first century. Photos of the Conservatives looked like they were taken in the fifties. And this insurgency within our own party found an echo in women all around the country. They, too, wanted to push forward and, while they could see Labour women trying to do the same, all they could see from the Tory women was a defence of the status quo. I got the sense that, while any concerns the Tory women had about their own party were publicly muted, privately, as we advanced, Tory women MPs were starting to become insistent on change in their own party. However, they remain implacably opposed to positive action and, without all-women shortlists, progress on increasing their number has been slow. Tory women remain outnumbered by men four to one. It was our demands for more Labour women MPs, the arrival of those Labour women in the House of Commons and their prominence in our front-bench teams that, ironically, provided some momentum for Tory women and that has seen their MPs grow from only ten in 1982 to sixty-eight in 2015. The battles we fought to raise the number of women MPs have not only changed the Labour party, they've helped Tory women make progress within their party, too.

The 2015 and 2017 intakes of women Tory MPs not only added to the number of women on the Tory benches, they brought with them a very different attitude to feminism from that of the previous intakes. Though they represent a party which is against the progressive objectives we espouse, they are of the generation which now believes instinctively in a woman's right to equality. We fought to change attitudes as well as rights and, as the culture evolved, that affected the new generation of Tory women. On many issues, their attitudes are now much more like ours. They argue for more childcare and for equality at work. But, as a party which remains rooted in reducing public spending and shrinking the state, it remains impossible to envisage that a Tory government would ever deliver the massive investment and strong rights at work which would bring us equality for women.

The new Tory women, especially the outspoken ones, experience the rebuffs from their own side that will always be the fate of women in a minority. Having experienced it myself, I recognize the resentment I see in many of them when they suffer marginalization within their party. Though I disagree with her on many issues, not least her opposition to abortion, I admire Nadine Dorries, MP for Mid Bedfordshire, for her refusal to tolerate the condescension of the Tory grandees. As a woman who was brought up on a housing estate in Liverpool and became a nurse and then a successful author, she feels she has no reason to look up to male colleagues who were born with a silver spoon in their mouth. Nor should she. If she was a man, her independence would be admired. As a woman, she is vilified. I don't like to see that and cringe when our side join in.

I'm glad to see that Tracey Crouch is determined to stay on in her position as minister having had a baby, the first woman Tory MP to do so. Of course, in general, I'd rather see fewer Tory MPs, but I do believe that it's better for women in this country if both parties of government have more women MPs.

The fact that not just the first, but the second ever woman prime minister of the UK was a Conservative is a particular conundrum. Margaret Thatcher was not a feminist. However, it was undeniably the case that having a woman prime minister was a milestone. It fundamentally challenged the notion that there were some things women couldn't do, because here was a woman running the country. And that was a good thing. But what Margaret Thatcher did as Prime Minister set back, in our view, rather than advanced, the cause of women. She cut back public services and employment regulations. She only ever appointed one woman to her Cabinet, and that was Baroness Young, safely tucked away in the House of Lords. We criticized Margaret Thatcher for what she did, but it rankled that the Tories had managed to have a woman leader while Labour, which prides itself on being the party for women and equality, hadn't, and still hasn't.

And then the Conservatives chose their second woman prime minister, Theresa May. Again, that is undoubtedly a step forward for women. And Theresa May now speaks the language of equality. But, as with Margaret Thatcher, the issue is not just that she herself is a woman but what she does for women in the country she leads. Whether, under her term as Prime Minister, she will have helped women should, I believe, be measured according to the following criteria, among others:

- Is the gap between women's and men's income (taking into account pensions, benefits and tax credits as well as pay) narrowing, or is it widening again?
- Has the rate of domestic homicide fallen?
- Are women entitled, and enabled financially, to take more time off work after having a baby?
- Are men entitled, and enabled financially, to take more time off work after having a baby?
- Are more men working part-time when their children are young?
- Are there more childcare places for pre-school children, and more after-school and holiday clubs?
- Is public policy addressing the issues of older women?

Lib Dem women have long espoused feminist ideology. Within their party, they have had the influence of Shirley Williams, a former Labour Cabinet minister who was one of the founding MPs of the SDP, and Polly Toynbee, a feminist journalist and commentator (who is now Labour). However, despite this, their party has lagged behind on women's representation in Parliament, though one of their four women MPs, Jo Swinson, is now deputy leader. They oppose all-women shortlists not only because they were hostile to positive action but also because they are not prepared to withstand the resistance from local parties to the involvement of Lib Dem headquarters in local parliamentary selections.

It was sad to see the impact on some of the Lib Dem women when they went into coalition with the Tories. Lynne Featherstone, sharp and witty, is clearly a feminist, but on becoming a minister in the Tory-led government she voted for tax cuts for millionaires (mostly men) and inflicted the bedroom tax on council tenants (mostly women). She stayed in government to do what she could on issues like tackling human trafficking and ensuring there was a focus on women in the government's work in international development. But, being in a coalition, she was hopelessly compromised and lost her seat to Labour in 2015, when the Lib Dems were wiped out in London.

The SNP have learned the lessons that Labour in Scotland was too slow to recognize. Although we instituted positive action to ensure that 50 per cent of our MSPs were women, and got more women MPs from Scotland, Labour's political culture in Scotland remained resolutely male. As a long-standing party of power in the country, with strong connections to a male-dominated trade union movement, Labour in Scotland proved resistant to the inclusion of women on equal terms. While Labour clung to its traditions, the SNP, as the insurgent rather than the established party, swept to power by championing the contemporary values of equality. It now has a woman leader, and more than a third of their MPs and 43 per cent of the members of the Scottish Parliament are women. It's harder to make internal change in a party when it's in power. When you are holding office, the power is more keenly fought for. Just as we made our biggest structural changes in the party when we were out of office before 1997, the power that we had always held in Scotland made it harder to effect change there. The SNP, on the outside, were able to modernize and reaped the electoral benefits of doing so. In 2015 Labour's vote in Scotland collapsed. We went from forty-one Scottish Labour MPs down to just one. But the whole-sale rebuilding of Labour's support, necessitated by that disastrous general election result, is underway. The 2017 general election saw our parliamentary representation increase from one to seven, of which two are women. And from 2015 to 2017 Labour had its first woman leader in Scotland – Kezia Dugdale.

However, there are some issues where women MPs reach across the party divide and work together in the House of Commons, such as changing the hours at which the Commons sits and resisting the move to revert to late-night sittings. Labour women led this change initially, with Joan Ruddock MP playing a key part in reaching out to build cross-party working among women MPs, both to achieve change and to stop it being rolled back. I was able to use my official position as Mother of the House, the longest-serving woman MP, to galvanize cross-party working in support of women. I initiated a campaign for 'babyleave' for MPs that won strong support from many Tory and SNP women as it did from Labour women MPs. And Jo Swinson, now back in parliament and Lib Dem Deputy Leader, who herself had a baby while an MP, has ensured that the Lib Dems are backing 'babyleave' to give men and women MPs six months off after the birth of a child.

One issue that has engendered cross-party action amongst women has been tackling sexual harassment by MPs who use their position of authority to prey on young women working in Parliament, particularly researchers and journalists. The revelations in 2017 that Harvey Weinstein had used his position as one of the most powerful men in the US film industry to sexually assault and harass women, and had got away with it for decades, unleashed an outpouring of complaints about sexual harassment here in the UK. Women who had put up with it for years saw the opportunity to speak out and demand that it stop. Most men MPs would not dream of making unwanted sexual advances to young women. But some do, and for the victim the fear of notoriety and being accused of lying has deterred them from complaining. So MPs, like other men in positions of power, had impunity. Those men who grope young women (or indeed young men) are unlikely to do so only once and that, together with the outpouring of revulsion about Harvey Weinstein, provided the opportunity to tackle it.

What was key in empowering women to complain was that large numbers of women were speaking out. A man can brush aside the allegations of one woman by denial, vilifying her and traducing her reputation. But the public besmirching of women sexual harassment victims prompted other women who'd had the same experience with the same man to come forward and tell their story. With each accused man facing allegations not just from one but from many women, they could no longer escape accountability by smearing the victim. For once, attacking the victim's reputation didn't silence her, but served only to motivate more victims to make their complaints public. Again I was able to use my position as Mother of the House to work with women MPs from all parties to bring the issue for debate to the House of Commons, assert that it was a pervasive problem and demand that it be stopped. Finally, Parliament has faced up to what had been, for decades, an ugly reality. Each of the political parties has reviewed their complaints system. The House of Commons, with the enthusiastic support of Speaker John Bercow, has also revised their complaints procedure. Men in all parties have been exposed and lost their positions of seniority, including the Secretary of State for Defence, Sir Michael Fallon.

There has inevitably been a backlash, with men protesting that innocent flirting is being misinterpreted by oversensitive women. Disappointingly, these protests have been backed by some older women asserting that complainants are 'snowflakes' and should simply be more robust. But the combination of the revelation of the abuse of power by Harvey Weinstein, the exposure of senior men in Parliament as harassers, determined work by women MPs in all parties, new rigorous complaints procedures, and a new sense amongst women that they no longer have to put up with it, means that a historic change has taken place. We will, as ever, have to be vigilant that things don't slip back. And we will be, so I'm confident that this important and long overdue change will endure.

When it comes to restricting abortion law, which is regarded as a matter of conscience for MPs rather than party policy and as such is always on a free vote, it is usually a woman Labour MP and a woman Tory MP working together who mobilize women and men MPs on both sides to protect the law. Indeed it was Labour's Stella Creasy who by working with women in other parties made the government change the rules so that women from Northern Ireland could get abortions on the NHS in England. This is in marked contrast to the position in the US, where there is a deep party political divide between women Republicans, who oppose abortion, and women Democrats, who support a woman's right to choose.

As women have made progress there has been a backlash. It is always the case that when a progressive movement advances, its opponents mobilize to try and turn the clock back. It's a mistake to believe that gains made cannot be reversed. Opposition to progress never simply melts away but seeks its champions, its moments and methods. There remains an ugly resistance to women having the temerity to being in public life, being in leadership, making decisions and being authoritative. Donald Trump has re-legitimized disparagement of women. As President of the United States, Trump has emboldened misogynists throughout the western world. In social media such as Twitter, Facebook, Snapchat and Instagram the backlash against women's advances has found new, instant and anonymous routes for aggression and abuse. And this hostility is particularly virulent when directed at younger women and where the misogynist motivation is combined with racism. Luciana Berger MP was subjected to such violent and anti-Semitic threats the offender was sent to prison. Labour's Diane Abbott, the highest-profile black woman MP, has been subjected to a relentless torrent of racist, sexist abuse. Cornish Conservative MP Sheryll Murray received social media incitement to 'burn the witch', her office was urinated on and swastikas carved into her election campaign posters. As Nus Ghani MP said after enduring abuse on Twitter, 'I am a Conservative, I am a woman, I am an Asian and I am Muslim and that makes some people very angry and the fact that I had the audacity to stand for public office causes some people offence'.

Women political journalists, particularly those such as the BBC's Laura Kuenssberg and Channel 4's Cathy Newman who are most successful, are singled out for abuse. This is all about silencing women who speak out. Women should not have to endure vitriolic abuse as the price of being in the public domain. Being a woman

MP should not mean constantly having to look over your shoulder. Voters are entitled to choose a woman to represent them and then to have that woman get on with her work without hindrance. This is not just part of the 'rough and tumble of politics', requiring women to 'man up'. It is an insidious undermining of our democracy. The abuse that women in politics face is just another facet of that inflicted on women who are prominent in any walk of life and that which is endured by too many girls at school. But as women politicians we can do more than just endure this abuse, we can take action not only on behalf of women politicians but on behalf of all women and girls who are subjected to it. To do this we need to expose the fact that it is happening and not suffer it in silence. We must identify it as oppression of women and an attempt to silence us and push us out of the public domain. We must demand of all organizations, whether it be political parties, the media, Internet Service Providers, employers, schools or public agencies such as the police, that they take it seriously, don't minimize it and take the action they can to stop it. The Home Affairs Select Committee, chaired by Yvette Cooper MP, is working on this, as is the Women and Equalities Select Committee chaired by Maria Miller MP. The Labour Party should set an example by having a 'one strike and you're out' rule that in future any Labour member who perpetrates misogynist abuse would be permanently expelled from the party.

We should tackle those aspects of the political process which make women vulnerable. For example electoral law requires candidates' home addresses to be made public and put on all the posters pasted up around the constituency notifying voters of the election. The candidate's home address is also printed on all ballot papers. While there is a provision enabling a candidate to withhold their address and disclose only the constituency that they live in, this is not satisfactory because as the default position is to publish your home address, the candidate who doesn't looks as though they are hiding something and is thereby put at a disadvantage. The default position for all candidates should be only the constituency in which the home is located is made public.

We should recognize that misogynist abuse and vilification of women in the public domain covers a broad spectrum from anonymous insults on Twitter through threats, through to physical violence. Jo Cox was the Chair of Labour Women's Network and a dynamic, exceptionally able feminist. When I was Deputy Leader I pleaded with her to come to head up my office. But she had her young son with her and was pregnant with her daughter and turned me down saying, for the moment, they had to be her priority. She continued with Labour Women's Network and was then selected as Labour candidate for her home town of Batley. Elected to parliament in 2015, she immediately made an enormous impact, combining huge political energy with empathy, strongly Labour but able to work cross-party too. On 16 June 2016 she was attacked and killed outside her constituency surgery. It is impossible to describe the sense of loss we feel at her death.

Despite the horror of Jo Cox's murder and their routine subjection to abuse, women remain in parliament and there are ever more women determined to take up a place in Westminster to press for further change. Instead of being deterred, it has strengthened their resolve. We have to protect women and tackle abuse because it is right in principle that we make politics safe for women. But it is remarkable that despite the inevitability of abuse and the prospect of attack there are, for every woman MP, dozens more exceptionally able women ready and waiting to move into parliament. Women pay a high price for political activity, but the efforts of those who would push them out are doomed to fail.

The women's movement is an established force now, in Parliament as well as outside it, and women work together across the globe. For the future, much will change, but throughout the more than forty years I've been involved in the women's movement, there are some tenets of feminism which I think are enduring.

1. We should be gratified that we have made so much progress, but we should never be grateful. The rights that

we have made progress in achieving should always have been ours. The discrimination which we have beaten back should never have been inflicted on us. We have not been asking for anything that we were not always entitled to. We have no one to thank except ourselves and those women who went before us.

2. We should analyse and be clear about the extent to which inequality persists – and certainly never minimize it. To recognize that we still have such a long way to go is simply to face the facts. It doesn't detract from acknowledging how far we have already come or sap our determination to go further.

3. We should seek the support of men and work in partnership with them, but women must never surrender the leadership of this movement for change. It is not for men, however progressive, to tell women how to be feminist. It is not the case, yet, that we are 'all in it together'. In the words of the women's liberation movement, 'Women must be the engine of their own liberation.' Some men are now starting to describe themselves as feminist, which is welcome, but they need to remain as supporters, not leaders.

4. The women's movement doesn't belong to any particular generation of women. It belongs no more to the older generation than it does to young feminists. Both older women and younger women have their part to play. The new generation of feminists is neither better nor worse than the older generation, but they will do things differently.

5. Support other women – and draw on their support. The women's movement is a collective endeavour, not an individualistic quest. It's important to support women in leadership positions who are fighting for change. No woman manages to achieve change on her own so our support will help them make progress. They won't get everything right – no one does – and it's hard to be a

pioneer and break new ground. They'll frequently be undermined by those who are anti-feminist. Don't join in with this. Draw on the support of other women when you are trying to bring about change. There is a silent majority of women who will be backing you.

6. Resist being drawn into disputes about which sort of discrimination is 'worse'. There should be no hierarchy of inequality. Discrimination is wrong whether it is rooted in class background, racial prejudice, homophobia, prejudice against those with a disability, or those who are older, or any combination of these. Some people will campaign against all inequality, others against just one aspect of it, and, whichever they do, it is worthwhile and important.

7. Expect, as you press for equality, constantly to have arguments. It doesn't mean you are going about it in the wrong way. The status quo will always be defended by those whose interests it serves. Those who resist change have always characterized women who demand it as unreasonable, irrational, aggressive or divisive. If you are not having arguments, you are probably not making a difference.

8. Don't be lulled into a false sense of security by 'passive resistance' from men. It is sometimes harder to deal with those who say they agree with you and don't argue against you but who nonetheless resist change.

9. Recognize that the women's movement is a global movement for progress. We should support women in other parts of the world who face infinitely greater challenges than we do. That doesn't mean that the progress we make is any less important. The progress we achieve on our own behalf in our country encourages and inspires those women who have even further to go. And we have much to learn from and admire in their struggles.

10. Help the women who will come after you, and try to make it easier for them. Breaking new ground by getting

yourself into a certain position is important, but do more than that: help the women who join and strengthen the cause, and who will take things forward after you.

2018 marks the landmark of the centenary of the first women winning the right to vote and women have spent much of the ensuing one hundred years trying to get women into positions of power – into parliament and into government. Much of the energy of the women's movement has been consumed in tackling women's exclusion from power, in getting women 'into the room'. Now we must focus more on what we want now we, as women, are in that room. Hitherto our demands have been self-limited, reflecting that it's hard, as the most recent arrival, to make the biggest demands. But as we pass the centenary of women's right to vote surely it's about time that we asked ourselves, and answered the question, 'what would a government fully committed to women's equality do?' We need to raise our ambition for what we can achieve in tackling the continuing inequality of women and not be deterred if it seems like a big change, would engender resistance or would be expensive. For example, fully paid twelve-month's leave for both mothers and fathers would cost a considerable amount of public money. But it is necessary for both parents and for babies. On other issues, such as defence, we ask ourselves whether it's necessary and then work out how we can pay for it. That should be our approach on equality for women. High quality childcare for any child over one year old whose parents want it would cost billions. But just as we spend billions of pounds on the NHS because it is necessary, so too is it necessary for women's equality for there to be comprehensive, free childcare. There's no point waiting till we are told the country can afford it – that moment never seems to come when it comes to women's demands. So, to set us on the right path for the next one hundred years we should slough off the burden of self-censorship of our demands, be clear what we want and insist that it is done. We need to go from asking to insisting, from proposing to demanding, from persuading to asserting. And to achieve that, the women's movement will need to be stronger than ever before.

Acknowledgements

I'd always denounced political memoirs as male vanity projects and vowed never to write mine – so this book requires an explanation. I read the mounting pile of memoirs of the men who'd been my Cabinet colleagues. They wrote about themselves and each other but there was nothing about women. Nowhere could you see the huge changes in women's lives over the past thirty years, nor the transformation women have wrought in our politics, nor the battles the women's movement have fought and won. There was no mention of women's votes having been key to Labour's victory in 1997, or of how there being 101 Labour women MPs changed not just the policies of our government but the face of British politics. Our work as women in the Labour party, as the political wing of the women's movement, was being written out of history. And, since my thirty years in politics, twenty-eight years on Labour's front bench, eight years as Deputy Leader and two stints as Leader of the Opposition were not going to get an airing in the memoirs of my male colleagues, I'd clearly have to write my own.

My first piece of luck was happening on my agent, Clare Alexander. As a woman who's lived through the times described in the book, she understood exactly what I wanted to do before I did and found me the 'dream team' at Penguin. It has been a revelation to work with my editor, Helen Conford, and to benefit from her fierce intelligence and deep empathy. And Annabel Huxley brought total commitment and enthusiasm to the book as Penguin's Senior Publicity Manager.

Writing this book gave me the excuse to relive the highs and lows, the triumphs and defeats, with those whom I've worked over the years, and the opportunity to thank them. The essence of the women's movement is that it is about women doing things together, not on their own. It's not about heroines or leaders – above all, it's about the solidarity of women working together. The NCCL Women's Rights Committee – Anna Coote, Tess Gill and Patricia Hewitt – inducted me into the women's movement and were the most dynamic, supportive sisters anyone could hope for. The members of the Peckham Labour Party took a big gamble when in 1981 they selected me to be their next MP, and I'll always be grateful to them. The Wentworths, the Kennedys, Vicky Naish, Mary Ellery, Bill Skelly, Barrie Hargrove, the Situs, and so many more were the backbone of the Peckham party in good times and bad and always gave me wise counsel. My constituency staff have, over the years, done so much for me, and for the people of Peckham, and I'd like to thank them all, especially, Alun Hayes, Charlotte Hill, Charlotte Montague and Dora Dixon-Fyle.

No MP, let alone any minister, does it on their own, and one of the most exhilarating aspects of politics is working with a great team. It has been such a privilege to work with outstanding special advisers, Labour party staff and civil servants. Liz Kendall, Ed Miliband and Yvette Cooper were excellent advisers who then went on to become MPs. Scarlett McGwire and Deborah Mattinson have been key both to the advance of women in the Labour party and in helping me navigate the byzantine obstacles of the Labour party and government. With Anna Healy heading up my team as my special adviser when I was Leader of the House and Labour Deputy Leader, I was able to rely on great wisdom and unassailably good values. She and Ayesha Hazarika were integral to the progress we were able to make in our last years of government and in the nerve-wracking times I spent as interim Labour Leader and Leader of the Opposition. Sophie Wingfield and Mabel McKeown supported me in my role going all around the country as Deputy Leader. Clare Gosbee has been a rock, by my side in the constituency, in the House of Commons and on the road, in both the pink bus and the EU Referendum bus. Kate Wilson and Amanda Jordan have been my lifelong friends.

After a lonely start in Parliament, I ended up surrounded by good friends and allies. I'd like particularly to pay tribute to Joan Ruddock, Margaret Hodge, Ann Coffey, Vera Baird, Julie Morgan, Margaret Curran, Fiona Mactaggart, Anne Campbell and all the women Labour MPs, councillors and party members who constitute the political wing of the women's movement. There were, especially in the early days, few journalists who thought it worth reporting 'women's issues', so those who did were very important. Polly Toynbee, Jackie Ashley and Yvonne Roberts, in particular, could always be counted on to take what we were trying to do seriously.

I wouldn't have enjoyed the triumphs, let alone weathered the political storms, without the endurance, advice and support of my amazing family; my mother, my late father, my sisters and my three children. And Jack, with whom I've shared this great political and personal journey, has surely more than earned the right to be regarded as an honorary member of the sisterhood.

Because I didn't plan to write my memoirs, I never wrote a diary during my time in politics. I thoroughly disapproved of colleagues who sat in meetings writing theirs; I thought they should have been focusing on getting things done in the here and now, rather than anticipating their place in history. So, I had no diaries to remind me of events that go back over forty years. But what I do have are three sources, which I've used as the basis of this book. From 1981, I wrote, every month, a report for Peckham Labour Party. These reports, which I typed initially on an ancient typewriter, told my local party members what I was doing and what I thought of the politics of the time. MPs then did not report to their local parties in writing, but I did, for a number of reasons. When they selected me to be their candidate, my local party members hardly knew me. My reports showed them who I was. My political agenda, full of concerns about childcare, domestic violence and women's equality, was so profoundly different from that of my predecessor, Harry Lamborn, that I had to spell out what I was doing and why it mattered. And as a pregnant MP, and later one with three young children, I felt I needed to show them that I was fully on the job and not sitting at home. In addition, as the party was so turbulent and so bitterly divided in the eighties, I felt I needed to put down on paper what I was doing and saying in order to protect myself against malicious rumours. I am a lawyer, so recording meetings and actions and keeping those records is second nature to me, and I'd seen how Patricia Hewitt used her written reports as NCCL General Secretary to shape the agenda of the organization. So this book is based firmly on what I was saying and doing at the time, rather than on private reflections. My second source was press clippings, which, from 1981, local party members pasted into scrapbooks for me. I took these to my monthly party meetings to show the members that I was making Labour's case publicly. My third source was the people I was working with over those decades, who generously sat down with me to remember what we did together.

I'm grateful to Scarlett McGwire, Sarah Harman, Sarah Childs and Patricia Hewitt for reading the draft and to Joyce Gould for delving into the annual reports of the National Labour Women's Conferences right back to the eighties, to check what I remembered.

Looking back at these documents, I've been struck by how identical my analysis and demands in the eighties are to what I implemented in government. And while it's gratifying to see the consistency – even down to the same language and arguments being used over the forty-year period – it's startling to reflect on how long it took. We went from having ten Labour women MPs to having 101, but our arguments about the low proportion of women MPs started in the seventies and we didn't breach the 20 per cent barrier until 1997. Our demands for childcare, which fill my reports of the eighties, did not start to be rolled out until the first decade of the new century. In 1985, I reported to my General Committee my protest about the 'provocation defence' for domestic homicides, but it was abolished only in 2009. At least those demands of the women's movement which were so controversial then are generally accepted now. But I hope the next wave of progress doesn't take so long.

This is my personal story, but I was only one of thousands of women in a mighty movement for change. It has been my great good fortune to be part of the women's movement, and it is to them that this book is dedicated.

A Woman's Work, 1975–2015

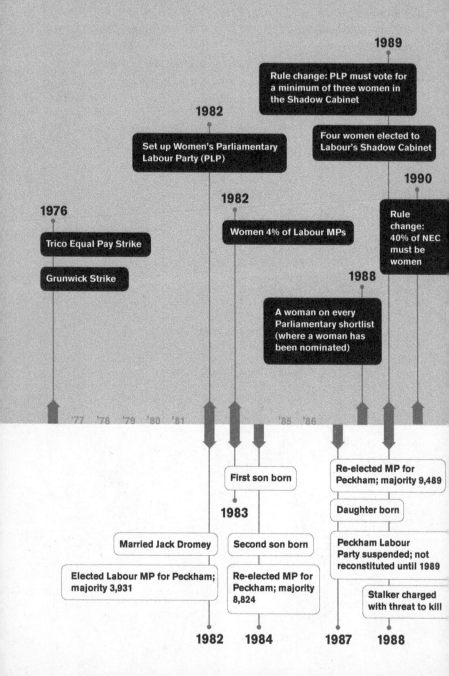

1989
Rule change: PLP must vote for a minimum of three women in the Shadow Cabinet

Four women elected to Labour's Shadow Cabinet

1982
Set up Women's Parliamentary Labour Party (PLP)

1990
Rule change: 40% of NEC must be women

1982
Women 4% of Labour MPs

1976
Trico Equal Pay Strike

Grunwick Strike

1988
A woman on every Parliamentary shortlist (where a woman has been nominated)

'77 '78 '79 '80 '81   '85 '86

First son born

1983

Re-elected MP for Peckham; majority 9,489

Daughter born

Married Jack Dromey

Second son born

Peckham Labour Party suspended; not reconstituted until 1989

Elected Labour MP for Peckham; majority 3,931

Re-elected MP for Peckham; majority 8,824

Stalker charged with threat to kill

1982   **1984**   **1987**   **1988**

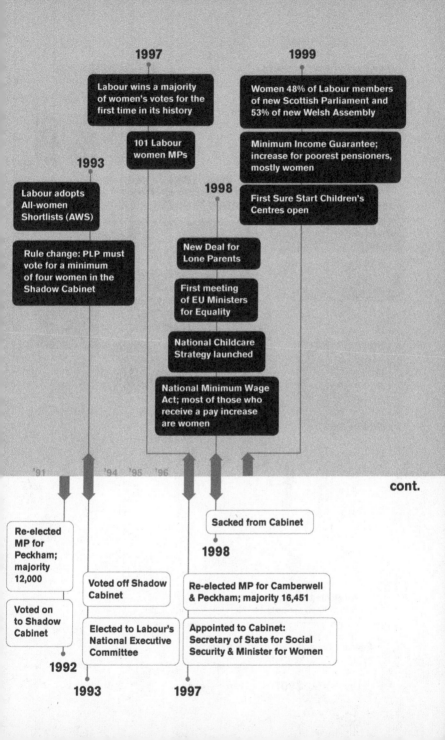

1997

Labour wins a majority of women's votes for the first time in its history

101 Labour women MPs

1999

Women 48% of Labour members of new Scottish Parliament and 53% of new Welsh Assembly

Minimum Income Guarantee; increase for poorest pensioners, mostly women

1998

First Sure Start Children's Centres open

1993

Labour adopts All-women Shortlists (AWS)

Rule change: PLP must vote for a minimum of four women in the Shadow Cabinet

New Deal for Lone Parents

First meeting of EU Ministers for Equality

National Childcare Strategy launched

National Minimum Wage Act; most of those who receive a pay increase are women

'91   '94 '95 '96

cont.

Re-elected MP for Peckham; majority 12,000

Voted on to Shadow Cabinet

1992

Voted off Shadow Cabinet

Elected to Labour's National Executive Committee

1993

Sacked from Cabinet

1998

Re-elected MP for Camberwell & Peckham; majority 16,451

Appointed to Cabinet: Secretary of State for Social Security & Minister for Women

1997

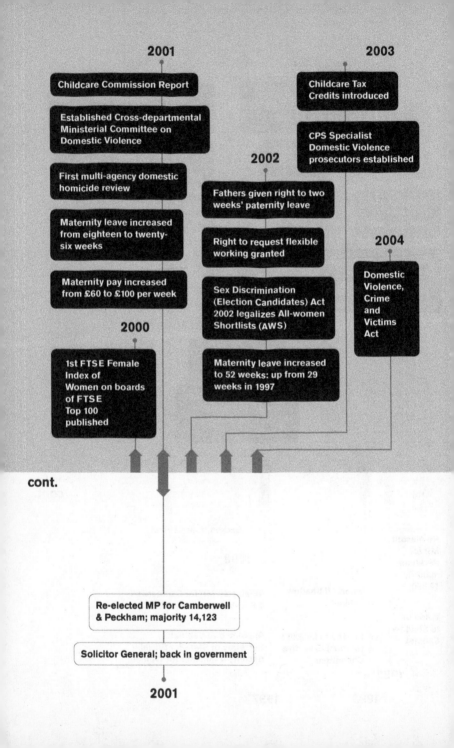

2001

Childcare Commission Report

Established Cross-departmental Ministerial Committee on Domestic Violence

First multi-agency domestic homicide review

Maternity leave increased from eighteen to twenty-six weeks

Maternity pay increased from £60 to £100 per week

2003

Childcare Tax Credits introduced

CPS Specialist Domestic Violence prosecutors established

2002

Fathers given right to two weeks' paternity leave

Right to request flexible working granted

Sex Discrimination (Election Candidates) Act 2002 legalizes All-women Shortlists (AWS)

Maternity leave increased to 52 weeks: up from 29 weeks in 1997

2004

Domestic Violence, Crime and Victims Act

2000

1st FTSE Female Index of Women on boards of FTSE Top 100 published

cont.

Re-elected MP for Camberwell & Peckham; majority 14,123

Solicitor General; back in government

2001

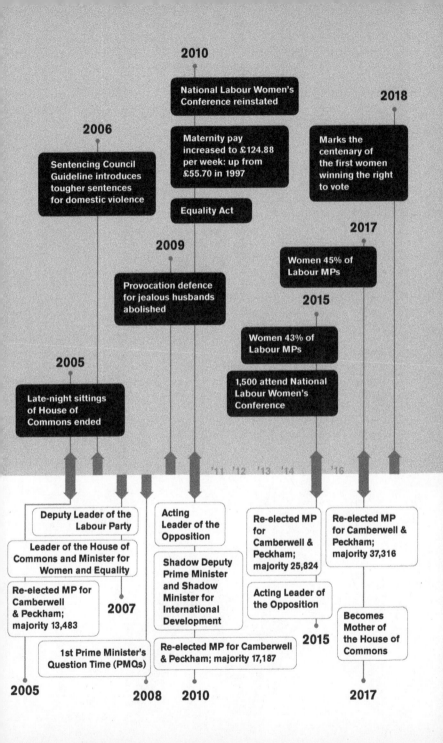

2010

National Labour Women's Conference reinstated

Maternity pay increased to £124.88 per week: up from £55.70 in 1997

Equality Act

2006

Sentencing Council Guideline introduces tougher sentences for domestic violence

2018

Marks the centenary of the first women winning the right to vote

2017

Women 45% of Labour MPs

2009

Provocation defence for jealous husbands abolished

2015

Women 43% of Labour MPs

1,500 attend National Labour Women's Conference

2005

Late-night sittings of House of Commons ended

'11 '12 '13 '14 '16

Deputy Leader of the Labour Party

Leader of the House of Commons and Minister for Women and Equality

Re-elected MP for Camberwell & Peckham; majority 13,483

2007

1st Prime Minister's Question Time (PMQs)

Acting Leader of the Opposition

Shadow Deputy Prime Minister and Shadow Minister for International Development

Re-elected MP for Camberwell & Peckham; majority 17,187

Re-elected MP for Camberwell & Peckham; majority 25,824

Acting Leader of the Opposition

2015

Re-elected MP for Camberwell & Peckham; majority 37,316

Becomes Mother of the House of Commons

2005

2008

2010

2017

Index

'HH' in subheadings refers to Harriet Harman